China: Radicalism to Revisionism 1962-1979

Bill Brugger

CROOM HELM LONDON

BARNES & NOBLE BOOKS
TOTOWA, NEW JERSEY

© 1981 Bill Brugger
Croom Helm Ltd, 2-10 St John's Road, London SW11

British Library Cataloguing in Publication Data

Brugger, William
  China, radicalism to revisionism.
  1. China — Politics and government
  — 1949-1976
  2. China — Politics and government
  — 1976-
  I. Title
  951'.05   DS777.55

  ISBN 0-7099-0610-2
  ISBN 0-7099-0611-0 Pbk

  First published in the USA 1981 by
  Barnes & Noble Books,
  81 Adams Drive,
  Totowa, New Jersey, 07512

  ISBN: 0-389-20087-5

  Printed and bound in Great Britain

CONTENTS

ACKNOWLEDGEMENTS

To the many students who commented on the first edition of this book. To colleagues at Flinders University and elsewhere who pointed out the shortcomings and errors in that text, and especially to Graham Young, Dennis Woodward, Steve Reglar and Michael Sullivan. To the many reviewers who persuaded me to change the book's organisation and approach. To Michelle Grieve for her help on the first edition and to Ron Slee for carrying on her good work into the second. To Andrew Little for map work. To Catherine Cameron for logistic support, through both editions, and to Marie Baker, Heather Bushell, Ann Gabb, Linda Kelly, Elizabeth Neil and Mary Saunders for typing the latest manuscript. Finally, to Suzanne Brugger for the many hours I spent closeted with the text and for her refreshing criticism.

Once again, I can only reiterate that it would be presumptuous for me to claim responsibility for a work which contains so much plagiarism. I must, however, carry the burden for the many errors which remain. Once again, I can only express adherence to the Chinese slogan 'collective initiative and individual responsibility'.

Bill Brugger

The Flinders University of South Australia
December 1979

ABBREVIATIONS

ACFTU All China Federation of Trade Unions
ASEAN Association of South East Asian Nations
ANU   Australian National University
BR   *Beijing Review* (formerly *Peking Review*)
CB   *Current Background*
CC   Central Committee
CCP   Chinese Communist Party
CMEA   Council for Mutual Economic Assistance
CPSU   Communist Party of the Soviet Union
CQ   *The China Quarterly*
EEC   European Economic Community
FBIS   *Foreign Broadcast Information Service*
FEER   *Far Eastern Economic Review*
GMRB   *Guangming Ribao*
GNP   Gross National Product
IMF   International Monetary Fund
JPRS   *Joint Publications Research Service*
NATO   North Atlantic Treaty Organisation
NCNA   New China (Xinhua) News Agency
NPAD   National Programme for Agricultural Development
NPC   National People's Congress
PFLP   Peking Foreign Languages Press
PLA   People's Liberation Army
PR   *Peking Review*
RMRB   *Renmin Ribao*
SALT   Strategic Arms Limitation Talks
SC   State Council
SCMM   *Selections from China Mainland Magazines* (later *SPRCM*)
SCMP   *Survey of China Mainland Press* (later *SPRCP*)
SPRCM   *Selections from the People's Republic of China Magazines* (formerly *SCMM*)
SPRCP   *Survey of the People's Republic of China Press* (formerly *SCMP*)
SW   *Selected Works*
SWB   *Summary of World Broadcasts* (British Broadcasting Corporation) Pt 3 *The Far East*
TPRC   *Translations from the People's Republic of China* (*JPRS*)

URI   Union Research Institute
US   United States
USSR Union of Soviet Socialist Republics.

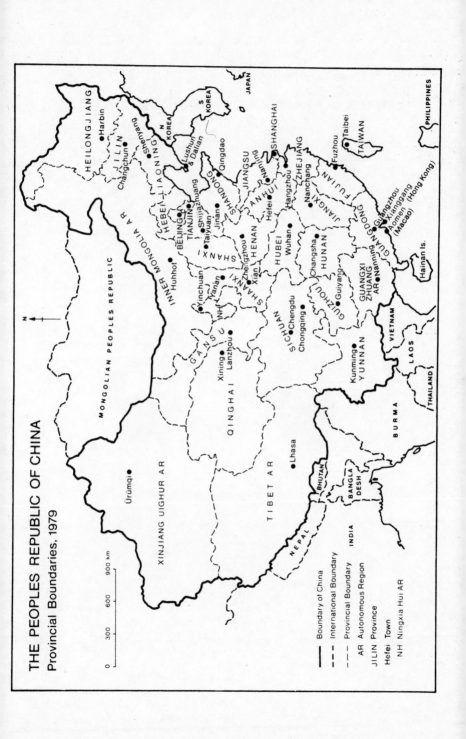

THE PEOPLES REPUBLIC OF CHINA
Provincial Boundaries, 1979

Boundary of China
International Boundary
Provincial Boundary
AR Autonomous Region
JILIN Province
Hefei Town
NH Ningxia Hui AR

INTRODUCTION

This volume is the sequel to *China: Liberation and Transformation, 1942–1962* which traced the history of contemporary China from 1942–62. That volume noted that, up to 1962, no fundamental split had occurred in the Chinese leadership concerning developmental strategy. This volume will trace the split which did occur in the leadership after 1962. To set the scene, therefore, I can do no better than to repeat part of the concluding section of the first volume and request that those who have read it proceed straight to the first chapter.

In the early years of the People's Republic, debates on developmental strategy centred on the applicability of the wartime experiences of the Chinese Communist Party, in the revolutionary base areas, to problems of running the whole country. In Yan'an, in the early 1940s, a model of administration had been worked out which was felt to have contributed much to the eventual victory of the Communist Party. The Yan'an model depended upon a new type of leader—the 'cadre'—committed to change within a network of human solidarity and with an orientation which was both 'red' and 'expert' (or, in the idiom of that time, 'virtuous' and 'talented'). He was kept on his toes by a process of rectification in which he was required to answer for his conduct in the field and to learn how to apply Marxism-Leninism and generalised Party policy to a concrete environment. The cadre operated in a situation of decentralised authority where only broad policy was centrally determined. In operational decisions, he was granted much leeway in interpretation and wide scope for initiative. The cadre's initiative, however, was constrained by the requirement that he adhere to the Mass Line technique of reconciling central policy with mass sentiments. According to the prescriptions of the Yan'an model, administration was organised according to a principle of dual rule, where local cadres were enjoined to be responsive not only to vertical chains of command but also to local Party committees. In practice, this meant that the many political campaigns, which characterised that time, were led by the local Party branches and, thus, the horizontal component in the dual rule scheme was strengthened. To prevent a growing division of labour between leaders and led, a programme of *xiaxiang* (later called simply *xiafang*) was introduced whereby cadres were transferred to lower levels of administration and were required to work for a time as ordinary peasants. In this process, they were able to help the peasants construct informal or semi-formal *minban* (people-run) education units. Throughout the whole process, units (both civilian and military) were encouraged to become self-sufficient and competent in both production and other duties. Rural co-operativisation, therefore, was much more than an agricultural programme. It was the first step in a process of integrating agriculture, industry, administration, education and defence.

During the Civil War of 1946–9, fighting over rapidly shifting fronts led to an erosion of the principles of Yan'an. At the same time, the confusion generated by a much more intense process of land reform gave rise to a rectification movement very different from that of Yan'an. China's first experiment with open-rectification (where people outside the Party were involved in disciplining cadres) was not a great success and, with the restoration of order at the end of the Civil War, a much tighter system of central control was gradually imposed.

The experiences of 1947–8, the sheer problems of administering large urban as well as rural areas, the general inexperience of cadres, the Cold War and economic blockade, all led to a decision to implement a model of administration which derived from the Soviet Union. As an imported model, it was applicable neither to the objective situation in China in the early 1950s nor to the tradition of the Chinese Communist Party. The Soviet model, which was often implemented dogmatically, tended to prescribe a leadership type which was more that of the manager than that of the cadre. The leader was still committed to change but within a network of technological solidarity (between roles and structures rather than human beings). In a situation where both policy and operational decision-making were centralised, the commitment of leaders was to 'expertise' rather than political values and the quality 'virtue' ('red') was interpreted increasingly in technological terms. The culture hero frequently became the engineer and model worker rather than the political activist and the powers of local Party branches tended to be eclipsed in a centrally-organised, vertical bureaucracy. In such a situation, *xiaxiang*, *minban* education and the Mass Line became less important, a slow programme of co-operativisation tended to be run from the top down and the army became separated from the rest of society.

The Soviet model of administration, however, was only imperfectly implemented and, in the mid-1950s, certain of its features came under attack. By the Great Leap Forward of 1958–9, which saw the culmination of rural collectivisation, the model was dismantled and many elements of the Yan'an tradition were adapted to the changed situation. The original Yan'an model had been formulated in a period of moderate radicalism. In 1958–9, however, the political climate often went to radical extremes and an excessive concern for production and 'ultra-left' idealism resulted in 'mistakes'. The debates of the early 1960s focussed on these mistakes. At issue here was the role of the Great Leap Forward in bringing about the economic crisis of 1960 – 2. Various leaders disagreed on the extent to which one should assign blame to the policies of 1958 – 9 or to the three years of very bad harvests which China experienced at that time. In 1962, when Mao decided that the policies of post-Great Leap retrenchment had gone far enough, a major cleavage occurred amongst the leadership and this volume will document its development.

China: Liberation and Transformation 1942 – 1962 speculated on the reasons why disputes remained constrained by a basic policy consensus until 1962. Though no definitive conclusion was reached, it was argued that 1962 was important in marking the beginning of Mao's fundamental reappraisal of the process of socialist transition. The 'new democratic' formula, adopted in the 1940s and early 1950s, was not particularly concerned with defining socialism, since the current 'new democratic revolution' was seen as a species of 'bourgeois democratic revolution'. During that revolution, it was believed that a 'four-class bloc' would eradicate the landlords together with the bureaucratic and comprador bourgeoisie. By the 1950s, however, as the Chinese engaged in 'socialist construction', they came to see socialism as a static model in much the same way as Stalin had conceived the term in 1936. At that time, Stalin had outlined a number of features of 'socialism' in order to demonstrate how the Soviet Union had basically achieved them. The Stalinist model had been criticised by Trotsky on the grounds that socialism had been pitched at too low a level.[1] What was more to the point, however, was that the Stalinist model lacked a diachronic element. Mao was to remark on Stalin's poor knowledge of dialectics. But when he made those remarks, Mao did not see that China, in abandoning the Soviet model of administration, had not abandoned the Soviet model of socialism.

Thus Mao's seminal essay, 'On the Correct Handling of Contradictions among the People' (1957), whilst rejecting many of the Soviet ways of doing things, still adopted a managerialist method of 'handling contradictions' in order to make the model work more effectively. What was new about Mao's conceptualisation of 'uninterrupted revolution', in January 1958, was his attitude towards the periods of consolidation between the various stages in the construction of socialism.[2] It was, however, still informed by the 1936 Stalinist view, reiterated in 'On the Correct Handling . . .', that 'large-scale turbulent class struggles, characteristic of times of revolution [had] in the main come to an end'. Though it might have been the case that Mao was not entirely unsympathetic to those who claimed, in 1958, that the socialist revolution might be growing over into communism, there is no evidence that he was prepared, at that time, to incorporate such considerations into his theoretical view of socialist transition. He thus found it quite easy, in the subsequent period, to condemn the 'communist style'.

It was a consideration of events in the Soviet Union which led Mao Zedong to reformulate his views on socialist transition. In analysing what was particularly 'leftist' about the mistakes of Stalin, Mao began to come to a view of what constituted 'revisionism'. By 1962, 'revisionism' was seen not simply as a behavioural characteristic but also as the fostering of conditions under which policies appropriate to a superseded stage of development might be implemented. It arose from a disjunction between three elements of the relations of production (the pattern of ownership, the relations between people at work and the reciprocal interrelation between production and distribution). As Mao began to move away from a behavioural to a more substantive conception of 'revisionism', he must surely have begun to take stock of conditions in China which, in many ways, mirrored the 'reforms' then under way in the Soviet Union. The decentralisation of decision-making power to local areas, fostered during the Greap Leap, was giving way to a mixture of recentralisation and decentralisation of power to units of production. Atomised units, therefore, began to be linked more by the market than by the plan and economists had come forward to promote the virtues of 'market socialism'. These were the same conditions which had produced 'revisionism' in Yugoslavia—a country which Mao became convinced was no longer socialist. The Soviet Union, moreover, seemed to be heading in the same direction.

The reason why Mao did not come to this view until 1962 might have been because he was preoccupied with the economic damage resulting from natural calamities and from the Great Leap. It might also have been the case, however, that he had not had time to study political economy until after he had retired to what he referred to as the 'second front' in 1959 when Liu Shaoqi took over many of his former duties. Whatever the reason, the period 1960–2 did see Mao's first serious study of political economy. But he was still a novice and his notes, written at that time, reveal much inconsistency and confusion. As this volume will go on to show, his inconsistency was to have quite serious results in later years.

Mao's new thoughts about the structural conditions for 'revisionism' led him quite naturally to a reformulation of 'class struggle'. There had been much talk of 'class struggle' during the Great Leap, but one gets the impression that it was still seen in the old Soviet sense; it resulted from the persistence of remnant classes and ideologies which were supported by external forces. But, by the early 1960s, Mao began to feel that, in socialist society, certain structural conditions might produce *new* bourgeois elements. This generative view of class had very important implications for domestic politics. It implied that the revolution was constantly in danger of sliding backwards. Thus, socialism came to be seen not as a model to be achieved and consolidated but as the whole process of transition from the old society to communism. It was, moreover, a *reversible* process. Mao had, indeed, begun to add a diachronic element to his view of socialist transition. There was now no room for models.

Inner-Party Struggle

Mao's move away from considerations of behaviour to considerations of structure had very important implications for the way debate was conducted in the top policy-making circles. The conscientious adherence to Party norms of debate was no longer to be any guarantee that one would not be seen as the promoter of 'antagonistic' structures. Up to 1962, it seemed that the process of decision-making was able to accommodate all sorts of deviant and heterodox views, provided that organisational norms were adhered to. The Gao Gang and Peng Dehuai cases, however, appear as major aberrations. This may have been because Mao believed, in each case, that the existence of an independent power base suggested a conspiracy to seize supreme power. In each case also, a belief in a Soviet connection lent weight to such a view. But the important point is that, whereas in the case of Gao Gang most Party leaders were prepared to support the conspiracy theory, in the case of Peng Dehuai many were not. To such people, it must have seemed that Peng had been victimised simply for his views on the Great Leap and a very unfortunate precedent had been set. Earlier, Chen Yun had lost power because of a similar opposition to the Great Leap but the case of Peng Dehuai did seem to be the first time that a senior leader had been publicly humiliated for such a position. Whether that assessment was correct or not is an open question. Suffice it to say that the case of Peng Dehuai was to be a major element in the events which led up to the Cultural Revolution and which will be explored in this volume. In that revolution, many more cases like that of Peng Dehuai were to occur and the resentment continues to this day.

At lower levels of the Party organisation, the norms of inner-Party debate had started to break down much earlier than the Peng Dehuai case. The collapse of consensus at the highest levels was not to occur until Mao had discarded much of the Soviet model of socialism. At lower levels, concerned more with operational matters, consensus began to break down as soon as the Soviet model of administration had been discredited. Thus, many people were capped as 'rightist' in 1957–8 purely because of their expressed attitudes and not because of any physical act of opposition. Such a situation was to affect quite profoundly the way rectification movements were carried on. Following Teiwes, [3] one might draw a clear distinction between the closed type of rectification movement which had occurred at Yan'an and the open type of movement of 1947–8 which had resulted in confusion. The movement of 1950 was once again a closed movement as the Party strove to restore order, though elements of open rectification appeared in the subsequent three and five anti movements of 1951–2. When the Soviet model was implemented, the rectification movements were, once again, closed, but, unlike that closed movement in Yan'an, were not reliant on material solicited by Mass Line techniques. Thus, the Party became more and more exclusivist and cut off from the masses. This prompted Mao's call for an open process of rectification in 1957 which, after much opposition, finally got off the ground and then quickly got out of hand. One cannot be sure whether Mao supported the sudden decision to terminate open debate in mid-1957, but that reversal did signify a return once again to closed rectification. If Solomon is right and Mao was able to steer the subsequent anti-rightist movement on to specifically economic targets, then we might have the basis for an understanding of the excessive 'commandism' which sometimes developed during the Great Leap. Ideally, at that time, since open rectification could no longer be implemented, the closed process of rectification should have been informed (in the Yan'an style) by a parallel development of the Mass Line. But, when the pace of change was too quick for mass comments to be solicited, the Great Leap might actually have contributed to the exclusivity of the Party and occasioned the complaints which were voiced in 1960–1. In contrast to the 1959 campaign against 'right opportunism' in the aftermath of the Peng Dehuai case, the movement of 1960–1 was again relatively open but took place in such an atmosphere of demoralisation that one wonders whether the masses were mobilised actively to remedy the situation. All too often, it seems, the masses might have been persuaded merely to endorse the decision of work-teams and to blame the bad economic conditions on local cadres, regardless of their actual guilt. But significantly, the campaign of 1960–1 did give rise to the formation of new peasant associations and these were to become quite important in the period covered in this volume. In the first two chapters, much will be said about the relationship between peasant associations and work-teams.

It would seem, therefore, that, after Yan'an, closed rectification movements led to Party exclusivity and open rectification movements led to confusion. By the early 1960s, the attempt to get back to the spirit of Yan'an by combining closed rectification with the implementation of the Mass Line had failed. What was more important, however, was that, once Mao had decided that elements of a new bourgeoisie might develop in the Party structure itself, then the only kind of rectification movement which he would promote would be the open type. Mao, therefore, had to take the risk of whatever confusion might occur. Such was the thinking which led eventually to the Cultural Revolution.

The Decision-making Process

The apparent ease with which Mao returned to the 'first front' in 1962, which marks the starting point of this volume, has given much weight to a view of Chinese politics which sees Mao as the consistent drafter of the political agenda. According to this view, Mao constantly shifted his position between radical and more conservative policies. This was because of changing information from below, produced either by Mass Line techniques or invented by his close advisers such as Chen Boda or Kang Sheng. Thus, a 'conservative' or an 'ultra-leftist' was simply someone who did not keep up with Mao's changing position. There can be no doubt about the extraordinary power enjoyed by Mao both before and after the Party began to talk about 'collective leadership' in the 1950s. Indeed, the case of Peng Dehuai could be interpreted as showing that Mao was quite capable of taking a personal initiative and launching a surprise attack against someone who thought he was adhering to the norms of inner-Party debate. At times, Mao must have been a very difficult person to live with. Yet, if one looks at the whole period up to 1962, one finds that Mao did not often act in that way.

After 1962, however, Mao's political style began to change. As more and more of his political initiatives were blocked by a Party machine which feared the consequences of renewed radicalism, Mao began to work out a series of strategies to remove a large number of senior leaders from their posts. Mao certainly changed the rules of the game. How justified one deems him to have been in this will depend upon one's view of Mao's diagnosis of the changing orientation of the Party leadership. Implicitly, the post-Mao leadership has criticised Mao for violating the accepted rules of procedure. Mao would probably have criticised them for violating the process of socialist transition. Yet, right to the end, Mao maintained some respect for the rules of procedure and was to criticise many other people for violating them. That is why current (1976–9) recapitulations of history have been able to prise Mao apart from many of the advisers who surrounded him. This volume will perhaps help one to come to an assessment as to whether that attempt is credible.

NOTES

1. Trotsky, 1972 (original 1937), pp. 62–3.
2. Mao Zedong, 28 January 1958, *Chinese Law and Government*, Vol. I, No. 4, Winter 1968–9, pp. 13–14.
3. Teiwes, 1979.

I
ATTEMPTS AT RADICALISATION
(1962–1964)

The Tenth Plenum of the Eighth Central Committee, held in Beijing from 24 to 27 September 1962, was the culmination of two months extensive discussions at a central work conference which met first at Beidaihe and then in Beijing. The result of those discussions was an endorsement of Mao's call to combat 'revisionism' and to promote 'class struggle'.

As Mao saw it, the issues of 'revisionism' and 'class struggle' were the same both within China and internationally. Constant attention needed to be paid to the continued existence of classes in socialist society and the fact that imperialism was as powerful as ever. Party cadres, moreover, were falling into the morass of 'revisionism' in exactly the same way as some socialist countries were drifting back into capitalism. Unless there was constant vigilance, therefore, China could develop into another Yugoslavia; such he believed was happening to the Soviet Union.[1]

But how was the principle of class struggle to be operationalised? Here, Mao was extremely vague. The logic of the generative view of class was that, since 'new bourgeois elements' had begun to appear in the Communist Party, a large-scale 'open' process of rectification ought to be undertaken. Yet, the last such open rectification movement in 1960–1 had been directed at penalising cadres who had been too enthusiastic about the Great Leap Forward. Mao, therefore, first had recourse to a Yan'an-style movement, which combined closed rectification with mass mobilisation.[2] He was soon, however, to depart from this and introduce external elements into the process. Mao's position, therefore, tended to become quite ambiguous and such ambiguity led to many different interpretations of his directives. As a result of this, scholars are divided as to Mao's aims in the period 1962–5. Some tend to see Mao's consistent initiatives constantly being thwarted by an entrenched Party machine which feared the consequences of mass mobilisation. Others, however, see the oscillations in policy resulting from unexpected obstacles or the fact that Mao could not make up his mind about the relative merits of an open or closed movement. The chairman felt, for example, that the immediate task, in 1962, was not to go around persuading the masses everywhere to root out 'rightists', neither was it to reverse the verdicts on people already 'capped' as 'rightist' unless such verdicts were wrong.[3] But one was never sure how Mao's criteria for determining 'rightists' were to be interpreted nor who was to do the interpreting. Thus, when Mao objected to the rehabilitation of large numbers of 'rightists' (particularly in Anhui)[4] in 1962, it is difficult to know whether his policy had been deliberately violated.

Another source of confusion lay in the association between the new radical policies and the Great Leap Forward. Prior to 1962, Mao had been quite critical of many of the developments of 1958 – 9. In that year, however, he decided to strengthen his affirmation of the Great Leap Forward, though not its excesses. But what had been its excesses? This was an important question since the Socialist Education Movement, launched at the Tenth Plenum, took its name from that movement in 1957 which paved the way for the original Great Leap. Was there now to be a new 'leap forward'? If so, what might constitute its permissible constraints? But one thing did seem clear; satirical comments on the original Great Leap would no longer be tolerated. Mao was quite forthright:

> Writing novels is popular these days, isn't it? The use of novels for anti-Party activity is a great invention. Anyone wanting to overthrow a political régime must create public opinion and do some preparatory ideological work. This applies to counter-revolutionary as well as revolutionary classes.[5]

Yet even such an apparently unambiguous statement has led some commentators to suggest that Mao might not have been talking about the efforts of people such as Wu Han and Deng Tuo.[6] After all, they were criticised for writing plays and essays and not novels. The scope for scholarly interpretation in this period was, therefore, very wide. All we can say with certainty is that Mao did call for a reform of work in literature and the arts which, coupled with the Socialist Education Movement and the struggle against 'modern revisionism', was to provide the major themes for policies over the next few years.

The Socialist Education Movement

The Socialist Education Movement was probably accepted by most members of the Party, since very serious problems had arisen in the countryside. According to some documents pertaining to Lianjiang *xian* in Fujian province, which found their way to the West via one of the many Guomindang raids carried out in this period, there was a general 'spontaneous inclination towards capitalism' in the countryside. Many peasants were devoting an excessive amount of time to their private plots or had abandoned farming to go into business. Some cadres were corrupt and had appropriated public funds for their own use. Speculation and gambling were rife and there had been a revival of 'feudal' practices such as religious festivals, bride purchase and witchcraft.[7]

But how were these problems to be dealt with? At first, according to the Yan'an tradition, Party-led work-teams were sent to the countryside to rectify the situation. These work-teams were to be complemented by 'poor and lower-middle peasant associations' which had begun to reappear in the rectification movement of 1960 – 1. At the same time, the educational content of the Socialist Education Movement was taken very seriously and attempts were made to revive the old *minban* concept, through the establishment of 'part-work, part-study schools'.[8] But what was the relationship between formal and semi-formal education to be? What initiative, moreover, should be accorded to the peasant associations in relation to the work-teams? According to the Yan'an formula, the work-teams had to take the major initiative but, as more and more elements of 'open rectification' entered the picture, there was a basis for much disagreement.

As the movement got under way in the autumn of 1962, however, differences had not yet polarised at lower levels. At first, the movement was implemented in a number of trial areas, notably in Hebei and Hunan[9] (also in Lianjiang *xian*),[10] but, although some progress was made in raising cadre morale, there still remained the problem of ineffective leadership. In January 1963, therefore, cadres were instructed to pay particular attention to the health of the leading group within the brigades when carrying out the annual task of 'readjusting communes'.[11] When promoting cadres, stress was to be placed on those from poor and lower-middle peasant backgrounds (although others should not be automatically excluded.)[12] In carrying out rural work, cadres were instructed to be severe in their ideological criticism but, at the same time, organisational treatment should be lenient. Such a contradiction was in accord with the Yan'an principle of operating through existing organisations rather than pulverising them, but it might also have reflected the beginnings of divergencies in fundamental approach.

By the new year, moderate progress had been made in the movement in some areas. A number of economies in administration had been effected and a few private plots had been restricted, but the peasants had not been mobilised and, in some cases, cadres had insisted that the amount of money available for peasants to spend in the free markets should be increased.[13] The spirit of Yan'an had, once again, become Party policy but cadres interpreted that spirit in different ways. Some, for example, quoted from the documents of the early 1940s to correct what were felt to be excessively radical actions. Thus, the call to 'develop the economy and safeguard supplies', made by Mao in 1942,[14] might have had a dampening effect on the policy of mass mobilisation.

The Party was dragging its heels in the Socialist Education Movement. This may have been due to the lack of specificity in central policies or to conscious opposition to those policies. The army, however, which under Lin Biao had undergone a kind of Socialist Education Movement of its own, actively sought to propagate the spirit of the movement. Army cadres addressed gatherings of civilian leaders on the need to strengthen rural collective organisations and more and more study materials were published with obvious civilian application. Articles by army cadres began to appear in the newspapers calling for greater radicalism but, at the same time, these same newspapers carried articles by some Party leaders urging caution.[15]

In January 1963, a considerable amount of army propaganda material centred on the conduct of a model soldier by the name of Lei Feng. Lei Feng was remarkable in his devotion to the 'three red banners' of the Great Leap Forward, his selfless devotion to his comrades and the civilian population. After a short life of utterly devoted service, Lei Feng died a rather unspectacular death but fortunately left behind his diaries which became study materials for the new campaign. The point of the Lei Feng model was a fairly obvious one—that true glory did not consist of spectacular deeds and dying conspicuously for one's country but might be achieved in one's everyday activities. The model was that of a 'rustless screw' in the revolution—obviously above any form of corruption.[16] In February 1963, the Lei Feng documents became basic study material for a newly revamped militia organisation[17] and it was precisely that militia organisation which was to provide the backbone of the new poor and lower-middle peasant associations. Though it is very difficult to generalise about the Lei Feng movement, it is my impression that it was very effective. To Western eyes, Lei Feng might have appeared a prig. One might doubt the selflessness of a man who had himself photographed so many times and kept a diary which seemed written for a mass audience or even wonder whether he existed at all. That, in my opinion, would be to miss the point, for Lei Feng was presented as a normative model and it did not matter much whether he existed or not.

A second feature of army involvement in the Socialist Education Movement was the launching of a campaign for the 'living study and living use of Mao Zedong Thought'. This campaign, originally initiated in the army, was later to lead to the publication of *Quotations from the*

Works of Chairman Mao in red plastic covers[18] which was to become famous in the subsequent Cultural Revolution. The aims of the movement were many. First, and most obvious, the movement was aimed at countering individualism and the 'spontaneous development of capitalism' by presenting as many people as possible with a radical view of China's development. Secondly, the movement might provide the ideological cement which Mao and Lin Biao hoped (in the Yan'an tradition) would be much more effective than mere organisational engineering. On the other hand, it also promoted the person of Lin Biao who was now designated as the one who most creatively applied Mao Zedong Thought.[19]

A third feature of army involvement was that many of the key slogans put forward during the army reform after 1960 (such as the 'three-eight working style') were now seen as having applicability to the civilian sphere, though this came initially through the militia. The implication here was that the army should be involved in civilian life in a way not seen for over a decade. Again, this was in accordance with the Yan'an model, which sought to prevent the growth of a gap between army and civilians and to prevent military professionalism. Such a movement was, from Mao's point of view, healthy so long as it did not violate one of his cardinal principles, which held that although 'political power grows out of the barrel of a gun', it is the Party which wields the gun[20] and not vice versa.

With the partial radicalisation of the Socialist Education Movement in the new year of 1963, attempts were made to specify guidelines for the movement. In February, at a central work conference, Mao Zedong commented on the relatively successful experiences of the movement in Hunan and Hebei and urged that it be extended to cover the whole country. Experience in those areas had shown that the movement should be conducted in three steps. First, devote some 20 days to train a group of cadres; secondly, use this core to train more cadres and activists among the poor and lower-middle peasants (which I take to mean form the nucleus of poor and lower-middle peasant associations); thirdly, conduct all-out efforts (to mobilise the masses).[21] In this formula for mass mobilisation, Mao called for a movement which would go far beyond the simple process of closed rectification currently being carried out by the Party machine.

At another central work conference in May, the experiences of conducting the Socialist Education Movement were codified in a 'Draft Resolution of the Central Committee on Some Problems in Current Rural Work'.[22] This document, commonly known as the 'Early Ten Points', which was said to have been compiled under Mao's personal supervision, stressed the importance of class struggle. The notion 'four clean-ups' (*siqing*) was introduced which signified cleaning up accounts, granaries, property and work-points and ending cadre corruption. Cadres were to participate in productive labour and, most important of all, the Party formally proposed to re-establish poor and lower-middle peasant associations at commune, brigade and team levels to lead the movement.

After the promulgation of the 'Early Ten Points', the Party could hardly drag its feet on *policy* but it could, and indeed did, drag its feet on operations. The crux of the problem was exactly how the poor and lower-middle peasant associations should be established, what their functions were to be and how these related to the work-teams sent down from above. When the first 'poor peasants' representative groups' (*pinnong daibiao xiaozu*) were set up after the directive, they were charged with fostering the collective economy but under the leadership of the Party and as assistants to management committees.[23] The key question was—under the leadership of the Party *at what level?* What were they to do when a local Party branch was corrupt, or when the work-team was slothful? For their part, Party committees were enjoined to *submit* to the supervision of the peasant associations and yet also *lead* them. There was much confusion, therefore, as to whether rectification should be an open or a closed process.

There was very little, however, that bureaucratic cadres could do about avoiding participation in manual labour, since very detailed regulations were issued setting quotas on the number of days they must work in the fields and reducing the number of subsidised work-points they received for office duties. These latter were commonly reduced from 4 per cent to 1-2 per cent.[24]

By the summer of 1963, therefore, the main task in the Socialist Education Movement was to activate the poor and lower middle-peasant associations. As work-teams, concerned not to interfere too much with production, tried to keep control of the movement and as newly formed militia organisations, often with army instructors, pressed for further radicalisation of the associations, the situation became more confused. There was a need, therefore, for distinct Party instructions on the degree of permissible activism.

In September, the Party Centre attempted to satisfy the need for more specific instructions by the publication of a set of directives known as 'Some Concrete Policy Formulations . . . in the Socialist Education Movement'.[25] The ostensible aim of these directives, commonly referred to as the 'Later Ten Points', was to clarify a number of general issues enunciated in the 'Early Ten Points'. In fact, it was subsequently claimed in the Cultural Revolution that these 'Later Ten Points', which were issued under the direction of the Party general secretary Deng Xiaoping with the aid of Beijing's mayor Peng Zhen,[26] in 'clarifying' certain issues actually negated the spirit of the earlier document. Instead of 'struggle' (which was now confined to a very limited number of people), the later document preferred to speak of 'appropriate criticism'. Contradictions were to be seen as 'among the people' and 'non-antagonistic'. People were not to be branded as 'rightists'. 'Prosperous middle peasants' were not to be considered 'rich peasants'; more important still, the work-teams were to control the peasant associations and were not to disrupt existing organisations in the countryside. The 'Later Ten Points', which are riddled with contradictions, give one the overall impression that the new organisations created in the countryside were not to become vehicles for horizontal mobilisation but were to be ancillary 'staff' in a rigid vertical staff-line system of command which would carry out a disciplined movement from the top down. Though Mao probably authorised the publication of the 'Later Ten Points', one doubts whether this was his original intention. The detailed class analysis in the document, far from clarifying how to analyse class elements in the countryside, confused the situation and must have left cadres unsure of exactly what were the movement's targets.

Attempts were now made to ensure that leadership from above was strengthened by demanding that cadres 'squat on the spot' (*dundian*) in specific areas. On the surface, the demand that cadres spend more time in the country would seem to be a radical move in line with the injunction of the 'Early Ten Points', yet one might also interpret the requirement to 'squat on the spot' as a desire to prevent any unruly actions by peasant activists. Cadres were now not to wander aimlessly about convening meetings here and there and occasionally participating in manual labour, but were to stay in one area and thoroughly understand the situation.[27] Such a policy would only be effective if the cadres were sufficiently oriented to radical policies. If they just sought a quiet life, there could be no more effective way of preventing peasants criticising them.

To supplement the rural Socialist Education Movement, Mao and Lin Biao launched a movement in February 1964 to 'learn from the People's Liberation Army'.[28] This, in the spring, led to the establishment of a system of political departments in various branches of the economy based on that of the PLA.[29] As the movement unfolded, meetings were held having particular relevance for the Socialist Education Movement. Units were encouraged to 'compare' themselves with advanced units, in particular in the army, 'study' these units, 'catch up' with them and 'help' the less advanced (*bi xue gan bang*).[30] Large numbers of people were transferred permanently or temporarily out of the PLA to work in urban and rural economic units and militia training was given much greater stress. Army cadres, transferred to help militia units, now began to propagate more radical policies in the Socialist Education Movement in a spirit much more thoroughgoing than that of the 'Later Ten Points'. These cadres could easily call upon lecturers from the PLA to come down and give reports,[31] thus bypassing the regular administrative network.

Even in the somewhat more radical atmosphere of 1964, however, most of the policy directives put out by the Party from Beijing were cautious. However much Lin Biao promoted *political* emulation, other leaders still stressed *economic* emulation. Industry all over the country was still urged to emulate Shanghai.[32] This may have been because Shanghai was industrially the most advanced city in China. It was, however, also the most bourgeois city and yet contained a Party leadership which had been extremely enthusiastic about the Great Leap. Though, once again, interpretation is difficult, it is unlikely that Shanghai was seen in a Great Leap context in 1964. The emulation campaign was, it seems, part of a process whereby smaller towns were urged to emulate the industrial achievements of larger towns.[33] With greatly improved harvests after 1962, the central planners were proud of the economic achievements obtained since the years of natural calamities and wished to avoid any disruption. Significantly, a much publicised pamphlet by Tao Zhu concerning people's communes, written in 1964, made no mention of the army, at a time when the whole country was being urged to study its experiences.[34]

During the Socialist Education Movement, meetings were held to recall the past and peasants compiled their 'three histories' (personal, family and village) so as more easily to compare the present with the past.[35] Peasant associations were strengthened and cadres conducted lessons in 'class education'. In this atmosphere, a central work conference and Politburo Standing Committee conference met in June 1964 to discuss progress in the Socialist Education Movement. During this conference, Mao Zedong, taking the initiative, laid down six criteria for evaluating the Socialist Education Movement. The first of these was the degree to which poor and lower-middle peasants had been truly mobilised.[36] They could surely not have been mobilised according to the 'Later Ten Points' but, by then, this document seems to have been brushed aside. Mao further went on to demand that when rich peasants, counter-revolutionaries and bad elements who engaged in destructive activities were discovered, they should be 'struggled against' by the masses rather than dealt with by higher authorities.

The June conference finally formulated an 18-point document entitled 'Organisational Rules for Poor and Lower-Middle Peasant Associations'.[37] These associations were still circumscribed by the leadership of local Party committees but the tone of the document was somewhat less cautious than hitherto. Cadres, for example, were strictly warned not to 'strike retaliatory blows' against peasants who criticised them. But the overall impression one gets of progress in the Socialist Education Movement, by mid-1964, was that Mao was still finding it very difficult to achieve the degree of radicalism he had aimed at.

Ambiguity in Economic Policy

It was not just in the Socialist Education Movement in the rural sector that ambiguity reigned. In the economy as a whole, the new radical spirit coexisted uneasily with policies which dated from the consolidation period of 1960 – 2.

The new radical climate after 1962 seems to have prevented any of the Liberman-type proposals, advanced at that time, from being put into practice. It is probable, moreover, that the issue of the profit-motive was effectively squashed even before the new period of radicalism began. The 'Seventy Articles on Industry' must have left any advocate of 'leaping forward' very dissatisfied in that they paid little attention to political work in industrial enterprises, but they did stress the priority of output targets over profit targets.[38] An out-and-out 'revisionist' policy, according to Chinese criticisms of the later Soviet economic reforms, would have been to allow enterprises to produce directly for the market and to judge their performance solely according to the profit they made in that arena. In China, there seems to be no evidence that this kind of policy was introduced in the early 1960s.[39]

Another development of 1962 which became a major issue in the Cultural Revolution was the reversal of the priority Mao had given to collectivisation over mechanisation. In that year, Liu Shaoqi was said to have advocated a policy of selective mechanisation based on tractor stations separate from the people's communes. Liu is reported to have selected some 100 – 130 *xian* in which full mechanisation was to be introduced. The initiative here would be taken by tractor stations which would work for a profit. The profits generated during this first stage of mechanisation would be used to provide mechanisation for a similar batch of *xian* after ten years.[40] As Jack Gray points out, since there were some 2,000 *xian* in China, this road to mechanisation would have taken an extraordinarily long period of time.[41] But again, this conservative policy does not appear to have been carried out during the Socialist Education Movement, although Liu is reported to have advanced his ideas several times during the years after 1962.

In 1963, Liu was said to have extended his ideas for rural mechanisation by advocating the establishment of an agricultural machinery trust[42] and later other trusts covering various sectors of the economy. One must distinguish here between horizontally integrated local trusts (often known as joint enterprises) which were set up in ever increasing numbers in China, even during the radical period of the middle 1950s,[43] and the vertically integrated trusts advocated in the 1960s. These latter were, in fact, to be state corporations with monopoly control of the manufacture and distribution of certain products. They were to operate autonomously, free from ministerial control and also free from the influence of local Party and government organisations.[44] Such trusts not only negated the dual rule policies but were profit-making concerns which might quite easily grow into 'independent kingdoms'. The vertically integrated trusts seem to have been effective mainly at provincial level.[45] Nevertheless, even such a limited implementation does not suggest that they occasioned much opposition at the time.

Another feature of economic policy, which perhaps caused some concern to those who wished to close the urban-rural gap, centred on the question of employment and wages. During the period 1957–63, average industrial wages fell by 0.8 per cent,[46] which was encouraging from the point of view of those who wished to close the urban-rural gap. In 1963, however, a mild wage reform was carried out which raised industrial wages somewhat. It is fair to say, however, that the effects were not very significant. In general, the average industrial wage remained almost static[47] during the period 1957–63, which was a remarkable achievement in countering inflation.

To look at average wages, however, may perhaps give one a somewhat distorted picture since the first half of the 1960s saw an enormous growth in the number of temporary contract workers recruited from the rural areas. In 1958, there were about 12 million such workers, whereas in the early 1960s this figure increased to some 30–40 per cent of the total non-agricultural workforce.[48] One might argue that the employment of this cheap labour actually served to close the urban-rural gap but it also created sharp *intra-urban* differentials which were potentially very divisive. Furthermore, an excessive reliance on temporary labour unassimilated into any communal-type organisation was a violation of the radical vision of the late 1950s.

Though wage reform and the growth of temporary labour were later to cause disquiet, there were some areas of economic administration during the Socialist Education Movement which, from the perspective of the Cultural Revolution, were encouraging. Though vertical rule in industry was much stronger than hitherto, workers and staff congresses were revamped[49] and, in some enterprises, experiments were undertaken whereby factory general managers were elected.[50] Although 'one-person management' was occasionally revived, experiments were undertaken in 1964 to introduce a non-bureaucratic functional system of management which accorded well with the old Yan'an principle of 'concentrated leadership and divided operations'.[51] Although, occasionally, Party committees and senior management were in fact the same people, the principle of 'responsibility of the factory general manager under the enterprise Party committee' was retained and, as Andors has pointed out, the Great Leap Forward legacy could never be completely negated.[52]

A second source of encouragement lay in the remarkable success with which China's petroleum industry had developed since the Great Leap

Forward. An object of great pride was the Daqing oilfield in north-east China. In recent years (1977–9), the development of this oilfield has been portrayed as a triumph of those who sought to develop the productive forces against the 'idealist' schemes of their radical opponents.[53] In fact, the field was named after the 'great celebration' of the tenth anniversary of the Chinese People's Republic and thus signified the spirit of the Great Leap. In the early 1960s, it was considered to be a model of self-reliance and improvisation and a triumph of the human spirit over the pessimism of technologists. Before 1949, Western surveys had shown China to be very poor in oil. It was soon to become self-sufficient in this vital energy source. Daqing became the symbol of that self-sufficiency, and its heroes, such as the famous 'Iron Man' Wang Jinxi, symbols of the right combination of 'red' and 'expert'.[54] Before long, the oilfield was also to become a model of social organisation as many of the features of the old urban commune were recreated.[55] Mao Zedong was most insistent in his call for industry to 'learn from Daqing'.[56]

The agricultural counterpart of Daqing was the Dazhai production brigade in the poor loess lands of Shanxi. This had been criticised by one of the work-teams in the Socialist Education Movement but had been praised by Mao. Before liberation, there had only been some 53 hectares of land in Dazhai, scattered over seven gullies, eight ridges and one mountain slope with a per hectare yield of only one tonne. Most of the output went to one landlord and three rich peasants. Of the village's 64 households, 48 were in the category of poor and lower-middle peasant, many of whose members had to work outside the village and some of whom had been reduced to begging. After land reform, a fierce struggle had apparently occurred between those who saw little chance of improvement without considerable state aid and those who believed that co-operativisation could be undertaken before mechanisation. At one stage in the early 1950s, it was claimed that two mutual aid teams had existed embodying these different approaches to modernisation, though finally the radical team under the leadership of Party Secretary Chen Yonggui was victorious and set about organising a co-op. The early life of the Dazhai co-op was very precarious since a conservative local government had little confidence in its chances of success in such a climatically hazardous region. When the co-op wanted to expand beyond the limits set by the *xian* authorities, Chen Yonggui was forced to keep two sets of accounts, one showing the production of a co-op of 41 households, and one showing the production for a co-op of 30 households as prescribed by the *xian*. By the early 1960s, yields in Dazhai had begun to surpass the average for the Huanghe region but, in the autumn of 1963, there occurred the worst floods for a century and some brigade members again began to think of asking for state aid. Resisting this demand, Chen Yonggui persuaded the brigade members to adhere to the principle of self-reliance and to repair the broken stone walls which held up the terraces. By 1964, Dazhai's harvest was a spectacular 310 tonnes with a yield of 6.2 tonnes/hectare.

Not only was Dazhai held out as a model for 'self-reliance' (according to the spirit of the Great Leap), it was also designated a model for the 'living application of Mao Zedong Thought'. A practical example of what this meant lay in the reform of the work-point system. The old system of designating a number of points for each job of work was abolished and a new system introduced whereby each peasant said what he thought his work deserved and the other members of his team discussed and amended his appraisal. As a consequence, the average number of workdays per person went up from 260 in 1963 to 280 in 1964. Thus, an attempt had been made to get away from the idea of piece-work and to move nearer to the payment ideals of the Great Leap. True, this was not payment according to 'need' such as was advocated in some areas during the Great Leap. It was still the 'socialist' principle of payment according to work, but it reintroduced the idea of labour attitude and consciousness and, as such, was said to have contributed much to work enthusiasm.[57] Dazhai was a remarkable model even though the work-team which brought it to national attention considered that it had falsified its achievements.[58] Visiting Dazhai in the summer of 1966 after another, though less serious, downpour of heavy rain, I was impressed by the way every bit of land had been preserved behind stout walls, and how, after the rains of that year, they were being rapidly repaired. Dazhai seemed to provide an example of what could be done relatively quickly and cheaply in many other regions.

Economic policy, therefore, was ambiguous. Policies which might be considered to be 'revisionist' were still voiced though rarely imple-mented. At the same time, impressive models had been put forward though one was not always sure how to establish them in other areas. What probably preoccupied rural cadres were simply petty instances of capitalism and the lack of clarity in central policies. They were never quite sure whether the targets of their criticism ought to be their fellows or senior people in authority.

Reform in Literature and the Arts

May 1963 saw not only the publication of the 'Early Ten Points' which were designed to spread the Socialist Education Movement over the whole country, but also Mao Zedong's first attempt to promote a campaign to reform literature and the arts. It was claimed, in 1979, that Mao embarked on this campaign on the basis of false information concocted by his close associate Kang Sheng. Kang, apparently, had wrongly informed the chairman in 1962 that literature and art had been used for anti-Party purposes.[59] Enough has already been said in the previous volume, however, to suggest that a good case might be made out to show that literature was, in fact, being used for, if not anti-Party, at least, anti-Mao purposes. In any case, the launching of a campaign in literature and the arts would follow naturally from Mao's previous thinking about superstructural push.

The National Conference of Writers and Artists, convened in 1963, sought to mobilise intellectuals to 'play their full militant role' in the struggle against 'modern revisionism' and to help them identify with the 'broad masses of the labouring people, with the workers, peasants and soldiers'. They were instructed not to avoid conflict[60] or, in the terminology soon to become popular, they were to adhere to the proposition that 'one divides into two'.

The proposition 'one divides into two' was not, as it might seem, an esoteric philosophical point, but was to have considerable relevance in the following years. It signified an injunction to look at everything in terms of its internal contradictions and to separate out the contradictory elements. Once those elements were separated, one could determine whether the relationship between them was antagonistic or non-antagonistic and so formulate a policy for dealing with them. The alternative premiss, soon to be put forward by some philosophers, was 'two combines into one' whereby one looked not at the inherent division within a thing but at the way divisive elements ceased to be divided and came together in an entity. The former proposition, therefore, was an obligation to criticise, analyse and struggle whereas the latter was to smooth over differences. In politics, the former advocated the theme of the Tenth Plenum—class struggle—whereas the latter was held to concentrate on the way classes died away. In literature and art, the former portrayed heroic and villainous characters as models whereas the latter was merely a continuation of the conservative policy of portraying 'middle characters'.

About the same time as the May 1963 National Conference of Writers and Artists, Mao's wife Jiang Qing began to take a direct part in the process of literary and art reform. She was said to have carried out investigations into the intent of Wu Han's play about Hai Rui and to have examined a series of stories allegedly written in early 1961 by one of the 'Three Family Village' trio, Liao Mosha.[61] In retrospect, it would seem that this collection, entitled *Stories About Not Fearing Ghosts*, was particularly significant though the precise meaning of the stories has yet to be satisfactorily explained. One explanation, put forward by He Qifang (in the preface to the volume), was that the aim was to publicise Mao's slogan that 'all reactionaries are paper tigers' by showing that imperialists and reactionaries, like ghosts, were not to be feared.[62] On the other hand, it has been argued that He's preface and the intent of the book was to de-emphasise Mao's slogan by declaring that imperialists and reactionaries were merely 'ghosts',[63] in the same way that Deng Tuo was said to have implied that Mao's statement about the 'East wind prevailing over the West wind' was merely 'wind'.

Throughout 1963 and early 1964, most Party statements on the question of reforming literature and art were usually qualified,[64] and Beijing operas continued to be played. It was subsequently revealed that, by mid-1964, Mao was profoundly impatient and, at a meeting of the All China Federation of Literary and Art Circles in June, declared that unless Chinese intellectuals remoulded themselves they would, at some future date, develop groups like the infamous Hungarian Petöfi Club.[65] Mao was profoundly pessimistic about the lack of advance made in literature and art since 1949 and was particularly worried about the return to old 'feudal' themes. He commented:

> Problems abound in all forms of art . . . and the people involved are numerous; in many departments very little has been achieved so far in socialist transformation. The 'dead' still predominate in many departments . . . Isn't it absurd that many communists are enthusiastic about promoting feudal and capitalist art, but not socialist art?[66]

In 1979, it was claimed that Mao's increasing dissatisfaction with the state of literature and art was not an appropriate response to the actual situation. This was because the chairman had been misled by Jiang Qing and her supporters. Apparently, in response to a criticism of literature and art made by Mao in December 1963, the literary authorities had produced a report on the current situation which was said to be erroneous and not to have reflected the objective situation. The report, moreover, failed to take into account the new climate which had developed in early 1964. As a result of the criticisms of Deng Xiaoping and others, the report was not submitted officially to Chairman Mao. Jiang Qing, however, obtained a copy of the report and inserted in it further material to support her nefarious designs. She then submitted the adulterated report to Mao Zedong as an official document. It was on the basis of this that Mao's denunciations had been made.[67] The implication was that, had Mao known that the document he received had not been endorsed officially, he might have come to a different conclusion. But one wonders if such would have been the case and whether Mao, in early 1964, had such a naive faith in the literary authorities.

In any case, regardless of what had really happened in the corridors of power, the June Party central work conference approved Mao's demand to rectify the field of literature and art and, in the second half of

1964, the movement was to be vigorously promoted within the Federation of Literary and Art Circles. The question was, however, who was to do the promoting? After Mao had complained about literature and art in December 1963, it was said that Liu Shaoqi, Deng Xiaoping, Peng Zhen and Zhou Yang had discussed the question and, in January, had declared that they would promote socialist art.[68] As of June 1964, however, classical theatre still flourished and nothing much seems to have been done. In that situation, Mao came to rely more upon the efforts of Jiang Qing, her army colleagues and the Shanghai literary critic Yao Wenyuan who had assisted her in denouncing *Stories About Not Fearing Ghosts*.[69]

Jiang Qing's initial attempts to get the First Beijing Opera Company to produce Beijing operas with modern themes came to nothing. Apparently, her first attempt to get produced a piece, which subsequently became the opera *Shajiabang*, was rebuffed by the opera company which insisted on producing time-honoured classical pieces.[70] After the initial failure, however, Jiang Qing was to have more success with modern ideas during and after a national festival of Beijing opera on revolutionary themes in the summer of 1964.

Formal responsibility for the rectification movement in the field of literature and art, which began in mid-1964, however, was not entrusted to Jiang Qing but to Peng Zhen. One wonders why the immediate superior of Wu Han, Deng Tuo and Liao Mosha should have been chosen for such a task.[71] One might posit a number of explanations. First, it is possible that Mao was not in the least concerned about the satirical writings of 1961 – 2 and had every confidence in a man who had played a major role in the Socialist Education Movement and who had been designated 'Mao's close comrade in arms'. Secondly, if Mao were worried about Peng, he might have thought that Peng might see the error of his ways once he was put in a position of rectifying his subordinates. Thirdly, Peng could have been the appointee of those Party leaders who had rejected the draft report on literature and art of early 1963 and who resented the fact that Jiang Qing had submitted it to Mao. Fourthly, it is possible that Mao had observed Peng's unwillingness to do very much after his call in December 1963 and had realised that, once a mass movement could be launched from below, Peng would attempt to suppress it and so expose himself. As to which, if any, of the above explanations is correct, we can only guess.

Closely allied with the movement for the reform in literature and the arts was an attempt to inject fresh radical blood into the propaganda network.[72] Deng Tuo, Wu Han and Liao Mosha had quite easily found outlets for their writing in the Beijing press and indeed, at one time, Deng Tuo had been the editor-in-chief of *Renmin Ribao*. With the radicalisation of 1964, it was claimed that attempts were made in the

Beijing press to check the dissemination of Mao Zedong Thought.[73] The fresh blood to be injected into the press was to come from the People's Liberation Army though it is my impression that the injection was initially rather unsuccessful, at least judging from the way certain newspapers remained highly cautious in the early days of the subsequent Cultural Revolution.

The Campaign to Cultivate Revolutionary Successors[74]

It was not, however, only the older intellectuals who worried Mao and the Party radicals. In different conversations with foreign visitors in 1964 – 5, Mao remarked time and again that contemporary youth lacked real experience in class struggle and were becoming soft.[75] He felt that the youth should participate in a much more radical version of the Socialist Education Movement and actively prevent the rural revolution from slipping backwards. The Communist Youth League seemed to be degenerating into a corps where youth were apprenticed to become members of an élite.[76] Clearly it was not only the Party which should be rectified from the outside.

As Mao saw it, the current education system, far from doing anything to rectify the situation, was geared to creating a technocracy[77] devoid of sufficient political consciousness. Mao was to tell Edgar Snow in early 1965 that it was possible that today's youth might

> make peace with imperialism, bring the remnants of the Jiang Jieshi clique back to the mainland, and take a stand beside the small percentage of counter-revolutionaries still in the country.[78]

Mao's view of current teaching practices was equally stringent:

> The present method of education ruins talent and ruins youth. I do not approve of reading so many books. The method of examination is a method for dealing with the enemy; it is most harmful, and should be stopped.[79]

Mao's answer, however, did not lie in educational reform from above. Youth must be actively mobilised to reform their own educational system even if it meant overthrowing the academic authorities. What was required was to extend the Socialist Education Movement into the sphere of formal education. For the time being, however, Peng Zhen did not seem to be the kind of man who could take a lead in that process.

The Campaign in Philosophy

The first major explosion to take place in the field of education occurred in the summer of 1964 and centred on the issue of 'two combining into one'. In May, a rather obscure article appeared in *Guangming Ribao* to the effect that such was the universal law of materialist dialectics and the notion of 'one dividing into two' was merely an analytical method used by Marxists in analysing society and nature.[80] As I suggested earlier, the debate hinged upon the whole question of handling social contradictions. What the *Guangming Ribao* article seemed to be advocating was a class conciliationist position, which echoed that of Khrushchev. The philosophical polemics were to rage unabated for three months and occasioned a forum held by the Higher Party School on the issue. The final result was to be the dismissal of the head of the Higher Party School, Yang Xianzhen, who was charged with provoking the debate with ulterior motives.[81]

In retrospect, the debate in philosophy appears extremely significant. It was probably too early at this stage to attack Wu Han's and Deng Tuo's treatment of history for having ulterior motives but it was possible to attack Yang Xianzhen for covertly adopting a class conciliationist line under the guise of academic debate, if indeed that was what he was doing. The Yang Xianzhen debate was to set a precedent which was to become increasingly important in the Cultural Revolution. In the meantime, subsequent victims of the Cultural Revolution such as Zhou Yang had 'tested the wind' and had become most vocal in their application of the principle of 'one divides into two'.

The Sino-Soviet Dispute—Open Polemics

The principle of 'one divides into two' was advanced by Zhou Yang in January 1964 as the ideological rationale for developments in the International Communist Movement.[82] Indeed, between the Tenth Plenum and that date, the point of no return in Sino-Soviet relations seems to have been reached. Even prior to the Tenth Plenum, Mao had made it clear that 'revisionism' was not just a domestic concern. Shortly after the plenum, international events occurred which seemed to confirm Mao's diagnosis of the Soviet Union.

On 22 October 1962, two days after the outbreak of the hostilities between China and India, President Kennedy announced that the Cuban missile crisis had begun.[83] As Gittings points out, there is no evidence that China sought to take advantage of Soviet and American distractions, since no one surely could have predicted the events in Cuba and such an explanation avoids any consideration of the state of India's 'forward policy'.[84] Although *Pravda* cautiously endorsed the Chinese proposal to negotiate with India on 25 October during the height of the Cuban crisis, the Soviet Union soon swung back to its so-called 'neutral' attitude. Khrushchev's 'neutrality' allegedly included an apology to Nehru for supporting China's bid for negotiations[85] and a continued supply of arms to India. China, for its part, had supported the Soviet Union in the Cuban crisis, also significantly on 25 October, but once the Soviet Union backed down under American threats, the Chinese began to analyse the Cuban situation and found the Soviet Union guilty of 'capitulationism' for withdrawing the missiles under threat.[86] The Chinese were particularly indignant at what they considered 'a betrayal of proletarian internationalism' during the Indian war and were probably particularly incensed that, after they had supported Soviet actions which they considered adventurist in Cuba for the sake of that internationalism, the Soviet Union should now actively aid China's enemy. Anyway, now that the Soviet Union could be seen to be guilty of bad faith, there was no point in masking Chinese disquiet concerning the whole Cuban adventure. The Soviet view of the Cuban crisis, however, was that, in obtaining a guarantee from the United States not to invade Cuba, they had scored a victory and the Chinese tough line, if implemented, would have threatened world peace.[87]

In the winter of 1962 – 3, a series of Communist Party congresses were held in Bulgaria, Hungary, Italy, Czechoslovakia and East Germany which saw the continuation of the polemic and during this period *Renmin Ribao*, on 15 December, openly criticised the behaviour of anti-Chinese delegates to the congresses.[88] Such was the beginning of a furious open polemic which reached a climax in March 1963. By that time, a number of Communist parties, anxious to bring about a compromise, proposed an international conference which both the Soviet Union and China accepted. On 30 March, a Soviet letter spelt out questions of principle to be discussed[89] and in May agreement was reached to hold bilateral talks on 5 July. On 17 June, the Chinese published a reply to the Soviet letter of 30 March[90] setting out what they considered a suitable agenda, but this was taken by the Soviet Party to be a breach of the agreement to suspend polemics. The Soviet government, in response, demanded the recall of three Chinese diplomats from Moscow. On 5 July, the bilateral talks opened in a very strained atmosphere and by 13 July the publication of open polemics was resumed. Following the opening of the test-ban treaty talks in mid-July, Sino-Soviet negotiations ceased.

As the Chinese saw it, the partial test-ban treaty between the Soviet Union, Britain and the United States, signed on 25 July, was the ultimate sell-out. The Soviet Union had given up the idea of complete disarmament and a total ban on nuclear weapons in favour of a partial treaty which banned tests in the atmosphere. Such a treaty froze the nuclear status quo since, with the current state of technology, any country which had begun to manufacture nuclear weapons would be obliged initially to test them in the atmosphere, particularly since it was much cheaper. Most aspiring nuclear powers could, therefore, not sign the treaty, for those that did would be unable to produce nuclear weapons at all. In the meantime, both the superpowers could go on increasing their stockpiles. To the Chinese, the test-ban treaty was a supreme example of 'great power collusion' and China could only propose a total and universal ban on the production, stockpiling, testing and use of all nuclear weapons.[91] In the meantime, China's own nuclear weapons programme would continue and China fully intended to test in the atmosphere once it was ready. Few people foresaw, in July 1963, that China would be ready in only 15 months.

The open publication of the Sino-Soviet polemics in the first half of 1963 led to a Chinese reappraisal of the structure as well as the orientation of the International Communist Movement. It has never, to my knowledge, been satisfactorily demonstrated that there were significant differences among the Chinese leadership on this question, though Jim Peck has suggested possible divergencies which deserve mention.[92] In Peck's view, Mao, as a dialectician, was concerned primarily with orientations and the direction of change, whereas Liu Shaoqi was primarily an organisation man. It is probable, therefore, that Mao's view of the world in the early 1960s was one of a global United Front constantly shifting in composition while Liu's view was one of tightly organised blocs. The combination of both of these views resulted in 1963 in a policy which sought both to unite with whomever could be united with to oppose the principal enemy (United States imperialism) and an attempt to create a new and separate International Communist Movement.[93]

Within international organisations during this period, the Chinese delegates made much of United States-Soviet collusion and the Soviet Union attempted to capitalise on China's denunciation of the partial test-ban treaty. Sino-Soviet clashes occurred within the World Peace Council, the World Federation of Trade Unions and the Afro-Asian Peoples' Solidarity Organisation.[94] Amongst Communist parties, the issue of Soviet 'revisionism' was hotly debated and a number of new Marxist-Leninist parties were formed with enthusiastic Chinese support. In the next two years, such parties appeared in Belgium, Ceylon, Australia, Colombia, India, Lebanon, Nepal and Paraguay. In Brazil, an 'anti-revisionist' party had been set up as early as February 1962 and was now supported by the Chinese. In 1963–4 a number of established Communist parties also took a firm line against Soviet 'revisionism', among them those of New Zealand, Japan, Indonesia, Malaya, Thailand and Burma. Other parties took a more moderately critical line, among them those of the Democratic Republic of Vietnam and the Democratic

People's Republic of Korea.[95] In subsequent years, the International Communist Movement was to experience further splits and realignments, but it was fairly clear by 1964 that the movement was irreconcilably split. One had indeed divided into two!

Conclusion

By mid-1964, Mao's attempts to combat 'revisionism' had met with only limited success. The Socialist Education Movement had developed a head of steam though it seemed that the Party machine was not performing as well as it might in the task of revitalising the rural areas. Part of the fault for this might have been due to the fact that Mao himself was not too clear about what he wanted. The campaign in literature and the arts had also made only moderate achievements. It was, moreover, in the charge of Peng Zhen, a man who was at odds with one of the major influences on Mao on that subject—Jiang Qing. Mao also was apparently quite dispirited with the political consciousness of most of China's youth and the only major issue to rock the academic world was the debate in philosophy over 'one dividing into two'. By 1964, the Sino-Soviet split had reached serious proportions and had caused a complete rethink about the content of the 'socialist camp'. The polemics directed against the Soviet Union were, it seems, also in part directed at a 'revisionist' Chinese audience. Thus it was within this inter-Party polemic that a new initiative was taken to promote radical policies.

NOTES

1. Mao Zedong, 24 September 1962, Schram, 1974, pp. 188-96.
2. Ibid., p. 193.
3. Ibid., p. 194.
4. SCMM 651, 22 April 1969, p. 39.
5. Mao Zedong, 24 September 1962, Schram, 1974, p. 195.
6. Chan, 1980, p. 176.
7. Chen and Ridley, 1969, summarised in Baum and Teiwes, 1968, p. 12.
8. Price, 1973, p. 7; Gardner, 1971, p.247.
9. Baum and Teiwes, 1968, p. 63.
10. Chen and Ridley, 1969, pp.140−8, *passim*.
11. Ibid., p. 151.
12. RMRB, 11 January 1963, p. 1.
13. Vogel, 1971, p. 302.
14. Ibid.; Gao Xiang, SCMP 2939, 15 March 1963, pp. 1−9.
15. Vogel, 1971, pp. 303−4.
16. Chen, 1968.
17. SCMP 2947, 27 March 1963, pp. 7−8.
18. The English edition of this is Mao Zedong, 1966.

19. See p. 145.
20. Mao Zedong, 6 November 1938, *SW* II, 1965, p. 224.
21. Baum and Teiwes, 1968, pp. 63 – 4.
22. Text in ibid., pp. 58 – 71; see also Selden, 1979, pp. 536 – 41.
23. Baum and Teiwes, 1968, pp. 16 – 17.
24. Ibid., p. 18.
25. Text in ibid., pp. 72 – 94. This document is discussed in Baum, 1975, pp. 44 – 59.
26. Baum, 1969, p. 94; Baum, 1975, p. 43; Teiwes (1979, pp. 521 – 2) assigns primary responsibility to Peng Zhen.
27. Baum and Teiwes, 1968, p. 23.
28. *SCMP* 3164, 24 February 1964, pp. 1 – 8.
29. Ibid. 3200, 16 April 1964, pp. 3 – 7.
30. Vogel, 1971, p. 310; *SCMP* 3179, 16 March 1964, pp. 1 – 5.
31. Vogel, 1971, p. 316.
32. On the movement for 'comparing with, learning from and overtaking the advanced and helping the backward in industry' *(bi xue gan bang)*, see *CB* 731, 11 May 1964.
33. Vogel, 1971, p. 312.
34. Tao Zhu, 1964. Moody (1973, pp. 284 – 5) describes this pamphlet as 'left in form and right in essence'.
35. Hu Yaobang, *PR* 28, 10 July 1964, p. 15.
36. Mao Zedong, June 1964, Baum and Teiwes, 1968, p. 27.
37. Text in ibid., pp. 95 – 101.
38. Perkins, 1968, p. 607. See also Selden, 1979, pp. 485 – 8.
39. Perkins, 1968, p. 607.
40. Gray, 1973, p. 144.
41. Ibid. For Mao's views on agricultural mechanisation, see Mao Zedong, 12 March 1966, *JPRS*, 1974, pp. 373 – 4.
42. *SCMM* 644, 10 February 1969, pp. 35 – 8.
43. Schurmann, 1966, p. 300.
44. Gray, 1973, p. 145.
45. *SCMM* 644, 10 February 1969, pp. 35 – 8. Liu and Tan Zhenlin did set up the 'China Tractor and Internal Combustion Engine Industrial Corporation' with branch companies in 7 areas, though it is uncertain how effective the corporation was (ibid., p. 28). According to *Nongye Jixie Jishu*, its activities were 'checked in time' by Mao and 'boycotted by the masses'.
46. Howe, 1973(b), p. 237.
47. Ibid.
48. Ibid., p. 235.
49. *SCMP* 2604, 24 October 1961, pp. 15 – 17.
50. Richman, 1969, pp. 255 – 6.
51. Chang Dakai and Song Jinsheng, *Renmin Shouce*, 1965, pp. 564 – 6.
52. Andors, 1974.
53. See Chan, 1980, p. 178.
54. PFLP, 1972 (b), pp. 5 – 8.
55. *PR* 53, 31 December 1971, pp. 6 – 9.
56. Mao Zedong, 13 February 1964, Schram, 1964, p. 199.
57. Pien Hsi, 1972.
58. Teiwes, 1979, pp. 554 – 5.
59. See Chan, 1980, p. 180.
60. *PR* 22, 31 May 1963, p. 8.
61. *SCMP* 3686, 28 April 1966, p. 2.
62. He Qifang, *PR* 10, 10 March 1961, pp. 6 – 10.

63. See Solomon, 1971, p. 414.

64. Vogel, 1971, pp. 309 – 10.

65. Mao Zedong, June 1964, *CB* 891, 8 October 1969, p. 41.

66. Mao Zedong, December 1963, ibid.

67. Li Zhi, *Renmin Wenxue* 1, 1979, p. 99.

68. Esmein, 1973, p. 49.

69. Solomon, 1971, p. 450.

70. The opera *Spark in the Reed Field* was a Shanghai opera. It was allegedly called off one day before the opening night on the orders of Peng Zhen. *SCMM* 639, 6 January 1969, pp. 15 and 23.

71. See the discussion in Bridgham, 1967, p. 12. Dittmer (1974, p. 70) argues the alternative thesis that there was no *necessary* connection between Wu Han's actions and Peng's defence of them.

72. Bridgham, 1967, p. 13.

73. *SCMP* 4253, 9 September 1968, p. 25.

74. See Mao Zedong, 16 June 1964, *JPRS*, 1974, pp. 356 – 60.

75. Snow, 1965, p. 21.

76. Gardner, 1971, pp. 276 – 86. See also Funnell, 1970.

77. See Mao Zedong, 13 February 1964, *JPRS*, 1974, pp. 329 – 30.

78. Snow, 1965, p. 23.

79. Mao Zedong, 13 February 1964, Schram, 1974, p. 205.

80. Ai Hengwu and Lin Qingshan, *CB* 745, 2 December 1964, pp. 1 – 5 (particularly p. 3).

81. A post-Cultural Revolution Chinese account of the debate may be found in PFLP, 1973. See also *PR* 37, 11 September 1964, pp. 9 – 12. For an early Western account, see Munro, 1965.

82. Zhou Yang, 26 October 1963, *PR* 1, 3 January 1964, pp. 10 – 27.

83. For China's response to the Cuban crisis, see ibid. 44, 2 November 1962, pp. 3 – 7.

84. See Gittings, 1968, p. 174. For a full treatment of India's forward policy, see Maxwell, 1972, pp. 179 – 273.

85. Dallin, 1963, p.660.

86. Ibid., pp. 656 – 9.

87. Suslov, quoted in Gittings, 1968, pp. 176 – 8.

88. PFLP, 1962 (b).

89. Gittings, 1968, p. 185.

90. Text in PFLP, 1965 (b), pp. 1 – 54.

91. *PR* 31, 2 August 1963, p. 8.

92. Peck, 1972.

93. Ibid., p. 293, in particular.

94. Gittings, 1968, pp. 193 – 5.

95. Ibid., pp. 200 – 1.

II
THE LAUNCHING OF THE
CULTURAL REVOLUTION
(1964–1966)

In the last chapter it was noted that Mao's attempts, in 1963 and early 1964, to promote new radical movements to evoke once again the spirit of the Great Leap Forward, met with only limited success. It was perhaps because of the frustration engendered at that time that Mao came, in 1964–6, to see the need for a denunciation of the most senior leaders of the Chinese Communist Party. With the publication of the document 'On Khrushchev's Phoney Communism and its Historical Lessons for the World',[1] a series of events was set in train which was to result in that momentous and most contentious political movement—the Cultural Revolution.

'On Khrushchev's Phoney Communism and its Historical Lessons for the World'

'On Khrushchev's Phoney Communism . . .', published on 14 July 1964, was, in fact, the ninth comment on the open letter of the Central Committee of the CPSU. Allegedly written under Mao's guidance,[2] it represented the culminating point of the Sino-Soviet polemics, begun in December 1962. But its significance went far beyond the question of peace, war and relations with the United States. It represented a distillation of all the criticisms of 'revisionism', made both internationally and domestically in the preceding years, and included a reference to Mao's generative view of class arrived at in the years 1960–2. Even more important, it put forward an action programme reaffirming many of the principal non-economic themes of the Great Leap Forward.

As its major theme, 'On Khrushchev's Phoney Communism . . .' took the Khrushchevian notion of a 'state of the whole people' and a 'Party of

43

the whole people' and compared them with the Marxist-Leninist notions of 'dictatorship of the proletariat' and 'vanguard Party'. It noted that, in the Soviet Union, capitalist vestiges still existed and had existed in Stalin's day (even though he did not see them). The fundamental difference, however, between Stalin and Khrushchev was that, though Stalin did not make the correct class analysis, he did in fact adhere to the Leninist principle of dictatorship of the proletariat, whereas Khrushchev not only knew that capitalist vestiges still existed, but actually profited by them and sought their preservation. More important, there was developing in the Soviet Union a *new* stratum of 'capitalists' which was committed to a policy of material incentives, the profit motive and high salary differentials. The document went on to give many examples of corrupt practice in the Soviet Union, taken from the Soviet press, and noted that these had been made possible by the active connivance of the Soviet leadership. Since the state was, in Marxist terms, an instrument whereby one class exercised power over other classes, a 'state of the whole people' could only be the instrument of this privileged stratum and not of the proletariat. In class terms, the privileged stratum could only be defined as *bourgeois*. Under such circumstances, the Soviet state, far from withering away, was becoming stronger. It was precisely this privileged stratum, representing a capitalist class, which controlled the Soviet Party. The Soviet Party, therefore, in being designated as a 'Party of the whole people', was in fact becoming a *bourgeois Party*. As for the declaration in Khrushchev's new Party programme that the Soviet Union was building 'communism' which would be attained within 20 years, this was an 'economist' fantasy, for communism was surely much more than the provision of a 'plate of goulash'!

In case anyone should have any illusions that 'On Khrushchev's Phoney Communism . . .' was merely a discussion of the Soviet Union, the document went on to explain Mao Zedong's 15-point programme to prevent the same sort of thing happening in China. The theme of Mao's speech 'On the Correct Handling . . .' was reaffirmed but was supplemented by the new stress on class struggle in socialist society. The document warned that socialism was not simply a matter of transforming the economy and communism could not be reached until after a very long period of struggle had been experienced. During this period, the principle of dictatorship of the proletariat should be maintained with an emphasis on 'democratic centralism' within the ranks of the 'people'. The Mass Line, mass movements, great debates, the 'hundred flowers and hundred schools' should be given full play. In the Socialist Education Movement, reliance should be placed on the poor and lower-middle peasants and cadres should participate in manual labour. The socialist economy should be expanded upon a broad scale and wide salary differentials should be narrowed. The people's commune was hailed as an appropriate organisational form for effecting the transformation from collective ownership to 'ownership by the whole people'. The idea of 'everyone a soldier', anti-careerism in the army, officers serving in the ranks and Party and mass supervision of the PLA and public security organs was reaffirmed. The necessity to train 'revolutionary successors' who were both 'red' and 'expert' and to develop a socialist culture was a matter of prime importance. In foreign policy, cadres were warned to avoid 'great power chauvinism' and 'national egotism' (such as charac-terised the Soviet Union) and to replace them by genuine 'proletarian internationalism'. Finally, and perhaps most important, cadres were enjoined to watch out for hidden conspirators who sought to reverse this (the Great Leap Forward) programme.

Radicalism and Resistance (September-December 1964)

In the late summer and autumn of 1964, events moved rapidly. In July, the Chinese had spelt out the relevance of the Sino-Soviet polemic for domestic politics. Soon, the Tonkin Gulf incident provided ample evidence that the United States was as predatory as ever and, as the Vietnam War escalated, the relationship between international tension and Chinese domestic politics began once again to resemble 1958. By mid-October, Khrushchev had been forced out of office and the Chinese leadership began hastily to reassess the new situation. At almost the same time, China conducted its first nuclear test, signalling to the world that its foreign policy was now to be completely independent. It was to be in this rapidly changing environment that the Socialist Education Movement radicalised.

In September 1964, the 'Later Ten Points', now defunct, were replaced by another document known as the 'Revised Later Ten Points'.[3] Here the Socialist Education Movement was seen not as a moderate closed rectification movement but as something which required long and bitter struggle and which might perhaps last five or six years or even longer. The document warned against superficiality and called for the reregistration of Party members. For the first time since land reform in the early 1950s, a general reclassification in the Chinese countryside was to be undertaken and particular attention was to be devoted to those cadres who had degenerated into becoming class enemies and who had committed 'four uncleans'.[4] The 'Later Ten Points' had warned against excesses and, although this point was taken up again, a far more serious deviation was now seen to be excessive leniency. The 'Revised Later Ten Points' laid particular stress on mass mobilisation to criticise errant cadres at whatever level.

Experience . . . has revealed that cadres in basic-level organisations who have committed serious mistakes are usually connected with certain cadres of higher-level organisations . . . and are instigated, supported and protected by them. In such cases we must go to the origin and get hold of the responsible persons. No matter to what level the cadres belong, or what positions they hold . . . they should be subjected to open criticism before the people . . .[5]

The radicalisation of the Socialist Education Movement in the second half of 1964 signified a change in the effective leadership of the movement from Peng Zhen to Liu Shaoqi.[6] Liu, it appears, had come to see the need for a much more radical process of mass mobilisation after his own and his wife Wang Guangmei's experiences in the Taoyuan production brigade in Funing *xian*, Hebei.[7] He inaugurated, therefore, a new stage in the campaign known as the 'big four clean-ups' in which huge work-teams descended on the countryside and engaged in disciplining up to one million basic-level cadres.[8] In the subsequent Cultural Revolution, it was claimed that Liu's intention was to redirect the focus of struggle away from senior Party cadres 'taking the capitalist road' and towards cadres at the basic level. It was, therefore, 'left in form and right in essence'. Some scholars have, however, challenged this interpretation of Liu's position, noting that his personal investigations in the earlier part of 1964 had led to a very pessimistic view of the successes in the movement. This occasioned that massive campaign which many referred to as the 'second land reform'. Mao, moreover, endorsed his policies.[9]

Though the primary initiators of the new intensified campaign were the work-teams, the poor and lower-middle peasant associations were also strengthened. One way of effecting this was to expand the militia organisation in accordance with Mao's renewed call for 'everyone to be a soldier'. At a time of growing tension in south-east Asia, militia expansion was felt to be particularly necessary.[10] As work-teams and militia-backed peasant associations swung into action, those who were found to be guilty of 'unclean practices' were denounced, fined or dismissed from office.[11] The movement was no longer confined to key points but became general. At first, struggle was directed against obvious targets such as 'counter-revolutionaries' and unregenerate landlords but gradually extended to include most cadres. As in land reform, there was often initial reluctance to 'struggle' as peasants feared retaliation once work-teams left, but soon the power of the peasant associations was such that critics might be protected. The poor and lower-middle peasant associations were further strengthened by the extension of their organisation above brigade level to the communes and even higher.[12] Indeed, it would appear that such strengthening was necessary, once cadres began to hit back and utilise their organisational position to quell criticism, and

Renmin Ribao constantly warned against retaliation.

One of the major criticisms, during the more radical period of the Socialist Education Movement of late 1964, was that cadres had permitted or even encouraged the earlier 'spontaneous development of capitalism'.[13] There was now pressure for the restriction of free markets in the countryside in the spirit of the Great Leap.[14] By December, Mao Zedong was once again using the term 'Great Leap Forward' to describe future policy:

> We cannot follow the old paths of technical development of every country in the world, and crawl step by step behind the others. We must smash conventions, do our utmost to adopt advanced techniques and, within not too long a period of history, build our country up into a powerful modern socialist state. When we talk of a Great Leap Forward, we mean just this. Are we boasting or shooting off our mouths? Certainly not. It can be done.[15]

The last Socialist Education Movement had been the harbinger of the Great Leap of 1958 – 9. This time, however, resistance to Great Leap policies was to be much greater than in the mid- and late 1950s. It was to grow stronger as the Socialist Education Movement expanded into a new five anti movement in the cities and merged with all the other parallel movements which had been going on since 1963.

Resistance was later said to have been quite marked in the field of pro-paganda and education. It was the Propaganda Department of the Party Central Committee, together with its Beijing municipal counterpart, which had launched much of the alleged criticism of the Great Leap in the so-called 'blooming and contending' period of 1961 – 2. In the subse-quent more radical period, propaganda organs still seemed unprepared to have any confidence in mass consciousness and mass enthusiasm.[16] The same might be said for many senior university administrators. In Beijing University, in particular, the chancellor Lu Ping came under very serious attack from a work-team, much to the apparent chagrin of Peng Zhen.[17] There were blockages too in less prestigious institutions and, to counter this, renewed stress was laid on the 'part-work, part-study' principle of education and the selection of people from worker, peasant and soldier backgrounds for enrolment in tertiary institutions.[18] It was evident, however, that the 'two-track' system of education still made the 'part-work, part-study' schools poor adjuncts to the more traditional school system[19] and students with better academic records from hardly pro-letarian backgrounds were still enrolled in universities in substantial numbers.

The 'learn from the People's Liberation Army' campaign, likewise, was greeted with much fanfare and, with the establishment of political work departments, PLA cadres engaged more frequently in what was formerly considered to be exclusively civilian Party work. Nevertheless, the fact that the political work departments found it difficult to extend their network down beyond the central level might be taken to reflect resistance on the part of civilian cadres[20] and the inability of outside organisations to crack the very strong established Party structure.

By the end of 1964, the Socialist Education Movement had still not achieved much success. As a response to blockage and inertia, the rural movement had escalated to the point where very repressive measures had been taken. In such a situation, Mao was to come to the view that the movement had been mishandled and that Liu Shaoqi ought to be removed from his position of authority over it. The disciplining of basic-level cadres had not brought much new vitality to the countryside. The fault, therefore, must lie with more senior members of the Party who had failed to provide the conditions for the peasant associations to play a more constructive role.

Consolidation (1965)

The new mood was reflected by Zhou Enlai in his report on the work of the government to the Third National People's Congress in December 1964. At one level, Zhou affirmed the new radical interpretation of the movement. He made it clear that the focus was now on the 'big four clean-ups' (politics, economics, ideology and organisation)[21] rather than the earlier narrower concentration on things like accounts, granaries, property and work-points. He demanded also that the movement be much broader in scope and not confine itself to petty misdemeanours. At another level, however, Zhou paid much attention to the need to concentrate on modernising the country. For that task, stability was a prerequisite.

In the new year, the theme of 'antagonistic contradictions' was taken up in a new policy document which was to govern the Socialist Education Movement. This document, 'Some Problems Currently Arising in the Course of the Rural Socialist Education Movement' (commonly known as the 'twenty-three articles'),[22] was said to have been written by Mao himself. At the level of policy, the document made the extremely radical demand that the Socialist Education Movement focus its attention on 'persons in authority taking the capitalist road' at all levels up to and including the Central Committee itself. At an *operational* level, however, the 'twenty-three articles' suggested merely that peasants combine with basic-level cadres and work-teams in a 'triple alliance', reminiscent of that organisational form which characterised the immediate post-liberation period. In the villages the stress was on patient persuasion.

There has been much debate amongst scholars as to what the 'twenty-three articles' were designed to do. In one sense, they were clearly intended to further radicalise the Socialist Education Movement. The central work conference which adopted them inaugurated a programme of rectifying *xian* Party leadership.[23] At the same time, a campaign to study Mao Zedong Thought was launched to strengthen the educational component in the movement. In another sense, however, the 'twenty-three articles' were quite cautious and the work conference criticised Liu Shaoqi's handling of the movement in late 1964[24] for leftist excesses. The 'twenty-three articles', therefore, like most other documents of the time, were radical in their policy commitment but moderate in their operational prescriptions. Thus, once the 'twenty-three articles' were approved, Peng Zhen, who was brought back to take charge of the Socialist Education Movement, attempted to restore the prestige of some of his colleagues (such as Lu Ping) who had come under attack.[25]

Once the focus of attention shifted away from basic-level cadres to 'top persons in authority taking the capitalist road', the movement in the villages was blunted and, though 'spontaneous capitalist tendencies' were still criticised, it was with less vigour than before. It is possible that those who shared Mao's view intended to open a new stage of mass mobilisation once 'top persons in authority taking the capitalist road' had been designated. In early 1965, however, the Party machine appeared too strong to allow its senior members to come under criticism.

By the spring of 1965, a new period of consolidation had been inaugurated. Though the Socialist Education Movement wound down over two or three months, a decision to deradicalise seems to have been taken quite abruptly. This was the only major deradicalisation decision the effects of which I personally experienced. Teaching at that time in Beijing, I found quite suddenly that my teaching time was cut by a third and extensive discussions were held on combining work with leisure. Not only were work schedules cut but also the amount of time people spent attending political meetings.

One cannot be certain how the decision to deradicalise was taken and exactly why it came about in 1965. I feel that the major reasons were internal and linked to the situation of stalemate in the Socialist Education Movement and the relative lack of success in reforming literature and the arts, though alternative explanations have been put forward which focus on the international situation.[26] In February 1965, the United States commenced large-scale bombing of the Democratic Republic of Vietnam and there was a fear that the war might escalate into China. It is possible that the Party's response to this threat was to call a halt to any radical pro-grammes under way and to promote unity in the face of external threat. It is equally possible, however, that those who sought to revive the Yan'an tradition saw the threat of war as an even more urgent reason why the masses should be mobilised. I shall return to the strategic debate of 1965 shortly. In the meantime, we must note a major consequence of deradicalisation.

It was subsequently alleged that, in 1965, the campaign to cultivate revolutionary successors was dealt a heavy blow by a change in the policies of the Communist Youth League. In 1964, the League secretary, Hu Yaobang, admitted that 'bad and degenerate elements had wormed their way into the League'.[27] Many of its leaders were clearly above the upper age limit for the League and new, younger leaders were not coming forward. In the radical period of 1964, an attempt had been made to impart new vigour to the League in the campaign to cultivate revolutionary successors but, in 1965, policy was reversed and a massive recruitment drive launched. In that one year, eight million new members were taken into the League (a jump of nearly 25 per cent) and many of these new recruits were from dubious class backgrounds.[28] Those who had condemned Khrushchev's 'Party of the whole people' could not but look askance at an organisation which was rapidly turning itself into an élite training corps. As concessions were made to petty capitalism in the Chinese countryside and some of the reforms undertaken in industry proved ineffective in the summer and autumn of 1965, it seemed that the only hope for radical reform lay in mobilising the youth—but clearly not through the bureaucratised Communist Youth League. New organisations had to be established.

The Consequences of 'Revised Soviet Internationalism'

The adoption by the Chinese, in early 1963, of what Peck has called 'revised Soviet internationalism' convinced Khrushchev that China had to be expelled from the International Communist Movement. But due to the efforts of the Rumanian and other Communist parties, Khrushchev's two attempts at collective mobilisation to oppose China, in October 1963 and the late summer of 1964, came to nothing, and it is possible that his fall in October 1964 was not unconnected with his handling of the International Communist Movement.[29]

In political style, the new Soviet leadership could not have been more different from Khrushchev. Khrushchev had appeared as an irascible, unpredictable adventurer. From Mao's perspective, he was clearly a 'revisionist', but at least he was concerned primarily with Marxist-Leninist theory (however distorted his interpretation) and it is probably for this reason that the Chinese coined the term 'Khrushchevism'. They were not to honour any of his successors with the title 'ism', for they seemed dull grey pragmatists, committed to the same goals as Khrushchev but perhaps not so worthy of the really eloquent invective which had been produced in the polemic of 1963–4.

The new Soviet leaders believed that, although there was not much that could be done on a party-to-party basis, since they affirmed Khrushchev's position from the Twentieth to the Twenty-second Congresses, it might be worth while calling an international conference and attempting to improve state-to-state relations. Following the demise of Khrushchev, the polemics ceased for a while and Zhou Enlai led a high-powered delegation to Moscow in November 1964.[30] Neither side held out much hope for its success. The Soviet position on most of the contentious issues was adamant and the Chinese press continued to print Albanian and other criticisms of the Soviet Union.[31] On 21 November, a major *Hongqi* editorial entitled 'Why Khrushchev Fell' attributed his demise to a 'revisionist' general line[32] and all that both sides felt able to do was to agree that a preparatory meeting for an international conference be held in Moscow in March 1965. The March meeting was to be 'a gloomy and forlorn affair'.[33] It affirmed the principle of holding an international conference but did not say when and called for united action on Vietnam but did not say what. While the March meeting was in session, clashes occurred between Chinese demonstrators and Soviet police outside the United States embassy in Moscow[34] and, in this deteriorating atmosphere, open polemics were resumed.

Following the meeting in March 1965, one of the major bones of contention between China and the Soviet Union concerned the question of aid to Vietnam and exactly how unity of action might be achieved.[35] The Chinese rejected Soviet moves to use Chinese air bases to ship material to Vietnam. They did, however, allow the shipment of supplies by rail through Chinese territory, although the Soviet Union accused the Chinese of causing delays.[36] The Chinese, for their part, were suspicious of earlier Soviet initiatives to limit the fighting in Vietnam by concluding a deal over the heads of the Vietnamese.[37]

Another major bone of contention, in the spring of 1965, concerned the convocation of a second Afro-Asian conference to mark the tenth anniversary of the Bandung conference of 1955. On an extended tour of Africa and Asia in 1963–4, Zhou Enlai had lobbied actively for its convocation[38] and, in April 1964, a preparatory meeting in Jakarta fixed its date as March 1965. The importance of the conference lay in the fact that it might provide a forum for a Third World front against the United States and might give support to the more revolutionary movements in Africa and Asia. As the Chinese saw it, Africa in particular was 'ripe for revolution' and this had been demonstrated in the abortive Congo War of 1964. The conference, however, foundered on the issue of Soviet participation. It was first postponed until June 1965, to be held in Algiers, and then, following the Algerian coup of 19 June 1965, postponed again. It was never held.[39]

The Algerian coup and the abandonment of the second Bandung conference was only one of a series of events in 1965 which spelt failure for the policy of 'revised Soviet internationalism'. Not only did the new Marxist-Leninist parties remain small but attempts to mobilise the Third World to resist United States domination and Soviet blandishments were, in the main, unsuccessful. Nkrumah of Ghana was overthrown while on a trip to China, the Indo-Pakistan War left India far closer to the Soviet Union than ever before and, perhaps most important of all, the Indonesian coup not only rendered Sukarno powerless but led to the massacre of the second largest Communist party in Asia and China's most consistent supporter. The time had come to rethink foreign policy and the most important contribution, in this respect, was to come from Lin Biao.

The Strategic Debate of 1965

To understand the evolution of the Lin Biao position in foreign affairs, some attention must be given to the strategic situation in 1965. Though I doubt that the major reason for the deradicalisation in the spring of 1965 was a response to events in Vietnam, it is impossible to deny that China's leaders, of whatever perspective, looked with grave concern at events beyond China's southern frontier. It has been argued that, following the bombing of North Vietnam in February, a furious strategic debate occurred in China which was ultimately to see the demise of PLA Chief-of-Staff Luo Ruiqing and the assertion of Lin Biao's version of Mao Zedong's concept of people's war. Different commentators have described the debate in different ways. Donald Zagoria, for example, has pointed to three tendencies amongst the Chinese leadership—the 'doves' (who favoured peace at any price), the 'hawks' (who pressed for a hard line and reliance on the Soviet Union if necessary) and the 'dawks' (who were prepared for war, if it came, but who believed that a national liberation war had to be waged by the country invaded and China should not be actively involved in Vietnam unless the war escalated).[40] Others have rejected this ornithological fantasia and have even denied that there is evidence for any strategic debate at all.

The argument which has achieved most support, even though it is based on shaky evidence, is that of Michael Yahuda.[41] In May 1965, Yahuda argues, China saw a massive American build-up in Vietnam and the bombing of targets very near the Chinese frontier. Faced with this situation, Chief-of-Staff Luo Ruiqing wrote an essay in May 1965[42] commemorating the twentieth anniversary of victory in Europe in which he implied that the United States could be deterred by a United Front (with the Soviet Union). If invaded, the tactics China should employ were those used by the Soviet Red Army in defeating Hitler. The stress should not be on guerrilla-type engagements, luring the enemy in deep, but on a kind of mobile war based on a defensive line within Chinese territory. In Yahuda's view, Luo thus revealed a kind of positional mentality out of keeping with Mao's notion of people's war, an undue confidence in the Soviet Union and far too great a stress on modern armaments as opposed to the human factor. It is possible that Yahuda has read too much into Luo's published speeches but what one can say with confidence is that, in the summer of 1965, Luo Ruiqing's position in the army was severely weakened, at the same time as an exchange of notes between China and the Soviet Union revealed that no joint action on Vietnam was possible.

In late May, the radicalisation of the PLA, in which both Lin Biao and Luo Ruiqing had been involved, was intensified with the abolition of ranks[43] and, in August, the veteran military commander He Long warned against 'overlords' with heads 'stuffed full of foreign ideas'.[44] At the same time Peng Zhen, in a speech in Indonesia, struck a new note revealing, it is claimed, the radical response to Luo's position. Peng took up a theme of Aidit, the chairman of the Indonesian Communist Party that, in the current situation, 'the world's countryside was surrounding the world's cities',[45] which implied that Mao's theory of people's war could be generalised on a world scale, in contrast to Luo's positional approach.

Significantly, in this changed situation, the speech commemorating the twentieth anniversary of victory over Japan was given not by Luo Ruiqing but Lin Biao. This was his famous 'Long Live the Victory of People's War'[46] which reaffirmed the idea of the world's cities being surrounded by the world's countryside and saw that the response to any American attack on China must be the same as the Eighth Route Army's response to Japanese attacks during the Second World War—not positional war but essentially a combination of guerrilla and mobile war, waged by armed forces with deep roots among the people. Such a war had been effective in the 1940s because the policy of the Party had been moderately radical. There could, therefore, be no strategic reason for continued deradicalisation. As such, 'Long Live the Victory of People's War' was one of the first shots in the Cultural Revolution.

I do not know how one would go about substantiating the above highly imaginative exercise in Pekingology but, even if it were only half true, it does explain the extraordinary importance given to Lin Biao's 'Long Live the Victory of People's War' and the disappearance and subsequent criticism of Chief-of-Staff Luo Ruiqing who allegedly preferred military exercises to political work.[47] It also explains Mao's reported horror at a Japanese Communist Party question in 1966 as to whether joint action with the Soviet Union on Vietnam were possible.[48] Mao's point was fairly clear. Once you invite the Russians in, they come to stay. As things turned out, China and the United States came very close to war in late 1965 but they never had to put Lin Biao's essay to the test, at least in a military sense.

What is really significant about Lin Biao's 'Long Live the Victory of People's War' was its effect on foreign policy. If China were attacked, Lin proposed very active measures to deal with an aggressor. If, however, it were not attacked, China would remain an isolated fortress waiting for the 'world's countryside' to complete its work. China was no longer seen as the centre of a revised Soviet International, but as a base area awaiting the outcome of national liberation struggles it could support morally but in which it could not intervene. Thus Lin had taken the theory of people's war, which applied very well to China internally, and had projected it on to the international arena where it became a recipe for *passivity*.[49]

Mao's Strategy for Launching a Cultural Revolution

The passive implications of 'Long Live the Victory of People's War' were probably not very apparent in the climate of late 1965. At the time, it signalled a new orientation of China's view of the world in a situation where many Third World countries were lurching rather rapidly to the right and when China's only successes in foreign policy were moderate and were confined to what was referred to as 'the second intermediate zone' (notably France).[50] It was put forward, moreover, when economic conditions were more favourable to a revival of radical policies than at any time since the late 1950s. China was said to be free of debt.[51] Grain production was approaching 1958 levels[52] and industry had recovered from the crisis of 1960–2.[53] Vast new energy sources had been brought into production and any leap forward in future[54] would surely be able to build upon the very firm base of intermediate technology, which had been one of the enduring features of the Great Leap of 1958–9. From Mao's perspective, there was also room for optimism in the reforms which Lin Biao had carried out in the army. As a result of these, the army seemed to have become one of the most radical forces in society. It had helped propel forward both the Socialist Education Movement and the movement for literary reform and, with the transfer of cadres after 1964, had also come to provide a lot of new personnel for economic administration.

Yet, for all that, the case of Luo Ruiqing suggests that there were a number of people in senior positions of command in the PLA who were not at all happy about the reiteration of the theory of people's war. In other sections of society, the attempted radicalisation was still bogged down. The campaign to reform literature and the arts had met with only limited success. Some modern Beijing operas had been produced—but Wu Han and Deng Tuo were still unmolested in their Beijing offices and Zhou Yang still had his hand firmly on the controls. There was, as yet, no sign of the outpouring of mass creative work which had characterised the Great Leap. Economic policy was still riddled with contradictions. The idea of trusts and 'learning from Dazhai' were pushed at the same time. The slogan 'learn from Daqing' was proposed when the Anshan constitution was still buried under a mound of bureaucracy. Whilst Dazhai had scrapped the work-point system, some industrial enterprises had reintroduced piecework. It was a very confusing situation.

The confusion was nowhere more apparent than in the Socialist Education Movement. Though the 'big four clean-ups', in their revised form, were still promoted, the Socialist Education Movement had lost some of its vigour. By 1965, the rural movement had taken the form of a rectification of *xian*-level cadres and the many young PLA models that had been put forward since 1963 were now joined by a model *xian* Party secretary, Jiao Yulu. Whether Jiao Yulu, who died of hard work with a copy of Liu Shaoqi's book *On Self-Cultivation* under his pillow,[55] was a subtle criticism of models of the Lei Feng type is debatable. None the less, the stress laid on the movement does indicate the new importance attached to the rectification of middle-level cadres.

In 1965, the Socialist Education Movement had merged with the earlier five anti movement in the cities and the movement to learn from the PLA. As a result, urban economic departments were, like their national counterparts, frequently modelled on PLA political departments and even street committees sometimes employed political instructors *(zhengzhi jiaodaoyuan)*.[56] The plethora of parallel bodies attached to urban organs must have created organisational confusion. In addition to the formal office and its Party committee, there might also be a political department modelled on the PLA, a socialist education department and occasionally also a work-team.[57] Where these various bodies failed to co-ordinate their activities, it is perhaps understandable that the work-team might temporarily have taken over the administration[58] and thus have made the implementation of the Mass Line very difficult.

The above is a problem we have met time and again—the relationship between work-teams and mass organisations. In the Socialist Education Movement, the problem was perhaps more acute than at other times because the Party machine seemed bent on stopping the movement getting out of hand. In the autumn of 1965, Mao was to initiate a number of moves which were to ensure that the Party machine did lose control of the various movements which were going on. His aim was to transform the Party from without.

At a central work conference which met from September to October 1965, it is reported that Mao Zedong criticised Wu Han and called for a rectification of the Party.[59] Though current (1979) revisions of recent history have sought to deny it, Mao's strategy seems to have consisted of three components. First, expose the whole issue of Wu Han to the light of day so that people could make the association between reform in literature and the arts and the various policies associated with Peng Dehuai. Secondly, conduct a rectification movement in the army so that the PLA could give moral support to what became known as the Cultural Revolution, without the obstruction of military technocrats. Thirdly, support movements amongst students for educational reform so that they could see that the Youth League and the Party machine had departed from the revolutionary goals of Yan'an. Each of these strategies had been initiated by November. On 10 November, the Shanghai literary critic, Yao Wenyuan, published an article entitled 'On the New Historical Play *Hai Rui Dismissed from Office*', in which he bitterly attacked Wu Han.[60] It was said, in 1966 – 7, that Yao's action was taken under Mao's personal guidance but current (1979) accounts make no mention of Mao's role, claiming that the publication of the article was simply the result of a conspiracy between Jiang Qing, Zhang Chunqiao (a propaganda official in Shanghai) and the author Yao Wenyuan.[61] Secondly, on 18 November, Lin Biao issued a five-point directive to the PLA to rectify its style of work. Thirdly, perhaps as early as September, May Zedong himself was said to have given his support to a group of students at Beijing University who remained opposed to Chancellor Lu Ping[62] after Peng Zhen had reversed the verdict of the critical work-team.

The publication of Yao Wenyuan's attack on Wu Han was undertaken not by the Shanghai Party press but by the non-Party newspaper, *Wenhuibao*. An attack on the deputy mayor of Beijing, and by extension on his superior the mayor, Peng Zhen (the very man charged with rectifying the literary and art world), was regarded by those in charge of the Party machine as unforgivable. The immediate response of the Beijing Municipal Party Committee was an urgent telephone call to the Shanghai Party Committee demanding the reasons for the publication of Yao Wenyuan's article and expressing doubts about that committee's 'Party character'.[63] Not only would the Beijing municipal press not reprint the article but the Central Committee newspaper *Renmin Ribao* remained silent. On 29 November, however, the organ of the PLA—*Jiefangjunbao*—reprinted the article and thus ensured it a nationwide readership.[64] On the following day, *Renmin Ribao* was finally forced to reprint Yao's criticism and it immediately became study material for cadres and people throughout the country.

A speech attributed to Mao, however, suggested that Yao Wenyuan had not gone far enough.

Yao Wenyuan's article . . . is . . . very good; it has had a great impact on theatrical, historical and philosophical circles. Its defect is that it did not hit the crux of the matter. The crux of *Hai Rui Dismissed from Office* was the question of dismissal from office. The Jia Qing emperor dismissed Hai Rui from office. In 1959 we dismissed Peng Dehuai from office. And Peng Dehuai is Hai Rui too.[65]

Faced with the wide dissemination of Yao Wenyuan's attack, the Beijing municipal authorities still endeavoured to shield themselves. On 12 December, Deng Tuo wrote in *Beijing Ribao* that the question of Wu Han was an 'internal contradiction' and that the deputy mayor was not to be treated as an enemy; and, on 27 December, the same paper published Wu Han's self-criticism in which the deputy mayor tried to head off his critics.[66] Recent (1979) recapitulations of the events of that time suggest that Mao himself shared the view that the case of Wu Han was an internal contradiction—an explanation which, in the light of the above argument, I find very difficult to accept. The most, I think, that one can concede was that Mao's advice on how to deal with Wu Han might have been vague. If the above quotation is genuine, then Mao clearly intended to underline the association between Wu Han and Peng Dehuai's criticism. When, however, the 'group of five' appointed to look into the question of Wu Han met under the chairmanship of Peng Zhen in the new year, its members were apparently divided on whether the Peng Dehuai issue should be reactivated and it is said that the final report of the group, which was produced in February 1966, was actively opposed by one of the members, Kang Sheng.[67] The so-called 'February Outline' was in many ways reminiscent of the 'Later Ten Points' and specified the implementation of the Cultural Revolution in such a way as could be construed as negating its very spirit.[68] According to the 'February Outline', the main issue was not the radical policies of the Great Leap Forward but the correct interpretation of history; in short, was Hai Rui progressive or not? One should not resolve the debate by discussing the political viewpoint of individual writers, such as Wu Han, but by raising the level of competence of China's historians; to this end, a series of draft model articles was to be published.

The defensive strategy seemed to be exactly the same as the attempt to confine the 'two combines into one' debate of 1964 to academic discussion. It was, at first, moderately successful. Following the acceptance of the 'February Outline' in the name of the Central Committee (presumably by the Politburo Standing Committee chaired by Liu Shaoqi in Mao's absence),[69] a campaign of criticism was launched against historians who were felt to have interpreted history wrongly.[70] Recent revisions of official history have claimed that the savage criticism of historians was a tactic pursued by the 'conspirators' Jiang Qing, Zhang

Chunqiao and Yao Wenyuan,[71] though one might equally argue that the criticism was part of what was to become an increasingly common defensive strategy pursued by people who wished to prevent criticism escalating to include themselves. In any case, for a time, the attack was deflected from 'persons in authority taking the capitalist road' to relatively harmless historians. By March 1966, it seemed that, for the time being, Peng Zhen had held his own and had prevented the Cultural Revolution developing into a mass movement. He could not, however, halt the furious debate that had been going on in the press since December and was soon to face much sterner opposition.

The second component of Mao's September strategy was to rectify the PLA. We know little about the movement in the army, following Lin Biao's five points of mid-November, but we may surmise that Luo Ruiqing came under very severe criticism and 'Long Live the Victory of People's War' became required reading. It was probably opposition to this renewed radical line that led, in February 1966, to a spate of rumours concerning a possible military coup. It was later alleged that the Beijing military authorities, encouraged by Luo Ruiqing, strengthened the Beijing garrison under the pretext of war preparations.[72] At a time when government offices were being moved out of Beijing in preparation for a possible American attack,[73] it is more likely that what went on at that time were *genuine* war preparations. Though we do not know whether an actual coup was planned in February 1966, we do know that the events of February led to a renewed rectification movement in the army and the formal dismissal of Luo Ruiqing. After an unsuccessful attempt to commit suicide on 18 March,[74] Luo is reported to have been denounced on 13 April, finally stripped of office on 16 May and replaced by Yang Chengwu.[75]

By the spring of 1966, the army appeared to have been firmly committed to a radical line and its press actively propagated the radical interpretation of the Cultural Revolution. The army had also become extremely active in the field of literature and art. A meeting of the Military Commission on 30 March approved a document summarising the discussions of a forum on literary and art work in the armed forces, responsibility for which had been assigned by Lin Biao to Jiang Qing.[76] Another dimension had been added to the campaign to learn from the People's Liberation Army.

The third component of Mao's autumn strategy was educational reform. At the September meeting, Party general secretary Deng Xiaoping was said to have opposed any cultural reforms and changes in the schools,[77] but at the same time Mao reportedly backed some of the more militant members of Beijing University who were pressing for a less élitist approach to education. In a speech at Hangzhou in December, Mao insisted on the urgency of educational reform:

We should reform university education. So much time should not be spent attending classes. Not to reform arts faculties would be terrible. If they are not reformed, can they produce philosophers? Can they produce writers? Can they produce historians? Today's philosophers can't turn out philosophy, writers can't write novels and historians can't produce history. All they want to write about is emperors, kings, generals and ministers.[78]

By March 1966, a 'Red Flag Militant Team' had been formed in a secondary school attached to Beijing University,[79] in response to Mao's call, and pressure on Beijing University Chancellor Lu Ping mounted. Since Lu Ping was a close associate of Peng Zhen and the Beijing Municipal Party Committee, it was only a matter of time before the first and third components in Mao's strategy merged.

The Collapse of the Beijing Party Committee

By April 1966, it was apparent to many leaders of the Party that Peng Zhen's handling of the Cultural Revolution had resulted in no Cultural Revolution at all. Consequently, a meeting of the Secretariat, attended also by Zhou Enlai, Kang Sheng and the influential editor of *Hongqi*, Chen Boda, on 9–12 April, resolved to appoint a new leading group. After Kang Sheng had conveyed what was said to be Mao's personal criticism of Peng to the meeting, the 'February Outline' was repudiated and a resolution adopted to set up the new group to direct the reforms.[80] We are unfortunately unable to answer the crucial and intriguing question how it was that the change in orientation of the Cultural Revolution was brought about at a meeting of the highly bureaucratic Secretariat. Nor can we be certain exactly what the position of Liu Shaoqi might have been since he was abroad on a state visit to Burma. In fact, Liu returned just in time for the final stages of a Politburo Standing Committee meeting in Hangzhou. This meeting (16–20 April) resolved to turn the criticism of Peng Zhen into 'struggle' and Mao Zedong reportedly endorsed seven documents repudiating Peng's 'crimes'.[81]

In early April, there were still attempts to deflect the focus of criticism by selecting obvious old 'bourgeois' targets according to the radical injunction to repudiate the 'four olds' (old thought, old ideas, old habits and old customs). There was also, however, a renewed stress on the importance of the rectification movement of Party secretaries at *xian* level and above (the final stage of the Socialist Education Movement), and a determination to keep the focus very clearly on the Party. As warnings of a Petőfi Club again began to be heard,[82] the army renewed its call for a nationwide movement to study Mao Zedong's works. The famous 'May Seventh Directive' stipulated that the whole of the PLA should be a school (of Mao Zedong Thought)[83] with the obvious implication that such a 'school' would not be limited to the army. Since the whole of society was seen as a school, the formal school system was de-emphasized.

In the spring of 1966, most of the authoritative editorials on the Cultural Revolution were carried first in *Jiefangjunbao* and only later taken up by *Renmin Ribao*. On 8 May, attacks were launched against the Beijing municipal press[84] which had carried the original articles by Wu Han, Deng Tuo and Liao Mosha. Two days later, Yao Wenyuan published the first definitive attack on Deng Tuo,[85] who probably still had connections with *Renmin Ribao*. The following day, the literary critic Qi Benyu published a scathing attack on the Beijing municipal press[86] and the stage was set for the public repudiation of Peng Zhen's Cultural Revolution line.

At an enlarged meeting of the Politburo Standing Committee in Hangzhou on 16 May, at which Peng Zhen acknowledged his guilt,[87] another famous document was approved—the 'May Sixteenth Circular'.[88] The Secretariat's resolutions of April were ratified, the 'February Outline' was formally countermanded and the five-man group under Peng Zhen dissolved. To take its place, a new Cultural Revolution Group of 18 members was established. Though we are unclear as to the initial composition of the group, it soon came under the leadership of Chen Boda who, as well as being editor of *Hongqi*, had long been Mao's political secretary. Other leaders included Jiang Qing, the only dissident voice in the old group of five—Kang Sheng—and the two Shanghai figures who had helped launch the attack on *Hai Rui Dismissed from Office*—Zhang Chunqiao and Yao Wenyuan. As I have noted, the meeting of mid-May also approved the report of an investigation into the mistakes of Luo Ruiqing, who was formally dismissed, and Lin Biao warned against the possibility of a counter-revolutionary coup.[89]

Although Lin Biao's warning indicated that, even then, the situation in the army was not all it might have been, Peng Zhen's position had been completely undermined and the Beijing Party committee could be reorganised. By the end of May, the student movement in Beijing had acquired a momentum of its own. Around 21 May, a secondary school attached to Qinghua University had organised the first student group to call itself 'Red Guards'[90] and, on 25 May, Nie Yuanzi, a philosophy teacher at Beijing University, put up a large character poster *(dazibao)* denouncing Lu Ping and the Beijing University leadership.[91] A week later, on 2 June, this poster, with Mao's support, was hailed by *Renmin Ribao* as a major contribution to the revolution.[92] On 1 June, the official designation of the Cultural Revolution was changed from 'Great *Socialist* Cultural Revolution' to 'Great *Proletarian* Cultural Revolution',[93] signifying a new radical spirit, and it was quite clear that the various articles published in the press denouncing 'persons in authority taking the capitalist road' were a summons for others to make similar criticism. Nie Yuanzi's *dazibao* was to be a model. As the Cultural Revolution switched into high gear, it was announced on 3 June that Li Xuefeng had taken over from Peng Zhen[94] and the Beijing Party and Youth League committees had been reorganised. Just at this crucial moment, when the first thorough mass movement since the Great Leap Forward looked like getting under way, control in Beijing passed to Liu Shaoqi.

Liu Shaoqi's Fifty Days

Following the dismissal of Peng Zhen (although at this stage he was not named) and the reorganisation of the Beijing Municipal Party Committee, a wave of criticism engulfed the country. Initial criticisms centred on the Beijing committee but soon widened to include almost anything about which people had a grievance. On almost every wall, *dazibao* appeared in profusion. There were often just too many to read and people under attack knew that one of the surest ways of diluting criticism was to attack all and sundry, so that criticism of their individual actions was lost in the storm. Just as Peng Zhen had diverted the attacks upon him by criticising historians, so Party officials sought scapegoats and unimportant targets to turn the spotlight away from themselves.

In this early period of the Cultural Revolution, the main activists were students and it is understandable, therefore, that some of the most intense debates centred on education and examinations. The key questions were: how were politics to be integrated more fully into university or school life? What was the proper relationship between study and manual labour? What part should students play in the administration of their place of learning? To facilitate the debate, the State Council announced, in mid-June, that examinations for entrance into tertiary institutions the following year would be postponed,[95] and, in many places, all formal teaching stopped. At the same time, the Communist Youth League was dissolved because of its association with the academic establishment.[96] Now students were free to form their own groups to discuss educational policy and what lessons could be learned in their own university or school. They could discuss the charges that Beijing and other universities had been unduly élitist and had favoured the children of the well-to-do. One should, of course, avoid the mistake of thinking that Beijing University (or for that matter any of the other old élite universities) was typical of tertiary education. Certainly, in the institute in which I taught, the class origin of most students was very different from Beijing University. None the less, there was much that could be learned from the Beijing experiences.

Although the main activists in the Cultural Revolution in June 1966 were students and teachers, it was quite clear that the injunction to struggle against 'monsters and demons'[97] applied to all sectors of society. Up to that time, the Socialist Education Movement in the countryside had been concerned largely with the study of Mao Zedong Thought and the rectification of *xian*-level cadres, begun in 1965. Now poor and lower-middle peasant associations were called upon to join the great 'blooming and contending' and criticisms were voiced once again of basic-level cadres in suburban villages. Many of these lower-level cadres who had escaped the pre-1965 'small four clean-ups' and whose misdeeds had been neglected, as targets shifted upwards in 1965, were now required to answer for their 'economism' and other deviations.[98] The Socialist Education Movement and the Cultural Revolution were beginning to merge.

While the 'blooming and contending' developed, the newly-formed Cultural Revolution Group does not appear to have been very active, perhaps because it saw mass spontaneity needing little leadership, perhaps because it wanted to see just how Liu Shaoqi would react or perhaps because it did not know what to do. The group's activities seem to have been confined to intensifying the press campaign against what was referred to as the 'Black Gang'. In July, criticisms began to be voiced of the 'literary tsar' Zhou Yang[99] and, in the same month, Tao Zhu replaced Lu Dingyi as head of the Party Central Committee's Propaganda Department.[100] In the universities, however, the frightened Party machine strove earnestly to establish control.

In early June, under Liu Shaoqi's guidance, decisions were taken to send work-teams into schools and universities and an eight-point directive was adopted.[101] It seemed evident that Liu, the organisation man, was attempting to control the Cultural Revolution in exactly the same way that the Party machine had attempted to control the Socialist Education Movement. The work-teams consisted usually of middle-rank cadres often advised by some very senior Party cadre. At Qinghua University, for example, the senior cadre was none other than Wang Guangmei, the wife of Liu Shaoqi.[102] Having seen just how work-teams inhibited mass spontaneity in the Socialist Education Movement, Mao is reported to have cautioned against the hasty despatch of these teams as early as the Politburo Standing Committee meeting of 9 June.[103] None the less, the work-teams went into action and, in many cases, succeeded in stifling mass spontaneity. Just as student radicals began to link up with similar groups of industrial workers, attempts were made by the teams to confine criticism to the universities and schools. 'Excesses' were denounced and 'unruly' students detained.[104] Work-teams were said to have aided those in authority in diverting the heat of criticism away from themselves, either by broadening its scope to include the absolutely trivial or by focusing it upon targets which had little operational significance. It was now permissible to attack Peng Zhen or Zhou Yang but not one's own school principal or university chancellor. It was permissible to denounce the bombing of Hanoi and Haiphong, but not to criticise local Party cadres.

It is my impression that the work-teams were remarkably successful in dampening down the struggle in the universities and schools in June and July 1966 and the Minister of Public Security, Xie Fuzhi, was later to remark that the Cultural Revolution in Beijing was almost snuffed out.[105] There were some student groups, however, which would not toe the official Party line and they were sometimes helped by members of the Cultural Revolution Group. Jiang Qing, for example, actively supported groups at Qinghua University in resisting the pressure of the work-team sent down under the leadership of Wang Guangmei.[106] Though proto-Red Guard groups were in existence before the despatch of the work-teams, it was in those colleges where student groups struggled hardest against the work-teams that Red Guards developed their strongest organisation. In a sense, the Red Guards were the product of that struggle.

The struggles of June-July 1966 were very confusing. In many students, obedience to local Party committees was ingrained. Others were not quite sure just how far they should go in opposing the power-holders *(dangquanpai)*. Still others were infuriated at the way work-teams were defusing the struggle. Further confusion was caused by the fact that every group and every work-team claimed allegiance to Mao, and Mao's works (more particularly the 'little red book' now produced by the million) were used to justify almost any position. And yet Mao was silent! For a long period he had remained in the Changjiang (Yangtze) region watching events in Beijing and elsewhere. Suddenly, on 16 July, he gave a signal that heralded the end of Liu Shaoqi's 50 days' management of the Cultural Revolution. Mao Zedong went for a marathon swim in the Changjiang, thus signifying that he was not ill or infirm but ready to take a lead in the movement.[107] The next day he was back in Beijing and ready to inaugurate the most radical phase of the Cultural Revolution yet.

Three days later, on 20 July, a central work conference was convened, this time with Mao Zedong in the chair.[108] He was determined the student movement should not be suppressed. In a speech to the conference the following day, he demanded the total mobilisation of youth:

> I say to you all: youth is the great army of the great Cultural Revolution! It must be mobilised to the full. After my return to Beijing I felt very unhappy and desolate. Some colleges even had their gates shut. There were even some which suppressed the student movement. Who is it who suppressed the student movement? Only the Beiyang warlords. It is anti-Marxist for Communists to fear the

student movement. Some people talk daily about the Mass Line and serving the people, but instead they follow the bourgeois line and serve the bourgeoisie. The Central Committee of the Youth League should stand on the side of the student movement. But instead it stands on the side of suppression of the student movement. Who opposes the great Cultural Revolution? The American imperialists, the Soviet revisionists and the reactionaries.[109]

The conference, which went on to the end of July, finally criticised the current handling of the Cultural Revolution and probably resolved to recall the work-teams.[110]

By early August, the atmosphere radicalised once again. The 'May Seventh Directive' was reiterated[111] and Yang Chengwu confirmed as acting chief-of-staff of the PLA.[112] Although it is difficult to gauge the significance of the delay of his confirmation since the formal dismissal of Luo Ruiqing in May, it is my belief that the fact that a formal announcement could now be made signified that any trouble that may have occurred in the PLA, and to which Lin Biao had alluded in May, had now passed. In the new atmosphere, attacks shifted to the field of economics. A press campaign was launched, in early August, against the economist Sun Yefang and other followers of Liberman-type 'market socialism',[113] and it is not unreasonable to associate the campaign with the eclipse of Liu Shaoqi. By August, it was a completely different kind of revolution. However cultural the revolution had been before, it was now 'Cultural' in the widest sense.

The central work conference of late July was to pave the way for a far more significant meeting—the Eleventh Plenum of the Eighth Central Committee, the first plenum to be held since 1962. Its communiqué affirmed the radical policies adopted since the Tenth Plenum and thus disavowed those associated with Liu Shaoqi.[114] It adopted a 16-point programme for the Cultural Revolution[115] and confirmed Lin Biao as Party vice-chairman—'Mao Zedong's close comrade in arms'. The plenum took place in the enthusiastically radical atmosphere previously noted, in which not only were the press attacks on revisionism stepped up but Mao Zedong joined the Red Guards. In a letter to the Red Guards of Qinghua University secondary school on 1 August, Mao remarked:

Here I want to say that I myself as well as my revolutionary comrades in arms all take the same attitude. No matter where they are, in Beijing or elsewhere in China, I will give enthusiastic support to all who take an attitude similar to yours in the Cultural Revolution movement.[116]

Mao had, however, some words of caution to offer and the 'Sixteen Points' were not a recipe for unrestrained struggle. None the less, Mao supported mass action against the instruments of the Party machine. On 5 August, he even put up his own *dazibao*:

> China's first Marxist-Leninist big-character poster and Commentator's article on it in *Renmin Ribao* are indeed superbly written. Comrades please read them again. But in the last fifty days or so some leading comrades from the central down to the local levels have acted in a diametrically opposite way. Adopting the reactionary stand of the bourgeoisie, they have enforced a bourgeois dictatorship and struck down the surging movement of the great cultural revolution of the proletariat. They have stood facts on their head and juggled black and white, encircled and suppressed revolutionaries, stifled opinions different from their own, imposed a white terror, and felt very pleased with themselves. They have puffed up the arrogance of the bourgeoisie and deflated the morale of the proletariat. How poisonous! Viewed in connection with the Right deviation of 1962 and the wrong tendency of 1964 which was 'Left' in form but 'Right' in essence, shouldn't this make one wide awake?[117]

The stage was now set for the total reconstruction of the Chinese political system.

Conclusion

This chapter has traced the immediate origins of the Cultural Revolution. The evaluation of that revolution has caused much polemic both inside and outside China. Were the events of 1964 – 6 the prelude to a great act of liberation or a sequence of serious mistakes?[118] To answer that question one must evaluate the whole course of the Cultural Revolution and it was not until the late summer of 1966 that mass struggles were to begin. There seems to me to be no doubt that people such as Zhang Chunqiao, Yao Wenyuan, Jiang Qing and others did engage in conspiratorial activities to launch the movement in art and literature and, in so doing, violated the norms of the Chinese Communist Party. It seems clear also that army involvement in various sectors of society, under the instigation of Lin Biao, tended to violate the hitherto accepted principles of Party leadership. But is it fair to reduce the actions of those people to a simple striving for power, as the present (1979) Chinese leadership claims? Could the means justify the end of what might be seen as mass liberation? Can, moreover, one disassociate Mao Zedong from their actions? In this chapter, I have attempted to argue that the participants in the programme of criticism which developed after 1964 were acting according to a strategy worked out by Mao himself and this is quite apparent in speeches of the chairman released in the Cultural Revolution. It is unlikely that these speeches were forgeries, but even if that were the case, Mao's symbolic actions of mid-1966 cannot be interpreted in any way other than support for the campaign of criticism which was unfolding.

Yet the Cultural Revolution, which got under way in early 1966, seemed not to be informed by an adequate theoretical understanding of the problems it was to resolve. The basis for a theory had, of course, been established in the early 1960s and was reiterated in 'On Khrushchev's Phoney Communism . . .'. In 1965 – 6, however, little was said about the generative view of class and perhaps that is why energies could be diverted away from 'top persons in authority taking the capitalist road' on to relatively harmless 'remnants' of the past. The problem was an acute one since, without an adequate theory which specified where 'enemies' might be found and the structural basis of antagonism, one could designate anyone as an 'enemy' solely on the subjective evaluation of behaviour.

But why was it that Mao never fully explicated his views on the generative notion of class? Why was one never presented with a fully-fledged theory of 'continuous revolution'? Perhaps it was the case that Mao was frightened of the implications of his earlier ideas. If the sole *raison d'être* of the Party was its vanguard role—its superior grasp of the theory of socialist transition—and if that Party had been corroded by the generation of a new bourgeoisie, how did one decide when the Party's leadership was in the wrong direction? Who was it that decided? In the period under review, it was clearly Mao who decided. Remedial measures, however, were to be decided by the masses. Yet they were to decide without the guidance of an adequate theory. The result was to be a mixture of emancipation, creativity, chaos, brutality and violence. On that process, which is the subject of the next chapter, there can be, as yet, no consensus.

NOTES

1. Text in PFLP, 1965 (b), pp. 417 – 80.
2. Johnson, 1969, p. 24.
3. Text in Baum and Teiwes, 1968, pp. 102 – 17.
4. Just as there were two sets of targets for the four clean-ups: (1) accounts, granaries, properties and work-points, and (2) politics, economics, ideology and organisation, so one might assume there were two sets of four uncleans. The reference here is almost certainly to the latter set.
5. Baum and Teiwes, 1968, p. 115.
6. Teiwes, 1979, pp. 533 – 4.

7. *PR* 49, 1 December 1967, p. 17. On the 'Taoyuan experience', see Baum, 1975, pp. 83–101.

8. Teiwes, 1979, p. 545.

9. Ibid., p. 534.

10. Mao Zedong, 16 June 1964, *JPRS*, 1974, pp. 356–7.

11. Baum and Teiwes, 1968, p. 33.

12. Vogel, 1971, p. 318.

13. Ibid., p. 317; Baum and Teiwes, 1968, p.33.

14. Baum and Teiwes, 1968, p. 33.

15. Mao Zedong, December 1964, Schram, 1974, p. 231.

16. Neuhauser, 1967, p. 22.

17. Teiwes, 1979, p. 552.

18. Neuhauser, 1967, p. 23.

19. See the collection of articles in *CB* 868, 31 December 1968. Also Bastid, 1970, p. 20; Gardner, 1971, pp. 247–50.

20. Neuhauser, 1967, p. 25.

21. Zhou Enlai, *PR* 1, 1 February 1965, p. 13.

22. Text in Baum and Teiwes, 1968, pp. 118–26.

23. Ibid., pp.95–6.

24. Teiwes, 1979, pp. 553–63.

25. Ibid., pp. 563–9.

26. E.g. Bridgham, 1967, pp. 14–15.

27. Hu Yaobang, *PR* 28, 10 July 1964, p. 19.

28. Israel, 1967, p. 3; Oksenberg, 1966, p. 4; *SCMP* 3554, 8 October 1965, pp. 4–9.

29. Gittings, 1968, pp. 212–17.

30. *PR* 46, 13 November 1964, p. 6.

31. E.g. ibid. 6, 5 February 1965, pp. 22–5.

32. Ibid.48, 27 November 1964, pp. 6–9.

33. Ibid.13, 26 March 1965, p. 7.

34. Ibid.11, 12 March 1965, p. 15.

35. See Gittings, 1968, pp. 256–8.

36. *PR* 1, 1 January 1966, pp. 16–17.

37. Chen Yi, ibid. 33, 14 August 1964, pp. 8–9; Gittings, 1968, pp. 254–60.

38. Adie, 1964.

39. Gittings, 1968, pp. 247–8.

40. Zagoria, 1968, p. 67.

41. Yahuda, 1972.

42. Luo Ruiqing, *PR* 20, 14 May 1965, pp. 7–15.

43. Ibid. 22, 28 May 1965, p. 4.

44. He Long, ibid.32, 6 August 1965, pp. 8–9.

45. Peng Zhen, ibid.24, 11 June 1965, p. 11.

46. Lin Biao, ibid.36, 3 September 1965, pp. 9–30.

47. *SCMM* 641, 20 January 1969, pp. 4–6.

48. Yahuda, 1972, pp. 70–1.

49. Peck, 1972, pp. 294–5.

50. Erasmus, 1964.

51. Li Chengrui, *PR* 1, 1 January 1966, p.19.

52. Eckstein, 1973, pp. 216–17.

53. Ibid., p. 224.

54. In early 1966 there was talk of a new Great Leap. See e.g. *SCMP* 3628, 1 February 1966, p. 8.

55. *PR* 9, 25 February 1966, pp. 5–8.

56. White, 1972, p. 342.

57. Ibid., p. 344.
58. Ibid., p. 345.
59. *PR* 21, 19 May 1967, p. 6.
60. Text in URI, 1968 (a), pp. 235–61.
61. *BR* 10, 9 March 1979, pp. 6–7 and 27.
62. Israel, 1967, p. 7.
63. Qi Benyu, *SCMM* 529, 20 June 1966, p. 2.
64. Ibid., 640, 13 January 1969, p. 3.
65. Mao Zedong, 21 December 1965, Schram, 1974, p. 237.
66. *SCMM* 640, 13 January 1969, pp. 3–4.
67. Ibid., p. 6. The 'May Sixteenth Circular' absolved Kang Sheng from any blame (URI, 1968 (b), p. 21). The final report was said to have been adopted on 4 February though the text gives the date 3 February when Kang Sheng and the radical wing were in attendance (URI, 1968 (b), p. 7).
68. Text in URI, 1968 (b), pp. 7–12.
69. *SCMM* 640, 13 January 1969, p. 7. Note, Dittmer (1974, p. 74) argues that there was no necessary connection between Peng Zhen and Liu Shaoqi.
70. See Yin Da, *SCMM* 517, 28 March 1966, pp. 1–11. Qi Benyu, Lin Jie, Yan Changkui, ibid. 521, 25 April 1966, pp. 28–44.
71. *BR* 10, 9 March 1979, p. 7.
72. Esmein, 1973, p. 78.
73. CCPCC, 16 May 1966, in URI, 1968 (b), pp. 31–3.
74. *SCMM* 641, 20 January 1969, p. 11.
75. Yang Chengwu's appointment was not announced until 1 August, and it is not certain exactly when he was appointed.
76. Text in PFLP, 1970, pp. 201–38.
77. Bridgham, 1967, p. 16.
78. Mao Zedong, 21 December 1965, Schram 1974, pp. 236–7.
79. Israel, 1967, p. 7.
80. *SCMM* 640, 13 January 1969, p. 12.
81. Ibid., pp. 13–14.
82. *PR* 20, 13 May 1966, p. 42.
83. Mao Zedong, 7 May 1966, *CB* 891, 8 October 1969, pp. 56–7.
84. Gao Ju, 8 May 1966. Text in Schurmann and Schell, 1968, pp. 603–6.
85. *PR* 22, 27 May 1966, pp. 5–18.
86. Qi Benyu, *SCMM* 529, 20 June 1966, pp. 1–10.
87. Dittmer, 1974, p. 77.
88. Not published until 16 May 1967, *PR* 21, 19 May 1967, pp. 6–9.
89. Chang, 1970, pp. 193–4.
90. Israel, 1967, p. 7.
91. Mao apparently saw the poster on 1 June and ordered it to be published throughout the country. *SCMM* 648, 24 March 1969, p. 18. On the early stages of the Cultural Revolution at Beijing University, see Nee,1969.
92. *RMRB*, 2 June 1966, p. 1.
93. *PR* 23, 3 June 1966, pp. 4–5. The article 'Sweep Away All Monsters' refers to Great *Proletarian* Cultural Revolution. The editor of *Peking Review* was probably unaware of the significance (ibid., p. 1).
94. Ibid. 24, 10 June 1966, pp. 3–4.
95. Ibid. 26, 24 June 1966, p. 3.
96. Dittmer, 1974, p. 81.
97. The term 'monsters and demons' (literally 'ox-ghosts and snake-spirits') was the same term that was used in 1957.
98. Baum, 1969 (b), p. 99.

99. *PR* 33, 12 August 1966, pp. 32–8.

100. No formal announcement was made concerning Lu Dingyi's dismissal. The first reference to Tao Zhu's appointment was made by NCNA, 10 July.

101. *CB* 834, 17 August 1967, pp. 26–7.

102. Liu Shaoqi, 23 October 1966, URI, 1968 (b), p. 358, and *CB* 834, 17 August 1967, p. 27. For a detailed account of Wang Guangmei's activities, see Hinton, 1972.

103. Chang, 1970, p. 194.

104. Liu Shaoqi, 9 July 1967, Liu, 1968, Vol. III, pp. 371–2.

105. Daubier, 1974, p. 56.

106. Hinton, 1972, p. 65.

107. *PR* 33, 12 August 1966, pp. 17–19.

108. *CB* 891, 8 October 1969, pp. 58–60.

109. Mao Zedong, 21 July 1966, Schram, 1974, p. 253. The Beiyang warlords were a group of graduates from a military academy of that name in Tianjin which exercised tremendous power in China in the second and third decades of the twentieth century.

110. Chang, 1970, p. 194, based on *CB* 891, 8 October 1969, pp. 58–60. A conference was certainly held at which regional party secretaries and members of the Cultural Revolution Group were present. I am not sure, however, about the dates, nor am I sure that it was at that meeting that a decision was taken to withdraw the teams.

111. *PR* 32, 5 August 1966, pp. 8–10.

112. Ibid., p.4.

113. *SCMP* 3765, 22 August 1966, pp. 4–13.

114. *PR* 34, 19 August 1966, pp. 4–8, and in URI, 1968 (b)., pp. 62–70.

115. Text in *PR* 33, 12 August 1966, pp. 6–11; URI, 1968 (b), pp. 42–54; Selden, 1979, pp. 549–56.

116. Mao Zedong, 1 August 1966, Schram, 1974, p. 260.

117. Mao Zedong, 5 August 1966, *PR* 33, 11 August 1967, p. 5.

118. This was the official view in 1979. See Ye Jianying, 29 September 1979, *BR* 40, 5 October 1979, p. 15.

III
RED GUARDS AND RED REBELS
(1966 – 1967)

The Eleventh Plenum of the Eighth Central Committee, in August 1966, was to inaugurate the Cultural Revolution as a major mass movement. The 'Sixteen Points', laid down by the plenum, had attempted to prescribe the limits beyond which the Cultural Revolution was not to go. But the very logic of a movement which was aimed at bringing about a restructuring of the Communist Party from without, seemed to deny that there were any limits. In the period considered in this chapter, the Cultural Revolution was to escalate far beyond the limits of the 'Sixteen Points' and, indeed, beyond what even Mao had thought possible, to the point where the chairman may have lost his nerve. It seemed that most Party and state leaders who tried to control the movement were to become its victims. Thus, by early 1967, the only leadership role remaining at a national level was exercised, on the one hand, by the Central Cultural Revolution Group which urged people to be more and more bold in their denunciations and, on the other, by those like Zhou Enlai who strove to protect what remained of the central government apparatus without antagonising people who believed that it was 'right to rebel' (*zaofan youli*).

The Emergence of the Red Guards and Red Rebels

The violation of the 'Sixteen Points' seemed to occur almost immediately after their promulgation. According to 1979 reports, Lin Biao, in a speech to a central work conference as early as 13 August 1966, signalled his rejection of the position that the 'overwhelming majority of cadres were good or comparatively good'. In another speech to the first major rally of Red Guards in Beijing's Tiananmen Square on 18 August, Lin adopted a tone which was far more radical than the prescriptions of the document endorsed by the Eleventh Plenum.[1] I have little doubt, however, that Mao endorsed Lin's position, since the chairman symbolically donned a red armband at the same rally and indicated his support for the Red Guard movement. From then on, Red Guards spread rapidly outside the universities and schools and large numbers of new Red Guard groups formed.[2] The nuclei of such groups had already been in existence for some time in the form of Cultural Revolution study groups (formed after the dissolution of the Communist Youth League) or more militant groups formed to oppose the work-teams. All that was needed to galvanise them into action was the despatch of Red Guards from Beijing following the 18 August rally.[3] As the campaign against the 'four olds' achieved nationwide proportions, many different kinds of Red Guard groups formed, all with different action programmes. Opinions differed amongst groups as to what attitude to take to the former work-teams, to the leading personnel in various organisations, to the criteria for membership and to the priority between old intellectuals and specifically Party targets. The degree of Red Guard spontaneity was such that they could choose their targets at will and could organise themselves however they saw fit. In such a situation, factionalism was bound to occur and Party authorities, which sought to limit their activities, strove to keep targets confined either to the already discredited Peng Zhen 'Black Gang' or harmless 'bourgeois' targets outside the Party. When Red Guards busied themselves changing the names of streets and shops, Party bureaucrats, who sought to preserve their position, were probably delighted, since they hoped that such actions would keep the heat off themselves.

One of the few things which all Red Guards seemed agreed upon was that the Youth League had been hopelessly bureaucratic and, on 20 August, its organ *Zhongguo Qingnian bao* (*China Youth News*) ceased publication.[4] Disagreements on how to evaluate Liu Shaoqi's 50 days, however, resulted in two separate Red Guard headquarters forming in Beijing. One group felt that the repressive activity of the work-teams was merely an unfortunate episode in the Cultural Revolution which should now return to the criticism of the line of Peng Zhen, while the other felt that a profound analysis of the reasons why the work-teams had been sent in the first place should be undertaken.[5] In this situation, Party leaders, who feared for their positions, willingly lent their support to those who wished to confine the Cultural Revolution to the matters under discussion in June and thus prevent the movement escalating to a wholesale condemnation of Liu Shaoqi, Deng Xiaoping and the Party machine.

Perhaps the most important figure in this debate was the new head of the Party Central Committee's Propaganda Department, Tao Zhu. Following the overthrow of the Propaganda Department after the demise of Lu Dingyi and Zhou Yang, Tao Zhu had acquired an extraordinary importance in the Cultural Revolution and, like Peng Zhen and Liu Shaoqi before him, he tried to keep it within bounds. Clearly he could no longer advocate the despatch of work-teams but what he could do was to make use of 'liaison personnel' to limit the targets and attempt to direct Red Guard activities through 'Cultural Revolution committees'.[6] Provision for such committees had been made in the 'Sixteen Points' and thus this revised work-team approach had the stamp of legitimacy. At the same time, Tao himself, who was not sparing in his criticism of all and sundry,[7] appeared to support the extension of radical criticism. In practice, we have seen that such a procedure only confused issues and the more targets there were the harder it was for anyone to reach conclusions about any of them.

Though it is probably true that Tao Zhu abetted the confusion which occurred in September 1966, it was probably the dynamic of the movement itself that constituted its primary cause. As early as the mass movements of the early 1950s, it had been anticipated that any mass movement would initially be characterised by confusion but that, eventually, water would flow along clearly defined channels.[8] In September 1966, however, such channels were very difficult to discern. Almost anyone in a position of authority came under criticism and, at the highest level, not only did posters appear criticising Peng Zhen and his group but also Liu Shaoqi, Deng Xiaoping[9] and even the new first secretary of the Beijing Party committee, Li Xuefeng.[10] Not only did senior cadres in the Party attempt to channel criticism in certain directions but different Red Guard groups formed their own control organisations[11] to impart a sense of discipline, to limit targets and prevent the movement becoming too generalised.

At this point, some of the more radical students in Beijing, notably from Qinghua University and the Aeronautical Institute (in which Lin Biao had considerable influence), became tired of the rather sterile debate about the episode of the work-teams and sought once and for all to concentrate criticism on Liu Shaoqi and Deng Xiaoping. Such was the origin of Beijing's Third Red Guard Headquarters which received the enthusiastic support of Chen Boda and the Central Cultural Revolution Group.[12] The process of splitting and realignment, characteristic of Beijing's Red Guards, was duplicated in the provinces and municipalities and further confusion was caused by the injunction that Red Guards should travel round the country spreading revolutionary experiences. It was perhaps necessary that free travel should be granted to Red Guards if the mass movement should truly be nationwide, but this 'revolutionary exchange' (*chuanlian*) led to certain problems. There were severe logistic problems (Beijing's population swelled by some two million, some provincial bus services were denuded of vehicles and the rail service became overloaded).[13] Furthermore, much criticism became uninformed and ineffective since the constant movement of people prevented Red Guards in any particular locality having a detailed knowledge about the leadership in that area. On the other hand, 'revolutionary exchange' did lead to links being formed between university-based Red Guards and factory-based Red Rebels.[14]

The factory-based rebel groups which began to form in August and September 1966[15] were once again very disparate in aims. The more radical amongst them demanded a greater say in management and protested that the labour unions had once again become 'economist' to the detriment of political goals. In the early rallies, after 18 August, a few worker groups had become quite active in support of Red Guard activities[16] although, once organisations became formalised the following month, more conservative groups formed, with labour union support, to protect the privileged position of workers as opposed to some other groups in society. These conservative groups came increasingly to oppose radical Red Guard activity. In early September, the press was most insistent in its demand that the Cultural Revolution should not interfere with production and many of the radical workers were persuaded to return to the factories,[17] not to emerge again until later in the year. There is evidence, however, that ferment within the factories continued throughout October and was seen as being particularly significant. In Mao's view, university and school students could only initiate the revolution. The orientation of the working class would decide its fate.

The process of 'revolutionary exchange' led also to the forging of links between Red Guard groups and rural poor and lower-middle peasant associations. Although the cautious 'Sixteen Points' still saw the Cultural Revolution's main target[18] as cultural and educational units and that of the Socialist Education Movement as communes and factories, that document did point out the complementary nature of the two movements. Care had to be taken, however, not to launch the Cultural Revolution in villages and urban enterprises 'where original arrangements for the [Socialist Education] movement are appropriate and where the movement is going well'.[19] Such an injunction confused the nature of the two movements. Though peasant associations were much stronger than hitherto, work-teams still played an important part in the Socialist Education Movement whereas, in the Cultural Revolution, work-teams were by August the object of much vilification. It was thus still possible to control the Socialist Education Movement from above. Was it possible to exercise the same kind of control over the Cultural Revolution without it ceasing to be a mass movement proceeding according to its own momentum?

Not long after the beginning of 'revolutionary exchange', urban-based Red Guard units acted as the catalyst for the formation of groups of suburban peasant Red Rebels which sought resolution of economic and other issues left over from the Socialist Education Movement.[20] Like their urban counterparts, peasant Red Rebels were subject to splits and, like the small rebel groups in the universities before July, came into conflict with the still active work- teams.[21] The rural work-teams were probably no different from those in the cities and responded character- istically by branding many rebels as 'counter-revolutionaries'.[22] As conflicts began to occur in the suburban countryside, however, the central leadership was concerned that the gathering of the autumn harvest might be affected. On 14 September, a directive was issued 'Concerning the Great Cultural Revolution in Rural Districts Below the *Xian*-Level' stipulating that the Cultural Revolution in rural areas should be conducted in communes and production brigades 'in asso- ciation with the original "four clean-ups" arrangements'.[23] This quite extraordinary order was tantamount to saying that, in the rural areas, work-teams were still permissible. Cadres were to remain at their posts, urban-based Red Guard units were forbidden to interfere in the communes and, to all intents and purposes, a halt was called to the Cultural Revolution in the countryside. But not long after the directive, *Hongqi*, realising probably what the 14 September directive implied, modified its terms by declaring that urban-based Red Guards were only forbidden to 'make revolution' in rural units 'where the "four clean-up" provisions were considered appropriate by the masses'.[24] The boot was now clearly on the other foot. Earlier in the Socialist Education Movement, radical policies had been modified by cautious operational instructions. The *Hongqi* article indicated that the reverse was now the case.

Though the major slogan in the autumn of 1966 was 'grasp revolution and promote production', with a very clear emphasis on the second part of the slogan, propaganda teams still continued to operate in the country- side and the work-teams seemed to fade from view. By the time the Socialist Education Movement was formally brought to an end on 15 December,[25] nothing much had been heard of them for some time.

The Focus on Liu Shaoqi

By October 1966, the degree of mass mobilisation had increased to such an extent that even Mao Zedong was surprised:

> I had no idea that one big character poster, the Red Guards and the big exchange of revolutionary experiences would have stirred up such a big affair.[26]

Amongst the Red Guards, there was still turmoil but it was a turmoil in which young people were receiving a practical political education which no formal classes could achieve. Large numbers of weapons, hoarded gold and even pictures of Jiang Jieshi were unearthed.[27] The continued payment of 'fixed interest' to former 'national capitalists' was criticised.[28] Excessive Party secrecy and the keeping of dossiers on people of dubious political background (the so-called 'black documents') were denounced.[29] Literally millions of Red Guards still toured the country spreading experiences and the influx of people into Beijing to attend mammoth rallies created many headaches for the city authorities; it may be argued that one of the functions of the rallies was to give the Red Guards a chance to see Chairman Mao and then go home.

With the publication (by the Military Commission and the PLA General Political Department) on 5 October of an 'Urgent Directive on the Cultural Revolution in Military Academies',[30] it was apparent that the Cultural Revolution had radicalised even further. Such schools (and by extension all schools) were required to do away with 'all the bonds which have shackled the mass movement' and 'daring' was to be 'put above everything else'. Cultural Revolution groups were now seen as 'organs of power'. It is possible, however, that at that time the PLA command and the central Party press (under the influence of Chen Boda) took a line slightly to the left of Mao Zedong. After the appearance of the early October edition of *Hongqi*, which noted that repression still continued and had to be combated,[31] *dazibao* appeared critical of Liu Shaoqi and Deng Xiaoping.[32] Although Mao was undoubtedly determined to restrict Liu's organisational power, he was probably a little more cautious than either the press or the radical Red Guards. At a central work conference on 26 October, he remarked:

> You find it difficult to cross this pass and I don't find it easy either. You are anxious and so am I. I cannot blame you, comrades, time has been so short. Some comrades say that they did not intentionally make mistakes, but did so because they were confused. This is pardonable. Nor can we put all the blame on Comrade [Liu] Shaoqi and Comrade [Deng] Xiaoping. They have some responsibility but so has the Centre. The Centre has not run things properly. The time was so short. We were not mentally prepared for new problems.[33]

Mao was obviously alluding here to the 'self-criticism' made by Liu Shaoqi to the same conference when he admitted that his handling of the Cultural Revolution during the '50 days' had been inadequate. Liu was most contrite:

> Comrade Lin Biao is better than I in every respect: so are the other comrades in the Party. I am determined to abide by a Party member's

discipline and do nothing before anybody that amounts to 'agreement by mouth but disagreement at heart'.[34]

But, unlike Mao, the radical Red Guards would not, in any way, accept the self-criticism of Liu and made every effort to escalate criticism. On 18 October, some senior cadres in the Central South Bureau of the Party came under attack[35] as part of a general denunciation of the alleged diversionary line pursued by Tao Zhu, and it seemed that, whatever reserve Mao and others may have felt, their only course was to let the revolution work itself out.

In the last two months of 1966, attempts were made by local authorities to limit Red Guard activity, though it was by no means certain whether their motives constituted anything more than just a practical response to logistic problems. The problem of the vast influx of Red Guards into Beijing, in the autumn of 1966, had been partially solved by their participation in gathering the autumn harvest. In October and November, however, more stringent efforts were made to reduce the burden Red Guards had imposed upon the transport system. Announcements appeared curtailing free travel[36] and Red Guards were encouraged to spread revolutionary experiences by undertaking new 'Long Marches'[37] rather than going everywhere by bus and train; though, to be sure, there were educational objectives pursued here as well as the purely economic.

At the same time, warnings appeared threatening both authorities and Red Guards with punishment if they employed violence,[38] and stories began to circulate about a particularly violent Red Guard group in Beijing known as the United Action Committee (*Lianhe Xingdong Weiyuanhui*).[39] The United Action Committee had been formed at a time of furious debate about the proper response to old cadres and about whether admission to Red Guard organisations should be limited to the sons and daughters of workers, peasants, soldiers and others with impeccable class or revolutionary backgrounds. Most groups had denounced any requirements concerning parental background as 'the reactionary theory of lineage', but there were a few others who saw themselves in a vanguard role and it was they who formed the backbone of the United Action Committee. The United Action Committee, which comprised former members of the Red Guards' First and Second Headquarters, tended towards a far less radical position than the Third Headquarters, whose parental credentials were less impeccable. It accused the Third Headquarters, which was supported by the Cultural Revolution Group, of violating the moderate 'Sixteen Points' and, significantly, of being infiltrated by 'bourgeois elements'. This accusation the radicals considered to be 'waving the Red Flag to oppose it'. For a while, it was claimed that the United Action Committee imposed a reign of terror over

Red Guard organisations in Beijing and availed itself of money and vehicles supplied by unnamed Party officials who saw in the committee a force which might contain radicalism. The United Action Committee demanded the dissolution of the Cultural Revolution Group, denounced Lin Biao as a 'conspirator'[40] and was joined in its opposition to the Third Headquarters by conservative worker organisations backed by the labour unions.

The above situation in Beijing was duplicated many times with many different variations in the provinces. It has yet to be established what (if any) co-ordination existed between the various conservative groups which became active in the latter part of 1966. We may surmise, however, that whatever reservations Mao and other senior Party leaders may have had about pressing home the attack against Liu Shaoqi and the Party machine must surely have been dissipated once it became clear that any call for moderation of radical criticism would play precisely into the hands of these conservatives.

In early December, the ever prudent Zhou Enlai emphasised the support of Mao Zedong and Lin Biao for the Central Cultural Revolution Group[41] and the mid-December edition of *Hongqi* called for a counter-offensive to crush the 'bourgeois reactionary line'.[42] Probably as a result of this support, the Third Headquarters, now greatly augmented in numbers, stepped up its denunciation of Liu Shaoqi and Deng Xiaoping, the work of 'liaison personnel' (organised by Wang Renzhong with the support of Tao Zhu) and the United Action Committee.[43] Before long, the name of Tao Zhu had been joined to those of Liu Shaoqi and Deng Xiaoping as targets for overthrow[44] and the militant Red Guards prepared for a new onslaught.

The further radicalisation of the Cultural Revolution in December 1966 had three consequences. First, the Cultural Revolution superseded the Socialist Education Movement in the countryside. Secondly, the workers' movement now became the main focus of 'struggle' and, thirdly, the army became much more involved in the revolution.

Following a very successful autumn harvest, the 15 December directive ending the Socialist Education Movement[45] cleared the way for a more thoroughgoing rural Cultural Revolution. An immediate consequence of the directive was the strengthening of poor and lower-middle peasant associations which were now to form their own Cultural Revolution committees.[46] The associations seemed no longer subject to the leadership of local Party branches and could transcend all the limitations imposed upon them by the earlier 'four clean-ups'.[47] Together with special groups formed to promote production,[48] the peasant Cultural Revolution groups could now go into action against local cadres. The situation was, however, highly confused. During the earlier Socialist Education Movement, large numbers of peasant rebels had been denounced by the work-teams and branded as 'counter-revolutionaries'. These rebels now demanded the reversal of verdicts but were joined in their demands by rightists, ex-landlords and people said to be 'genuine' counter-revolutionaries. The peasant Cultural Revolution committees were to find new evaluations extremely difficult.[49]

The new radicalisation in the industrial sphere was considerably influenced in late 1966 by events in Shanghai. The growth of worker Red Rebel groups in the autumn resulted in a massive outpouring of all kinds of grievances concerning conditions of work, bonuses, piece-rate systems, participation in management, the role of the labour unions etc.[50] A major bone of contention was the status of temporary workers recruited on contract from the countryside.[51] Some advocated that the wages and working conditions of these workers should be raised to the level of regular industrial workers whilst others could not see how job opportunities could be created to accommodate such a demand.

On 9 November, a radical alliance was formed between workers and students in Shanghai known as the Shanghai Workers Revolutionary Rebel Headquarters.[52] It was in this organisation that Wang Hongwen first achieved prominence. Wang, together with Jiang Qing, Zhang Chunqiao and Yao Wenyuan, was later considered to be one of the 'Gang of Four' which had used the Cultural Revolution to seize power for itself. The headquarters, which promoted the establishment of Revolutionary Rebel groups in factories, was opposed by the Shanghai Party committee, which may have been responsible for ensuring that a train carrying a delegation from the headquarters to Beijing was shunted into a siding 18 kilometres outside Shanghai and left there. Zhang Chunqiao, who had been active in the Central Cultural Revolution Group in Beijing, flew hurriedly back to Shanghai to sort out the situation and signed a document acceding to the workers' demands. Though Zhang may have gone further than the Central Cultural Revolution Group may have wished, the group could only endorse his action, much to the chagrin of Shanghai's mayor Cao Diqiu. At first, there was little the Shanghai authorities could do, but following the occupation by rebels of the editorial offices of *Jiefang Ribao* (*Liberation Daily*, the Shanghai Party newspaper) in early December, they came more and more to rely upon a much less radical formation known as the Scarlet Guards (*Chiweidui*) which inaugurated a period of intense conflict with other Red Rebel groups. As clashes occurred in December, a directive was issued in the name of the Central Committee calling for the extension of the Cultural Revolution into factories and mines and the toleration of criticism.[53] Faced with what seemed to be Beijing's endorsement of the Revolutionary Rebel position, the Scarlet Guards now made a bid for power and attempted to consolidate their hold over the city's factories. The result was a wave of strikes in late December, to which the Revolutionary Rebel

Headquarters could only respond by demanding that the Revolutionary Rebels 'seize power' and run the factories themselves. Before the end of the year, Jiang Qing endorsed demands for such 'power seizures' not only in factories but in the Ministry of Labour and the 'economist' All China Federation of Trade Unions,[54] the Shanghai branches of which had supported the Scarlet Guards.

The third consequence of the radicalisation of December concerned the army. Through the autumn, the PLA had been ordered, time and again, to confine its support for Red Guards and Red Rebels to the logistic and the symbolic. The army was not to involve itself actively in the civilian Cultural Revolution.[55] By December, however, the Cultural Revolution had spread to military academies and some regular troops had taken up the rebel cause.[56] At the same time, worker rebel groups became active in factories under military control,[57] such as those under the Seventh Ministry of Machine Building. On 18 December, Jiang Qing called for mass action to seize power over the public security network and the courts,[58] and, where this was resisted by the police, the army sometimes took over public security duties.[59] The PLA, therefore, was gradually being pulled into the Cultural Revolution and found itself in a curiously ambiguous position. Sometimes troops supported rebel organisations and, at other times, adhered to the official policy of non-involvement; occasionally troops actually tried to dampen rebel ardour.[60] Not only did troops find themselves in support of Zhang Chunqiao[61] but also Tao Zhu.[62] There was clearly a need for some kind of specific directive on PLA involvement in the Cultural Revolution. It is perhaps significant to note here that, at the turn of the year, when Peng Zhen was arraigned before a Red Guard rally, Luo Ruiqing and Peng Dehuai were also arrested.[63] Those who arrested the former Chief-of-Staff and Minister of Defence were in fact students of military academies,[64] acting, it is now claimed (1979), under direct instructions from Lin Biao.[65] Even if we discount the current (1979) assertion that Chen Boda had decided that the army was 'turning bourgeois',[66] there is enough contemporary evidence to suggest that the army could not, for long, remain neutral.

By new year 1967, it was clear that the Cultural Revolution was not to be allowed to run down. Attempts were made to fuse together the rebel movements in the universities, schools, factories and perhaps also the countryside. There was probably some pressure also for greater PLA involvement. Rebels were now enjoined not only to 'seize power' and to 'struggle' actively against the 'handful of people in authority taking the capitalist road', but also to model their organisations on the Paris Commune of 1871.[67]

The January Revolution

One of the immediate consequences of the policies announced in late December was the disintegration of the All China Federation of Trade Unions. It was accused, notably by Jiang Qing, of permitting the exploitative contract labour system,[68] but in January there seemed little that could be done, given the employment situation.[69] Radical workers, who began to seize power in January 1967, however, were concerned immediately not with major economic questions but with how to take over and run their own factories. It was a period of great excitement.[70] Semi-literate workers now put pen to paper without the slightest reservation and almost every printing press was devoted to the publication of broadsheets and newspapers. The rather abstract notion of 'politics in command' now began to mean something very concrete as workers showed a genuine interest in the politics that affected them. Worker organisations themselves entered into heated discussion on exactly how factories were to be organised and how they could develop their own potential.

In Shanghai, the seizure of power was carried out with frantic urgency because of the need to end the strike caused, it was believed, by the Scarlet Guards. The Scarlet Guards were, however, probably numerically superior to the Revolutionary Rebels and were supported to some extent by the Municipal Committee.[71] As has been noted, their motive in carrying out the strike was probably to prevent the Municipal Committee giving in to the pressure of the Central Cultural Revolution Group and its Shanghai spokesman, Zhang Chunqiao.[72] But the strategy of the Revolutionary Rebels, backed by Beijing, was to create new organisations to get production moving and so discredit both the Municipal Committee and the Scarlet Guards. They were remarkably successful. In early January, the Shanghai *Wenhuibao* was seized by the rebels[73] and an appeal made to the people of Shanghai denouncing both the Municipal Committee and the Scarlet Guards.[74] The appeal, which was reportedly supported by Mao Zedong,[75] greatly swelled the ranks of the Revolutionary Rebels who, by 9 January, had the railways moving once again. Before long, production committees in power stations and shipyards restored operations there too[76] and resistance crumbled.

The problem of 'economism'[77] still remained. It was perhaps inevitable that amongst the mass of demands put forward by workers in January 1967, there should be included those for shorter hours and better pay. It was also inevitable that those demands should have been fostered by what remained of the labour unions and utilised by the Party machine to protect its own position. The 'economism' of January 1967 took the form of the advance payment of wages and an increase in bonuses, on the one hand, it was said, to buy off a section of the workers and, on the other, to split them. This second objective had also been pursued in late 1966 by encouraging work stoppages[78] although, with the seizure of power in 1967, this option no longer remained. A third method of causing splits derived from the commitment of the new ACFTU Centre to rationalise the contract labour system in a situation where it had not the economic resources to do so. Not only could the resentment of contract workers be capitalised on but so could that of the peasants, who feared that rural-urban mobility might be restricted.

A further set of problems resulted from the difficulties of seizing power in a situation where a number of different Revolutionary Rebel groups coexisted. It was never clear which rebel group was to seize power. Sometimes repeated power seizures took place between rival rebel groups and, at a municipal level in Shanghai, power was seized four times before a city-wide organisation was constructed.[79] Sometimes the old administration formed its own group to seize power through which it could still manipulate the organisation from backstage. Such, some Red Guards felt, was the policy of the Minister of Agriculture, Tan Zhenlin, in Beijing.[80] On other occasions, the old administration concealed records and plans from rebel groups seizing power so that the new administration would be unable to function and request the return of old cadres. Sometimes a successful seizure of power might take place but, following that seizure, the rebels would send too many cadres down to the factory floor and leave themselves with insufficient technical advice to keep the organisation running.[81] The situation was sometimes chaotic and yet, for the first time, many ordinary workers were being drawn into administration. If one wanted to learn something about administration, there was surely nothing like engaging in it oneself, even if one initially made great mistakes.

Although the Shanghai strikes did not last for very long, they were sufficiently serious for Zhou Enlai and Chen Boda, while endorsing the rebel seizure of power, to warn that the seizure and control of everything on the Shanghai pattern should not be repeated elsewhere.[82] As most of the central leadership saw it, groups which had seized power should *supervise* cadres but not dispense with them.[83]

Despite the warnings not to seize power indiscriminately and the reprinting of one of Mao's earlier essays opposing egalitarianism, the Shanghai pattern did repeat itself in some other areas. In the countryside, the movement to seize power was further complicated by the fact that different kinds of proscribed elements (so-called 'five category elements') had demanded the reversal of verdicts reached in the Socialist Education Movement. Attempts were made to recall the original work-teams to undergo criticism.[84] To prevent proscribed elements usurping the leadership of the new radical movement, the central leadership had no course but to endorse the (now defunct) Socialist Education Movement, despite its shortcomings, and prohibit the reversal of any verdicts at all,[85] at least for the time being. With the rural Cultural Revolution now proceeding in low gear, the problem of 'economism' again reached serious proportions.[86]

A problem even more important than the seizure of power within production units concerned the links between organisations in which power had been seized. Somehow a structure had to be created which would prevent the cities, or for that matter the countryside, dissolving into atomised units. Since the summer of 1966, there had been much talk of modelling organisations upon the Paris Commune, whereby leaders at various levels of civil administration might be elected by popular assemblies and subject to immediate recall by their constituents. In Shanghai, there was to be more than just talk but the Shanghai People's Commune proved to be extraordinarily difficult to organise. After three weeks of discussions, a Preparatory Committee led by Zhang Chunqiao and Yao Wenyuan was finally established on 5 February.[87] The Preparatory Committee which represented 38 Red Rebel organisations organised a Provisional Committee which was vested with supreme power. The Provisional Committee consisted of eleven permanent members plus the heads of a number of commissions. Two student organisations ran the Liaison and External Relations Commission, revolutionary cadres from the old Municipal Committee ran the Control Commission, the Workers Revolutionary Rebel Headquarters ran the Organisation Commission and the Revolution and Production Front (set up to deal with the strike) ran the Operations Commission. The Provisional Committee consisted of seven workers, three students, two peasants, two cadres and two soldiers. It formally proclaimed the abolition of the Shanghai Municipal Committee and the Shanghai Party Committee, declared all their decisions since 16 May 1966 null and void and urged rebels to seize power in all units.[88] Provision was made for other rebel organisations to join the new government but negotiations concerning membership might be protracted since there were still serious ideological and organisational problems which had to be overcome. Although the original intention had been for the Commune Provisional Committee to be chosen by popular elections, the body which was proclaimed on 5 February was really just an amalgam of revolutionary organisations. In fact, popular elections for the Shanghai People's Commune were never held since events in other parts of the country were beginning to overtake Shanghai and new organisational forms were emerging.

The events of Shanghai in January 1967 were profoundly exciting as more and more people were drawn into city and local administration, yet the problems were serious and power seizures elsewhere in the country were much less abrupt. As Mao saw it, there could only be one organisation which could provide the cement necessary to hold the various institutions together after power had been seized; there was only one institution which could prevent highly destructive faction fighting and negate the influence of proscribed elements, while the rural Cultural Revolution developed. That was the PLA. Without army involvement, rebel clashes would continue and localism would develop. Army-supported mass action had, after all, constituted the pattern of power seizure in 1948 – 9. At that time, worker picket organisations often took over the factories and peasant associations took over the villages but they were linked to municipal and *xian* government by the army and guided by army representatives. In the period immediately prior to January 1967, army schools had undergone their own internal rectification under the leadership of a special army Cultural Revolution Group and, on 11 January, this group was reorganised, presumably to prepare it for a greater civilian role. Significantly, the army Cultural Revolution Group was now subordinated to the Central Committee's Cultural Revolution Group.[89] As has been noted, the army had already to some extent been drawn into the civilian Cultural Revolution by the actions of its military academies and factories and its involvement in public security work. It had, however, performed somewhat ambiguously for sometimes it had backed rebels and at others had supported the status quo. By mid-January, Mao was determined that the involvement of the army in the Cultural Revolution had to be on the side of the 'left' and called upon the army to help in the seizure and consolidation of power.[90] Finally, at the end of the month, a definitive order went out for the PLA to 'support the left'.[91]

Though excited by developments in Shanghai, Mao Zedong saw great problems in the Shanghai People's Commune. In February 1967, Zhang Chunqiao and Yao Wenyuan reported Mao's position:

> With the establishment of a people's commune, a series of problems arises and I wonder whether you have thought above them. If the whole of China sets up people's communes, should the People's Republic of China change its name to 'People's Commune of China'? Would others recognise us? Maybe the Soviet Union would not recognise us whereas Britain and France would. And what would we do about our ambassadors in various countries? And so on. There is another series of problems which you may not have considered. Many places have now applied to the Centre to establish people's communes. A document has been issued by the Centre saying that no place apart from Shanghai may set up people's communes. The Chairman is of the opinion that Shanghai ought to make a change and transform itself into a revolutionary committee or a city committee or a city people's committee.[92]

By February, Mao's preferred model of organisation was clearly that of 1949, now known as the 'revolutionary committee' based on a triple alliance of revolutionary rebels, old cadres and PLA. Such a committee had already been set up, at a provincial level, in Heilongjiang on 31 January[93] and a number of other committees were soon established on the same model.[94] Mao, therefore, advocated a limited support role for the military until the Party could be rebuilt along more revolutionary lines. As Zhang Chunqiao reported Mao's words:

> With the Commune inaugurated do we still need the Party? I think we need it because we must have a hard core, whether it is called a Communist Party or a social democratic party . . . In short we still need a Party.[95]

This statement was made just before the Shanghai People's Commune itself was transformed into a revolutionary committee based on the triple alliance formula.[96] The chairman was convinced that mass action should no longer be as anarchistic as some of the 'ultra-left' manifestations in Shanghai had been.

> The slogan of 'doubt everything and overthrow everything' is reactionary. The Shanghai People's Committee demanded that the Premier of the State Council should do away with all heads. This is extreme anarchism, it is most reactionary. If instead of calling someone the 'head' of something, we call him 'orderly' or 'assistant' this would really be only a formal change. In reality, there will always be 'heads'. It is the content which matters.[97]

The proponents of radical criticism were now faced with an extremely serious problem. How was one to define 'ultra-left anarchism' and how was one to deal with it? They were soon to be faced with an even more serious problem. The army was to support the 'left' but how was one to define the 'left' and how was one to prevent the army actually exercising control?

The Foreign Ministry Drags its Feet

Before discussing the short period of consolidation in February 1967, it might be useful to look at the 'seizure of power' in one particularly crucial ministry—Foreign Affairs.[98] The aim here is not to describe a typical case, since the Foreign Ministry was regarded as being responsible for a particularly sensitive area of government policy, but an examination of the events of January 1967 will help one understand the peculiar direction Chinese foreign affairs took in mid-1967.

In mid-1966, Foreign Minister Chen Yi was personally responsible for the despatch of some 15 work-teams to subordinate departments and schools attached to the Foreign Ministry. He was, therefore, accused by Red Guards of excessive conservatism. When pressure mounted in the autumn of 1966 to establish Cultural Revolution committees, Chen still resisted the Red Guards. Not only did he not condemn Liu Shaoqi's earlier work-teams but he refused to withdraw his own work-teams from departments of the ministry. At one point, Mao himself is said to have despatched Zhou Enlai to find out why Chen was still violating Cultural Revolution policy.

In November, when other people in authority were adopting covert means to protect their position, the irascible Chen Yi actually went on the offensive and accused the Red Guards of indiscipline. In fact, the impression one gets of Chen Yi, in the autumn of 1966, is of a man who was not terribly worried about Red Guard criticism at all and was more concerned about the deterioration of China's foreign relations during the escalation of the Vietnam War and the changed situation in Asia following the Indonesian coup. Between his foreign policy statements and his personal reaction to the Cultural Revolution, there seemed to be a severe contradiction. On the one hand, he embraced the Lin Biao thesis, welcomed the growing anti-imperialist struggle, noted that temporary setbacks were part of a 'zigzag' pattern of development and affirmed the importance of the Chinese Cultural Revolution internationally, yet, on the other, he regarded the growth of the Cultural Revolution in his own ministry as a tiresome interference.

By the end of 1966, however, Chen's position had been undermined. He could no longer maintain work-teams or work-team surrogates and all China's ambassadors were gradually recalled (with the one exception of Huang Hua in Cairo). By the beginning of January, the lack of progress of the Cultural Revolution in the Foreign Ministry began to result in what was considered to be 'ultra-leftist' pressure. A key figure here was the influential Wang Li (a member of the Central Cultural Revolution Group) who tried to get rid of Chen, in defiance of Premier Zhou Enlai. On 18 January, a Ministry of Foreign Affairs Revolutionary Rebel Liaison Station (*Waijiaobu Geming Zaofan Lianluozhan*) was established to inspect work and criticise policies. Although committed to the position urged by Jiang Qing, its setting up hardly constituted a 'seizure of power'.

On 24 January, Chen Yi was forced to give a self-criticism before a mass rally where he was accused of a number of 'crimes' including his support of the work-teams, fostering bureaucratism and adopting a conservative position on education in 1961-2. Unlike many other confessions, however, Chen's was accepted and the Foreign Minister retained his post. Confirmed in office, he then launched a counter-attack, criticised the rebel liaison station and reinstated a number of people accused of 'revisionism'. Admitting that his confession had been forced out of him, Chen demanded that, if the Red Guards really wanted to make revolution, they should leave him alone and go to Vietnam. Almost unbelievably, he reportedly went on to say: 'Comrade [Liu] Shaoqi speaks correctly ... Comrade Shaoqi is my teacher.' After what amounted to a declaration of war upon the Red Guards, one might have expected Chen Yi to be bitterly denounced and removed from office. In fact, Chen's position was stronger in February 1967 than ever before.

As I see it, there are two explanations for the extraordinary tolerance accorded to Chen Yi in early 1967. First, he was protected by Zhou Enlai who was concerned that China's foreign relations might deteriorate further and, secondly, Chen's counter-attack coincided with the beginning of a new and short period of consolidation following some of the 'ultra-leftism' of January. But the consequences of Chen's declaration of war were to be very far-reaching. There was to remain, within the foreign affairs network, tremendous resentment against Chen, and his reaction to Red Rebels gave rise to an 'ultra-leftism' which was eventually to cause more havoc than might have occurred in January 1967 had Chen been less instransigent. Perhaps the most implacable of Chen's critics was a man still employed as chargé d'affaires in the beleaguered embassy in Jakarta—Yao Dengshan.

The 'February Adverse Current'

Foreign Minister Chen Yi was probably saved by what became known as the 'February Adverse Current'. Since this 'adverse current' constituted an attempt to impose severe restrictions upon the development of the Cultural Revolution, it has become the source of much controversy. Recent (1979) accounts deny that the current was 'adverse' at all and assert that the events of February 1967 were merely an attempt to counter some of the effects of 'ultra-leftism' and to get back to the spirit of the 'Sixteen Points'. To support this position, it is claimed that Mao Zedong himself endorsed the 'current' in late 1971, indicating that it had been an appropriate means to deal with the extremism of Lin Biao and Chen Boda.[99] Mao's comments, however, were to be made in a very different political climate.

It was quite clear that Mao Zedong wished to curtail unrestrained faction-fighting. To this end, his order to the PLA in late January gave rise to a new policy of 'three supports and two militaries' (support the workers, peasants and the 'left' and adopt leadership and training by the military). This policy was not, however, intended to halt the Cultural

Revolution but merely to make the army hold the ring whilst mass organisations formed their own alliances. The interpretations of 1979, however, suggest that another important consideration of Mao was to stabilise the army and thus field armies were forbidden to proceed further with their own internal Cultural Revolution. Indeed, the only part of the army which was allowed to engage in Cultural Revolution activities were the military academies and these were forbidden to establish ties with non-military Red Rebel organisations.[100] The result of this was that, in 'supporting the left', the army was to become the arbiter of various groups' political position in a struggle which was defined as purely civilian. In retrospect, it seems that Mao's confidence that the political consciousness of military commanders was sufficient to enable them to do this was often misplaced. Having no internal experience of the criteria for arbitration, a number of units responded with a very heavy hand. In a study of PLA reaction to the order of late January, Jürgen Domes notes that the army firmly supported Red Rebel groups in six out of the 29 administrative units at provincial level, gave moderate support in four, remained neutral in nine but either refused to 'support the left' or actively opposed it in ten.[101] I do not know how accurate Domes's evaluation is but it is certainly true that, in some areas, the military 'support for the left' was highly questionable. In Qinghai[102] and Guangdong, in particular, military reaction seemed to be particularly harsh and the Guangdong military commander Huang Yongsheng earned the title of 'Guangzhou's Tan Zhenlin',[103] after the Minister of Agriculture who was soon to be accused of organising his own power seizures.

In many ways, the subsequent literature has identified the 'February Adverse Current' with the person of Tan Zhenlin. This, 1979 accounts claim, was because he had written a letter to the Central Committee protesting about the activities of Jiang Qing and she, therefore, had chosen him as a major target for overthrow.[104] In fact, though Tan was one of the most outspoken opponents of the January Revolution, it was claimed that his position was shared by most of the old leaders of the Party. They felt that the Cultural Revolution had violated the provisions of the 'Sixteen Points' and thus opposed the efforts of the Central Cultural Revolution Group to extend it. Though the Party leadership may not have been as united as the 1979 accounts claim and though, for symbolic reasons, the role of Mao has probably been distorted, the recent recapitulations of the events of mid-February are worth considering.[105] They describe a decisive confrontation between the bulk of the old central Party leadership and the Central Cultural Revolution Group at a fortnight-long series of meetings in Beijing's Huairen Hall. At those meetings, a number of former marshals of the PLA, led, it is said, by Ye Jianying and Xu Xiangqian, protested about the continued disruption of the army which the order of late January had been designed to curtail. Apparently, the houses of a number of senior military cadres had been searched and secret military documents had been stolen. They protested also about the continued denunciation of senior cadres. Mao, it is alleged, ordered that various senior officials from the provinces be brought to Beijing to enjoy the protection which had already been accorded to Liu Shaoqi. When, however, it appeared that Chen Pixian, the first secretary of the East China Bureau of the Party, had been detained in Shanghai, according to what Zhang Chunqiao described as the will of the 'masses', Tan Zhenlin exploded:

> What masses? It's always the masses! The masses! There is also the question of Party leadership. You don't want Party leadership and constantly go on about the masses liberating themselves. What is that? It is metaphysics . . . Your object is to overthrow the veteran cadres one after another and bring to ruin the family of revolutionaries of forty years standing . . . This is the cruellest struggle in our Party's history—bar none . . . If you think that is the way to do things, go ahead. But I won't stand for it. I'll fight you to the end, even to the point of decapitation, imprisonment or expulsion from the Party.[106]

Herein lay the crux of the dissension. The Cultural Revolution was negating the leadership of the Chinese Communist Party. Such was the logic of the policies which Mao had instituted. But, perhaps Mao was too much of a Leninist to follow his ideas through to their logical conclusion. I suspect that Mao did, in fact, offer protection to senior cadres under attack and we have already seen Mao's withdrawal of support from the Shanghai Commune, which was the logical outcome of his promotion of mass activism. Perhaps Mao feared the recrudescence of the same kind of resentment which had existed for a quarter of a century after the harsh criticism of certain veteran cadres in Yan'an. Recalling that criticism, Chen Yi implied that the Cultural Revolution was sowing the seeds of new and more bitter resentment.[107] He was more than prophetic. Indeed, much of China's history since 1967 may be understood in that context.

The 1979 account of the meetings in Huairen Hall concentrates largely on attacks made by members of the Central Cultural Revolution Group on senior members of the Party accused of 'negating the Yan'an tradition'. Much also is made of statements of Mao aimed, it is said, at moderating the campaign and of the protection given to veterans by Premier Zhou Enlai. Yet, although sympathetic reference is made to groups like the United Action Committee, little is said about the counter-attack on radical criticism. Throughout February 1967, accounts appeared far and wide of an extension of military control. On 26 January, the army took control of civil aviation.[108] In late January, military representatives were dispatched to factories, mines and stores.[109] In early February, many public security organs were placed firmly under military control.[110] At provincial levels and below, military control commissions were formed[111] prior to the establishment of revolutionary committees in exactly the same way as 1948 – 9. In the countryside, the army also became increasingly involved in administration.[112] Yet one should not conclude from the simple fact of military involvement that the Cultural Revolution was being stifled any more than radical change had been stifled by military involvement during the Civil War. What we must look at is the way the army restored order, and this was sometimes peremptory. We must look also at policy. In late January, for example, the Cultural Revolution was actually *postponed* (whatever that may mean) in a number of military regions until order could be restored.[113] In the countryside, peasants were forbidden to take any action against members of the former work-teams[114] and leniency was stressed during the spring planting season.[115] Long Marches of students exchanging revolutionary experiences were curtailed[116] and numbers of former officials, who had been considered to be 'revisionist', were returned to office.[117] In the light of such evidence, it would seem that the Cultural Revolution was winding down.

Conclusion

By February 1967, many problems had occurred in the Cultural Revolution and had occasioned a counter-attack on the part of senior leaders of the Party. In some places, the hand of the army had been applied quite heavily and there were many local leaders who had carried out what were considered to be bogus power seizures. The revolutionary committees, which had begun to form on the basis of the 'triple alliance', were much less ambitious than the radical schemes for a Paris Commune, which had been discussed in January, and occasionally the initiative in the formation of these committees had come from the army rather than the masses.

Despite this, however, something quite remarkable had been achieved. Not only were students and teachers asking questions about political power which they had never considered before, not only were peasants now free from bureaucratic control from above, but there had occurred, in Shanghai and some other places, an explosion of popular participation in decision-making. The Party machine had been dismantled and could be built on less bureaucratic lines and the way was open for a complete restructuring of China's educational system. More people than ever before had become involved not only in operational decision-making, not only in policy-formulation, but also in macropolitics. In some ways, the situation in China resembled that of 1949, though this time there was a much more literate and, it was hoped, more politically conscious population.

The situation was similar to 1949 also in the sense that military control commissions and military representatives were active in helping (and sometimes forcing) the process of consolidating new forms of political power. One suspects that this was not what had been intended in early 1966 and, once Mao had appeared to lose his nerve and once opponents of the Central Cultural Revolution Group rallied, there was nothing that could be done except to return to well-tried forms of administration. Yet if the mistakes of the early 1950s were not to be repeated, much depended upon the support role of the military. In 1949 – 50, soldiers turned themselves into civilian Party cadres and their inexperience sometimes led to the adoption of organisational forms which negated the ideals for which they had fought. Would this happen again or would the army merely hold the ring until new administrative bodies from the masses were formed and consolidated? If the army representatives in the factories, schools and communes did retain their military positions, however, was there a danger that the army might replace the Party? What kind of army would it be, moreover, if the military became affected by the same kind of faction-fighting as had occurred in the civilian sector?

Faced with situations like that of Guangzhou, where Huang Yongsheng had created his own 'left' to support, it was evident to the Central Cultural Revolution Group that the above problems would not be solved without a continuation of the mass struggle. Large numbers of Red Guards and Red Rebels had been infuriated by military overreaction and it was felt that their initiative had to be sustained if a new order was to be built out of the confusing situation. Capitalising on the resentment of rebel groups, the Cultural Revolution Group was able, once again, to take the initiative. This was done, however, against the protests of many senior leaders of the Party and thus, in my view, could only have been carried out with the approval of Mao. But one is never quite sure of Mao's position and his authority was invoked by all the various parties to the struggle.

Whatever Mao's actual position might have been, it was clear that the 'February Adverse Current' was to be terminated. On 9 March, a *Hongqi* editorial stated quite clearly that the main component in revolutionary alliances should be the *masses*.[118] Tan Zhenlin began to be condemned as the architect of false power seizures and there was no more talk of postponing the Cultural Revolution. At a mass rally on 14 March, the 'February Adverse Current' was denounced and calls were made for the dismissal of five vice-premiers and four vice-chairmen of the Party's Military Commission.[119] At the same time, the army was ordered to examine itself and on 6 April was instructed not to take any action against mass organisations without prior clearance from Beijing[120] (which presumably meant Lin Biao). A new chapter of the Cultural Revolution was to begin and this time it was to be a much more bitter and more violent chapter.

NOTES

1. *RMRB*, 26 February 1979, p.2.
2. *PR* 35, 26 August 1966, pp. 3 – 8. In some places, such as Xi'an, this stage began a few days earlier. Personal information from A. Watson.
3. E.g. Zhengzhou (Hinton,1972, pp. 83 – 7) and Xinjiang (ibid., pp. 87 – 94), where the movement was initially unsuccessful. Also marked by initial resistance, Guangzhou (Bennett and Montaperto, 1971, pp. 74 – 7) and Shanghai (Hunter, 1969, pp. 88 – 110).
4. Soviet and Yugoslav reports, *CQ* 28, 1966, p. 187.
5. Hinton, 1972, p. 72.
6. Daubier, 1974, pp. 89 – 90.
7. Hinton, 1972, p. 97. For an explanation of Tao's contradictory behaviour, see Moody, 1973, pp. 288 – 91.
8. Zhu Pu, *Zhongguo Gongye*, Vol I, No. 12, 24 April 1950, p. 13.
9. The first posters to appear, criticising Liu Shaoqi, were probably those at Qinghua University in late August. Hinton,1972, pp. 74 – 5.
10. Israel,1967, p. 16. Note, Liu Shaoqi claimed he had despatched work-teams through the *new* Beijing Committee (Liu Shaoqi, 23 October 1966, in Liu, Vol III, 1968, p. 358).
11. Personal observation.
12. Daubier, 1974, p. 100.
13. Personal information. See also Bennett and Montaperto, 1971, p. 105. Many different estimates of Beijing's population were made at the time and the two million figure can be no more than a guess.
14. Daubier, 1974, p. 82.
15. Ibid., p. 79.
16. Personal observation and ibid. p. 80.
17. Esmein,1973, p. 113. In some places such as Xi'an, many workers did not return to the factories. Personal information from A. Watson.
18. Baum, 1971, p. 378.
19. *PR* 33, 12 August 1966, p. 11.
20. Baum, 1969 (b), p. 101; Wylie, 1967.
21. *SCMP* 4128, 29 February 1968, pp. 22 – 4.
22. Chen Boda, *SCMM* 617, 29 April 1968, p. 8.
23. Text in URI,1968 (b), pp. 79 – 80.
24. Baum,1969 (b), p. 103.
25. CCPCC, URI,1968(b), pp. 139 – 42.
26. Mao Zedong, 24 October 1966, Schram,1974, p. 268.
27. Israel, 1967, p. 13: report of Xie Fuzhi, 3 October 1966.
28. Personal observation. These criticisms appeared as early as late August.
29. CCPCC, 16 November 1966, URI,1968 (b), pp. 103 – 5.
30. Military Commission and General Political Dept., 5 October 1966, ibid., pp. 89 – 91.
31. *PR* 41, 7 October 1966, pp. 15 – 17.
32. Daubier, 1974, p. 93.
33. Mao Zedong, 25 October 1966, Schram, 1974, p. 274.

34. Liu Shaoqi, 23 October 1966, Liu, Vol III, 1968, p. 363.

35. Notably Wang Guang, *CQ* 29 1967, p. 184.

36. E.g. CCPCC, SC, 16 November 1966, URI, 1968 (b), pp. 109–11; CCPCC, SC,1 December 1966, ibid., pp. 127–9.

37. E.g. *PR* 44, 28 October 1966, pp. 16–19; Hinton, 1972, p. 100.

38. CCP, Beijing Municipal Committee,18 November 1966, URI, 1968 (b), pp. 122–3, forbidding specifically kangaroo courts, arrests, torture and detention.

39. Daubier,1974, pp. 102–5.

40. Ibid., p. 104.

41. Ibid., p. 106.

42. *PR* 51, 16 December 1966, pp. 5–7.

43. Daubier,1974, p. 106.

44. Ibid., p. 107.

45. CCPCC,15 December 1966, URI, 1968 (b), pp. 139–42, Selden, 1979, pp. 619–21.

46. CCPCC, 15 December 1966, URI, 1968 (b), p. 140.

47. Baum, 1971, p. 406.

48. CCPCC, 15 December 1966, URI, 1968 (b), p. 140.

49. Baum, 1971, p. 410.

50. Esmein, 1973, p. 174.

51. *Current Scene*, Vol VI, No. 5, 15 March 1968, pp. 1–28; Esmein,1973, pp. 174–5.

52. The following account is taken from Hunter,1969, pp.. 132–220; Esmein, 1973, pp. 179–83.

53. CCPCC, 17 November 1966, URI, 1968 (b), pp. 116–19.

54. Bridgham, 1968, p. 8.

55. Esmein, 1973, p. 81.

56. Ibid., p. 83.

57. Ibid.

58. Bridgham, 1968, p. 8.

59. Esmein, 1973, p. 84.

60. Ibid., p. 85.

61. Hunter, 1969, p. 238; Esmein, 1973, p. 86.

62. Esmein, 1973, p. 86.

63. Peng Dehuai was arrested in Changsha (URI, 1968 (a), p. 391). Luo Ruiqing seems to have been arrested in Beijing (Esmein, 1973, p. 83).

64. Esmein, 1973, p. 83; URI, 1968 (a). p. 391.

65. *RMRB*, 26 February 1979, p. 2.

66. Ibid.

67. *PR* 1, 1 January 1967, p. 21.

68. *Current Scene*, Vol VI, No. 5, 15 March 1968, pp. 9–10.

69. The joint notice of the National Rebel General Corps of Red Labourers, Ministry of Labour and ACFTU, 2 January, was repudiated by the CCPCC and SC on 17 February 1967. URI, 1968 (b), pp. 305–6.

70. Esmein, 1973, pp. 195–201.

71. According to *Asahi*, there were 800,000 Scarlet Guards and 600,000 Revolutionary Rebels. Esmein,1973, p. 184. On the limited support for the Scarlet Guards, see ibid., pp. 182–5.

72. Ibid., p. 183.

73. Hunter, 1969, p. 208.

74. Text in *PR* 3, 13 January 1967, pp. 5–7.

75. Mao Zedong, 9 January 1967, Schram, 1974, p. 275. Message of support from CCPCC, Military Commission and Central Cultural Revolution Group, *PR* 4, 11 January 1967, p. 5, and URI, 1968 (b), pp. 157–8.

76. *PR* 4, 20 January 1967, p. 28.

77. Ibid., pp. 7 and 12–15; URI, 1968 (b), pp. 165–70.

78. Daubier, 1974, p. 127.

79. On 14, 22, 24 January and 5 February 1967. Esmein, 1973, p. 192, and *SCMP* 4147, 27 March 1968, p. 3.

80. Robinson, 1971, p. 217.

81. Daubier, 1974, pp. 139–40.

82. *SCMP* 3898, 14 March 1967, pp. 1–7.

83. Bridgham, 1968, p. 10; Robinson, 1971, p. 203.

84. CCPCC, 25 January 1967, *CB* 852, 6 May 1968, p. 52.

85. CCPCC, 25 January 1967, URI, 1968 (b), pp. 204–5.

86. *RMRB*, 27 January 1967, p. 2; ibid., 1 February 1967, p. 2; Wylie, 1967.

87. Esmein, 1973, p. 187.

88. Ibid., pp. 187–90.

89. Ibid., pp. 87–90. For details of the reorganisation, see URI,1969, p. 201. There was a further reorganisation of this group in August 1967.

90. Mao Zedong, 1967, *CB* 892, 21 October 1969, p. 50.

91. CCPCC, SC, Military Commission and Central Cultural Revolution Group, 23 January 1967, URI, 1968 (b), pp. 195–7.

92. Mao Zedong, February 1967, Schram, 1974, p. 278.

93. *PR* 7, 10 February 1967, pp. 12–13.

94. This is dealt with in the next chapter.

95. Esmein, 1973, p. 189; *SCMP* 4147, 27 March 1968, p. 7. This remark was attributed to Mao.

96. *PR* 10, 3 March 1967, pp. 10–12.

97. Mao Zedong, February 1967, Schram, 1974, p. 277.

98. The following is taken from Gurtov, 1971, pp. 313–66. Chen Yi's 'self-criticism' is in *Chinese Law and Government*, Vol I, No. 1, Spring 1968, pp. 52–3.

99. *RMRB*, 26 February 1979, p. 2.

100. Ibid.

101. Domes, 1973, p. 181.

102. CCPCC, SC, Military Commission and Central Cultural Revolution Group, 24 March 1967, URI, 1968 (b), pp. 385–7.

103. Vogel, 1971, p. 332.

104. *RMRB*, 26 February 1979, p.2

105. Ibid., pp. 2 and 4.

106. Ibid., p. 2.

107. Ibid.

108. SC, Military Commission, 26 January 1967, URI, 1968 (b), p. 208.

109. Vogel, 1971, p. 332.

110. Ministry of Public Security, PLA Beijing Garrison HQ, URI, 1968 (b), pp. 667–8.

111. E.g. Vogel, 1971, p. 332.

112. Baum, 1971, pp. 422–1.

113. Military Commission, 28 January 1967, URI, 1968 (b), p. 216.

114. CCPCC, 17 February 1967, ibid., p. 294.

115. CCPCC, 20 February 1967, ibid., pp. 331–3.

116. CCPCC, SC, 3 February 1967, ibid., pp. 227–9; Military Commission, 8 February 1967, ibid., pp. 244–5.

117. Robinson, 1971, p. 217.

118. *PR* 12, 17 March 1967, pp. 14–16.

119. *RMRB*, 26 February 1979, p. 2.

120. Text in URI, 1968 (b), pp. 409–11.

IV
MILITARY REACTION AND THE
PROBLEM OF 'ULTRA-LEFTISM'
(1967 – 1968)

Much of the politics in China during 1967 and 1968 may be understood as a reaction to what was felt to have happened during the 'February Adverse Current'. That, I am sure, is the reason why the Chinese press went to such pains, in 1979, to argue that the current was not 'adverse' at all. This reaction was to be referred to as 'ultra-leftist' and 1979 accounts ascribe responsibility for this position to Lin Biao and the whole of the Central Cultural Revolution Group.[1] It is very difficult to evaluate such an assertion since the Chinese press is somewhat vague about what it means by 'ultra-leftism'.

To many people, the term 'ultra-left' meant little more than being more radical than oneself. On the other hand, at a highly abstract level, it signified an idealist faith in human capacity regardless of socio-economic constraints. It is, however, an extraordinarily difficult task to locate any particular action on the continuum between freedom and necessity. In the first edition of this book, I suggested that the criterion for identifying an 'ultra-left' position was whether or not actions violated the Mass Line. 'Ultra-leftist' policies, therefore, were those which had the effect of coercing the masses into becoming socialist. It was pointed out, however, that the operation of the Mass Line was dependent upon a functioning Party apparatus which could process mass demands and, by March 1967, the Party machine had broken down. There was, in short, mass activity without the Mass Line.[2] I was forced, therefore, to fall back on the behavioural position suggested by Benjamin Schwartz. 'Ultra-leftism', in the context of 1967, signified the belief that only one's own organisation possessed true virtue.[3] Such was the position of Lin Jie, whom I can only describe as a Jacobin. Lin, faced with what was felt to be the moral corruption of both the Party and the army, wished to strengthen the power of provisional organs by infusing the ranks of particular groups of Revolutionary Rebels with a military-type iron discipline.[4] Such was the position also of the Qinghua University activist, Kuai Dafu, who regarded his own faction as the only source of correct revolutionary commitment.[5] To ask such persons to form alliances with other groups, with or without military support, seemed a forlorn hope. In the face of people such as Lin or Kuai, many people in the central leadership, who were perhaps not so extreme, were caught in a quandary. They realised that the army had often gone too far in February 1967 but, if they criticised the army too severely, the initiative would be taken by those who believed they had a monopoly on virtue.

This chapter will describe the 'ultra-leftism' which grew in response to military action and the further military action which was needed to deal with it. The result was a very violent situation.

The Growth of the 'Ultra-left'

By March 1967, a number of decisions were taken in Beijing concerning the military overreaction during the preceding 'February Adverse Current' and attempts were made to see that similar actions did not occur in future. The harshest criticism was directed against the military commander, Zhao Yongfu, who was accused of carrying out a coup in Qinghai on 23 February and of deceiving both the Central Committee and the masses.[6] In the weeks which followed, documents were issued dealing with mistakes in PLA 'support to the left' in Anhui,[7] Inner Mongolia,[8] Sichuan[9] and Shandong.[10] The suppression, carried out by the Guangdong commander Huang Yongsheng, however, which seemed to provoke quite considerable resentment from the rebels,[11] was spared official censure, probably because he was protected by Lin Biao, his long-time associate.[12]

The official line in March-April 1967 was to restrict military reaction and to correct some of the mistakes made in February, while still adhering to a policy of military involvement. Army participation in the triple alliance formula for revolutionary committees was seen as essential. Yet the distrust of the army, engendered by military overreaction, was to weaken the effectiveness of that participation and soon calls were made to 'drag out the handful of capitalist roaders in the army'. Those who made such a demand seemed to concentrate on denouncing individual persons rather than the line they represented. This was nowhere more apparent than in the treatment of Liu Shaoqi. At an enlarged meeting of the Politburo, in March 1967, it was decided to criticise the line of Liu Shaoqi[13] and it was stressed that what was being carried out was 'line struggle' rather than 'unprincipled civil war'. This position was reflected in the various articles which appeared criticising Liu Shaoqi's book *On Self-Cultivation*. Particularly singled out for denunciation was Liu's tendency to play down class struggle.[14] It was felt that the revisions which Liu had made to his book in 1962 were part of a concerted campaign to reinstate the line of Peng Dehuai with its Khrushchevian denunciation of 'left dogmatism'.[15] Bearing in mind the works of Wu Han and Deng Tuo, written at the same time as Liu's 1962 revisions, some people felt that *On Self-Cultivation* contained implied criticisms of Mao.[16] The point which was perhaps of the greatest importance, however, was that the very notion of 'cultivation' (*xiuyang*) was individualistic and élitist. The aim was to create men of superior moral qualities who were essentially self-trained, whereas Mao's view was that the qualities of leadership were acquired in dialectical interaction with the masses. It was felt, therefore, that Liu's prescription for leadership had more in common with ancient Confucianism than with the Mass Line.[17]

Those whose position might be described as 'ultra-left', however, seemed not to be satisfied with an analysis of 'revisionist' line and were more interested in disgracing Liu himself. One such person, Qi Benyu, took a far more aggressive position in his opening press attack entitled 'Patriotism or National Betrayal?'.[18] He accused Liu of propagating a film entitled *The Inside Story of the Qing Court* which portrayed the Guang Xu Emperor, at the turn of the century, as a progressive element struggling against the reactionary Empress Dowager and which painted the *Yihetuan* ('Boxers') in an unfavourable light. In Qi's view, the Qing court was hopelessly corrupt from top to bottom and the *Yihetuan* were just about the only progressive anti-imperialist force in 1900. Qi was, however, unwilling to let the matter rest with a denunciation of the film. Having warmed himself up for a full-scale attack, he accused Liu of capitulating to the Guomindang during the war against Japan, opposing the socialisation of industry and commerce, dissolving co-ops, liquidating the class struggle, attacking the Great Leap Forward, advocating *sanziyibao*, pursuing a revisionist foreign policy, propagating 'self-cultivation' to oppose Mao Zedong Thought, perverting the Socialist Education Movement and colluding with Deng Xiaoping to sabotage the Cultural Revolution. As Qi saw it, Liu was a ' sham revolutionary, a counter-revolutionary . . . a Khrushchev lying right beside us'.[19] The logical extension of Qi's position was to reduce the Cultural Revolution to a witch-hunt. An excessive concentration on the *subjective* villainy of a few people such as Liu Shaoqi hindered an analysis of the objective reasons for their standpoint. Qi's focus was on the *person* not the line.

Later, in the summer of 1967, Liu attempted to defend himself.[20] On the question of capitulating to the Guomindang, he pleaded ignorance. He blamed Deng Zihui for the dissolution of co-ops and others for the 'revisionist' policies of the early 1960s. He admitted, however, that the Eighth Party Congress had made mistakes in line and that his book *On*

Self-Cultivation contained errors. Though he had made mistakes in the Socialist Education Movement, he defended his own and Wang Guangmei's participation. Finally, in his handling of the early stages of the Cultural Revolution, he confessed an inability to see what he had done wrong and, if anything, went back on his earlier 'self-criticism'.[21] Those who shared Qi's position probably saw Liu's defence as perfidious lying whereas it would surely have been more useful to have examined the roots of Liu's ignorance.

It is likely, as Esmein argues, that Mao Zedong was critical of the personalised nature of the criticism of Liu.[22] In the weeks after Qi Benyu's initial attack, this criticism reached quite savage proportions and various leaders were accused before mass meetings.[23] In the new, highly-charged atmosphere, a number of new targets appeared, among them Zhou Enlai who was felt to have given unnecessary protection to Chen Yi and Tan Zhenlin.[24] As the number of targets increased, so the content of criticism became more trivial, focusing on things such as the dress Wang Guangmei wore on her visit to Indonesia and her 'shameful exhibition' of dancing with President Sukarno.[25] In such a situation, there was a great danger that the educative effect of the Cultural Revolution might be lost and that the campaign to criticise Liu Shaoqi's works might fail to provide a focus for Red Guard and Red Rebel unity.

In contrast to her subsequent portrayal as the fount of 'ultra-leftism', Jiang Qing was as active as Zhou Enlai in the spring of 1967, patching up quarrels and helping to form revolutionary alliances. At the same time, she warned time and again against 'anarchism' and 'factionalism' because these deviations would cause the masses to become disenchanted with the Cultural Revolution. In February, attempts had been made to get students back into school[26] although, in the new period of ferment, Qi Benyu was said to have maintained that 'to go back to classes after making revolution for six months would be an admission of defeat'.[27] But despite his exhortations, many students did in fact go back to school where the army busied itself organising intensive political training classes.[28] In some of the major universities, however, the army seems to have played little part and various 'headquarters' continued to hurl insults at each other. In Beijing, when the three Red Guard headquarters joined in February 1967 into a single organisation,[29] it appeared that some kind of unity had been achieved. In reality, the new Red Guard Congress was largely a creature of the Third Headquarters led, amongst others, by the Qinghua 'hero' Kuai Dafu.[30] In the universities, 'factionalism' was probably worse than ever before.

An immediate consequence of what was called 'bourgeois fac-tionalism' (which was equated with 'bourgeois parliamentarianism')[31] was that the new moderate policy towards the rehabilitation of cadres could not go into effect. It was Mao's view that a majority of cadres could, after a while, be rehabilitated.[32] But whenever one side in the universities put up a slate of cadres for rehabilitation, it would usually be vetoed by the other side and the result was chaos.[33]

It was extremely difficult to get any kind of agreement amongst students on attitudes towards the army. Many persisted in seeking revenge for the events of February and in their demands to 'drag out the handful'. In Beijing, for example, demonstrations were held opposing the new chairman of the Red Guard Congress, Nie Yuanzi, the once popular philosophy teacher who put up 'China's first Marxist-Leninist *dazibao*' but who had recently been criticised for indulging in luxuries.[34] When clashes developed, troops were sent in and incensed activists then shifted their attacks to the deputy commander of the PLA Beijing garrison and detained some PLA cadres. In such a situation, all the leaders of the Central Cultural Revolution Group could do was convene a meeting in mid-April and chastise the 'ultra-left' for attacking the PLA and engaging in 'unprincipled civil war'.[35]

Although the above picture of China in March-April 1967 is one of increasing tension, one should note that the phenomenon of 'ultra-leftism' was largely confined to the intellectuals. In the suburban countryside, the incidence of factional struggle seems to have declined at a time when spring planting was under way[36] and criticism within industry seems to have been confined within factories.[37] In the urban residential areas, there was considerable criticism of street cadres,[38] exacerbated in many cases by the return of young people from the countryside or the frontier regions whence they had gone during the Socialist Education Movement.[39] As urban residents' committees organised themselves into 'newspaper reading groups'[40] to formulate criticisms, they made frequent contact with Red Guard organisations but do not seem to have been greatly influenced by 'ultra-leftism'. The main problem in the residential areas seems to have resulted from the breakdown of the public security network and occasionally residents' vigilante groups were formed to deal with petty crime.[41] In the spring of 1967, therefore, the main arena of conflict seemed confined to the universities and the army. There were also the beginnings of a decisive confrontation between intellectual activists and regional army commanders. Convinced that these contradictions were as yet 'non-antagonistic', the central leadership strove to speed up the formation of revolutionary committees.

As we have seen, the model for provincial-level revolutionary committees was established in Heilongjiang on 31 January under the leadership of the old first secretary of the Provincial Party Committee, Pan Fusheng. The formation of this committee had been relatively smooth since there was a good working relationship between Pan and the local PLA commander and both joined the revolutionary rebels.[42] The key to success here, it would seem, was the relative ease with which Red Rebels identified revolutionary cadres. The Guizhou committee was established on 12 February, again fairly smoothly because the PLA identified clearly with the revolutionary rebels,[43] and a similar pattern developed in Shandong where a revolutionary committee was established on 23 February.[44] In Shanghai (28 February)[45] and Shanxi (22 March),[46] the new revolutionary committees grew out of Paris Commune-type organisations though, in the latter, PLA support was not as strong as it might have been.[47] It is probable that the Shanxi revolutionary committee represented something of a model in that it was composed of some 50 per cent Red Rebels, 25 per cent PLA and 25 per cent rehabilitated cadres. In its standing committee, however, over half were revolutionary cadres,[48] although, of course, this tells us little about their actual orientation.

By April, the Beijing leadership felt that the time had come to set up a revolutionary committee there too, amongst other things to provide the framework for reconciling hostile groups. At one time, Beijing's Red Guards and Red Rebels had formed an organisation called the 'Preparatory Committee for the Beijing People's Commune' but, following the promulgation of the triple alliance model in February, attempts were made to set up a Heilongjiang-type committee under the leadership of the Minister of Public Security, Xie Fuzhi.[49] The rather questionable Red Guard Congress, established in February, was the first of a number of organisational building blocks which were to form the revolutionary committee. On 19 March, a similar Congress of Poor and Lower-Middle Peasants was formed[50] and, on 25 March, with military support, a secondary school Red Guard Congress.[51] After protracted discussions, these various congresses agreed finally on the composition of a Beijing Revolutionary Committee which was established on 20 April.[52] Of its 97 members, only 17 were soldiers and 13 revolutionary cadres. Of the remainder, there were 24 workers, 20 students, 13 peasants, six members of cultural and social organisations and four urban residents.[53] Such was the new model which was designed to show that diverse groups could work together. As we shall see, there were some groups who clearly could not.

Zhou Enlai and the 'Ultra-Left'

Flushed with their successes in the campaign against Liu Shaoqi in April 1967, the 'ultra-left' critics began to step up their attacks upon Zhou Enlai in early May. What provided fuel for their fire was the fact that, in the May Day celebrations, discredited ministers such as Tan Zhenlin, Chen Yi and Chen Yun still appeared to have retained their posts.[54] This, it was claimed in 1979, was achieved with Mao's explicit approval[55] though one cannot be sure how reliable such an assertion was. As far as his critics were concerned, Zhou's record in the Cultural Revolution, to date, had been a series of actions designed to pour cold water on the revolutionary upsurge. During the process of 'seizing power', Zhou had established a complex set of criteria which were designed to prevent precipitate action. He had demanded that 'power seizures' should only take place 'within systems' and not across organisational boundaries (which made horizontal mobilisation extremely difficult). He had demanded that power be seized gradually, after extensive preparations from the bottom up. He had spoken much of 'revolutionary order' and had precluded direct elections on the Paris Commune model.[56] This, the 'ultra-left' felt, protected senior 'persons in authority taking the capitalist road'.

Since the beginning of the year, Zhou had not only protected Chen Yi but also four other vice-premiers including Tan Zhenlin. It was only on 23 May that Zhou associated himself with Red Rebel attempts to overthrow Tan and only on 15 June that he agreed to join in the criticism.[57] Although Zhou found it impossible, in the end, to protect Tan, he remained steadfast in his protection of Chen Yi, whose difficulties were multiplying daily. On his return from Indonesia on 30 April,[58] the 'red diplomat' Yao Dengshan became the centre of an 'ultra-leftist' faction in foreign affairs which intensified its attacks on Liao Chengzhi's Overseas Chinese Affairs Commission, charged with the 'crime' of denationalising overseas Chinese.[59] At a time when overseas Chinese in Indonesia were subject to savage repression,[60] these charges seemed particularly serious. At the same time, the 'ultra-left' criticised the 'bourgeois habits' of China's diplomats abroad and demanded that the Cultural Revolution should apply to them also.[61]

In June and July 1967, 'ultra-leftist' pressure on the Foreign Ministry and the inability of Chen Yi (and presumably Zhou Enlai) to control the situation resulted in a series of setbacks in foreign relations. Faced with the growth of the revolutionary White Flag Communist Party of Burma, the group surrounding Yao Dengshan was no longer content to offer it merely lukewarm support and still maintain 'correct' relations with Ne Win's government. Following anti-Chinese riots, connected amongst other things with the distribution of Mao badges, the Chinese government reversed its previous policy and branded the Burmese government 'fascist'.[62] At almost the same time, Sino-Cambodian relations soured as Sihanouk perceived (rightly or wrongly) some connection between 'Khymer Rouge' activities and the increased militancy of Chinese embassy staff.[63] In Kenya, Nepal and Ceylon a similar deterioration of relations occurred partly, at least, as a result of 'ultra-leftist' pressure.[64]

The 'ultra-left' activists were not content merely to criticise Chen Yi's and Zhou Enlai's defence of officials they considered 'revisionist' and to demand changes in China's foreign policy. They were concerned also with the structure of the State Council itself. The record of power seizures in the State Council in the first half of 1967 was hardly impressive. Officially or unofficially sanctioned power seizures had taken place in only three of the nine state committees, 30 of the 40 ministries, six of the 24 bureaux and none of the six staff offices. Of the 49 commissions and ministries at the core of the State Council, only one of them—the Scientific and Technical Commission—had established a revolutionary committee. Far from creating new organs of power in the central government, the system of ministerial Party committees had been re-established in February and maintained administrative continuity throughout the turbulent period which followed.[65]

What must have been particularly galling to the 'ultra-leftists' was the fact that the army seemed firmly behind Zhou Enlai's protection of the central government.[66] Whatever friction might have existed between Lin Biao and Zhou Enlai, Zhou enjoyed great prestige in the army. He attended meetings of the Military Commission, defended the army from attacks and, at times, even gave orders to the troops on his own initiative.[67]

In the period May-July 1967, the orientation of the army was considered to be absolutely crucial by the moderate leadership which Zhou Enlai seemed to symbolise. In the face of provocation, the army was under no circumstances to respond in a way similar to February 1967 and, on the anniversary of the 'May Seventh Directive', Lin Biao ordered an intensive two-week rectification campaign in the PLA to correct mistakes made in the previous period of 'supporting the left'.[68] Army units were ordered to undergo a process of self-criticism on the model of the Shandong Military District Party Committee, though even there it was revealed that the committee was reluctant to publish the results for fear that they might be used to reinforce an attack upon the military leadership.[69] Although the army was forbidden to use force, it was not to sit passively by and watch the new series of clashes which occurred in the period after May. It was still enjoined to reconcile groups by patient persuasion although, as the summer approached, this became more and more difficult. In Yunnan, the Party first secretary, Yan Hongyin, under attack for persecuting Red Guards and sending them to undergo reform, committed suicide.[70] In Xinjiang, Wang Enmao, who had called for an end to the Cultural Revolution, was still faced with considerable radical opposition.[71] In Sichuan, the repression of radical activity by First Secretary Li Jingquan resulted in bloody clashes and his replacement by Zhang Guohua—the commander of troops in Tibet.[72] In Beijing itself, the Minister of Public Security and chairman of the new revolutionary committee, Xie Fuzhi, reported that struggles in the capital were still going on and that production had declined by 7 per cent in April.[73] In such a situation, the army could only respond with patience and issue orders forbidding armed struggle, assaults, destruction, raids and unauthorised arrests. The army newspaper, *Jiefangjunbao*, saw the only response to mass criticism as patient discussion even when the army considered the masses to be wrong.[74] Although the army occasionally violated the non-intervention order, one cannot but be struck by its considerable forbearance and discipline during these trying months. In the countryside (though not always in suburban communes), the army seemed to have been remarkably successful in its use of Mao Zedong Thought propaganda teams to effect reconciliation and in its establishment of 'front-line commands for grasping revolution and promoting prodution'.[75] It is highly unlikely, however, that the turbulence of the towns extended far into the rural areas.

It was probably to test the efficacy of its orders prohibiting armed struggle, assaults and unauthorised arrests that the Centre sent to the provinces a number of investigation teams in June and July 1967. Perhaps the most famous troubleshooters of all were the Minister of Public Security, Xie Fuzhi, and Wang Li, who were sent first to Yunnan to find out about the case of Yan Hongyin.[76] But a more immediate danger in early July was the convocation of the first congress of an organisation known as the 'May Sixteenth Group'.[77] Though it is said that the origins of this group go back to September 1966, it did not achieve national prominence until after 16 May 1967 when, on the first anniversary of the circular repudiating Peng Zhen's 'group of five', a 'May Sixteenth Notification' was issued attacking Zhou Enlai as a 'double dealer playing with counter-revolution'.[78] The origins of the May Sixteenth Group were allegedly found in the Department of Philosophy and Social Sciences in the Chinese Academy of Sciences which produced such prominent and powerful 'ultra-leftists' as Lin Jie and Mu Xin. To this group was added Guan Feng, Wang Li and later Qi Benyu, who held powerful positions in the Central Cultural Revolution Group and thus constituted a real threat to Zhou's position. The May Sixteenth Group was joined in mid-1967 by another extreme 'ultra-left' group known as the 'June Sixteenth Group', based on the Beijing Foreign Languages Institute,[79] presumably with connections with Yao Dengshan and those who wished to overthrow power-holders in the Foreign Ministry. It was apparent, therefore, that if large-scale violence broke out in the Cultural Revolution, not only would Zhou's position be in danger but the whole focus of the Cultural Revolution would be thrown in an 'ultra-left' direction. Just at this crucial point, large-scale violence did, in fact, break out in the city of Wuhan where, for the first time in the Cultural Revolution, a large military unit mutinied.

The Wuhan Incident and its Aftermath[80]

The Wuhan incident of July 1967 might be traced back to the beginning of that year when the military commander, Chen Zaidao, had been actively engaged in suppressing Red Rebels and had earned the reputation as something of a militarist. In the period April – June, a number of armed incidents occurred in the city and a large number of factories, including the massive Wuhan Iron and Steel Works, either suspended production for a time or were reduced to half capacity. By June, the city authorities and PLA units were co-operating with an anti-radical formation consisting largely of industrial workers known as the 'One Million Workers' in suppressing student and worker rebels.

To rectify the situation, no less a person than Zhou Enlai himself flew to Wuhan where he issued a four-point judgement declaring that the 'One Million Workers' were conservative, that the military district command should not support them and that the revolutionary workers and student organisations, together with their headquarters, should be rehabilitated. To help Zhou sort out the situation, the now experienced troubleshooters, Xie Fuzhi and Wang Li, arrived in Wuhan on 14 July, whereupon Zhou left them to implement his judgement. Almost immediately, however, Xie and Wang entered into argument with Chen Zaidao about a certain organisation which had been disbanded by Chen because of radical activities. Accusing Xie and Wang of prejudging the case, Chen threatened to have the 'One Million Workers' cut off the city's water, power and transport if his verdict was reversed. Apparently, Chen, said to be in good standing with Lin Biao, refused to negotiate with such relatively minor personages as Xie and Wang and merely let them carry out inspections from 15 to 18 July. In the meantime, however, the 'One Million Workers' continued their work of repression and, by 19 July, Xie and Wang felt they had seen enough to make a report on the situation. After hearing the report, which reaffirmed Zhou's original judgement, one military commander, Niu Hailong, immediately mobilised his troops and, together with members of the 'One Million Workers', laid seige to Xie and Wang's hotel. On the following day, when Chen declared that the 'One Million Workers' were beyond his control, Xie and Wang were seized and beaten up and the whole of the city taken over by the 'One Million Workers' backed by Niu Hailong's troops.

The reaction from Beijing was immediate. Acting Chief-of-Staff Yang Chengwu ordered Chen to release Xie and Wang and escort them to Beijing, ordered an airborne division, the 15th Army and five gunboats from the East Sea Fleet into action and prepared to take Wuhan by force. Zhou Enlai flew back to Wuhan taking care not to land at the main airport (in order to avoid any kidnap attempt) and Lin Biao himself went to Wuhan to assess the situation and appoint, as field commander, Yu Lijin, the political commissar of the air force. Meanwhile, both Xie and Wang were either released or managed to escape and, on their arrival in Beijing, were greeted by the whole of the central leadership,[81] minus Mao Zedong, and supported by several days' demonstrations in the capital. On 26 July, what was left of the Central Committee convened a special meeting to deal with the situation, dismissed Chen Zaidao, replaced him by Zeng Siyu [82] and, on the following day, sent a letter of support to the PLA units now moving against the insurgents.[83] Fighting in Wuhan probably continued until 4 August, by which time Xie and Wang could return to the city to witness the final victory; but it was a victory won at a considerable price.

The most immediate consequence of the Wuhan incident was a violent 'ultra-left' reaction. Many activists were now convinced that there was indeed a 'handful' in the army taking the 'capitalist road' which they sought immediately to 'drag out'.[84] In the army itself, some people revived the case of Peng Dehuai in *Jiefangjunbao* as a focus for mobilisation.[85] In the period following the Wuhan incident, a series of violent incidents occurred in over a dozen provinces.[86] The new 'hero', Wang Li, returned from Wuhan immediately to join Yao Dengshan in his bid to oust Chen Yi from the Foreign Ministry and topple, once and for all, the 'handful' there too.[87] For 14 days they were successful. Yao Dengshan virtually appointed himself Foreign Minister and brushed the protests of Zhou Enlai contemptuously aside.[88] On 11 August, the Foreign Ministry rebels held a mass rally in Beijing's Great Hall of the People to denounce Chen, and all Zhou Enlai could do was to suggest smaller rallies in future.[89] Though Chen still continued to officiate at formal functions, policy was clearly in the hands of the 'ultra-left' who managed, in its short term of office, to alienate Cambodia,[90] deliver an ultimatum to the British government concerning the suppression of Chinese rebels in Hong Kong and, on its expiry, to burn down the British mission in Beijing on 22 August.[91]

With the burning of the British mission, it was clear that the 'ultra-leftists' had overplayed their hand. Confident of military support, Zhou Enlai was now able to issue an order restricting Red Guard activities around foreign missions[92] and, on 1 September, the Beijing Municipal Party Committee reprimanded the 'ultra-left' and banned the May Sixteenth Group.[93] Red Guards were now forbidden to move around the country and were required to 'support the army'.[94] On 5 September, Jiang Qing, once a great supporter of the movement to seize power, criticised the Red Guards' attacks on the army and the seizure of guns,[95] and her appeals were endorsed in the name of the Central Committee.[96] Now that the army was prepared to counter 'ultra-left' violence, Yao Dengshan disappeared from view and Chen Yi was reinstated. The sick Chen Yi was, however, never the same man again.[97]

In the weeks following the burning of the British mission, Mu Xin, the editor of *Guangming Ribao*, Lin Jie, the editor of *Hongqi*, and Zhao Yiya, the editor of *Jiefangjunbao*, were arrested and the May Sixteenth organisation rooted out.[98] At the same time, the influential Guan Feng and Wang Li were placed under surveillance and Qi Benyu disappeared from view. As the May Sixteenth organisation was systematically dismantled, *Hongqi* suspended publication for a time[99] and, in an article criticising two books of Tao Zhu, Yao Wenyuan signalled that those 'opportunists' who had come to power with Tao Zhu were to be carefully examined.[100] Clearly a new stage of consolidation was to begin.

An Attempt at Consolidation

1979 accounts of the events of September 1967 suggest that it was only the second level of 'ultra-left' leaders who were removed from their posts. Those who had masterminded the 'ultra-left' activities—Lin Biao, Chen Boda, Zhang Chunqiao, Yao Wenyuan, Jiang Qing, Xie Fuzhi and Kang Sheng—remained in power.[101] Contemporary evidence, however, seems to suggest that there was a qualitative difference between those removed in September and the above leaders who tended towards a more moderate position. It is possible that, once arrests were under way, the more senior leaders of the Cultural Revolution Group feigned a conciliatory position in order to protect themselves. But there is, as yet, insufficient evidence to evaluate such an hypothesis. What we do know, however, is that the removal of prominent 'ultra-leftists' in Beijing was not followed immediately by the establishment of a more orderly climate in the provinces. In the autumn of 1967, complaints were heard that the new triple alliance organs were 'dominated by the bourgeoisie' but Mao was quite adamant that the Cultural Revolution should now be carried on relatively peacefully. In a Red Guard publication of 23 October he is quoted as saying:

> This nationwide disturbance is the last of its kind. The army is also disturbed this time. After this disturbance, the whole country will be at peace and become the régime of the Revolutionary Rebels. It is the Party Central Committee that allows this nationwide disturbance.[102]

Though Mao always advocated the efficacy of struggle, it was apparent that many workers and peasants had become quite alienated by the faction-fighting of the 'ultra-left'. If, ultimately, the Cultural Revolution was indeed 'proletarian', the working class organisations, which had been little affected by 'ultra-leftism', should play a much greater role.

In the autumn of 1967, Mao Zedong himself undertook an extensive tour of China, issuing as he went a series of 'supreme instructions', calling for the formation of 'grand alliances' and the reconstruction of the Communist Party.[103] With the formation of the Qinghai Revolutionary Committee on 12 August 1967,[104] only seven of the 29 provincial-level administrative divisions had established revolutionary committees and Mao set the end of 1967 as a target for the formation of such bodies over the whole country. By the Spring Festival of 1968, the whole country was to have consolidated the new structure of power.[105]

But it proved extremely difficult to establish the necessary 'grand alliances' to form the basis of the provincial-level committees. Although the hands of the army were no longer as tied as they had in the period prior to the Wuhan incident, the army was under strict orders not to allow the situation of February 1967 to recur. At that time, some military units had decided quite arbitrarily which group constituted the 'true left' that they would support and had suppressed others. The disastrous consequences of such actions have already been noted. Now, the army was still prevented from supporting particular groups but, in addition to undertaking the task of patient persuasion, the PLA could insulate certain organisations from outside contact and so prevent the influence of 'ultra-leftist' groups which cut across organisational lines.[106] Factories and schools were now to form their own alliances and then affiliate with larger bodies, rather than the previous situation where 'ultra-leftist'-dominated alliances (such as the Beijing Red Guard Congress) descended upon the schools and fanned into flames the already smouldering faction-fighting. The army, therefore, was to hold the ring, and to do this effectively it was required, in October, to undergo a new round of rectification.[107] Progress, however, was to be very slow indeed. Only one more provincial-level revolutionary committee was to be formed in 1967, that of Tianjin municipality[108] (which was raised to provincial status early in 1967). In other parts of China, 'grand alliances' took a very long time to form. An even more difficult problem was how to reconstruct the Party. Where revolutionary committees were in existence, 'nuclear core groups' of Party members were sometimes formed but under no circumstances were the revolutionary committees allowed to appoint them. The 'nuclear core groups' were required to 'emerge from the struggle' and, as yet, not play a leading role in the revolutionary committees' policy formation.[109] The new relationship between Party and state bodies had still to be worked out.

Perhaps nowhere was the new stress on consolidation more bedevilled by 'ultra-leftist' demands than in the field of education. On 25 October, *Renmin Ribao* once again put forward a plea that regular classes should be resumed, though this time according to the stipulations of Mao's 'May Seventh Directive'.[110] Integration was to be effected between units of education and units of production. Schools were to run factories and

factories to run schools. To inculcate the idea of 'revolutionary discipline', schools might be organised on a military basis with battalions and
companies, each with their own political instructor from the PLA.
Examinations were under no circumstances to be reintroduced and
recruitment was to be based on a combination of recommendation by
units of production and selection by school revolutionary committees.[111]
Though the reform proposals were very bold, they still did not satisfy the
'ultra-leftists' who rejected categorically any 'slave mentality' requiring
the subordination of students to authority. They seemed to advocate
nothing less than the dismantling of the formal school system, the
abolition of the universities and any form of organisation based on what
they called the 'three in one conglomeration'.[112]

The Shengwulian

One of the main difficulties in forming 'grand alliances', in the autumn of
1967, was the fact that the 'ultra-left' was often still quite strong in the
provinces. In Hunan province, in particular, there emerged in late 1967
an organisation which was unashamedly 'ultra-leftist' and which categorically rejected the policy of consolidation embarked upon in
September. Though the programme of the Hunan 'ultra-leftists' might
be atypical, I shall describe it here at length in order to give some idea of
what an 'ultra-leftist' position was after the 'August storm'.[113]

Following Mao Zedong's visit to Changsha (the capital of Hunan) on
17 September, the chairman's call for a 'grand alliance' was interpreted
by the Hunan 'ultra-left' as a demand for a Paris Commune-type organisation which would reverse the drift towards the restoration of the pre-
Cultural Revolution situation. The idea of the commune was taken very
seriously indeed. The Hunan Provincial Proletarian Revolutionaries'
Grand Alliance Committee (abbreviated as *Shengwulian*), which was
formed on 11 October, stated (probably wrongly) that Mao had been in
favour of the original Shanghai Commune of February 1967 and was
hard put to explain why he finally turned against it. Its only explanation
was that the Shanghai Commune had failed to measure up to the
standards of the Paris Commune of 1871, in that the proletariat had not
been armed and Mao could only postpone the implementation of
communes until the Cultural Revolution had truly removed the
'handful' in the army. To this end, Mao had demanded that the People's
Liberation Army 'support the left' and thus become involved in the
Cultural Revolution.

As the *Shengwulian* saw it, the January Revolution had been a glorious
experience. Proletarian power had been achieved and 90 per cent of
cadres had been forced to stand aside. Since workers had shown that they

could manage factories, there was surely no need for so many cadres to be rehabilitated. Though it did not say so in so many words, the *Shengwulian* completely reversed Mao's statement that 90 per cent of cadres might be rehabilitated. It sympathised with Mao's call for revolutionary committees based on the triple alliance formula, but emphasised that such bodies were only temporary organs of power which were to remain in existence until the army was fully integrated into the Cultural Revolution. Now that the army had been so integrated, there was no reason for their continued existence and communes and 'soviets' might be set up immediately.

The *Shengwulian* regarded it as a matter of extreme urgency that revolutionary committees and their preparatory committees be eliminated. Since the February Adverse Current, these committees had provided an opportunity for power to be seized by a 'red capitalist class' of whom Zhou Enlai was the major symbol. This class had wrested power and property away from the revolutionaries and had imprisoned some of the Red Rebels. The *Shengwulian* considered it utopian to believe that revolutionary committees would provide the basis for a transition to communism since they had imposed their rule from the top down and had been dominated not only by 'capitalist roaders' among the old Party cadres but also by 'capitalist roaders' in the army. The 'People's Commune of China' was the only answer.

The *Shengwulian* was particularly heartened by the events of the August storm. Looking back with nostalgia to the old days when the army and people maintained very close relations, it felt that the only way this relationship could be recaptured was by an internal revolutionary civil war such as almost developed in August. At that time, more and more 'ultra-left' organisations seized arms from the PLA and were convinced that many cities were in a state of 'armed mass dictatorship'. It was the masses in arms which had provided the cement for the old Paris Commune and this was something that the 'facade' of the people's militia could never achieve. What the 'ultra-left' found most impressive about the August storm had been the extent to which everyone had become soldiers and even primary school students had carried out the work of communications and public security.

The *Shengwulian* firmly believed that it had been Mao Zedong himself who had called for the mass seizure of arms in August and regarded the 5 September directive ordering the surrender of arms as a betrayal. At that time, 'ultra-leftists' had launched a movement to conceal arms from the troops in preparation for future armed struggles. The new period of consolidation launched in September was, in the eyes of the *Shengwulian*, comparable only to the situation in Russia after February 1917 where soviets had been formed but political power had been usurped by the bourgeoisie. Its 'October Revolution' was just around the corner. The *Shengwulian* was witnessing merely the last struggle of the 'bourgeoisie', represented in Hunan by the Preparatory Committee for the Hunan Provincial Revolutionary Committee, upon which (the soon to be famous) Hua Guofeng was a major figure. Hunan would perhaps see the triumph of the *Shengwulian* policy of 'victory first in one or several provinces'.

The *Shengwulian* seemed supremely confident that it would be swept to victory. It castigated those who just sat waiting for a second Cultural Revolution and believed that the revolution should be one continuous process, not punctuated by stages of consolidation (though perhaps to avoid being branded as Trotskyist it did, in fact, make some reference to the idea of 'stages'). In the meantime, it rejected the idea of building up the Party in preparation for the Ninth National Congress by rehabilitating old cadres. What was needed was a new 'Maoist' (*Mao Zedong zhuyide*) party (a term never used in the official media), and not a party of the 'bourgeois reformers'.

On 24 October Lin Biao was reported to have said:

The rubbish heap of Hunan is large and the three black lines are thick and long. Hunan is a counter-revolutionary 'three in one' patchwork. Hunan has not gone through disturbances thoroughly.[114]

This speech, which I have never seen in full, was taken by the *Shengwulian* to herald a new stage in the Cultural Revolution. Similarly, speeches by Jiang Qing on 9 and 12 November,[115] which called for further reforms in the field of art and literature, were taken as a signal that the period of consolidation was to be brought to an end. After all, that would be in accordance with theories about 'superstructural push'.

Whatever Jiang Qing's intentions might have been in late 1967, she was most bitter in her denunciation of the *Shengwulian* programme in early 1968.[116] She was joined by Kang Sheng[117] and Yao Wenyuan[118] who were already engaged in a denunciation of the May Sixteenth Group. The *Shengwulian* was considered to be guilty of forming 'independent kingdoms', a 'mountain-top mentality' and above all 'anarchism'. Though it is possible that the *Shengwulian* and other organisations of an 'ultra-left' persuasion might have been committed to a coherent anarchist philosophy, it is my own view that all 'anarchism' meant, in the context of early 1968, was a sectarian rejection of discipline and authority, a romantic commitment to disorder, a premature rejection of the state in all its forms and, consequently, an implied negation of the principle of the dictatorship of the proletariat. Such anarchism was seen in early 1968 as a 'petty bourgeois' deviation which negated proletarian discipline, and cadres and people were enjoined to 'make a class analysis of factionalism'.[119]

The Case of Yang Chengwu

The mounting criticism of the May Sixteenth Group and other 'ultra-leftist' organisations such as the *Shengwulian*, in early 1968, led to some surprising developments in the army. Yu Lijin, the air force political commissar who had commanded the PLA forces during the capture of Wuhan, and Yang Chengwu, the acting chief-of-staff who had so promptly ordered troops into action, were removed from their posts.[120] Chen Zaidao, on the other hand, who had appeared as the hard-headed conservative military commander at Wuhan, was treated most leniently in contrast to the 'ultra-leftist hero' Wang Li. It would be rash, however, to conclude from an analysis of the Wuhan incident that Lin Biao felt he had made a mistake and that the discrediting of the 'ultra-left' should be followed up by the removal of those who had taken a strong stand against those who had resisted Red Guard attacks in Wuhan. Many other reasons have been put forward for Yang's dismissal. He has been accused of undue ambition and of forming his own power group to become sub-stantive chief-of-staff, of 'bugging' the houses of Mao Zedong and Lin Biao and of attempting to play off different groups to advance his own position.[121] Yang has sometimes been accused of supporting the conservatives and sometimes the 'ultra-left'. To add to the confusion, 1979 accounts allege that Yang Chengwu was dismissed as a result of false charges made by Jiang Qing that he had attempted to 'reverse' the 'correct verdict on the February Adverse Current'.[122]

Whatever the reasons for the removal of Yang and other senior military officers in March 1968, they cannot be disassociated from a clearly conservative drift within the PLA command. Yang was replaced by none other than Huang Yongsheng, who had been one of the more repressive commanders during the February Adverse Current, and who seemed to have been universally detested by all shades of radical opinion. In fact, Huang had just completed a programme of dealing with 'ultra-leftists' in Guangdong when he was appointed. It has been argued that Huang was the representative of a powerful group of scarcely radical regional military commanders such as Han Xianchu (Fujian), Chen Xilian (Liaoning), Xu Shiyu (Jiangsu) and Yang Dezhi (Shandong) who had been opposed to Yang Chengwu's policy of centralised command and the placing of his own appointees in the provinces.[123] I am not altogether convinced by the argument. First, if the regional commanders wanted independence, why should they club together and select a former Fourth Field Army man likely to continue to enforce a policy of central-isation via the Fourth Field Army network? It must surely have been clear that the source of the policy of military centralisation was, in fact, Lin Biao. Secondly, is it likely that regional commanders, hoping for a quiet life, would select someone who was likely to provoke an extreme reaction from what 'ultra-left' were still active? The role of Lin Biao in the events of 1968 has yet to be explained but I suspect that, if Lin was half as ambitious as he was claimed to be, the appointment of Huang Yongsheng was his way of satisfying regional demands for a conservative appointment while still maintaining very tight control over regional appointments and thus enhancing his own position.

Whatever the truth in the Yang Chengwu incident, it is certainly the case that the regional military played a much more important role in the formation of revolutionary committees in late 1967 and early 1968. Jürgen Domes has divided the formation of provincial-level revolutionary committees into three waves.[124] The first, as has been noted, was from January to April 1967 in which mass organisations either played a very active role or, at least, where the role of the military was unclear. During this period, six committees were established. During the turbulent period of mid-1967, no provincial-level revolutionary committees were set up and the only committee to be established before November was in Qinghai (12 August). Beginning in November, however, the formation of provincial-level revolutionary committees came thick and fast—Inner Mongolia (1 November), Tianjin (6 December), Jiangxi (5 January), Gansu (24 January), Henan (27 January), Hebei (3 February), Hubei (5 February), Guangdong (21 February), Jilin (6 March), Jiangsu (23 March) and Zhejiang (24 March).[125] Of these committees, Domes argues, the majority were set up under strong regional pressure from the army. A third wave was to begin in April and, between then and September, the remaining eleven provincial-level units set up committees, again under strong military pressure.[126] Although it is very difficult to argue with Domes's assertion as to the role of the military, one should beware of coming to too hasty a conclusion as to its significance. First, although revolutionary committees were increasingly established from above, the conclusion, shared by 'ultra-leftists' and Western élite theorists, that the mass component within them was insignificant, does not necessarily follow. Secondly, the formation of provincial-level committees from above tells us little about administrative units at lower levels where it seems that the mass organisation component was greater. One of Domes's conclusions is, however, inescapable. The ideals of the Paris Commune had, without doubt, receded.

Renewed 'Ultra-leftism' (1968)

March 1968 was perhaps one of the most confusing months in the whole Cultural Revolution. In the country as a whole, several contradictory trends were evident. In the first part of the year, renewed calls were made to 'support the army and cherish the people',[127] aimed at restoring army-civilian relations and countering the growth of factionalism in the PLA associated with the Yang Chengwu incident. None the less, there were still many people who were profoundly disturbed at what they believed was a conservative drift in the army marked by the increased power of regional commander:. In Beijing, a number of the former marshals such as Nie Rongzhen and Xu Xiangqian achieved new prominence[128] as a focus of loyalty, and efforts were made to reconcile the 'left' with the new military leadership.

In the cities, a new and intensified effort was made to stress the importance of working-class leadership. Experiments with worker self-management were publicised[129] and examples were given of the integration of education with productive activity. Tongji University, for example, was cited as a model of how engineering faculties could be integrated with construction engineering companies[130] and many articles appeared showing the creativity of workers in proposing technical innovations.[131] In the countryside also, great prominence was given to the Dazhai model.[132] The major slogan of the time was 'struggle, criticism, transformation' with the new stress on the third of these components.

Nevertheless, however successful the process of 'transformation' had been in the industrial and agricultural sectors, the situation in the universities was still chaotic. In late 1967 and early 1968, large numbers of former activists were sent down to the countryside in a new programme of *xiafang*,[133] in part to dampen down their élitist tendencies but also as part of a general programme of reforming China's education system. It is probably quite understandable that some of them resented their fall in status, and it is significant that some left China for Hong Kong. Such one-time rebels have provided accounts (however jaundiced) of Red Guard activity[134] which have informed many studies of the Cultural Revolution. Some of these former 'little generals' were sent as far away as Xinjiang or Inner Mongolia where they were to settle down, under PLA guidance, to the new task of building up the frontier regions. There were, however, still a large number of disgruntled 'ultra-leftists' within the universities who continued to engage in faction-fighting.[135]

The operative slogan in early 1968 had been 'support the left but not any particular faction' and, however successful this might have been in restraining those who might have wished for a repetition of the February Adverse Current of 1967, it did little to solve the problem of 'factionalism'. In Beijing some people, still to some extent under the influence of Qi Benyu, wished to reform the Beijing Municipal Revolutionary Committee and mounted an attack on its chairman, Xie Fuzhi.[136] Throughout March 1968, demonstrations were held in the capital both in support of and in opposition to Xie and, in Beijing University, troops were called in, though seemingly to no avail.[137] In Qinghua University (the subject of a graphic account by William Hinton),[138] strife intensified in the spring of 1968, as student organisations clashed, and the Yang Chengwu incident only added fuel to the flames.

Perhaps another source of inspiration for the 'ultra-left' in May 1968 were the events in Paris and elsewhere.[139] Until that time, little attention had been paid in China to the revolutionary movements in capitalist countries. The events in Paris, however, had an immediate impact upon China and called into question once again the old foreign policy notion of the progressive nature of the 'second intermediate zone', in which De Gaulle stood as a major figure. On 21 May, a massive rally was held in Beijing to support the 'progressive student movement in Europe and North America' and statements were issued in support of the French workers and students.[140] The Beijing rally was followed by similar rallies in other parts of the country and it was pointed out that the Thought of Mao Zedong had had a great impact upon the development of revolutionary movements in other parts of the world.[141] Nothing was said, however, about how this re-evaluation of the revolution in capitalist countries affected Lin Biao's 'Third World' thesis.

I am not arguing here that the Chinese attention to the events of Europe and North America in May 1968 was merely the result of 'ultra-leftism' because, clearly, these events were so important that anyone would have felt obliged to comment on them. It is significant to note here that it was precisely at this time (July 1968) that Beijing felt obliged to report a French comment on the élitism of some of the European 'new left' idols such as Régis Debray[142] (with implications for the arch-symbol Che Guevara). The implied association between Chinese 'ultra-left' élitism and that of Debray must surely have been apparent.

The events in Paris, which revived once again the slogan of the Paris Commune,[143] and the warnings of a new 'rightist' danger which came in the wake of the Yang Chengwu incident, boosted the confidence of the 'ultra-leftists'. They had been extremely heartened by statements of Zhou Enlai in March, for clearly Zhou was not one of their number.

> From last winter to the present, the extreme left has been criticised and repudiated. Now the right has risen again, the February Adverse Current has made a comeback, and the royalists have tried to emancipate themselves and launch a counterattack and retaliation.[144]

Now the official line seemed not to be an attack on all factionalism but only 'bad' factionalism in accordance with the injunction to make a 'class analysis of factionalism'. In such a situation, extremists went on to the offensive yet again, though their efforts were much less effective than in 1967. During this period, incidents occurred in various parts of the country, the most serious struggle being in south China (Guangdong, Guangxi and Yunnan).[145] Though fighting in Guangdong, in particular, was quite intense and bodies appeared floating down the river to Hong Kong, and although much was made of the seizure and attempted seizure of arms,[146] it is probably true that, overall, the fighting in the spring of 1968 was less severe than in the summer of 1967.

Though, after 28 July, the army helped to disarm factions,[147] it was quite clear that military action was no solution to the problems in any long-term sense. The army had intervened in February 1967 and in the summer of 1967 and had only stiffened resistance. Thus, it was now felt that, if some new revolutionary order was to be established, the principle of working-class leadership and the study of Mao Zedong Thought had to be actualised and brought to bear upon the problem of 'ultra-left' factionalism. In 1967 and early 1968, it had been the PLA-led Mao Zedong Thought propaganda teams which had tried to bring about 'grand alliances';[148] now it was to be the *worker-peasant* Mao Zedong Thought propaganda teams. On 28 July, Mao Zedong is reported to have presided over a conference of student leaders in Beijing in which he said, 'You have let me down, and what is more, you have disappointed the workers, peasants and soldiers of China.'[149]

At the same time, China's first worker-peasant Mao Zedong Thought propaganda team was dispatched to the embattled Qinghua University and, by mid-August, was achieving the impossible—discipline and reconciliation.[150] To celebrate the victory, Mao presented to the team a gift of mangoes which he had received from a visiting Pakistani delegation.[151] For the rest of 1968, 'mangoes' were to become the symbol of worker-peasant leadership. One of the original mangoes was preserved in formalin[152] and workshops started turning out plastic mangoes in celebration of the event. However odd such actions might seem, the symbolic importance of the mangoes was as great as that of Mao Zedong's Changjiang swim of 1966. Consolidation under working-class leadership and with peasant support was to be the order of the day.

Conclusion

By August 1968, the violent period of the Cultural Revolution was over and what remained of the central leadership started to pick up the pieces and reconstruct the new social order. In September, the process of forming provincial-level revolutionary committees was completed[153] (nine months behind the original schedule outlined by Mao) and the Party set about organising the Twelfth (and last) Plenum of the Eighth Central Committee which met from 11 to 31 October. Indicting Liu Shaoqi for a host of 'crimes', the plenum decided finally to dismiss him from all his Party and state posts.[154] Such action was, of course, quite unconstitutional, since only the National People's Congress had any authority over state posts. By 1968, however, it is doubtful whether people bothered much about such niceties. Now, for the first time, 'China's Khrushchev', reviled by name in thousands of Red Guard publications, could be referred to by name in the official press. Not long after the plenum, Liu is said to have died but I imagine that, despite the invective, Liu's end was a quiet one. When angry Red Guards stormed Zhongnanhai (where Liu lived) in mid-1967, he was never handed over to them and Mao himself probably prevented a public trial.[155]

One wonders, however, whether the quietude accorded to Liu was enjoyed by other senior leaders of the Party. In 1979, it was claimed that the Twelfth Plenum was the scene of a renewed attack by Lin Biao and others on a number of senior commanders of the PLA.[156] The struggle stage of the Cultural Revolution was coming to an end, but the same could not be said for the rancour which that revolution had caused.

Despite the bitterness in late 1968, the Party was able to contemplate a new congress and to set about making plans to reconstruct the social order. In the heady days of 1967 – 8, not much thought had been given to concrete developmental policies and most attention had been directed to 'criticising the old'. Now the question arose, if the spirit of the Great Leap Forward was to be restored, which elements of Great Leap policies would be retained? Arguments on this question were to become quite intense.

NOTES

1. *RMRB*, 26 February 1979, p. 2.
2. Young, 1978, p. 39.
3. See Schwartz, 1970.
4. Lin Jie, *PR* 27, 30 June 1967, pp. 27 – 31.
5. On Kuai Dafu, see Hinton, 1972.
6. CCPCC, SC, Military Commission, Central Cultural Revolution Group, 24 March 1967, URI, 1968 (b), pp. 385 – 7.
7. CCPCC, 27 March 1967, ibid., pp. 392 – 5.
8. CCPCC, 13 April 1967, ibid., pp. 417 – 19.
9. CCPCC, 7 May 1967, ibid., pp. 434 – 8, and 16 May 1967, ibid., pp. 443 – 5.
10. *SCMP* 4061, 16 November 1967, pp. 11 – 12.
11. Bennett and Montaperto, 1971, pp. 163 – 5, 169, 179, 184 and 188.
12. Baum, 1971, p. 434.
13. Esmein, 1973, p. 159.
14. *PR* 20, 12 May 1967, p. 7.
15. *SCMM* 652, 28 April 1969, p. 30.
16. Ibid. 651, 22 April 1969, p. 19.
17. *PR* 17, 21 April 1967, pp. 14 and 17 – 18.
18. Ibid. 15, 7 April 1967, pp. 5 – 15.
19. Ibid., p. 15.
20. Liu Shaoqi, summer 1967, Liu, Vol. III, 1968, pp. 365 – 8.

21. Compare ibid., pp. 357 – 9 and 368.

22. Esmein, 1973, p. 161.

23. Ibid., p. 163.

24. Robinson, 1971, pp. 209 – 10 and 219 – 20.

25. Daubier, 1974, p. 179.

26. CCPCC, 19 February 1967, URI, 1968 (b), pp. 321 – 4; *PR* 11, 10 March 1967, pp. 13 – 15.

27. Esmein, 1973, p. 130.

28. This was in response to Mao Zedong's 7 March directive. For text, see *PR* 11, 15 March 1968, p.5.

29. Ibid. 11, 10 March 1967, pp. 5 – 8.

30. Hinton, 1972, pp. 117 – 18.

31. Ibid., pp. 115 – 16.

32. *PR* 10, 3 March 1967, pp. 5 – 9; ibid. 12, 17 March 1967, p. 15.

33. Hinton, 1972, p. 112.

34. Hunter, 1969, p. 153.

35. Bridgham, 1968, p. 18.

36. Baum, 1971, pp. 440 – 1.

37. Esmein (1973, p, 203) notes a decline in worker activism after the January storm. This was rekindled in June.

38. White, 1971, p. 339; Salaff,1971, pp. 295 – 8.

39. White, 1971, pp. 338 – 40; Salaff,1971, p. 296.

40. Salaff, 1971, p. 304.

41. Ibid., pp. 307 – 8.

42. Esmein, 1973, pp. 220 – 2; Domes,1970, p. 116; *PR* 7, 10 February 1967, pp. 12 – 13; *PR* 8, 17 February 1967, pp. 15 – 17.

43. Esmein, 1973, pp. 225 – 6; Domes, 1970, pp. 117 – 18; *PR* 10, 3 March 1967, pp. 19 – 21.

44. Esmein, 1973, p. 225; Domes, 1970, p. 117; *PR* 11, 10 March 1967, pp. 17 – 19.

45. Domes, 1970, p. 117; *PR* 10, 3 March 1967, pp. 10 – 12.

46. Esmein, 1973, pp. 226 – 7; Domes,1970, pp. 118 – 19; *PR* 14, 31 March 1967, pp. 5 – 6.

47. Domes, 1970, pp. 118 – 19.

48. Ibid., p. 113.

49. Esmein, 1973, pp. 227 – 9.

50. *PR* 13, 24 March 1967, pp. 6 – 8.

51. Ibid. 14, 31 March 1967, pp. 11 – 14.

52. Ibid. 18, 28 April 1967, pp. 10 – 14.

53. Esmein, 1973, pp. 228 – 9.

54. *PR* 19, 5 May 1967, p. 7.

55. *RMRB*, 26 February 1979, p. 2.

56. Robinson, 1971, pp. 234 – 5.

57. Ibid., p. 221.

58. *PR* 19, 5 May 1967, p.14.

59. Gurtov, 1971, pp. 329, 332 and 334 – 5.

60. *PR* 19, 5 May 1967, pp. 11 – 13.

61. Gurtov, 1971, pp. 335 – 6.

62. *PR* 28, 7 July 1967, p. 17. See Gurtov,1971, pp. 338 – 44.

63. Gurtov, 1971, pp. 344 – 6.

64. Ibid., p. 346.

65. Robinson, 1971, pp. 213 – 14 and 237 – 8.

66. Ibid., p. 225; *CB* 844, 10 January 1968.

67. Robinson, 1971, pp. 228 – 9.

68. Bridgham, 1968, p. 20.

69. *SCMP* 4061, 16 November 1967, p. 12.

70. Chien, 1969, p. 14.

71. Ibid., pp. 20–1.

72. Ibid., pp. 26–7.

73. Bridgham, 1968, p. 21.

74. *SCMP* 3975, 7 July 1967, pp. 1–6.

75. Baum, 1971, p. 440.

76. Chien, 1969, pp. 15–16.

77. Robinson, 1971, p. 223; *CB* 844, 10 January 1968.

78. Robinson, 1971, p. 224; *CB* 844, 10 January 1968, p. 26.

79. Robinson, 1971, p. 224; *CB* 844, 10 January 1968, p. 4 *passim*.

80. Robinson, 1971, pp. 239–59.

81. *SCMP* 3989, 27 July 1967, pp. 1–2.

82. Robinson, 1971, p. 269.

83. CCPCC, SC, Military Commission, Central Cultural Revolution Group, 27 July 1967, URI, 1968 (b), pp. 484–8.

84. In particular, Lin Jie. For an indication of his views see his article commemorating army day (1 August) in *PR* 32, 4 August 1967, pp. 36–9. This article, originally published in *Hongqi*, was said to have been a factor that led to the journal's suspension in late 1967.

85. The campaign began on 16 August with the publication of the resolution of the Eighth Plenum on Peng Dehuai. URI, 1968(a), pp. 39–44. Other articles from the official and unofficial press of the time may be found in ibid. For a discussion of different views on the campaign and its contemporary significance, see Esmein, 1973, pp. 286–9.

86. Chien, 1969, pp. 9–57.

87. Gurtov, 1971, p. 347.

88. Ibid., p. 348.

89. Robinson, 1971, p. 263.

90. Gurtov, 1971, pp. 350–1.

91. For a detailed account, see Hinton, 1972, pp. 132–4. See also Gurtov, 1971, pp. 351–2.

92. Esmein, 1973, p. 283.

93. Ibid., p. 284.

94. On 25 August, the CCPCC, SC, Military Commission and Central Cultural Revolution Group issued a call to 'support the army and cherish the people'; see CCPCC, SC, Military Commission, Central Cultural Revolution Group, 5 September 1967, URI, 1968 (b), p. 508.

95. Jiang Qing, 5 December 1967, URI, 1968 (b), pp. 521–33.

96. CCPCC, 9 September 1967, URI, 1968 (b), p. 520, and CCPCC General Office, 6 October 1967, ibid., pp. 543–4.

97. Chen was suffering from cancer and died on 6 January 1972. *PR* 2, 14 January 1972, pp. 3–5.

98. Esmein, 1973, p. 283.

99. Ibid., p. 285.

100. *PR* 38, 15 September 1967, pp. 7–17. The interpretation here is that of Esmein, 1973, p. 285.

101. *RMRB*, 26 February 1979, p. 2.

102. Mao Zedong, *SCMP* 4075, 7 December 1967, p. 27.

103. CCPCC and CCPCC Secretariat Bureau and General Office, July-September 1967, URI, 1968 (b), pp. 550–6.

104. *PR* 34, 18 August 1967, pp. 22–3.

105. *SCMP* 4070, 30 November 1967, pp. 2–3.

106. The operative slogan in the army was 'support the left but not any faction', *PR* 5, 2 February 1968, pp. 8–9; Esmein, 1973, p. 292.

107. *PR* 47, 17 November 1967, pp. 7–8.

108. On 6 December, Ibid. 51, 15 December 1967, p. 11.

109. *SCMP* 4237, 13 August 1968, p. 9.

110. *CB* 846, 8 February 1968, pp. 15–17. The same plea was made one month later on 26 November 1967. *SCMP* 4071, 1 December 1967, pp. 1–3.

111. Bastid, 1970, p. 27; *CB* 846, 8 February 1968.

112. Bastid, 1970, p.28. The reference here is to the 'triple alliance'.

113. The following description of the *Shengwulian* is taken from *Shengwulian*, autumn 1967, 21 December 1967, and particularly 6 January 1968, Mehnert, 1969, pp. 74–100.

114. *Shengwulian*, 21 December 1967, in Mehnert, 1969, p. 79.

115. Text in URI, 1968 (b), pp. 596–601.

116. Jiang Qing, 21–4 January 1968, Mehnert, 1969, p. 117.

117. Kang Sheng,21 January 1968, ibid., p. 117.

118. Yao Wenyuan, 21–4 January 1968, ibid., p. 118.

119. *PR* 19, 10 May 1968, pp. 3–4.

120. Reportedly, the order dismissing them was read to a rally on 27 March by Zhou Enlai. Chien,1969, p. 131.

121. For speculations on the Yang Chengwu case, see T. Robinson, 1972, pp. 191–2; Esmein, 1973, pp. 293–300; Domes, 1973, pp, 193–4.

122. *RMRB*, 26 February 1979, p. 2.

123. Domes, 1973, p. 133.

124. Domes, 1970, pp. 114–15.

125. *PR* 46, 10 November 1967, pp. 29–31 (Inner Mongolia); ibid.51, 15 December 1967, p. 11 (Tianjin); ibid.2, 12 January 1968, pp. 5–7 (Jiangxi); ibid.5, 3 February 1968, pp. 11–13 (Gansu and Henan); ibid.6, 9 February 1968, pp. 11–12 (Hebei); ibid. 7, 16 February 1968, pp. 25–7 (Hubei); ibid. 9, 1 March 1968, pp. 5–7 (Guangdong); ibid. 11, 15 March 1968, pp. 17–18 (Jilin); ibid. 13, 29 March 1968, pp. 10–11 and 38 (Jiangsu); ibid. 14, 5 April 1968, pp. 8–10 (Zhejiang).

126. Domes, 1970, p.142.

127. This campaign started originally in 1967. On the 1968 campaign, see *PR* 4, 26 January 1968, pp. 9–10.

128. Esmein, 1973, p. 298. Particularly worth noting was the fact that a number of these old marshals appeared at the fourth congress of activists in the creative study and application of Mao Zedong Thought. (*PR* 10, 8 March 1968, p.12) and the subsequent reception by Mao (*PR* 11, 15 March 1968, p. 8).

129. E.g. *PR* 12, 22 March 1968, pp. 18–21.

130. Ibid. 47, 17 November 1967, pp. 9–10; ibid. 48, 24 November 1967, pp. 9–10.

131. E.g. ibid. 3, 19 January 1968, pp. 15–17.

132. Chen Yonggui, ibid. 49, 1 December 1967, pp. 19–22.

133. CCPCC, SC, Military Commission, Central Cultural Revolution Group, 8 October 1967, URI, 1968 (b), pp. 560–3..

134. E.g. the subject of the biography by Bennett and Montaperto who left in November 1967.

135. Hinton, 1972, pp. 145–82.

136. Daubier, 1974, p. 245.

137. Esmein, 1973, p. 309.

138. Hinton, 1972, pp. 145–70.

139. Mehnert, 1969, p. 62.

140. *PR* 21, 24 May 1968, pp. 18–19.

141. Ibid. 22, 31 May 1968, pp. 9–10.

142. Ibid. 30, 26 July 1968, pp. 11–12.

143. Ibid. 21, 24 May 1968, p. 19.

144. Zhou Enlai, 21 March 1968, *SCMP* 4166, 29 April 1968, p. 2.

145. For a very confusing overview of the period, see Chien, 1969, pp. 174–217. See also *SCMP* 4215, 11 July 1968, pp. 1–11.

146. E.g. *SCMP* 4215, 11 July 1968, p. 11; ibid. 4227, 29 July 1968, pp. 9–12.

147. Ibid. 4266, 26 September 1968, p. 13. This account depicts students at the People's University unilaterally handing over arms to the PLA.

148. Baum, 1971, p. 440.

149. Gittings, *FEER*, Vol.LXI, No. 35, 25–31 August 1968, pp. 377–9.

150. Hinton, 1972, pp. 185–233.

151. *PR* 32, 9 August 1968, pp. 5–6.

152. Hinton, 1972, p. 227.

153. *PR* 37, 13 September 1968, pp. 3–5.

154. CCPCC, 31 October 1968, ibid. 44, 1 November 1968, Supplement, p. vi.

155. Hinton, 1972, pp. 118–22.

156. *RMRB*, 26 February 1979, p. 4.

V
'FLYING LEAP'
(1968–1970)

In the period 1968–70, attempts were made to put together, once again, the Party and state structure shattered in the Cultural Revolution. There was to be some confusion, however, as to which of the innovations of the Cultural Revolution were to be retained. The restoration of order, it would seem, was cast in terms of policies which dated, in part, from Yan'an but which were implemented more thoroughly during the Great Leap Forward of 1958–9. It was, after all, the evaluation of the original Great Leap Forward which had brought about the Cultural Revolution in the first place. Yet there were few people who would deny that the Great Leap had given rise to problems and that some policies could never be reintroduced. But which were they? Here was a source of disagreement which was eventually to provoke a major crisis.

Foreign Policy, Czechoslovakia and the Sino-Soviet Border Crisis (1968 – 9)

Though there was disagreement about exactly which elements of the Cultural Revolution ought to be discouraged in late 1968, there was one field which was obviously a complete disaster. In foreign policy, the Cultural Revolution had seen the deterioration of China's relations with many countries. There were, however, a few exceptions, such as Tanzania where China began to fulfil its pre-Cultural Revolution under-taking to build the Tanzam Railway in order to give Zambia an outlet to the sea other than through Rhodesia.[1] There were also a few foreign Communist parties, such as those of Albania, Vietnam and Rumania, which still maintained good relations with the Chinese Party, and China continued to enjoy close relations with a few revolutionary groups in Burma, India[2] and elsewhere, in opposition to those backed by the Soviet Union. In general, though, the situation was bleak. Many states had severed relations with the Chinese People's Republic. Most Communist parties had expressed hostility to the Cultural Revolution and the revolutionary groups which China supported were rarely the most popular in the countries in which they operated. The 'ripeness' of Africa for revolution seemed to be illusory. In Latin America, upon which China had pinned high hopes for revolution, the constant splits in the revolutionary movements presented a very dismal prospect and, as the Cultural Revolution progressed, China became more and more disenchanted with Cuba which was seen as fast becoming a Soviet satellite.[3]

The Soviet Union was, of course, not slow to capitalise on the unpopularity of the Cultural Revolution in the Third World. The Soviet press gave support to the various leaders under criticism in China[4] and even resurrected the aged Wang Ming to condemn Mao's 'idealism'.[5] Mao, it now declared, was definitely not a Marxist.[6] Responding to this in May 1968, China made much of a 'Stalin group' in the Soviet Union which was determined to combat revisionism,[7] though such a move could hardly achieve much support outside China.

Throughout the whole period of the Cultural Revolution, innumerable incidents occurred on the Sino-Soviet border but were probably considered to be too unimportant to make the official press.[8] In August 1968, however, the Soviet Union began to emerge in a new light. Though the Chinese heartily condemned the Dubcek leadership in Czechoslovakia as 'revisionist',[9] the Soviet-led invasion of 20 August and the subsequent attempt to legitimise it according to the principle of 'limited sovereignty' was unforgivable. As the Chinese saw it, the invasion was not only an example of the Soviet Union behaving just like the United States but was also an instance of 'great power collusion'. 'The aggression by Soviet revisionism was carried out with the tacit understanding of U.S. imperialism.'[10] Provided the United States could do what it liked in its sphere of influence, then so could the Soviet Union.

Some analysts have suggested that the invasion convinced the Chinese leadership that the Soviet Union might be tempted to launch a pre-emptive strike against China, in the knowledge that the United States would just look on, though evidence for this is doubtful. It is significant, however, that in 1967–8 a massive Soviet military build-up occurred along China's northern borders[11] which hastened the formation of the last revolutionary committees in the frontier regions.[12] It is also significant that, in March 1969, the fifty-seventh border clash in the Zhenbao Island area blew up into a major incident.[13]

I find it inconceivable that the Zhenbao incident of March 1969 was either a prelude to a possible Soviet invasion of China, in the manner of Czechoslovakia, or an example of China's revanchist wish to take back territory occupied by the Tsars. It seems more likely that what the Soviet Union was engaged in was a masking operation to hide the clamp-down in Czechoslovakia which did not occur until several months after the invasion. What better distraction than a resurrection of the 'yellow peril'? From China's point of view, the border incident, though disturbing, had perhaps a beneficial side. It hastened the drive towards unity after the 'struggle' stage of the Cultural Revolution and provided a patriotic motive in the rapidly developing Great Leap atmosphere. I am, of course, not arguing here that the incident was manufactured by the Chinese. It was, after all, the fifty-seventh incident in that one small spot on the map. All I am saying is that the Chinese were not reluctant to publicise it as they had been with similar incidents in the past. In my view, there was never any danger of war in 1969, though the Zhenbao Island incident did serve to point up the Chinese view that the Soviet Union and the United States enjoyed equal status as enemies and it cannot be without significance that the Ninth Party Congress opened on 1 April 1969 to the cries of condemning 'The New Tsars'.[14]

The Ninth Party Congress (1969)

The Ninth Congress of the Chinese Communist Party was originally to have been held back in the early 1960s and, since that time, there had been constant talk of convening it, but due to the escalation of what Mao referred to in 1971 as the ninth crisis in the history of the Party it had been repeatedly postponed. With the expulsion of Liu Shaoqi in October 1968, however, the way was clear for its convocation and the Twelfth Plenum discussed a draft Party constitution.[15] Though the congress had been a long time coming, one cannot avoid the impression that it was convened in a hurry and perhaps, like the two sessions of the Eighth Congress, was pushed through by those who wished for stability rather than a new period of radical experimentation.

It was alleged, in 1973, that the report to the congress given by Lin Biao was not his original report but had been substantially revised by Mao.[16] The constitution of April 1969, though giving considerable stress to the role of the military and nominating Lin Biao as Mao's successor,[17] was much less army-oriented than the draft document of October 1968. The congress, moreover, like its predecessors, was followed by a new period of radicalisation which did not seem to be the result of its deliberations. Would it be rash to suggest that the congress had been rushed through to stabilise the situation before a new radical offensive was launched?

The desire to avoid rash radical experimentation might have been reflected in the composition of the new Central Committee. Though there were a few youthful people in its ranks, the average age (for those members whose ages we know) was 61 as opposed to 56 in 1956. Half of the new Central Committee had a military rank between 1955 and 1965 (as opposed to 40 per cent from the military in 1956). The percentage of cadres in state administration went down from nearly 60 per cent to 31 per cent, which meant that the percentage of model workers and representatives of mass organisations increased considerably but did not include many prominent Red Guard leaders.[18]

The new Party leadership, elected at the First Plenum immediately after the Ninth Congress, consisted of a number of groups. First there was the group of Cultural Revolution activists headed by Chen Boda, Kang Sheng, Jiang Qing, Zhang Chunqiao, Yao Wenyuan and possibly Ji Dengkui. Closely allied with that group was a number of senior Party members concerned with public security work such as Xie Fuzhi and Wang Dongxing (and, indeed, Kang Sheng had also engaged in this sort of work). A third group consisted of the central military leadership under Lin Biao, Ye Qun (his wife), Huang Yongsheng (Chief-of-Staff who was also a regional military commander), Wu Faxian (Commander of the Air Force), Li Zuopeng (First Political Commissar of the Navy) and Qiu Huizuo (Director of Logistics). Fourth came the representatives of the regional military commanders who had been engaged in restoring order, Xu Shiyu, Chen Xilian and Li Desheng. There was also a group of senior administrators of the State Council headed by Premier Zhou Enlai and Li Xiannian (Minister of Finance). Sixth came the group of former marshals of the PLA. These consisted of people like Zhu De and Liu Bocheng who appeared to be too old to be anything but symbols, but also included Ye Jianying who was later to play a very active role in Chinese politics. Finally there were other symbolic worthies like Dong Biwu (who, following the demise of Liu Shaoqi, acted jointly with Song Qingling, the wife of Sun Zhongshan, as Head of State).[19]

I doubt whether any statistical analysis of the Ninth Central Committee tells us much about the political orientation of its members. It is perhaps more fruitful to look at the congress documents which, although reflecting something of a compromise, still promised the continuation of some radical policies. The Party Secretariat was not mentioned nor the post of general secretary (though one might note that the former Party general secretary Deng Xiaoping was no longer under a cloud). The principle of 'open Party building' was adopted whereby candidates for Party membership had to be accepted not only by Party branches but also by non-Party people they worked with. It was also accepted, in principle, that Party members having grievances could bypass various levels of Party authority and, if necessary, appeal directly to the chairman himself. The Thought of Mao Zedong, moreover, was given pride of place in the constitution.

In retrospect, it would seem that Mao Zedong was far from happy at the tremendous power enjoyed by Lin Biao and the central military apparatus at the time of the Ninth Congress.[20] There can be no doubt, however, that he believed that the rebuilt Party Centre in 1969 was much less bureaucratic than the one it had replaced and was superior to that of the CPSU. At the First Plenum on 28 April 1969, he declared:

> The Soviet revisionists now attack us. Some Tass broadcast or other, the Wang Ming material, and the long screed in *Kommunist* all say we are no longer a party of the proletariat and call us a 'petty bourgeois party' . . . When they see there are many military men in our lists of personnel, they call us 'military' . . . They can say what they want. But their words have one characteristic: they avoid branding us as a bourgeois party; instead they brand us as a party of the petty bourgeoisie. We, on the other hand, say that they are a bourgeois dictatorship and are restoring the dictatorship of the bourgeoisie.[21]

As I have indicated, there were good reasons why the military had come to enjoy great power in the aftermath of the Cultural Revolution and, whatever latent conflict existed between the Lin Biao group and the regional military commanders who had been entrusted with restoring order, the army was still the only really unified organisation in the country.

The Rectification and Reconstruction of the Party (Zheng Dang Jian Dang)

Obviously, the pressing need in 1969 was to replace representatives of the army on revolutionary committees by a reconstructed Party. Army leadership would have to continue until Party reconstruction could be achieved. In the meantime, however, Mao seemed to be quite critical of the heavy hand of the military. In his speech to the First Plenum of the Ninth Central Committee on 28 April 1969, Mao noted that factory leadership was usually not in the hands of 'true Marxists', nor in the hands of the workers, nor indeed had sufficient numbers of old factory cadres been rehabilitated.[22] If the source of bad leadership was neither the old cadres nor the workers, then surely the blame must lay with the PLA cadres sent down to 'support the left'. Mao was critical of the excessive repression which had been applied to old cadres. Some had been kept in 'cattle pens' for two years, spoke the language of two years previously and had no idea of how the Cultural Revolution had developed. Mao also seemed concerned about the way revolutionary committees had been imposed by the army from above. Such a situation had led to resentment and the rise of 'ultra-leftists', whom some army commanders insisted on treating uniformly as 'enemies'. In Mao's view, the policy of rooting out 'ultra-leftists' everywhere was a violation of the 'correct handling of contradictions'. He rebuked, therefore, the Shandong military commander Yang Dezhi for regarding the contradiction between himself and the 'ultra-leftist' Wang Xiaoyu as 'antagonistic'.[23]

If the Party was to be built successfully in this new period of 'struggle, criticism and transformation', those who had to judge whether cadres were excessively 'revisionist' or whether individuals and groups were 'ultra-leftist' had to be the masses. Thus, the mass component in the triple alliance formula was given greater stress. Under no circumstances was the military to be allowed to squash that activism.

Although it is possible that I have read too much into Mao's speech of 28 April 1969, it cannot be denied that, after the First Plenum, mass activism gained a new importance and army representatives, at lower levels of administration, were often replaced by rehabilitated cadres. At the same time, however, the press continued to categorise the army as a 'pillar of the dictatorship of the proletariat' and emphasised the way the army continued to solve problems.[24] Though Mao would perhaps have liked to phase the PLA out of lower-level administration more quickly than actually happened, it proved to be difficult to dispense with its services as the political climate radicalised even further in July.

By the summer of 1969, it seemed that efforts to curb military suppression had given rise to a new bout of factionalism and, once again, military overreaction. Local activists of an extreme persuasion often took the rejection of Liu Shaoqi's policy of being a 'docile tool' of the Party as a licence for disruption. Serious cases of disorder were noted in Guizhou, Jilin, Anhui and Inner Mongolia.[25] In Shanxi, in particular, the authority of Mao was invoked to put a stop to activities reminiscent of the summer of 1968.[26] In that province, disruptive elements had stolen property, opposed the triple alliance, attacked the PLA, killed soldiers, destroyed railways and bridges, occupied warehouses and banks, caused work stoppages and sabotaged production. It was even claimed that these 'ultra-leftists' had set up their own banks though I cannot imagine what an 'ultra-left' bank might look like. In such a situation, the Centre could not but rely on the PLA to restore order and get workers back into the factories. Incidents such as these made any policy of phasing out military control very difficult to implement.

By the autumn of 1969, some progress had been made in Party rebuilding from the bottom up, for which Mao had called at the First Plenum, but the first *xian* Party committee was not established until mid-November.[27] It may have been dissatisfaction with the speed of Party rebuilding, therefore, that led to a decision to concentrate on the rebuilding of the Party at the middle levels of *xian* and municipality in the winter.[28] Here again progress was slow and, by the autumn of 1970, only 45 of the 2,185 *xian* in the country were said to have set up Party committees.[29] One may speculate on the reasons for this slowness. Factionalism led to military overreaction. Then, when attempts were made to restrain the military, activists took this as official endorsement for more struggle and there was thus more factionalism.[30] At the First Plenum, Mao had demanded that equal attention be given to the inclusion of mass activists and rehabilitated old cadres in the new organs of power. Yet so long as those mass activists contained former Red Rebels who had just spent three years denouncing old cadres, there could be little but recriminations and resentment. In such a situation, how could the Party be rebuilt? The problem was compounded by the stress on reforming ideological orientations, during the course of Party rebuilding, in a process known as 'purifying the class ranks'.[31] But who was to do that reforming? If the army was incapable of the task and just attempted to reconstruct Party branches by purely organisational means, then what would emerge would not be a Leninist Party but a pluralist amalgam of hostile groups. In 1969 – 70, the central leadership of the Party went to great pains to promote models of Party rebuilding[32] where a successful integration of 'the old, the middle-aged and the young' (a new form of triple alliance) had been achieved, but it must have seemed to many, by early 1970, that the problem would only really be solved by a concentration on the organisational rebuilding of the Party from the top down and the purge of Cultural Revolution activists.

'Flying Leap'

The rebuilding of the Party in 1969 – 70 was to take place within an atmosphere reminiscent of the Great Leap Forward of 1958 and the external threat posed by the Soviet Union provided a motivation similar to that offered by the Taiwan Straits crisis of that year. The term used to describe the situation, however, was not 'Great Leap' but 'flying leap'. References to such a 'flying leap' seem all to derive from provincial reports[33] and no general directive appeared on overall economic policy. This may have been because the central leadership wanted to see just how local activism developed before issuing a directive, in the same manner as it had done in the summer of 1958, or because it was irreconcilably split on economic issues. If the general direction of policy was to emulate the spirit of the Great Leap but to avoid the 'commandist' excesses of 1958, there had to be basic agreement on what those issues were. In retrospect, there seems to have been little such agreement.

Though there was no general directive on economic policy in the period 1968 – 70, a number of administrative decisions, taken by the Centre, do suggest very strong parallels with 1957 – 8. There was a new stress on the decentralisation of decision-making authority to geographical areas. As in 1958, greater autonomy was enjoyed at *provincial* level, to which many more factories (formerly centrally controlled) were transferred.[34] In the new drive to develop local industries, the provinces were to play a major co-ordinating role. There was, of course, the ever present danger of provincial 'localism',[35] which was perhaps made more serious by the increased power of local provincial military commanders. To counter this, demands were made that key *policy*, as opposed to *operational*, decisions should be taken in Beijing.

Within the provinces, a considerable amount of decision-making power was transferred down to the *xian* level. Here much of the responsibility for water conservation, electrification and road building was located[36] and particular attention was devoted to industries run by *xian*—level government.[37] The idea was for each *xian* to set up a relatively independent agro-industrial system. The operative slogan, therefore, was 'local self-reliance'.

As a consequence of this stress on local self-reliance, the old Yan'an idea of 'crack troops and simple administration' was voiced again.[38] In Beijing, the number of central ministries was reduced[39] and many cadres were transferred down to local administration or to the 'front line of production'. Such a dismantling of the bureaucracy meant that the old Yan'an ideal of the 'cadre' became more and more important and articles appeared specifying the qualities of good Party secretaries.[40] These secretaries were required to interpret creatively generalised central policy statements and to take over leadership of the poor and lower-middle peasants who were instituting reforms under PLA guidance.

The Cultural Revolution in the Chinese countryside had been a somewhat patchy affair. In some suburban areas, mass activism had been quite intense and had reached a high point in 1968 where 'five category elements' had sometimes been killed by fanatic 'ultra-leftists'.[41] In most areas, however, one gets the impression that the Cultural Revolution had had little impact and the winding-down of the Socialist Education Movement in late 1966 had left the old administration intact. Certainly, the reports of ex-Red Guards who went to the rural areas do not suggest a high level of peasant activism.[42] In such a situation, the ideals of the Cultural Revolution had often been imported into the countryside by the army which established 'front-line committees' to replace the existing administration and safeguard production.

The introduction of the army into rural administration in 1968 seems to have been reflected in the composition of the revolutionary committees at commune and brigade level which were to replace the 'front-line committees' and the old administration. Those revolutionary committees which were set up in 1967 usually had a larger mass component than those set up in 1968.[43] This was because they were mainly in suburban communes and were not the direct product of military guidance. After the suburban disturbances of 1968, however, when it was felt that the autumn harvest had to be safeguarded at all costs, the military personnel hastened the formation of revolutionary committees and accelerated the process of screening and reappointing rural cadres. With the stress on consolidation, the main cadre deviation was seen to be excessive 'tailism'. Cadres, for example, failed to prevent the eruption of feuds between lineages[44] and, in response, the PLA Mao Zedong Thought propaganda teams could only intensify ideological education.[45] The intensification of the military controlled Cultural Revolution in the countryside in the second half of 1968, however, was, as one might expect, a relatively quiet affair with the stress on 'criticism and transformation' rather than 'struggle'.

By early 1969, the process of cadre-screening in the rural areas seems to have developed to the point where some local cadres could take the initiative in promoting the ideas of the new 'flying leap'. We are not certain just who these cadres were but one may surmise that the PLA Mao Zedong Thought propaganda teams had taken seriously the injunction to foster leaders from the young as well as the middle-aged and the old. But what were the young and inexperienced cadres to do in the absence of central directives on rural policy? On a few questions, there were clear directives. For example, cadres were enjoined to propagate the idea of 'storing grain everywhere' both as a safeguard against war and to prevent a recurrence of the hardships of 1959 – 61, in the aftermath of the original Great Leap. They were also instructed to make provision for the *xiafang* of large numbers of former Red Guards. On other questions, however, cadres had to make their own interpretation of official policy on the basis of masses of material criticising the rural policies in the early 1960s and in particular concerning the distribution of farm machinery.[46]

One crucial question, on which the rural cadre lacked guidance, concerned policy towards the unit of account.[47] Officially, the team was to remain the basic unit of ownership in the rural sector at which work points were allocated and the harvest divided. Nevertheless, the brigades now enjoyed a degree of authority far greater than at any time since the early 1960s. They could supervise team activities and most commune industry was administered at brigade or commune level. In addition, the decentralisation of educational facilities and the commercial network provided the brigades with new administrative responsibilities.[48] It seemed clear, therefore, in the radical atmosphere of 1969 – 70, that it was only a matter of time before the brigade acquired more power over the production of basic foodgrains and it is worth bearing in mind that Dazhai (the model) was a *brigade* (if only a small one) and not a team. How quickly, therefore, should the rural cadre proceed with the task of up-grading the unit of account? The cadre was similarly beset with a host of problems concerning the private sector and the free markets. Officially, the 1965 rules on the amount of land allocated to private plots were still in force and yet, since that time, there had occurred the Cultural Revolution, aimed, amongst other things, at countering privatism. Officially, provision was made for rural markets,[49] and yet the extension of rural markets had been one of the 'crimes' of which Liu Shaoqi had been accused. What attitude should the cadre take?

At the root of the rural cadre's problem was the relationship between human will and objective economic conditions. To exaggerate human will was said to be a characteristic of 'ultra-leftism'. Yet the Cultural Revolution had made it clear that the mechanistic determinism of the 'theory of productive forces', attributed to Liu Shaoqi, should not be allowed to recur. In 1969–70, it would seem that this latter consideration weighed most heavily with rural cadres and considerable stress was, in fact, laid on the human factor in the productive process. This was the economic counterpart of Lin Biao's stress on 'man before weapons'. Thus, rural cadres were said to have committed many of the old errors of the Great Leap. They inflated production goals beyond realistic limits and then used coercion to achieve them.[50] They arbitrarily collectivised private property,[51] prematurely upgraded the unit of account[52] and even considered the restoration of a partial free-supply system.[53] Sometimes, they interpreted the Dazhai model as a blueprint for rural policy to be put into immediate effect over the whole country, despite the fact that certain of its features ran counter to general policy towards the countryside. For example, the Dazhai production brigade had amalgamated teams into the brigade administration and awarded work-points in a very egalitarian way. Though laudable as a radical ideal, many people felt that to implement the model over much of China too precipitately might result in 'commandist' deviations.[54]

'Commandism' in the rural sector was, in large part, a consequence of the belated extension of the ideals of the Cultural Revolution into the countryside. The factories, on the other hand, which had gone through the 'struggle' stage of the Cultural Revolution, were beset with a far more serious problem—factionalism.[55] In the countryside, the revolutionary committees were often set up by external agencies such as the PLA Mao Zedong Thought propaganda teams. In the factories, however, the revolutionary committees were expected to grow out of an alliance between cadres (technical or otherwise), non-unionised workers and PLA representatives (or, failing that, militia representatives). The formation of these committees in factories was reported to have been seen by Mao, in early 1968, as the first stage in establishing a new system of industrial management. After their formation, Mao demanded, the campaign to 'purify the class ranks' should be extended into the factories; the enterprise Party branches were to be rectified and rebuilt; administration was to be simplified; outdated rules and regulations were to be discarded; and a system was to be instituted for managers to work regularly on the shop floor.[56] This last stage was to signify a restoration of the old Great Leap policy of 'two participations and triple combination' and, before long, the Anshan constitution, which embodied that principle, was republished with much fanfare.[57]

The establishment of enterprise revolutionary committees, however, proved to be immensely difficult. Sometimes groups of workers used the management committees to advance the interests of their own particular faction and sought, during the process of 'open Party building', to dominate the formation of the new enterprise Party branches. Because of such factional struggles,[58] it was not until the second half of 1969 that enterprise Party branches began to be formed.[59] Moreover, even after such branches were formed, the Cultural Revolution heritage of self-motivated political action made it very difficult to work out systems of factory disicipline [60] and to decide which particular factory rules were outmoded and ought to be discarded.

Without an effective Party apparatus to give guidance on the process of management reform, the Centre had recourse first to the advocacy of internal control mechanisms, operated by 'worker sentinels', and then to the promotion of models, deliberately set up by the PLA State Council Guard Unit 8341 under the command of Wang Dongxing. Six factories were designated as models[61] for the correct balance between discipline and radical participation during the process of rebuilding the Party. Yet continued reports of waste, extravagance, a lack of concern for productivity and technical skill and general problems of indiscipline[62] suggest that these models were not emulated as thoroughly as might have been wished. At the First Plenum in April 1969, Mao had expressed much disquiet with the situation in factories.[63] I doubt whether he would have been more satisfied with the situation in early 1970. But how is one to assess the relative strength of, on the one hand, creativity, mass participation and mass experimentation and, on the other, factionalism, indiscipline and a decline in production?

The Heritage of the Great Leap in Education

Though the record of the 'flying leap' of 1968–70, in agriculture and industry, was not all that impressive, the situation in education was much more promising. By 1968, the Cultural Revolution glorification of informal education was replaced by the Great Leap combination of the formal and informal. As Mao saw it, institutions such as universities had to continue in existence:

It is still necessary to have universities; here I refer mainly to colleges of science and engineering. However, it is essential to shorten the length of schooling, revolutionise education, put proletarian politics in command and take the road of the Shanghai Machine-tools Plant in training technicians from among the workers. Students should be selected from among workers and peasants with practical experience and they should return to production after a few years of study.[64]

The Shanghai Machine-tools Plant stressed the promotion of workers to the status of technicians after short periods of study in tertiary institutions and rejected the old system of employing graduates from the universities with little practical experience. It rejected also the 'ultra-left' utopianism which completely underestimated the role of any technicians. Now, university graduates were only to be employed in positions of responsibility after they had been granted a 'qualification certificate' from workers and peasants.[65] In the following period, the Shanghai Machine-tools Plant model was extended to the whole field of university enrolment, whereby universities would not accept students until they had spent some time working in factories and communes and had been recommended by appropriate revolutionary committees.[66]

It will be evident that the stress on an integrated education system, with factories running schools and schools running factories, was but a restatement of the old *minban* idea of education which dated from Yan'an days and which had been implemented once again during the Great Leap Forward. But, as has been noted, in the 'flying leap' of 1968 – 9, many of the excesses of the Great Leap were to be avoided. During the Great Leap, an overconcentration on production had sometimes resulted in a concentration on educational *output* rather than the quality of inputs. Now, the operative slogan was *shaoerjing* (little but well).[67] Though the Great Leap stressed informal education, institutions such as the family were not considered as important in this regard. Now, attempts were made to ensure that family discussions were integrated with the activities of schools.[68] In general, however, the reforms of 1968 – 9 were remarkably similar to those of 1958. Modern equivalents of the old 'red and expert' universities and technical middle schools were established.[69] The expansion of the education system was assisted by a new *xiafang* of educated youth. Theoretical training was backed up by a new practical orientation in the spirit of *Kangda* (the Resist Japan University) of 1942 – 3,[70] and a considerable amount of local initiative was fostered.

In education, as elsewhere, no attempts were made to standardise the system, after the criticism of excessive bureaucratisation in 1966. Each area and each school tried to work out its own structure and programme and solve its own problems and 'advanced experiences' were propagated not as operational instructions but merely as 'reference material'.

Although these 'advanced experiences' did not have the force of directives, it would perhaps be useful to outline some of their features to give an indication of the type of education which was preferred. First, particularly praised were cases where more and more of the poorer peasants had been brought into the educational system; cases are cited where all sorts of problems, such as lack of classrooms and the obligation of rural children to help with farm work, were solved.[71] Secondly, schools were praised which dispensed with full-time administrators and brought workers and peasants in to help with the teaching.[72] Thirdly, communes and brigades were commended for reducing or abolishing tuition fees (though this was a very knotty problem).[73]

From an organisational point of view, it would seem the countryside was much more successful than the cities in working out a new structure.[74] Though it was relatively easy for urban factories to set up schools, it was extremely difficult for the worker propaganda teams to organise schools in residential areas where they did not exist before.[75] The main problem was availability of funds, though one might imagine that local conservatism was also significant. In the countryside, however, where peasants probably had a much clearer idea of what they wanted, 'user-control' of schools was more easily effected. In the Lishu district of Jilin province, in May 1969, a programme was adopted which was given great prominence in *Renmin Ribao*.[76] Here, secondary school revolutionary committees were to be placed under the authority of commune revolutionary committees and primary schools under the authority of brigade 'educational leading groups'. A distinction was made between policy and operations, in that only the latter was the responsibility of teachers and students. At a policy level, the triple alliance comprised (1) representatives of the poor and lower-middle peasants, (2) the PLA and (3) teachers-students, but each of the first two elements in the triple alliance formula could also be involved in operations (teaching). The draft programme stipulated that school education, social education and family education should be integrated and that the operation of the schools should mesh in with production tasks. To this end, primary school teachers were to be paid partly as ordinary peasants on a work-point basis, though secondary school teachers received a salary. Priority in enrolment was to be given to the children of workers, poor and lower-middle peasants and soldiers, and age qualifications were abolished. The number of subjects taught was reduced and excessive book-learning was opposed. The old examination system was also abolished though 'open-book tests' were permitted.

The Decentralisation of Urban Services

The principle of 'user-control' and decentralisation was applied not only to schools in the second half of 1968 and in 1969. Medical services were also reorganised on a local level and integrated with neighbourhood administration.[77] In the spirit of the Great Leap Forward, the stress was on producing *more* medical workers rather than specialised surgeons. Large numbers of paramedical workers were trained[78] who, after a short course of one or two years, could deal with routine medical cases and were responsible for spreading China's medical network to areas where it had hardly existed before. Such a development, in what must surely be one of the most conservative professions anywhere in the world, was truly remarkable, and it is perhaps salutary to consider that many doctors were sent down into the wards to serve for a time as nurses.[79]

The decentralisation of services in the cities was part of a general process of urban reorganisation. Here, as elsewhere, the problem was to improve the quality of local cadres. To achieve this, a particular institution was utilised known as the May Seventh Cadre School.[80] Such schools were, at first, temporary creations designed to reorient cadres criticised during the Cultural Revolution. They, however, gradually became regular institutions. Cadres, at various levels in administration and education, were required to spend a period of time in them, not just studying and discussing their orientation but also engaging in productive labour.

A major task of the newly rehabilitated cadres and propaganda teams was to rebuild neighbourhood committees (street committees and residents' groups) according to the triple combination and the old Yan'an slogan of 'simple administration'. The first residential committees were established in Shanghai as early as March 1967, though it took a whole year before neighbourhood revolutionary committees were set up over the whole city.[81] In other areas, the establishment of street revolutionary committees appears to have been undertaken a little later, though, by the second half of 1968, progress was quite rapid. As street revolutionary committees were articulated first to military control commissions and later to higher-level revolutionary committees, the number of rehabilitated urban cadres increased and their street-level mass component decreased.[82] Nevertheless, the integration of representative bodies, formal urban administration and urban public security, which was now effected for the first time, made mass participation in urban administration easier than before.[83]

By the end of 1968, many cities had established revolutionary committees at municipal, ward (*qu*), sub-ward (*fenqu*) and street level. Below that level, the old residents' groups had been reorganised into Mao Zedong Thought study groups on demographic and social rather than purely residential lines. Local public security was in the hands of 'citizens' public security enforcement teams', revived 'worker picket organisations' or bodies known as 'teams for the dictatorship of the masses',[84] though soon such bodies were to give way to the regular police force. In many ways, this was a revival of the 1949 system which had been changed once the Soviet model of vertical rule had been adopted. It was, however, something more than just a reversion to 1949. The Mao Zedong Thought study groups were seen as having not just a control or governmental function but also an important educational function. The fusion of education with other aspects of life was rather a reaffirmation of the Great Leap Forward tradition.

A more significant element of the Great Leap tradition in urban administration was the merging of neighbourhood co-operatives with street administration[85] and the transfer of independent concerns to local collective leadership. The stage was set, it would seem, for the revival of many of the key elements of the old urban communes. Indeed, the model Daqing oilfield had been set up according to the urban commune idea of fusing together units of industrial and agricultural production, education and administration. Yet the urban commune was not revived as such. Memories of the administrative problems of the late 1950s seemed to urge caution.

The Split in the Central Leadership

The above survey of the 'flying leap' of 1968 – 70 has suggested the basis for disagreements within the Chinese Party leadership. Different views seemed to exist on just how far the Great Leap of 1958 might be emulated, how quickly the army ought to be phased out of adminis-tration, whether the slow process of 'open Party building' ought to be replaced by a more orthodox process, what exactly constituted rural excesses, whether experiments in industrial participation should be abandoned in favour of the imposition of discipline and whether the education system should be regularised. It is possible also that some people might have considered that the decentralisation of urban services wasted trained personnel.

There was also a basis for disagreement concerning foreign policy.[86] As far as Zhou Enlai was concerned, the strategy based on a genera-lisation of Lin Biao's people's war thesis had manifestly failed to produce any results. In fact, during the Cultural Revolution, China's foreign policy record was one long series of estrangements, which was neither helping China nor advancing the cause of world socialism. Though parts of the 'world's countryside' (such as Vietnam) were weakening the 'world's cities' (the United States), the Third World prospect offered very little in terms of a United Front from below. Since the beginning of the Cultural Revolution, international relations had begun to show clear signs of change. There were distinct differences between the United States and some of its NATO allies on the question of Vietnam. Canada, once firmly in the United States orbit, had announced, in January 1969, that it would consider entering into diplomatic relations with China, and Italy and Belgium were rumoured to be about to follow suit.[87] Apparently, the United States bloc was disintegrating. Similarly, the Soviet Union, now placed on an equal footing with the United States as a major enemy, also seemed to be in difficulties. The invasion of Czechoslovakia had weakened rather than strengthened the Warsaw Pact. Rumania was now firmly in a neutral position and Soviet control over other countries in Eastern Europe had slackened. With both of the major world power blocs disintegrating, could China still maintain a purist stand-off position?

By 1969, a new foreign policy orientation, attributed to Mao Zedong and Zhou Enlai, had begun to take shape. Now, the United States and the Soviet Union, in their struggle for world 'hegemony', were seen as oscillating between policies of competition and collusion (when threatened from outside). It would be foolish, therefore, to regard both of them as an undifferentiated enemy. Rather, China should exploit the contradictions between them and between each of them and their client states. To do this, avenues of communication had to be kept open between China and the Soviet Union and reopened between China and the United States. The parallel between 1969 – 70 and 1945 was immediately recalled. At that time, the Chinese Communist Party negotiated with Jiang Jieshi and yet prepared actively for the resumption of hostilities. Within two years, clear allusions would be made to the Chongqing negotiations of 1945.[88]

Though border clashes with the Soviet Union continued throughout the summer of 1969,[89] China pursued a policy of negotiations[90] coupled with tunnel digging and air-raid precautions.[91] Towards the end of the year, it was decided to resume contacts with the United States at ambassadorial level but the United States invasion of Cambodia in March 1970 made this impossible. Nevertheless, as the summer of 1970 approached, it seemed that the United States might soon be willing to talk and China could then engage in exactly the same tactic with the United States as it had with the Soviet Union.

It is impossible to say exactly how various members of the Chinese leadership reacted to the above developments. Subsequent charges, however, that Lin Biao opposed the new foreign policy line[92] are extremely plausible. After all, the new strategy completely negated his whole generalised people's war thesis. Yet I doubt whether foreign policy issues were the most important element in the leadership split which occurred in mid-1970. What was probably much more crucial was the reaction to the continued role of the army and the perceived excesses of the 'flying leap' of 1968–70. Any attempt to reconstruct the possible divergencies of opinion in 1970 is fraught with danger. In the early 1970s it was said that, at the root of the problem, was Lin Biao and Chen Boda's personal ambition to seize supreme power. After October 1976, official Chinese comment added all the other members of the old Central Cultural Revolution Group to this 'conspiracy'. Writing at a time when the Chinese leadership is criticising the Cultural Revolution and the Great Leap Forward, it seems that questions of personal power cannot be disassociated from the evaluation of the Cultural Revolution and the 'flying leap'.

The most serious objection to the claim that the crisis of 1970 might be seen purely in terms of Lin Biao and others seeking merely to seize power is that they already held supreme power. After all, Lin Biao had been specifically named as Mao's successor in the 1969 Party constitution. What seems to have been at issue was that the problems generated by the 'flying leap' had provided others in the Party with the opportunity to wrest that power away from Lin Biao and implement less radical policies which might promote more rapid economic growth. It seems also that Mao himself, having removed 'rightist' obstacles to his developmental strategy, was now, in the manner of Stalin, prepared to move against those whom he considered veered too much to the left.[93] Mao, it was subsequently alleged, had serious misgivings about Lin Biao as early as 1966 and had written a letter to Jiang Qing to that effect.[94] He had apparently suppressed those misgivings so long as Lin Biao was active in the Cultural Revolution and so long as the army, under Lin Biao, was holding the ring whilst the policy of 'open Party building' was being pursued. When in 1970, however, it seemed that the army had not made sufficient progress in helping to reconstruct the Party and the only course was to forget about 'open Party building' and build the same sort of Party as before from the top down, Lin Biao could be dispensed with and the army support to the civilian sector could be criticised. Thus, articles began to appear in late 1969 talking about arrogance and rashness within military circles.[95] It was made quite clear that army cadres could not just get away with correcting deficiencies in their work style (zuofeng) but had to look to their whole ideological orientation from which errors in work style arose.[96] But who exactly was being criticised? Was it the conservative military commanders who wished for law and order at any cost, or those who were associated all along with the activism of the Cultural Revolution. Perhaps, in Mao's eyes, these were the same people and Lin Biao, as Minister of Defence, was felt to be responsible for excesses in both directions. After all, Lin was now closely associated with Huang Yongsheng, one of the more repressive regional military commanders who had been appointed chief-of-staff. It will be a long time before we are able to sort out the very murky evidence.

Though 1979 reports accuse Lin Biao and others of engaging in 'ultra-leftist' disruption of the economy, it is not easy to deduce from the contemporary evidence concerning Lin Biao that the crisis in 1970 resulted from a rejection of the 'flying leap'. We are on much firmer ground, however, when we consider that the first major target for criticism in 1970 was Chen Boda, the head of the Central Cultural Revolution Group and one of the major sources of inspiration behind the original Great Leap Forward of 1958. In retrospect, it would seem that the heightened campaign against the May Sixteenth Group in late 1969 was aimed at Chen and, after October 1969, Chen gradually retired from the public stage. Indeed, by the end of the year, no more mention was made of the Central Cultural Revolution Group.

As the activities of Lin Biao and Chen Boda came under suspicion in late 1969 and early 1970, the Party was engaged in lengthy discussions in preparation for the long-awaited National People's Congress which would legitimise a new state structure. No meeting of the National People's Congress had been held during the Cultural Revolution and the state posts, which existed in early 1970 (the NPC Standing Committee, the vice-chairmen of the People's Republic and the premier of the State Council), owed their legitimacy to a very different era. It was noted above that the Twelfth Plenum of the Eighth Central Committee in 1968 had taken the unconstitutional step of dismissing Liu Shaoqi from all his state posts. The body which was in fact constitutionally empowered to do this was the National People's Congress and, if a new state chairman was to be elected, that body would have to be convened.

This issue of state chairman was a very important one. The chairman of the People's Republic was no figurehead. Mao's resignation from that office in 1959 had caused a certain stir and it was because of his position as chairman that Liu Shaoqi wielded considerable power. During the Cultural Revolution, the ceremonial functions of head of state had been undertaken by the aged Dong Biwu and Song Qingling, but it was felt in 1969 – 70 that a more substantive formal chairman should be appointed. Accordingly, a draft constitution for the People's Republic was prepared[97] and circulated for comment prior to ratification at a future meeting of the National People's Congress. One cannot be sure what the original document looked like but the version which is available in the West and which dates from the autumn of 1970 nominates Mao as head of state (*yuanshou*) rather than chairman (*zhuxi*). This, it was subsequently alleged, was done in opposition to Lin Biao who saw himself as substantive vice-chairman and soon, maybe (like Liu Shaoqi), the substantive chairman,[98] outranking Zhou Enlai in *government* rank as he did in the Party. When, in March 1970, Mao recommended the removal of the post of chairman from the constitution,[99] implying that his successors were now to be collective, Lin Biao was said to have been very angry. But was this anger just because of his thwarted ambition, as the official comments claim, or also because Mao had changed his attitude towards Lin Biao in the first three months of 1970? One suspects the latter and can only speculate as to why Mao had changed his mind. It could have been because of the growing strength of opposition to Lin Biao amongst leaders of the Party. It could also have been because the 'flying leap' was not proceeding as anticipated and Mao was heartily tired of the Cultural Revolution. As he later confided to Edgar Snow, the growth of mass consciousness had been impeded by a personality cult which did little more than promote book-waving and ritual slogan-chanting.[100] The promotion of that cult had been a major task of Lin Biao and Mao seems to have been aware of the dangers as early as 1966.[101] Why then did Mao not criticise the cult much earlier?

The showdown was not long in coming. In the spring of 1970, stress was laid not so much on learning from the PLA but on the PLA studying Mao Zedong's instructions on (civilian) Party building.[102] At the same time, Lin Biao's earlier criteria for Party membership, which stressed ideological commitment,[103] were replaced by a demand that Party members should trust the masses and undergo self-criticism.[104] Eventually a showdown came at the Second Plenum of the Ninth Central Committee which, like that similar meeting eleven years before, was held at Lushan. Clearly someone had a sense of history!

Conclusion

The Lushan Plenum of August 1970 was to see the beginning of the end of the attempt to restore Great Leap policies in the aftermath of the Cultural Revolution. One wonders, however, just how successful that attempt could have been. Much could be done in education, because that was the field where the Cultural Revolution had begun and where activism had been most marked. In the factories, however, discipline was seen as so much more important and the relationship between participation and discipline could hardly be solved through the techniques of 'struggle'. In the countryside, a controlled Cultural Revolution under PLA guidance could perhaps not be expected to lead to the kind of creativity needed to advance rapidly to a more socialised system of agriculture. What seemed to be lacking was the euphoria of the original Great Leap. Perhaps, as the present leadership suggests, this was because of mass disenchantment with the Cultural Revolution. More likely, it stemmed from a lack of confidence in the new divided leadership. In 1958–9, it seemed that the original Great Leap had enjoyed the support of the whole Party leadership which was determined to discard the Soviet model and create a new specifically Chinese socialist system. In 1968 – 9, it was clear that different groups had different views on the optimum level of activism and that they looked on each other with mutual suspicion. The original Great Leap had depended on what was felt to be a strong Party machine. In 1968 – 70, the Party machine was going through a painful process of reconstruction under the scrutiny of non-Party people who could see that what existed was far from the united vanguard in which they might have confidence.

NOTES

1. See Yu, 1970.
2. *PR* 29, 14 July 1967, pp. 22 – 6.
3. Halperin, 1967, pp. 148 – 51.
4. E.g. *Pravda*,16 February 1967, cited in *CQ* 30, 1967, p. 244.
5. An article by Wang Ming, 'China: Cultural Revolution or Counter-revolutionary Coup', was published in *Canadian Tribune*,19 March 1969, and subsequently reprinted by the Novosti Press Agency. It is cited in Schram, 1974, p. 348.
6. *Kommunist*, quoted in *CQ* 35, 1968, p. 198.
7. *PR* 20, 17 May 1968, pp. 20 – 3.
8. Ibid.10, 7 March 1969, p. 12.
9. Ibid.6, 7 February 1969, pp. 15 – 16.
10. Zhou Enlai, 23 August 1968, *PR* 34 (Supplement), 23 August 1968, p. iv.
11. This had been going on at least since January 1967 (*CB* 892, 21 October 1969, p. 50), when Mao noted that there were over one million Soviet troops threatening China to the north and west. See Snow, 27 March 1971, p. 22.
12. The last two provincial-level revolutionary committees were set up in Tibet and Xinjiang on 5 September.
13. *SCMM* 650, 14 April 1969, pp. 5 – 12; *PR* 10, 7 March 1969, pp. 4 – 12; *PR* 11, 14 March 1969, pp. 3 – 21; *PR* 12, 21 March 1969, pp. 6 – 26 and 29 – 31; *PR* 13, 28 March 1969, pp. 14 – 26, 29 – 31; *PR* 14, 4 April 1969, pp. 16 – 27.
14. *PR* 10, 7 March 1969, pp. 6 – 7.
15. Text in Chien,1969, pp. 349 – 55 and in *CQ* 37 1969, pp. 169 – 74.
16. *PR* 35 – 6, 7 September 1973, pp. 17 – 18. The report is in *PR* Special Issue, 28 April 1969, pp. 11 – 30, and *PR* 18, 30 April 1969, pp. 16 – 35.
17. Text in *PR* 18, 20 April 1969, pp.36 – 9.
18. Domes, 1973, pp. 208 – 10.
19. For a list of the new CC, see *PR* 18, 20 April 1969, pp. 47 – 8; for the new Politburo elected by the First Plenum, ibid., pp. 48 – 9.
20. Gayn (1973, p. 305) claims that Zhou Enlai informed visitors that Lin's group forced a reluctant Mao to name Lin his successor in 1969.
21. Mao Zedong, 28 April 1969, Schram, 1974, p. 282. *Kommunist* was a theoretical journal of the CPSU.
22. Ibid., p. 283.
23. Ibid., p. 286.
24. *SCMM* 664, 2 September 1969, pp. 1 – 23.
25. *CQ* 40, 1969, p. 171.
26. CCPCC, 23 July 1969, *Issues and Studies*, Vol. VI, No. 1, October 1969, pp. 97 – 100.

140 *'Flying Leap'*

27. Domes, 1973, p. 215.

28. Ibid. Young (1979, pp. 493–5) disagrees that a shift in focus took place, noting that the rebuilding of the Party at higher and lower levels proceeded in tandem.

29. Domes, 1973, p.215. The source of this information is unclear.

30. *China News Analysis* 799, 1 May 1970, p. 6.

31. See Young, 1978, pp. 41–3.

32. In particular were the 'six factories and two educational institutions'. The factories are listed in note 61. The two educational institutions were Qinghua and Beijing Universities.

33. This is the conclusion of D. Woodward. It will be discussed in his forthcoming PhD thesis on rural policy between 1969 and 1973.

34. Bastid, 1973, pp. 183–4.

35. On the importance of provincial power in the economy, see the two essays by Donnithorne, 1972.

36. Bastid, 1973, p. 181.

37. E.g. *SCMM* 650, 14 April 1969, pp. 37–40.

38. *SCMM* 654, 12 May 1969, pp. 28–33.

39. Snow, 27 March 1971 (from Zhou Enlai), p. 21. In late 1970, there were only 26 departments under the central government compared with 90 in the past.

40. Bastid, 1973, p. 185.

41. *SCMP* 4225, 25 July 1968, pp. 12–13; Baum, 1971, pp. 448–9.

42. See e.g. Bennett and Montaperto, 1971, pp. 220–4.

43. Baum, 1971, p. 447.

44. *SCMP* 4244, 23 August 1968, pp. 1–12.

45. Baum, 1971, pp. 449–53.

46. *SCMM* 643, 3 February 1969, p.34; ibid. 644, 10 February 1969, p. 40.

47. *Hongqi* 2, 26 January 1969, p. 29.

48. Bastid, 1973, pp. 177–80.

49. Ibid., p. 173: i.e. private plots were permitted but should not exceed 5 per cent of land under cultivation. The extent of free markets during this period should not be over-estimated. In 1969, for example, moves were undertaken in some areas to restrict the private trading in pigs (*China News Analysis* 778, 17 October 1969, p.5).

50. Bridgham, 1973, p. 445. For a survey of 'ultra-leftism' during this period see Woodward, 1978, pp. 161–5.

51. Party directives in 1972 called for the return of confiscated private property. This confiscation had probably taken place in the period under review. See CCP, Simao District Committee, Document No. 22, 26 March 1972, *Issues and Studies*, Vol. IX, No. 6, March 1973, p. 96.

52. *CQ* 49, 1972, p. 186.

53. *Current Scene*, Vol. VII, No. 9, 3 May 1969, p. 11.

54. See CCP, Simao District Committee, Document No. 22, 26 March 1972, *Issues and Studies*, Vol. IX, No. 6, March 1973, p. 92.

55. See Watson, 1968, pp. 179–80.

56. This was cited as a most recent instruction by Yao Yenyuan, *Hongqi* 2, 1968, p. 6.

57. A discussion of this constitution may be found in *PR* 14, 3 April 1970, pp. 11–15.

58. For analyses of different types of factionalism see *Hongqi* 1, 1970, pp. 61–7.

59. See Watson, 1978, p. 179. The Beijing Xinhua Printing Works, which was the major model for the formation of factory Party branches, dates from this time. See also *RMRB*, 16 December 1969, p. 1, and Young, 1978, pp. 44–6.

60. See Watson, 1978, pp. 179–81.

61. These were the Beijing General Knitwear Mill, the Beijing Xinhua Printing Works, the Beijing No. 3 Chemical Plant, the Beijing Beiqiao Timber Mill, the Beijing February Seventh Locomotive and Rolling Stock Plant and the Beijing Nankou Locomotive and Rolling Stock Plant.

62. See Watson, 1978, p. 181.
63. Mao Zedong, 28 April 1969, Schram, 1974, p. 283.
64. *PR* 31, 2 August 1968, p. 3.
65. Ibid., pp. 9–14.
66. Hinton, 1972, pp. 263–4.
67. Bastid, 1970, p. 41.
68. Ibid., p. 42.
69. *SCMM* 638, 23 December 1968, pp. 10–15.
70. E.g. *PR* 2, 10 January 1969, pp. 17–20.
71. *SCMM* 638, 23 December 1968, pp. 17–18.
72. Ibid., 647, 17 March 1969, p. 17.
73. Bastid, 1970, p. 35; *SCMM* 638, 23 December 1968, p. 18.
74. Bastid, 1970, p. 35.
75. Salaff, 1971, pp. 314–16.
76. *SCMP* 4418, 19 May 1969, pp. 9–15.
77. Salaff, 1971, pp. 316–17.
78. *PR* 5, 31 January 1969, pp. 17–18; Horn, 1969, particularly pp. 135–40.
79. Horn, 1969, p. 64.
80. Salaff, 1971, pp. 298–312.
81. Ibid., pp. 298–99.
82. Ibid., pp. 300–1.
83. Ibid., p. 303.
84. Ibid., p. 310.
85. Bastid, 1973, p. 174.
86. See O'Leary, 1978.
87. *CQ* 38, 1969, p. 189.
88. Certain direct quotes from Mao's essay on the Chongqing negotiations were made in a much publicised essay discussing Mao's 'On Policy' written not long after the visit of Henry Kissinger to China in 1971. See *PR* 35, 1971, pp. 10–13 and *Hongqi* 9, 2 August 1971, pp. 10–17.
89. E.g. *PR* 28, 11 July 1969, pp. 6–7; ibid. 33, 15 August 1969, p. 3 and 7; ibid. 34, 22 August 1969, pp. 4–5, 8–10.
90. An agreement to maintain the status quo on the border pending further negotiations was concluded by Zhou Enlai and Kosygin on 11 September 1969. Snow, 27 March 1971, p. 23.
91. Goodstadt, *The Times*, 1 December 1969, p. 5.
92. *CQ* 52, 1972, p. 768. *PR* (27, 2 July 1971, p. 21) notes that the new foreign policy line was attacked from the 'left' as well as the 'right'.
93. Mao's habit of siding with one group to attack another and then siding with another group to attack his former allies was noted by the group associated with the subsequent Lin Biao conspiracy. See CCPCC, *zhongfa* (1972) 4, 13 January 1972, *Issues and Studies*, Vol. VIII, No. 8, May 1972, p. 81.
94. Mao Zedong, 8 July 1966, *Issues and Studies*, Vol. IX, No. 4, January 1973, pp. 94–6.
95. *PR* 12, 21 March 1969, p. 4.
96. Ibid. 46, 14 November 1969, pp. 5–6.
97. Text in *Studies in Comparative Communism*, Vol. VI, No. 1, January 1971, pp. 100–6.
98. CCPCC, *zhongfa* (1972) 12, 17 March 1972, *Issues and Studies*, Vol. VIII, No. 12, September 1972, p. 67.
99. CCPCC, *zhongfa* (1970)56, 12 September 1970, *Chinese Law and Government*, Vol. V, Nos. 3–4, Fall-Winter 1972–3, p. 69.
100. Van Ginnekan, 1972 (from Burchett) describes the personality cult as part of a plot to remove Mao from effective decision-making. Snow (10 April 1971) describes Mao's

142   'Flying Leap'

unease about the cult.

101. Mao Zedong, 8 July 1966, *Issues and Studies*, Vol. IX, No. 4, January 1973, pp. 94–6.
102. Bridgham, 1973, p. 433.
103. Bridgham, 1967, p. 25.
104. *PR* 27, 3 July 1970, pp. 10–11.

VI
THE DEMISE OF LIN BIAO AND THE ESTABLISHMENT OF STABILITY
(1970–1972)

This chapter will examine the events which Mao described as the tenth major crisis in the fifty-year history of the Chinese Communist Party. This crisis centred on the person of Lin Biao, who first came under serious criticism at the Second Plenum of the Ninth Central Committee in August 1970 and who finally died after an alleged coup attempt in September 1971. The dates August 1970 and September 1971 are important in that they mark two watersheds in the general deradicalisation of policy in the aftermath of the 'flying leap'. The Second Plenum brought the 'flying leap' to an end but it was often not until late 1971 and 1972 that effective stability was achieved. On the surface, therefore, it would seem that the deradicalisation was intimately connected with the Lin Biao affair. This chapter will note, however, that it is difficult to document adequately such an association.

The Case of Lin Biao

The previous chapter outlined a number of reasons why Mao decided to remove Lin Biao from his position of supreme power. It is uncertain, however, just when Mao took that decision. All that is clear is that the crucial turning-point in Lin's fortunes was the Second Plenum. It was at that plenum that Mao was said to have reaffirmed his intention to oppose the election of a new chairman of the People's Republic,[1] though, as has been noted, the state constitution, discussed at the plenum, did have provision for a head of state. The plenum also denounced Chen Boda and his colleagues on the old Central Cultural Revolution Group and it was said that Lin tried to protect them. A consideration of such actions must figure in any analysis of the political demise of Lin Biao. It should be borne in mind, however, that much of the subsequent debate in the press was couched in theoretical terms, which ought not to be dismissed as mere rationalisations of a struggle for power.

At the root of the theoretical considerations was the growing feeling that Lin Biao was guilty of 'ultra-leftism'. It was perhaps the case that Lin had supported many of what were felt to be excesses both in the Cultural Revolution and the subsequent 'flying leap', but that may also have been true of many senior leaders of the Party who escaped censure at that time. The problem here is one of defining the term 'ultra-left'. Previous chapters have indicated a number of behavioural dispositions which at various times were labelled 'ultra-left' and have suggested that loosely the term might be seen as referring to those who wished to push ahead with eliminating capitalist and other economic forms regardless of objective economic constraints. But how was one to know what an economic constraint was until one had made an attempt to eliminate it? Was the term 'ultra-leftist' nothing more than a synonym for failure? Doubtless the fact that many people took it to be no more than that was because of the poverty of theory which had characterised the Cultural Revolution.

As was suggested earlier, much may be explained about the poverty of theory in the Cultural Revolution by Mao's unwillingness to develop his ideas on continuous revolution, first advanced in the early 1960s. If, perhaps, Mao had extended his ideas on the three aspects of the relations of production, we may have had the germs of a theory with which to evaluate 'ultra-leftism'. These aspects, according to Mao, were ownership relations, the relations between people at work and the reciprocal relation between distribution and production.[2] A tentative definition of 'ultra-leftism', therefore, might have been any action which promoted the socialist development of one of these aspects without regard to the other two. But Mao never developed his fragmented remarks or, if he did, was reluctant to publish them. It is difficult to see why! After all, Mao had been bold enough to promote the most momentous upheaval in modern Chinese history. Yet he remained theoretically rather timid. Even in the realm of practical politics, Mao occasionally lost his nerve. Perhaps in the field of theory, where one is open more to the direct judgement of history, Mao was less confident. This may be why the Lin Biao case was discussed in terms fundamental to Marxist theory yet without much theoretical guidance on the problem of 'ultra-leftism'.

At the core of the discussions concerning the Lin Biao case was the role of the individual in history. This was of particular relevance to one of the major problems of the 'flying leap' of 1968 – 70—that of discipline. During the Cultural Revolution, the more conservative wing of the Chinese Communist Party had come under attack for its stifling *organisational* discipline. The Party, legitimised by substantive rationality,[3] could only be reformed by appeal to the masses, led by a charismatic leader. But what was the nature of the discipline which was expected to grow out of the relationship between the leader and the masses? It could not be organisational discipline, which depends on the separation of particular organisations from the rest of society and the infusion of those organisations with *esprit de corps* (defined in relation to other *corps*). It had to be a form of *individual* discipline, in which the individual political actor subordinates himself or herself to the will of the leader. This ascetic individual discipline was most marked in those Jacobin philosophers, such as Lin Jie, who had been prominent in 1967. After 1968, however, it had been criticised as 'petty bourgeois' (and here the term Jacobin is most apposite). Such a form of discipline was, after all, at variance with the old Bolshevik tradition, which Mao was prepared to violate from time to time in practice but not in theory.

Here one may see one of the reasons why Lin Biao was later transformed from an 'ultra-leftist' to an 'ultra-rightist'. I shall go on to argue that there were also mundane political reasons why such a transformation was made. Suffice it to say here that, in purely theoretical terms, the association makes sense. What is at issue is the relationship between 'ultra-leftism' and 'fascism'. Both tend towards individual discipline rather than organisational discipline. Both stress the power of human will and believe that history is made by great men. Both rate the 'hero' as more important than ordinary people and turn the 'masses' into a metaphysical category. Both, moreover, are committed to a vague mystical ideal rather than a coherent ideology. I am, of course, not maintaining that Lin Biao was a 'fascist' in any philosophical sense; merely that one might make a behavioural association.

In the above context, the charges that Lin Biao and others peddled the 'ideology of individual genius' in the period after the Ninth Party Congress[4] is quite credible. At that time, much was made of Lin's 'heroic' role as Mao's 'close comrade in arms and successor' (and words to that effect were written into the 1969 Party constitution).[5] Much too was made of the 'genius' of Lin's son, Lin Liguo,[6] whose 'heroic' qualities earned him a very high post in the air force. Thirdly, and perhaps most important, Lin was later accused of wrongly portraying Mao Zedong himself as a 'genius'. This was the rationale behind the Mao cult, discussed in the last chapter. By the time of the Second Plenum in August 1970, Mao had become much more Bolshevik, in an orthodox sense, than in preceding years and was prepared to criticise the 'theory of genius'.[7] A major plank under Lin Biao's theoretical position had been removed.

To eradicate the power base of Lin Biao, it was evident, in the aftermath of the Second Plenum, that the process of Party reconstruction had to be accelerated. This demanded a modification of the policy of building the Party from the bottom up or even of concentrating on *xian*- and municipal-level Party committees. At provincial level, however, to which the focus of Party rebuilding was now switched,[8] power rested with revolutionary committees dominated by army representatives. It could not be certain that local military commanders would associate themselves with Mao or with Lin Biao if things came to a showdown. Nor was it clear whether an acceleration of Party rebuilding at provincial level would not snuff out the policy of 'purifying the class ranks' and giving full play to mass activism. Despite the dangers, however, the Party Centre pressed ahead in late 1970 with its new policy of *provincial* Party rebuilding and, in December of that year, the first provincial Party committee emerged from the Hunan Party Congress, headed by Hua Guofeng.[9] In the next nine months, Party committees appeared in all 29 provincial-level[10] units, though it is probable that the whole process was too quick and mass mobilisation was not undertaken. I suspect also that the reconstruction of provincial-level congresses and Party committees was effected with some military pressure.[11] In retrospect, it does not seem that such military pressure favoured the position of Lin Biao. In fact, it is possible that the role of *local* military commanders in provincial-level Party rebuilding was such as to counter the influence of the network of trusty followers which Lin Biao was said to have placed in positions of authority in the provinces.[12]

While the process of provincial-level Party rebuilding was going on, it was probably still not clear whether such a programme was sufficient to counter the efforts of that group of military men surrounding Lin Biao who began to develop conspiratorial measures to protect their positions. Mao decided, therefore, to take more decisive steps. At a meeting (work conference) in December 1970, he pressed for the reorganisation of the Beijing military region since, if in fact there was a conspiracy based on the Ministry of Defence, it was important that the military commanders in the capital should be loyal to the Party Centre.

In January 1971, the reorganisation took place[13] and this led immediately, it is said, to the formation of a plan of action by the Lin Biao group for a military coup. In February 1971, it was reported that Lin Biao's son, Lin Liguo (the young 'genius'), was active in the Shanghai region,[14] making preparations to neutralise opposition in the Party Centre and the reorganised PLA Beijing command. His efforts led, in late March, to the formulation of a document known as the '571 Engineering Outline' (*Wu Qi Yi Gongcheng Jiyao*).[15]

The words 'five seven one' (*wu qi yi*) are a Chinese pun on the words 'armed uprising' (*wuzhuang qiyi*). The conspirators, Lin Biao, Ye Qun (his wife), Lin Liguo (his son), Huang Yongsheng (chief-of-staff) and the other senior military commanders (and Politburo members), Wu Faxian, Li Zuopeng and Qiu Huizuo,[16] seem to have been a rather motley collection of people, united only in their belief that, if they did not immediately seize power, they would be dismissed by the forces of 'B-52'[17] (the codename for Mao, given because of his fondness for 'dropping bombs'). On issues of policy, their programme reveals a hotch-potch of complaints both of a conservative and 'ultra-left' variety. For example, they condemned *xiaxiang* as tantamount to labour reform; they asserted that the Red Guards had been deceived; they viewed the despatch of cadres to May Seventh Cadre Schools as a form of unemployment; and they demanded that the wage freeze for workers should be ended.

In assessing the strategic situation, the conspirators noted that they had considerable power within the air force. They felt also that the Soviet Union would look sympathetically upon any group which toppled Mao Zedong. On the other hand, they were uncertain as to what proportion of the PLA would rally to their cause and felt that some of the regional military commanders might be neutralised by the toleration of a degree of regional independence. At a tactical level, they planned to set up a training group, under the pretext of routine cadre re-education, and this group would attempt to assign to each military unit a trusty who could take over the unit when the time came. They proposed to offer favourable conditions to all old cadres who had been removed in the preceding few years, in the hope presumably of establishing a new administrative network. Finally, they chose as their centre of operations the Shanghai area whence air force units were to be deployed. If the worst came to the worst, Shanghai could provide a take-off point for a protracted guerrilla war waged, first of all, in Zhejiang province. It was crucial, therefore, that the commander of the Nanjing military region, Xu Shiyu, should be watched very carefully in case he began to move against them.

The '571 Engineering Outline' was truly an extraordinary document. I still find it extremely odd that Lin Biao, famed for his venom against the Soviet Union, should have entertained the idea of Soviet support or that such a staunch fighter against Japan should have spoken favourably of Eda Gima (the Japanese wartime naval school famous for propagating the Japanese military ethic of *bushido*).[18] I am inclined, however, to regard the document as genuine. It is too contradictory and incoherent to have been merely the product of a plot to besmirch Lin Biao.

In the spring and early summer of 1971, Mao and most Party leaders were, it is said, unaware of the existence of the '571 Engineering Outline'.[19] What they were painfully aware of, however, was a large-scale campaign to promote the qualities of Lin Biao which was sometimes aided by provincial military commanders. Since 1969, pamphlets and articles had appeared praising Lin's achievements with unparalleled extravagance,[20] in a way reminiscent of the articles praising Gao Gang after his transfer to Beijing under considerable suspicion in the early 1950s.

By the summer of 1971, it was clear that Mao had a very good idea about the impending coup and that the Nanjing military region was a crucial area of operations. From mid-August to September 1971, the chairman undertook one of his famous tours of inspection, in which the Nanjing military region and the Guangzhou military region (under the influence of Huang Yongsheng) figured prominently.[21] It was at this time that Mao noted that the crisis had been brewing since the Second Plenum and that it was the tenth major crisis in the Party's history.[22] It ranked, therefore, with the struggle against the lines of Peng Dehuai and Liu Shaoqi and was a 'struggle between two headquarters'. In Mao's view, however, the PLA would not follow Huang Yongsheng into rebellion[23] and there was a remote possibility that Lin Biao's errors in line might be corrected (or so he said).[24] Mao was most insistent that the three major slogans of the past few years were now inadequate. They had been: 'In industry, learn from Daqing; in agriculture, learn from Dazhai; in the whole country, learn from the PLA.' Now, most significantly, he added a fourth: 'The PLA should learn from the people of the whole country.' To counter military élitism, Mao once again stressed his 'three main rules of discipline' and the 'eight points for attention', but naturally omitted the various military slogans advanced since 1959.[25]

There has been much debate as to whether an attempted coup did or did not take place in September 1971 and whether Lin did or did not attempt to assassinate Mao.[26] Whatever happened, such seems to have been Lin's intention and, on 13 September 1971, it was reported that Lin and some others died as his escape plane crashed near Undur Khan in the Mongolian People's Republic en route for the Soviet Union.[27] There is conflicting evidence as to whether Lin was in fact on board[28] and who exactly was with him, but, in my view, it does not much matter. By mid-September, the Lin Biao conspiracy had been squashed and Lin Biao had been officially declared dead. As things turned out, the provincial military leadership had remained loyal to Mao Zedong but the Party was now determined to 'control the gun'. It was, however, still to be a long and tortuous process before the ideal PLA-Party relationship was settled. In the next few months, a large number of appointees of Lin Biao (especially in the air force which had been grounded during the September crisis) were removed from their posts[29] and a new military network was built up. At the same time, detailed investigations were made concerning the position of many senior cadres. Prominent in such investigations, some accounts claim, was the Hunan Party first secretary, Hua Guofeng, who moved to Beijing in late 1971. At the same time, the young Shanghai Cultural Revolution activist, Wang Hongwen, was summoned to Beijing and both men were given senior military posts.[30]

The death of Lin Biao in September 1971 was to see a renewed drive for stability in Chinese society though one must note that, of the two watersheds in the winding down of the 'flying leap' policies, the first (the

Second Plenum) was the more important. Most of the remainder of this chapter, therefore, will describe the deradicalisation after August 1970.

Consolidating the Rural Sector

Like the original Great Leap of 1958, the 'flying leap' of 1968–70 had seen the formulation of ambitious plans for agriculture in a number of provinces.[31] As one might have expected, constant reference was made to policies and documents which dated from the mid- and late 1950s. Once again, stress was laid on Mao's 'eight-character constitution' for agriculture[32] and how to implement the targets specified in the National Programme for Agricultural Development. This programme, it will be recalled, was first mooted in 1955, shelved in 1956 and resurrected in the Great Leap to take its final form in 1960.[33] It called for some quite spectacular increases in yields per hectare. Originally, the 1967 targets for food grain yields were six tonnes per hectare (south of the Changjiang), 3.75 tonnes per hectare (in the region between the Huai and Huanghe) and three tonnes per hectare (north of the Huanghe).[34] Few places had, however, reached these targets by 1967 and, even in 1970, the programme was a very long way from fulfilment. One should not, however, jump too readily to the conclusion that agricultural production had been seriously affected by the Cultural Revolution. Grain production in 1965 was estimated at 210 million tonnes. This figure rose to 230 million tonnes in 1967. In 1968, it fell to 215 million tonnes rising to 220 in 1969[35] and 240 in 1970.[36] It might be argued that the 1968 figure suggests that the Cultural Revolution had caused disruption though it is very difficult to say to what extent climatic conditions might also have been responsible. In any case, the decline was temporary and not of major significance. Of course, one might argue that, by the late 1960s, China had imported and adapted high-yielding seed strains which might have produced much higher output figures had it not been for the Cultural Revolution. Such a claim, however, is impossible to assess.

Nevertheless, despite the difficulty in proving the negative effects of the Cultural Revolution, it was quite evident by 1970 that elements of the Chinese leadership were worried about what were felt to be the disruptive effects of the Cultural Revolution and the subsequent 'flying leap'. Attempts were made, therefore, to formulate policy guidelines for the Fourth Five Year Plan which was to go into effect in 1971.[37] Material balance planning, it was felt, depended on stability. Thus, a series of policy documents appeared (both before and after the Second Plenum) which were to make up for the lack of central guidance during the preceding 'flying leap'.[38] Yet grain production still continued to be erratic. In 1971 it reached 246–50 million tonnes[39] and fell once again in

1972 to 240 million tonnes[40] (though this time there could be no doubt that climatic conditions were largely responsible).

The new stress on a stable increase in grain production in 1970 was to lead to a reinterpretation of the campaign to learn from Dazhai. Though the experiences of the Dazhai production brigade in increasing production had always been stressed, equal weight had been placed on the social experimentation carried on in the brigade, on the remuneration system and on the 'creative application of Mao Zedong Thought'. Now, what was to be emulated was not so much the Dazhai brigade itself but what were called 'Dazhai-type *xian*'. The model here was Xiyang *xian* (in which Dazhai was located). This, as time went on, was held up less as an example of social experimentation than as an example of how to improve production techniques. By 1969, it was said that nearly one-third of the brigades in Xiyang had 'crossed the Huanghe' (i.e. had reached the target yields specified in the National Programme for the area between the Huai and Huanghe) and 14 brigades had 'crossed the Changjiang'[41] (i.e. had reached the target yields for the south). In late 1970, a number of provincial-level conferences were held to study the methods of Xiyang *xian*[42] and a campaign to set up 'Dazhai-type *xian*' unfolded over most of the country. One year later, much success in this campaign was recorded in that north China had, for the first time, become self-sufficient in grain and no longer depended on imports of grain from the south.[43] This success was perhaps tarnished a little by the bad harvests of 1972, when a significant amount of wheat was imported from overseas, though it should be remembered that China remained an exporter of rice, the yields of which were much higher.

Perhaps the major limitations upon China's ability to profit fully from the development of new seed strains were the lack of capital to promote major new irrigation projects and inadequate production of chemical fertilisers. In the early 1970s, much was done to achieve control over the major rivers in north China, although water conservation projects were continually plagued by problems of silting. At the same time, large numbers of tube-wells were dug in the North China Plain, though these at times run dry.[44] In fertiliser production, developments after the Cultural Revolution had been quite dramatic. In 1971, 17 million tonnes of chemical fertiliser were produced rising to 20 million in 1972.[45] Yet this constituted only 30 per cent of the nutrients supplied to agriculture.[46] What is impressive about the 1971 figure, however, is that 60 per cent of the 17 million tonnes was produced by local (*xian* or lower level) factories.[47] Such was a glowing testimony to the policies, pursued in the 'flying leap', to achieve some kind of rural industrialisation. Yet those policies were now felt to be too slow and decisions were taken to import complete fertiliser plants from overseas.[48]

The eclipse of political goals in favour of simply increasing production led, in 1970, to a stress on sound economic management and the slogan 'increase production and practise economy' was interpreted quite strictly. There was an emphasis also on scientific farming and eleven high-yielding areas were singled out as models for the application of modern scientific techniques.[49] Now, although field experiments were still advocated, those who had neglected the activities of central research institutes were also criticised.[50] The ambitious plans for electrification and mechanisation, put forward in the 'flying leap', were interpreted in a more orderly way, as the country geared itself for the first stages of the new five year plan. In that plan, agricultural development was to proceed *step by step*.[51] There was to be no 'commandist' inflation of production targets and no falsification of statistics. Those who, in the 'flying leap', had committed the Great Leap error of advocating a reduction in the cultivated area were denounced[52] and those who had collectivised the private property of peasants were told to hand it back.[53] The emphasis was on stablity and to achieve this there was a renewed emphasis on the integrity of the production team.[54]

Back in the early 1960s, Mao had maintained that the point at which the unit of account might be upgraded was when a greater degree of income was generated at the higher level than at the lower.[55] Since very few communes or production brigades were in that position in 1970, the reiteration of Mao's criterion consigned most of the attempts at upgrading during the 'flying leap' to the category of 'ultra-leftist'. Yet when would brigades and communes be in a position to generate more income than the lower levels? Despite the fact that the promotion of rural industralisation (which generated income at brigade and commune levels) was still adhered to, it seemed that the process would take decades. In the meantime, brigades were enjoined not to encroach on the rights of teams, not to take labour away from them without due compensation[56] and not to draw on the teams' public accumulation funds.[57]

As the spirit of the 'flying leap' petered out in the period 1970–3, the new concern with increasing production at all costs resulted in an increase in private activity in the communes. Peasants were encouraged once again to keep pigs on their private plots, the aim being to reach the target of one pig per person or one pig per *mu* of land.[58] More liberality was shown in determining just exactly what constituted legitimate sideline occupations[59] and family-run rural craft industries developed once again.[60] At the same time, the restrictions on peasants selling the produce of their private plots on the open market were eased and rural markets began to thrive. In short, there was a slow drift back to 'petty capitalism' in the Chinese countryside. It was nothing like that which had occurred in the early 1960s but it was sufficient to cause the Party some concern. After all, it was the Party which had to decide on the optimum balance between private and public economic activity.

During the 'flying leap' of 1968–70, there had been much talk of leadership by the poor and lower-middle peasants. After 1970, however, as the Party was rebuilt in the rural areas, though the poor and lower-middle peasant associations remained in existence, there was more talk of leadership by the appropriate level of Party committee. As far as the revolutionary committees were concerned, more and more authority came to be exercised by Party secretaries and the mass representatives found themselves spending less time in decision-making than in performing productive labour.[61] It would seem, however, that the rebuilding of the rural Party branches was deemed to be insufficient to establish the balance between public activity and privatism and, in 1970, a major rectification campaign known as *yidasanfan* ('one strike and three oppositions') was extended into the rural areas to point cadres in the right direction.[62] This campaign, which did not involve much mass mobilisation, had all the characteristics of a 1950s-style top-down rectification campaign.[63] It was aimed at combating deviations both from the right and the 'ultra-left' yet, as time went on, it was to be the latter deviation which earned the most attention.

It was, of course, no use conducting a rectification campaign when the criteria for what constituted a deviation were constantly changing. Thus, to establish such criteria, teams of senior Party cadres were sent to the rural areas to monitor the current balance between productivity and mass activism and between public and private activity.[64] There was much that these teams had to decide and many contradictions which had to be resolved. They had to see that the new stress on adequate grain reserves was being implemented and that peasants were not consuming too much. Yet, at the same time, they had to ensure that rural units did not set their accumulation targets too high.[65] They had to monitor a renewed birth-control campaign which got under way in 1970[66] and yet promote a system of rural distribution which still discriminated in favour of those with large families. They had to propagate Mao's call for equal pay between the sexes[67] and yet foster a system of 'payment according to work' which favoured brute strength. They had to see that the peasants' standard of living was maintained and yet prevent peasant households obtaining advances greater than their annual income entitlement.[68] They had, moreover, to see that the large numbers of 'educated youth' who had been sent to the countryside in the wake of the Cultural Revolution were treated properly. But did this mean seeing that the youth were productive or well integrated? These two concerns might sometimes be in conflict.

In retrospect, it would seem that the campaign to resettle educated youth in the countryside in the years after the Cultural Revolution left much to be desired.[69] The original aim of the movement had been both economic (it helped to solve the urban employment situation and to resettle former Red Guards) and ideological (it helped to overcome what was felt to be the corrupting influence of an urban lifestyle and spread skills amongst the peasants). It was often implemented in such a way, however, that the ideological aims suffered. Though some youth managed to integrate successfully with the local peasants and got married, most lived in segregated quarters or even segregated villages. Only occasionally did those educated youth, who did integrate with the peasants, attain positions of authority in the communes. Frequently, educated youth complained that the peasants had no confidence in them and they were assigned to low grades in the system where work-point assessment was based on a hierarchy of skill. Sometimes they were welcomed by commune leaders so long as the initial resettlement subsidy from the *xian* lasted and, after that, regarded as a nuisance. As a result of this (and a general distaste for rural life), many went back to the cities without ration tickets where they became a burden on their relatives and friends or simply degenerated in the category of 'social youth' (a euphemism for members of street gangs). Clearly some remedial measures were necessary.

Consolidating the Industrial Sector

The restoration of Party authority in the rural areas, therefore, was to see a partial revival of some of the practices criticised in the Cultural Revolution. In industry, where problems of disorder had been more acute in the 'flying leap', this was even more the case.[70] As Party committees in factories were reconstructed, discussions were held concerning their relationships with the revolutionary committees. The official position, which harked back to the 1956 formula of 'responsibility of the factory general manager under the unified leadership of the enterprise Party committee', was that the Party committee should be responsible for policy and the revolutionary committee for *operations*. Cadres, once again, therefore, had to confront the possibility of conflict over how one defined these two spheres. One way of tackling the problem was to spell out, in detail, the precise division of labour between the two committees, but this could lead to bureaucratism. Another more common solution was to reduce the mass component on the revolutionary committees and allow for considerable overlap in the membership of both committees.[71] Such a development became easier as soldiers were phased out of factory administration and when, in the aftermath of the Lin Biao incident, the actions of the PLA came under criticism. Increasingly, therefore, in the years 1970–3, leadership in factories was in the hands of a body which was said to embody the long-term interests of the workers rather than directly representing those in the particular factory. At the same time, the need to restore production saw the rehabilitation of large numbers of old factory managers who were often restored to their original Party as well as managerial posts.

At factory level, worker representation was gradually effected through revamped worker congresses. The function of these bodies was at first political and managerial[72] though soon they began to perform many of the welfare functions hitherto exercised by the revolutionary committees. They thus resembled more and more the old labour union branches. Indeed, in 1973, they were renamed as such and attempts were made to rebuild the old structure of the ACFTU.[73] At lower levels, worker representative bodies took the form of elected shop workers' management committees, which continued to exercise a direct role in managerial decision-making. Such committees were concerned with the continued operation of the principle of 'two participations and triple combination' specified in the Anshan constitution. But, like so much else, this principle atrophied somewhat as the demands to increase production in an orderly fashion became more prominent after 1971. Pressure on the part of staff offices for greater independence from worker representatives and line management[74] hindered the operation of the 'triple combination teams' and, as 1974 criticisms reveal, there was a general return to old routines with reduction in the time spent by managers in productive labour.[75]

The restoration of many of the staff functions, abolished during the campaign to simplify administration during the 'flying leap', went together with a new stress on 'rational rules and regulations'. Even model factories, such as the Shenyang Locomotive and Rolling Stock Plant, were said to have abolished too many of the old rules and regulations and this had resulted in waste.[76] Workers were now enjoined to distinguish between production for the sake of the revolution and the pre-Cultural Revolution obsession with production to the detriment of politics. They were to understand that economic accounting for the revolution was not the same as 'profits in command' and that professional and technical work, carried on for revolutionary goals, was not the same as 'professional work in command'. Most important of all, revolutionary labour discipline was not to be taken to be the same as Liu Shaoqi's alleged policy of 'controlling, restricting and suppressing' the workers.[77] In practice, one might wonder how the distinction between revolutionary ends and revolutionary means might be made. After all, a denial of that distinction had been one of the hallmarks of the Cultural Revolution. It is clear that not everyone was comforted by assurances that the new rules and regulations were more 'rational' than those attributed to Liu Shaoqi[78] and instances of resistance were noted in the press.[79]

It is probably the case, however, that unease about the imposition of rules and regulations was offset, in large measure, by policies which significantly improved the living standards of many workers. In 1971, a partial wage reform was instituted. During the 'flying leap', no attempt had been made to change the eight-grade system for industrial workers though, by 1971, there had been no mass promotions for many years and workers had complained that they had remained on the first grade for a considerable period of time.[80] Thus, it was decided to promote all workers on the third grade who had started work before 1957 to the fourth grade, all those on the second grade who had started work before 1960 to the third grade and all those on the first grade who had started work before 1966 to the second grade.[81] This move, which was estimated to have raised the average wage by some 10 per cent,[82] probably did little more than restore the proportion of workers on each grade to that which existed before the Cultural Revolution,[83] but it probably did cause some disquiet amongst those whose primary concern was with closing the urban-rural gap. The preceding nine-year industrial wage freeze (and corresponding freeze on promotions) could be seen as a major factor in helping to overcome the 'three major differences'. It is uncertain, however, exactly how opinions divided on the issue of wage reform. According to the '571 Engineering Outline', it will be remembered, a (rightist) criticism had been put forward that the wage freeze had constituted a form of exploitation,[84] while other accounts lay responsibility for this policy on Lin Biao.[85] Suffice it to say that, in the aftermath of the Cultural Revolution, the wage reform, the stress on technical as opposed to political criteria in grading and the restoration of a 24-grade salary scale for cadres[86] must have caused some resentment. Though many workers were better off, it was at the expense of one of Mao's major concerns.

Another source of disquiet in the early 1970s concerned the importation of complete plants from overseas (though this time *not* from the Soviet Union). Such plants, as has been noted, could greatly make up for China's needs in fertiliser production etc. They did, however, require a sophisticated technology and, unless handled cautiously, might lead to the creation of differential wage systems applying to different sectors of the economy. The problem here is not just one of wages, however. Such plants can have a disruptive effect on national economic integration, since factory design embodies certain power relationships and (in a Marxist sense) certain relations of production which cannot easily be transferred from one society to another. In short, importation could hamper the policy of 'walking on two legs'.

The importation of technology had a direct bearing on a debate, carried on in the early 1970s, known as 'electronics versus steel'.[87] It is possible that this debate was, in some ways, connected with the Lin Biao case in that there were said to be people in the more technical arms of the PLA (notably in the air force in which Lin had considerable power) who wished to see the electronics industry serve the needs of national defence.

Lin Biao, for all his advocacy of people's war, was after all also a great advocate of nuclear technology and presumably also of missile technology, which requires a sophisticated electronics industry. But the advocates of electronics were opposed by those who saw the effects that such an emphasis might have on industrial integration and the linkage between local technology and urban industry. By 1973, the advocates of 'steel first' seemed to have won.[88] It is interesting to note, therefore, that although many radical policies were modified in the years 1970–3, the Chinese leadership still remained sensitive to the general policy goals of the Great Leap concerning economic integration.

The 'electronics versus steel' debate raises all sorts of questions about just what the orientation of Lin Biao might have been. It does show, however, that there were limits to the general retreat from the Cultural Revolution on the industrial front. Though greatly attenuated, the principles of the Anshan constitution were not discarded and it is possible to argue that the retreat of 1970–3 could have been but a period of consolidation whilst the basis for new radical policies was laid. In the light of accusations made in recent years (1978–9), it would seem that various leading members of the Chinese Communist Party took very different positions on this question. Some, in 1973, were ready to push ahead with a new radical campaign whilst others were delighted that the atmosphere of the Cultural Revolution had been dispelled. It was surely this latter group which interpreted the model Daqing oilfield not as an example of the Great Leap spirit but as a model for the orderly development of production. The success of Daqing, it was said, was due to policies summed up in the slogan 'three honest and four strict'. It was run by honest people, whose words and deeds were honest. However, it imposed strict demands, had a strict organisation and required strict behaviour and strict discipline.[89] Like the Dazhai model in the countryside, the Daqing model in industry had been recast to meet the needs of the new 'rational' order.

The Continued Legacy of the Great Leap Forward in Agricultural-industrial Integration

The reinterpretation of the Daqing model in the early 1970s as a model of productivity did not, however, alter the relevance of the model for agricultural-industrial integration. At Daqing, an attempt was made to build an oil-city complex which was integrated with the total environment.[90] In the oilfield, a cellular settlement structure was created with central points consisting of some 300–400 households, linked to small nodes of 100–200 households. Located at each central point and node were essential services and shops as well as agricultural technical stations, and the gaps between the central points and nodes consisted of farmland. At Daqing, in accordance with the May Seventh Directive, oil-workers were expected not only to engage in industrial pursuits, not only to help run neighbourhood services and schools, but also to work part of the time as peasants. By 1970, it was claimed that Daqing produced a certain amount of grain and was partly self-sufficient in meat and vegetables.[91] Discarded metals were processed into farm tools and household implements, and a plant had been set up to process refinery waste into phosphate fertiliser.[92] What persisted at Daqing, in the much less radical climate of the early 1970s, were many features of the old urban commune of the late 1950s. It was probably these, rather than the stress on 'strictness', which Mao Zedong had in mind when he called for the extension of the Daqing model even to large iron and steel complexes such as Wuhan.[93]

The continuance of the 'flying leap' policy of agricultural-industrial integration, as exemplified at Daqing, was also evident in the policy of rural industrialisation. There is no evidence that efforts to promote such a policy slackened in the early 1970s. On the contrary, plans were made further to develop rural industries within provincially integrated units. Great stress was given to the establishment of labour-intensive industries, managed at *xian* level and below, and care was taken in the vertical transfer of technology between province and unit of production.[94] Although decisions were taken to import huge nitrogenous fertiliser plants from overseas, rural fertiliser production continued and new developments were undertaken to produce phosphates within the communes. Equally impressive was the development of local cement plants—so necessary in a country where transportation facilities were not well developed. Local iron and steel production also showed significant development. In 1971, for example, 20 per cent of China's output of 20 million tonnes of pig iron was produced in local furnaces.[95] Though the quality was not up to the standard of the major iron and steel works, it was (unlike that produced in 1958) quite usable.

The above developments in the economy during the early 1970s suggest that the policy reversals, undertaken in 1970, were only partial and that attempts were still being made to preserve part of the Great Leap tradition. What continued to be preserved were policies of agricultural-industrial integration which, in the long run, were probably more important than the moderate extension of private economic activity in agriculture or the stress on greater discipline on the shop floor. People of a more radical persuasion might have had cause for disquiet concerning matters of micro-economic policy, yet this was not a field in which radical voices in the central leadership were very prominent. Zhang Chunqiao, for example, had yet to appear as an exponent of economic policy and Jiang Qing and Yao Wenyuan were mainly concerned with cultural and educational matters.

The Question of Art and Literature

The Cultural Revolution, it will be recalled, had started in the field of art and literature and yet, unlike the Great Leap Forward, the late 1960s were not characterised by much artistic vitality. Throughout the Cultural Revolution and the subsequent 'flying leap', the debate in art and literature focused on the reform of Beijing opera, in which Jiang Qing played a major role. Because of the highly charged political atmosphere of that time, instead of increasing the number of new Beijing operas, the same 'model' pieces were revised over and over again, reflecting more and more militancy in the search for 'correctness'.[96] As the tension became defused by 1972, however, the uncompromising militancy of the early model operas gave way to shades of grey [97] and they began to resemble more those of 1965. At the same time, the literary and art world began to think once again about how to revive classical opera without evoking the criticism of the 1960s.

The problem, in formulating an official policy towards literature and art, lay in the vagueness with which Mao's guidelines had been set. Back in 1942, Mao had affirmed that two sets of criteria should be applied to any work of art—the artistic and the political.[98] Yet one was never sure how one separated them. Thus, in the late 1960s, only the political criteria were taken seriously.[99] The statement that 'all art was propaganda' was probably uncontentious but, unless one attempted to flesh out just what the purely artistic criteria might be, there was a danger that some zealots might treat all propaganda as art. Problems occurred also in how one evaluated China's long artistic tradition. According to Mao, 'the old [must] serve the new' (gu wei jin yong),[100] but no one was quite certain how to give effect to such a slogan. Where the slogan could easily be operationalised was in the field of archaeology and, during the latter stage of the Cultural Revolution and the 'flying leap', archaeological research made unprecedented progress. It was, after all, easy to legitimise archaeological work by claiming that it depicted the creative role of labour and changes in class structure over the millennia.[101] In the creative arts, however, the problem was much more difficult and quite different principles of legitimation had to be sought.

After 1972, when publishing activity was stepped up once again, a number of classical novels reappeared such as the Water Margin (Shuihuzhuan) which could be legitimised by pointing out that they depicted peasant resistance against 'feudal' authority. But how was one to legitimise the importation of Western works of art? As Jiang Qing saw it, this could be done by reference to superior technique.[102] It was on these grounds that invitations were extended to Western orchestras to tour China, but such considerations were unable to prevent denunciation of works such as Beethoven's Pastoral Symphony for not reflecting class struggle. It is difficult to determine, however, just who originated such criticism. Could it have been Jiang Qing? After all, it was claimed that Jiang Qing had been responsible for extending the invitations in the first place. She had also recommended ten Western novels as required reading for workers in the field of art and literature. These included such curious items as *The Count of Monte Cristo* and *Gone With the Wind*[103] which do not suggest a concern with ideological purity. Nevertheless, Jiang Qing has been associated with the rejection of Western art and it is extremely difficult to explain just what her position actually was. Some writers have suggested that Jiang Qing, in the role of a new 'literary tsar', merely used the debate on art and literature to damn her opponents.[104] She was thus willing to countenance the importation of Western works when it suited her and then to condemn them when considerations of political power demanded. Such a conclusion, in my view, ascribes to Jiang Qing much too Machiavellian a disposition. Any reading of the interviews she gave to the American historian Roxane Witke[105] would suggest that Jiang was a very confused person, quite incapable of formulating a coherent policy from her position of quite peculiar isolation. One thing seems certain, however, and that is that Jiang did wield considerable power over artistic policy in the early 1970s and that the results were not very impressive.

My criticism of Jiang Qing, however, should not be taken as a total endorsement of the current (1979) official evaluation of literary policy in the early 1970s. This is a picture of complete artistic sterility across the board. It is true that the development of Beijing opera was rather miserable, that no new novels were forthcoming and intellectual writers had been reluctant to publish anything of worth since the Cultural Revolution. On the other hand, contemporary accounts do speak of considerable developments in mass art and mass theatre. There was, for example, a new flowering of local opera[106] which had always enjoyed popularity, even if eclipsed, in the official literature, by debates about Beijing opera. Such local opera had always been of a mass character and needed no official legitimation. Despite that, the conclusion is inescapable: the official promotion of literary forms was a miserable failure.

The Debate on Education

Though the literary and art worlds, in the 1970s, left much to be desired, the situation in education was much brighter. Throughout the period 1970–3, the various radical reforms in education, introduced after the Cultural Revolution, continued to be implemented.[107] The *minban* principle was stressed, with schools being taken to children rather than vice versa, and teachers' colleges frequently set up (often mobile) branch units to train the many new teachers who were required. Courses were shortened and emphasis continued to be laid on practical subjects and the integration of theoretical knowledge with activity in production. Literature students, for example, were required to compose *dazibao* and write political plays. The criticism of teachers was still encouraged, though with a new emphasis on politeness. Workers and peasants were still invited to help teach and lecture to students and, wherever possible, schools and colleges set up their own production units. Admission policy to universities still favoured mature students or those who had spent one or two years in productive labour. Furthermore, those who had worked for a period of five years or more continued to draw their wages at university. In general, then, the spirit of the 'flying leap' was maintained.

There were, however, a number of problems which did provoke some quite severe criticism. In mid-1970, Beijing and Qinghua Universities took in their first batch of first-year students for some years and, by 1972, most universities were functioning 'normally'. By 1972, the requirement that most entrants into the élite universities should be from worker and poor or lower-middle peasant backgrounds was relaxed somewhat and there was a danger that the pre-Cultural Revolution situation might, at some time in the future, recur. In line with the general criticism of 'ultra leftism', in the wake of the Lin Biao incident, some people decided that the policy of taking students from the communes and returning them to the communes was indeed 'ultra-leftist'.[108] The arguments advanced to support the conservative position were often quite ingenious. For example, it was sometimes suggested that since selection of students had to be based on the recommendation of their workmates, with the approval of the appropriate level of leadership, political criteria had to be treated as uniform. Thus, only academic criteria could be considered and the best way to do this was by reintroducing examinations. The result was that, although institutions which were reluctant to take students from among the workers and peasants were criticised, some forms of examination were reintroduced.[109]

Another major problem in tertiary education concerned the overwhelming emphasis given to practical subjects.[110] This was enshrined in the model nominated by Mao for emulation by all tertiary institutions—the July Twenty-First Workers College of the Shanghai Machine-tools Plant. Adherents to this model tended to believe that most knowledge which was not geared to the task of increasing production was useless. As one might have expected, such a position was objected to by senior academics in the old élite universities, in particular those of Beijing and Qinghua.[111] The most notable protest against the exclusively practical orientation was voiced by the physicist Zhou Peiyuan, the chairman of the revolutionary committee of Beijing University. What was important here was not the eminence of the protester but the fact that Zhou's views were carried in the national daily *Guangming Ribao*,[112] indicating that they enjoyed the support of some powerful leaders of the Party. One of these was probably the Minister of Education, Zhou Rongxin, and another may have been no less a person than Premier Zhou Enlai.[113]

Zhou Peiyuan's protest was published in the autumn of 1972, at a time when many radical policies were being eroded.[114] In universities and schools, the amount of time devoted to manual labour had been cut and a number of college-run factories had been closed down.[115] Textbooks had been revised and pruned of what was felt to be excessive sloganeering.[116] Indeed, within most educational institutions, teaching seemed to be more 'orthodox' than at any time since the turmoil of the late 1960s. Yet for all that, one does not get the impression that a major switch in policy had occurred in the education system as a whole.[117] For example, full-time educational institutions still coexisted with 'part-work, part-study' institutions in the manner of the Great Leap and 'flying leap'. In the absence of any programme for integrating these two types of institution, it was inevitable that the latter should be seen by some as poor cousins of the former. But, at least, the stress was still on broadening the base of education rather than élite specialisation. Indeed, after the Cultural Revolution criticism of 'bureaucratism', there was a reluctance to carry out any plans for standardising institutions and curriculum. Such standardisation as there was confined itself to things like the provision of teaching materials (published often at *xian* or municipal levels), and there was nothing like a return to the situation of 1965 when even *minban* institutions were often rigidly controlled by *xian* or municipal education bureaux. In general, rural communes and street revolutionary committees still had a say in the administration of local schools and local residents continued to sit on school revolutionary committees. These committees still had the power to determine course content and to hire or dismiss teachers (formerly the prerogative of *xian* or municipal education bureaux). Many primary teachers, moreover, continued to be paid on the same work-point basis as ordinary peasants, which was an effective way of making the peasants think about the teacher's relative worth.

The fact that rural primary school teachers (in schools at brigade level) were paid in a different manner to secondary school teachers (in schools at commune level) might be seen as a special case of the disarticulation of rural services and rural industry (according to the three-level system of ownership). It highlights also the recurrent problem of how to fund schools. In the rural areas, the three-level system of ownership made it easy to organise schools, yet the principle of 'self-reliance' often meant that lower-level schools were short of funds. In the urban areas, when 'factories ran schools', it was much easier to generate funds but there were often too many children. Thus, the normal pattern of educational administration was management by neighbourhood revolutionary committees which, like their rural counterparts, were short of cash. To add to the problem, there seemed to be no nationwide guidelines as to the extent to which local government might help schools in financial diffi-culties. Thus, the Cultural Revolution ideal of free education for all children could not always be implemented.

One wonders, however, whether funding was seen as a major problem. By 1972, China's education planners were contemplating the implemen-tation, before long, of a universal five-year programme of primary school education in rural areas and a seven-year programme in urban areas.[118] By 1972, some places had already enrolled 80 – 95 per cent of school-age children in schools.[119] Yet the fact that, by 1979, 6 per cent of school-age children still could not attend school[120] suggests that the plan for universal schooling was a little optimistic. My point is however, that despite the backlash at higher levels of the education system no serious plans had been put forward for retrenchment in education.

Foreign Policy—the Exploitation of Contradictions

The field of education was one in which most of the key elements introduced during and after the Cultural Revolution were retained. In most other areas discussed so far, certain elements were retained and it would be wrong to talk of a total rejection of Cultural Revolution inno-vations in any of them. In foreign policy, however, the 'mountain-top mentality' of the Cultural Revolution, already modified in the 'flying leap', was, in the early 1970s, completely discarded.

The American invasion of Cambodia in March 1970[121] and the suspension of the Sino-American ambassadorial talks[122] which followed, halted temporarily any moves the Chinese might have wished to make in opening channels of communication with the United States through third parties (such as Nikolai Ceaucescu of Rumania).[123] By the time of Edgar Snow's interviews with Mao Zedong and Zhou Enlai in late 1970, however, it appears that the new foreign policy course had been set.[124] In April 1971, a United States table-tennis team visited China[125] and, in July, Henry Kissinger flew secretly to Beijing to prepare for the visit of President Nixon which took place in early 1972.[126] The Shanghai communiqué, following the visit, secured a United States recognition that there was but one China, with Taiwan as a part, and a promise to withdraw United States troops and military installations from Taiwan as tension in the area diminished.[127] In the period which followed, relatively large numbers of Americans visited China and liaison offices were established in Beijing and Washington[128] in preparation for the eventual restoration of diplomatic relations.

There has been some debate as to whether China's desire to forge the new relationship with the United States was simply a response to the 1.2 million Soviet troops stationed along the 11,000-kilometre frontier. Undoubtedly, the threat was very real and improved Sino-American relations did allow China to redeploy troops to the northern frontiers.[129] If, however, China were simply reacting to the Soviet military build-up, one would have expected that the *rapprochement* would have taken place when the build-up occurred. Sino-American relations were established not when Sino-Soviet relations were at their worst (early 1969) but when they were, in fact, improving (late 1970). An alternative view maintains, therefore, that it was not just Soviet strength but also American weakness in Asia which caused China to see the possibility of driving a wedge between the superpowers.[130]

China's second major strategy was aimed at forging some kind of Third World identity. This was facilitated by the loosening of Soviet and American control over a newly formulated 'second intermediate zone' and by China's entry into the United Nations in 1971.[131] In the period 1972–3, China devoted considerable attention to strengthening state-to-state relations with as many countries as possible and backing the position of Third World countries in asserting political and economic independence, such as demands for a 200-nautical-mile extension of territorial waters[132] and various nuclear-free zones.[133] In doing this, China was perhaps too lavish in its praise of reactionary régimes and had begun to play down its support for national liberation movements in various countries. Two instances are usually cited here—Bangladesh and Ceylon (now Sri Lanka). China's support for Pakistan in the Bangladesh War of 1971[134] derived from a fear of being encircled by India's ally, the Soviet Union, and also by a belief that Bangladesh independence, if imposed with Indian bayonets, might create a state which was no more than nominally independent. As for China's support for Mrs Bandaranaike's suppression of the Ceylon rebellion of 1971,[135] explanations both to the effect that China was merely engaging in the game of *realpolitik*[136] and that it was trying to forestall a right-wing coup[137] are both rather unconvincing. With regard to the European Economic Community, which China supported,[138] it is probably true that, in the long run, Europe might constitute a power to offset that of the United States and the Soviet Union. In the meantime, however, the European economy had been penetrated by American-based multinationals and condemned by many of the indigenous left.

After the American *rapprochement* of February 1972, a major target in China's foreign policy was Japan. During the period 1970–2, China was concerned about the possibility of Japanese rearmament[139] and that Japan might step into American shoes following a United States withdrawal from south-east Asia. But in 1972, taking advantage of the Japanese government's desire to establish diplomatic relations, Premier Tanaka was invited to Beijing[140] and the issue of Japanese rearmament disappeared from the Chinese media, though I am sure not from people's minds. Following the breaking of diplomatic relations between Tokyo and Taibei, the Guomindang régime was more isolated than ever and, before long, the old general Fu Zuoyi, who had changed sides during the siege of Beijing in 1949, suggested strongly the possibility of the peaceful reabsorption of Taiwan into China.[141] Such appeals, however, seem to have fallen on deaf ears.

Having entered rapidly into the field of international power politics, it may be argued that China began to see itself as a major power. This the Chinese would have denied categorically. The extent to which China insisted on the 'Five Principles of Peaceful Coexistence', in particular mutual equality between nations, was quite strict. China professed to see a world in which two major powers vied with each other for hegemony and to feel that it could not counter this by adopting a hegemonist policy itself.[142] The aim was to insist on equality and exploit the contradictions between various shades of enemy and friend. In the words of the Chinese themselves:

> The view that all enemies are the same, that they are one monolithic bloc, is not in accord with objective reality. Moreover, with the development of the situation and the people's revolutionary forces daily expanding, the enemies' contradictions will become more and more acute. The proletariat and its party must learn to concretely analyse the situation in class struggle in the international and domestic spheres at different historical periods and be good at seizing the opportunity to *'turn to good account all such fights, rifts and contradictions within the enemy camp and turn them against our present main enemy'.*[143]

Conclusion

The period 1970–2 was one of a general retreat from the ideals of the Cultural Revolution. In foreign policy, the mentality of the Cultural Revolution had already been largely discarded in the preceding 'flying leap'. In agriculture and in industry, the most important policy watershed was the Second Plenum of 1970 though deradicalisation accelerated in the period after the reported death of Lin Biao. In education, the radical impetus seems largely to have been maintained thoughout the period 1970–2 though there was something of a backlash in the tertiary sector where examinations were reintroduced. In the field of literature and art, there was some relief from the sterility of officially sponsored art forms and some development of mass theatre though the general situation remained bleak and quite unlike the Great Leap Forward of 1958.

I have argued in this chapter that it is extremely difficult to document the association between the deradicalisation of policy and the case of Lin Biao. Recent interpretations of the history of that time do not help us at all to sort out that association, since each and every action of Lin's has been branded as 'ultra-leftist'. This is no more helpful than the interpretations made in the period 1973 – 7 which treated all Lin's actions as 'ultra-rightist'. I have suggested, however, some theoretical reasons why the association between these two terms might be made. There is no doubt, however, that the recategorisation of Lin Biao as 'ultra-rightist' in late 1972[144] also had an immediate *political* importance. It was to signify that many people thought that the retreat from the Cultural Revolution had gone too far. Thus, the term 'Lin Biao and his ilk' was to be directed at the architects of the consolidation of 1970 – 2. These were people very different from Lin Biao and included no less a person than Premier Zhou Enlai. This new radicalism will be the subject of the next chapter.

NOTES

1. CCPCC, *zhongfa* (1972)12, 17 March 1972, *Issues and Studies*, Vol. VIII, No. 12, September 1972, pp. 66 – 7; CCPCC, *zhongfa* (1972) 4, 13 January 1972, *Issues and Studies*, Vol. VIII, No. 8, May 1972, p. 78. This was confirmed by reports of unpublished speeches made in 1972. Personal information.

2. Mao Zedong,1960 (or 1961 – 2), *JPRS*,1974, p. 270.

3. The term 'substantive rationality' here is Weber's sense of rationality oriented toward absolute values or to ends given by a particular theory. It is distinguished from formal rationality (simple means-ends relationships). Weber clearly saw socialist rationality in the former sense. See Weber, 1964, pp. 185 – 6.

4. CCPCC, *zhongfa* (1972) 12, 17 March 1972, *Issues and Studies*, Vol. VIII, No. 12, September 1972, p. 67.

5. *PR* 18, 30 April 1969, p. 36.

6. CCPCC, *zhongfa* (1972) 12, 17 March 1972, *Issues and Studies*, Vol. VIII, No. 12, September 1972, p. 71. Mao here refers to a 'super genius' in his twenties. This is clearly a reference to Lin Liguo.

7. Ibid., pp. 66 – 7.

8. Domes,1973, p. 215.

9. *PR* 52, 25 December 1970, pp. 4 and 29.

10. For a list, see Domes,1973, pp. 224 – 5, note 47.

11. Domes (ibid., pp. 215 – 16), I think, grossly overstates the case. Though I am sure that the role of the military was excessive, an impressive list of military affiliations suffers from the classic flaw of all élite studies. It tells one little about actual behaviour.

12. Joffe,1973, pp. 456 – 8.

13. CCPCC, *zhongfa* (1972) 4, 13 January 1972, *Issues and Studies*, Vol. VIII, No. 8, May 1972, p. 78.

14. Ibid., p. 79.

15. Partial text in ibid., pp. 79–83.
16. Ibid., p. 78.
17. Ibid., pp. 80–1.
18. Ibid., p. 82.
19. Apparently the document was seized after Lin's coup failed. It was found on a helicopter arranged by Lin to remove incriminating evidence. Personal information.
20. The most remarkable pamphlet circulated in June 1969 has been translated in *CB* 894, 27 October 1969. This extravagant praise continued into 1971. See Bridgham,1973, p. 437.
21. Bridgham (1973, p. 438) specifies the Guangzhou and Nanjing military regions.
22. CCPCC, *zhongfa* (1972) 12, 17 March 1972, *Issues and Studies*, Vol. VIII, No. 12, September 1972, p. 65. The term used is 'line struggle'.
23. Ibid., p. 69.
24. Ibid., pp. 67–8.
25. Ibid., p. 70.
26. For one account of the assassination attempts, see Burchett,1973. Bridgham's account (1973, pp. 440–1) doubts whether Lin ever attempted to carry out his plan to assassinate Mao. According to unpublished speeches made by Chinese leaders in 1972, several attempts were made to assassinate Mao both before and during a quite horrific train journey from Shanghai to Beijing. Personal information.
27. Zhou Enlai, 24 August 1973, *PR* 35–6, 7 September 1973, p. 18.
28. According to Salisbury (1973, p. 273), there were at least three Soviet versions as to the people on board the crashed Trident aircraft. One said that no one of Lin's age was aboard. Another said that the bodies were too badly burnt to be identified. A third positively identified Lin through dental work done in the Soviet Union.
29. Bridgham,1973, pp. 442–3.
30. See *Issues and Studies*, Vol. XII, No. 3, March 1976, pp. 86–7.
31. These are discussed in a forthcoming PhD dissertation by Dennis Woodward at Flinders University, Adelaide. This section draws much from his work.
32. See e.g. *PR* 7, 13 February 1970, p. 8.
33. For a survey of changes in this plan, see Kuo,1970, pp. 7–9. The 1960 version of the plan is in ibid., pp. 241–62.
34. Ibid., p. 243 and map on p. 68.
35. Figures from Erisman,1975, pp. 328–9.
36. Snow, 27 March 1971, p. 20 (from Zhou Enlai).
37. The first announcement of this was made by Zhou Enlai on the eve of national day 1970. *PR* 41, 9 October 1970, p. 16.
38. E.g. ibid.7, 13 February 1970, pp. 3–9 and 20; CCPCC, *zhongfa* (1971) 82, 26 December 1971, *Issues and Studies*, Vol. IX, No. 2, November 1972, pp. 92–5.
39. *PR* (2, 14 January 1972, p. 7) gives a figure of 246. Other accounts round this figure off to 250.
40. Ibid.1, 5 January 1973, p. 12.
41. RMRB, 23 September 1970, pp. 1 and 4.
42. *Current Scene*, Vol. VIII, No. 11, June 1970, p. 5.
43. *RMRB*, 1 October 1971, *SCMP* 4994, 14 October 1971, pp. 167–74.
44. See Brugger,1980. It is not clear whether this was a phenomenon only of the mid-1970s or also of the early 1970s.
45. The 1970 figure was 14 million tonnes. Snow,27 March 1971, p. 20. *PR* (2, 14 January 1972, p. 7) speaks of a 20 per cent increase, making 17 million tonnes, and (1, 5 January 1973, p. 13) of a 20 per cent increase in 1972, making approximately 20 million tonnes.
46. Stavis,1974, p. 20.
47. *PR* 2, 14 January 1972, p. 8.
48. Some plants had been imported from the USSR in the 1950s. Two plants were

imported from W. Europe and Japan in the 1960s. In the early 1970s, China purchased several more. See Sigurdson,1975, pp. 416–17.

49. Stavis,1974, p. 20.

50. *GMRB*,17 September 1971, *SCMP* 4988, 5 October 1971, p. 19.

51. Statements by Mao to the effect were prominent in the press even before the Second Plenum. See *PR* 7, 13 February 1970, p. 5.

52. Zhao Fengnian, *RMRB*,23 September 1972, *SCMP* 5229, 4 October 1972, p. 94.

53. CCP, Simao District Committee (Yunnan), Document 22, 26 March 1972, *Issues and Studies*, Vol. IX, No. 6, March 1973, p. 96.

54. Article 7 of the draft constitution, discussed at the Second Plenum and adopted on 6 September 1970, specified that the three-level system of ownership should take the team as the basic accounting unit. Text in *Issues and Studies*, Vol. VII, No. 3, December 1970, p. 90.

55. Mao Zedong,1960 (or 1961–2), *JPRS*,1974, p. 267. Mao was talking here about ownership at commune level, though the same principle probably applied to brigades.

56. Minutes of the Yunnan Provincial Conference on Rural Work (draft), 24 December 1970, *Issues and Studies*, Vol. VIII, No. 2, November 1971, p. 107; CCPCC, *zhongfa* (1971) 82, 26 December 1971, *Issues and Studies*, Vol. IX, No. 2, November 1972, p. 95.

57. CCPCC, *zhongfa* (1971) 82, 26 December 1971, *Issues and Studies*, Vol. IX, No. 2, November 1972, p. 93.

58. Nanchang Radio, 30 October 1970 (from *Jiangxi Ribao*), *URS*, Vol. XLI, No. 16, 24 November 1970, pp. 218–20. There are 15 *mu* to the hectare.

59. *RMRB*, 17 June 1970, *SCMP* 4695, 13 July 1970, pp. 8–10.

60. Bastid, 1973, pp. 173–4.

61. Ibid., p. 186.

62. I.e. 'strike counter-revolutionaries, oppose corruption, oppose speculation and oppose extravagance and waste'.

63. See Woodward, 1978, pp. 161–2.

64. *RMRB* (14 July 1972, *SCMP* 5182, 26 July 1972, pp. 87–95) describes the activities of policy investigation teams.

65. CCPCC, *zhongfa* (1971) 82, 26 December 1971, *Issues and Studies*, Vol. IX, No. 2, November 1972, p. 93.

66. This was the acceleration of a campaign dating from 1962. See Orleans,1972. According to Snow, the campaign suffered in the Cultural Revolution due to Red Guard mobility. See Snow,1 May 1971, p. 21.

67. Bastid,1973, p. 181. This problem was noted in CCPCC, *zhongfa* (1971) 82, 26 December 1971, *Issues and Studies*, Vol. IX, No. 2, November 1972, p. 94.

68. CCPCC, *zhongfa* (1971) 82, 26 December 1971, *Issues and Studies*, Vol. IX, No. 2, November 1972, p. 95.

69. This is based on Bernstein,1977(a).

70. The following is based on Watson,1978.

71. Ibid., pp. 183–7.

72. Ibid., p. 194.

73. Beginning April 1973. *PR* 17, 27 April 1973, pp. 13–15.

74. Watson, 1978, p. 188.

75. For criticisms of this and other problems in factory management, see *SWB* FE/4534/B11/17–18, 23 February 1974; *SWB* FE/4538/B11/1–2 28 February 1974; *SWB* FE/4545/B11/2–14. 8 March 1974; *SWB* FE/4554/B11/5–12, 19 March 1974.

76. *Hongqi* 12, 1970, p. 58.

77. *RMRB*, 2 March 1972, *SCMP* 5093, 15 March 1972, pp. 85–91.

78. *RMRB*, 4 February 1972, *SCMP* 5076, 18 February 1972, p. 66.

79. E.g. Beijing Radio, 28 August 1972, *SWB* FE/4080/B11/13, 31 August 1972.

80. *Hongqi* 6–7, 1969, p. 29.

81. J. Robinson, 1972, pp. 2-3, cited in Watson, 1978, p. 196.

82. Howe, 1973(b), p. 251.

83. Watson, 1978, p. 196.

84. CCPCC, *zhongfa* (1972) 4, 13 January 1972, *Issues and Studies*, Vol. VIII, No. 8, May 1972, p. 80.

85. Howe, 1973(b), p. 252.

86. Meisner, 1972, p. 731.

87. See the discussion in Sigurdson,1973, pp. 227-32; Cheng, 1973, pp. 2-3; *GMRB*, 13 December 1971, *SCMP* 5045, 3 January 1972, pp. 1-8; Goodstadt, *FEER* 40, 2 October 1971, pp. 5-7 (on the military link).

88. According to Cheng (1973, p. 2), the advocates of steel gained the upper hand after 1970.

89. Watson, 1978, p. 192.

90. See Broadbent, 1972, pp. 49-51.

91. *PR* 53, 31 December 1971, p. 8.

92. Ibid.

93. *Hsinhua Selected News* 5, 29 January 1973. This is one of a series of five articles on Daqing. The remaining four can be found in ibid., pp. 21-2, and *CB* 979, 2 March 1973, pp. 4-15.

94. Sigurdson, 1973.

95. Ibid., p. 208.

96. To illustrate the importance of these models, some were reprinted in *Hongqi*. See *Hongqi* 5, 1970, pp. 23-46 (English in *SCMM* 681, 22 May 1970, pp. 1-42—*The Red Lantern*); *Hongqi* 2, 1972. pp. 22-48 (English in *SCMM* 723, 28 February 1972, pp. 23-73—*On the Docks*); *Hongqi* 3, 1972, pp. 36-62 (English in *SCMM* 725, 3 April 1972, pp. 37-92—*Ode to Dragon River*). These three operas and the revisions made to them are discussed in Mackerras, 1973, pp. 484-91. He notes that, in the last two operas, the role of the single hero is not so important, which might reflect the contemporary concern about heroes (pp. 490-1). On the hero of *The Red Lantern*, see *SCMM* 681, 22 May 1970, pp. 43-54.

97. Mackerras, 1973, p. 509.

98. Mao Zedong, May 1942, *SW* III, 1965, p. 89.

99. For a good contemporary example of the stress on politics, see Xin Wentong, *RMRB*, 29 May 1970, *SCMP* 4674, 11 June 1970, pp. 73-82.

100. Zhong An, *Hongqi* 5, 1972, *SCMM* 730, 5 June 1972, p. 85.

101. E.g. *PR* 34, 20 August 1971, pp. 8-11; *PR* 32, 11 August 1972, pp. 10-13; *PR* 4, 26 January 1973, pp. 13-16.

102. Chan, 1978, p. 113.

103. *RMRB*, 7 February 1977, p. 2.

104. See Chan, 1978, p. 113.

105. Witke, 1977.

106. Mackerras, 1973, pp. 493-4.

107. The following is based on Gardner and Idema, 1973, and Chan, 1978.

108. *Hongqi* 5, 1975, p. 69.

109. Chan, 1978, p. 116.

110. See the various articles on this point in *Hongqi* 9, 1972, pp. 36-60.

111. Ibid.5, 1974, p. 66.

112. Zhou Peiyuan, *GMRB*, 6 October 1972, pp. 1-2.

113. Chan, 1978, pp. 111 and 115.

114. For a reaction to this erosion, see *GMRB*, 22 January 1974, p. 2.

115. Jinan, Shandong Radio, 5 March 1974, *SWB* FE/4546/B11/4, 9 March 1974.

116. Chan, 1978, p. 113.

117. The following is from Gardner and Idema, 1973.

118. Robinson, 1973, p. 17.

119. Gardner and Idema,1973, p. 263.

120. Chen Muhua, *BR* 46, 16 November 1979, p. 24.

121. On events in Cambodia, see *PR* 13, 27 March 1970, pp. 13 – 28; ibid.14, 3 April 1970, pp. 16 – 33; ibid.15, 10 April 1970, pp. 31 – 5; ibid.16, 17 April 1970, pp. 17 – 27; ibid.17, 24 April 1970, pp.26 – 8; ibid.18, 30 April 1970, pp. 25 – 9; ibid.19, 8 May 1970, pp. 14 – 24; ibid.20, 8 May 1970, pp. 6 – 25; ibid., Special Issue, 23 May 1970, pp. 1 – 24. In particular, see Mao Zedong, 20 May 1970, in Special Issue, pp. 8 – 9.

122. China refused to take part in the next session of the talks scheduled for 20 May. A meeting of liaison personnel took place on 20 June with the promise that talks would resume at an appropriate time.

123. An account of these steps may be found in Nixon, 1972, pp. 327 – 31.

124. Snow, 27 March 1971, pp. 22 – 3.

125. *PR* 16, 16 April 1971, p. 3.

126. Ibid.7 – 8, 25 February 1972, pp. 6 – 9.

127. Ibid.9, 3 March 1972, pp. 4 – 5.

128. On 22 February 1973. See ibid.8, 23 February 1973, p. 4.

129. Lu Yung-shu,1971, pp. 898 – 906—an account of military redeployment.

130. See O'Leary,1978.

131. On the restoration of China's seat, see *PR* 45, 5 November 1971, pp. 6 – 8.

132. Ibid.1, 5 January 1973, pp. 18 – 20.

133. Qiao Guanhua, 24 November 1971, ibid.49, 3 December 1971, p. 15.

134. Ibid.50, 10 December 1971, pp. 6 – 15. For a very jaundiced view from the left, see Addy, 1972. See also the correspondence on his article in *Journal of Contemporary Asia*, Vol. III, No. 3, 1973, pp. 321 – 49. In the polemic, much has been made of a letter from Zhou Enlai to Yahya Khan, reprinted in ibid., Vol. IV, No. 1, 1974, p. 138.

135. See letter from Zhou Enlai to Mrs Bandaranaike, reprinted in *Journal of Contemporary Asia*, Vol. IV, No. 1, 1974, p. 139.

136. Addy, 1972, pp. 410 – 11.

137. Muthiram, 1973, p. 339.

138. For a discussion of China's relations with the EEC, see Wilson, 1973.

139. *SCMP* 4827, 17 January 1971, pp. 101 and 104; ibid.4849, 20 February 1971, pp. 120 – 1; ibid.4868, 30 March 1971, pp. 82 – 3.

140. For an account of the Tanaka-Zhou initiative, see Hsiao,1974. See also *PR* 40, 6 October 1972, pp. 12 – 13.

141. *PR* 10, 9 March 1973, pp. 11 and 21.

142. Significantly, the key slogan for the new year 1973 was 'dig tunnels deep, store grain everywhere and never seek hegemony'; ibid.1, 5 January 1973, p. 10.

143. Ibid.35, 27 August 1971, p. 12. Italics in original—a quotation from Mao Zedong, 27 December 1935, *SW* I, 1965, p. 159.

144. Gao Ge, *Hongqi* 12, 1972, p. 12.

VII
THE 'GANG OF FOUR'
AND DENG XIAOPING[1]
(1973 – 1976)

The recategorisation of Lin Biao as an 'ultra-rightist' in late 1972 heralded a change in the deradicalisation under way since 1970. It signalled a switch in the targets for criticism from those who had resisted the deradicalisation to those who had promoted it. It signified also a much more positive assessment of the achievements of the Cultural Revolution. There was much talk of the 'socialist new things', developed during the late 1960s, which included:

> the creation and popularisation of model revolutionary theatrical works, the enrolment of worker-peasant-soldier students in universities and colleges, settling educated youth in the countryside, participation of cadres in manual labour, the development of co-operative medical services, the emergence of barefoot doctors in the rural areas [and the] shifting of medical workers to the countryside.[2]

There was much talk also, in 1973, of educational reforms and the *xiaxiang* of youth. As the January Revolution of 1967 was assessed once again in positive terms,[3] the newly established labour organisations were urged to pay attention to the struggle against 'economism'.[4]

Though it is by no means clear that Jiang Qing, Zhang Chunqiao, Yao Wenyuan and Wang Hongwen constituted a coherent group in 1973, it does seem likely that these people, later known as the 'Gang of Four', were the main initiators of the new radical spirit. It is also likely that the claim made by the current (1976 – 9) leadership that Premier Zhou Enlai resisted their attempts is correct. Not long after the new radicalism was launched, Zhou was able to secure the rehabilitation of a number of senior leaders of the Party, who had been criticised in the Cultural Revolution, to shore up those members of the central leadership who did not wish for a new round of the Cultural Revolution. In April, Deng

Xiaoping, who had once been branded as 'the number two person in authority taking the capitalist road' re-emerged as vice-premier[5] and he was soon joined (in August) by Tan Zhenlin, the very symbol of the 'February Adverse Current' and Ulanhu, the former head of the Nationalities Commission, who had been accused of fostering narrow nationalism.[6] Such rehabilitations were highly provocative and were to cause much contention amongst the central leadership of the Party.

That there was no agreement on how far the rehabilitations were to go was reflected in the failure to celebrate Party day (1 July) and army day (1 August), when official photographs of the leadership are usually published. By August, however, the press gave every indication of the triumph of radical views. The Great Leap Forward, the people's communes[7] and political consciousness in industry[8] received renewed coverage and, on 18 August (the anniversary of the famous Red Guard rally in 1966), the achievements of the Red Guards were praised once again.[9] Prominence was given to the injunction 'never to forget the class struggle' and people were warned against 'bourgeois representatives' who sought to 'undermine socialism'.[10] Such was the atmosphere in which the Tenth National Congress of the Communist Party was convened.

The Tenth National Congress of the Chinese Communist Party

At first sight, the documents of the Tenth Congress reflected the radical atmosphere in which they were composed. Prominence was given to Mao's statement in 1966 that revolutionary upsurges would occur every seven or eight years[11] (in fact seven years had elapsed). The official account of the Lin Biao incident, moreover, now formally made public, was that it was a continuation of the struggle against 'revisionism'.[12] Much also was made of the fact that the Tenth Congress was a direct sequel of the Ninth Congress[13] (at which the influence of Lin Biao was said to have been removed in time and his report replaced by another one).[14] That congress had, of course, taken place in a more radical political climate. Yet there was a contradiction between the radical policy statements and the cautious measures taken to strengthen the Party leadership and to stabilise the state structure. It was announced, for example, that the National People's Congress would soon be convened.[15] At the same time, rehabilitated ministers received senior Party posts, thus diluting the influence of such people as Jiang Qing, Zhang Chunqiao and Yao Wenyuan.[16] If, in fact, another movement of nationwide proportions was to be launched, why was there a need to stabilise Party structure and predetermine the leadership? If the spirit of the Cultural Revolution was to be reinvoked, why was it that the decline in

the proportion of Central Committee members whose first identification
was with the PLA did not lead to a marked increase in the number of
members who had distinguished themselves as activists in the Cultural
Revolution?[17] One explanation would be that most members of the
central leadership desired not to promote the spirit of the Cultural
Revolution but to head off the moves towards radicalism which had been
so prominent in early 1973.[18] The Tenth Party Congress, like those of
1956, 1958 and 1969, was probably seen by many as an antidote to excessive radicalism and, again like the preceding congresses, was convened in
a hurry. This time there had not even been a preparatory plenum.

Though the congress was said to be a direct continuation of that of
1969, the leadership formula was quite different. No longer did Mao
make any attempt to nominate a 'close comrade in arms and successor'.
This time, a collective leadership was to be formed consisting of 'the old,
the middle-aged and the young'. Organisational conservatism, however,
did prevent young people achieving senior Party posts; but there was one
prominent exception. Wang Hongwen, later considered to be the fourth
member of the 'Gang of Four', was elected vice-chairman of the Party in
his thirties.[19] Wang had worked in the Shanghai No. 17 Cotton Mill and
had risen to a position of power in that city's Workers Revolutionary
Rebel Headquarters. In 1969, Wang was said to have been responsible
for ensuring that the No. 17 Cotton Mill was the first factory in Shanghai
to form a new Party committee after the Ninth Party Congress.[20] In the
aftermath of the Lin Biao incident, it will be remembered, Wang had
been summoned to Beijing and, together with Hua Guofeng, was
probably seen as a man destined for great things. But unlike Hua, whose
talents seem to have been organisational, Wang was promoted as a
symbol of 'correct' ideological commitment. He was thus invited to give
the address introducing the new Party constitution.[21]

Wang's address on the new constitution was in marked contrast to that
of Premier Zhou Enlai who reported on the work of the government.[22] Of
course, one would not expect such speeches to be the same in that the
former, of necessity, focused on matters of ideology whilst the latter was
more concerned with the more mundane tasks of government. Yet the
tone was so different that one might believe recent (1976–9) claims that
the two men represented very different interpretations of what ought to
happen in Chinese society. In short, Wang appeared to wish for a
continuation of the radical measures, initiated in early 1973, whilst Zhou
was more cautious. Though the proceedings of the Tenth Congress
might have represented a compromise, the stage was set for a new
confrontation.

The Campaign to Criticise Lin Biao and Confucius

The confrontation between senior members of the Chinese Communist Party was to take place in a movement, which was launched immediately after the Tenth Congress, to criticise Lin Biao and Confucius. The issue of Confucius had been hotly debated in the new radical climate in the summer of 1973[23] and, indeed, the latest round of academic reinterpretation of history may be traced back to mid-1972. At that time, Mao's old literary associate, Guo Moruo, had turned once again to the problem of how to periodise the history of the first millennium BC.[24] At various times in the past, Guo had placed the critical date of transition from slave to feudal society at around 770 BC, 206 BC and 475 BC. By 1952, however, he had settled on the last of these three dates and this he reiterated in 1972. In December 1972, a professor at Zhongshan University in Guangzhou, Yang Rongguo, continuing the debate,[25] adopted a broader period of transition and focused on the issue of Confucius who lived in this transitional period. As Yang saw it, Confucius attempted to block progress towards the more advanced feudal society, based on private ownership of land, and adopted a conservative position regarding the various slave revolts which took place at that time. In making this point, it was clear that Yang was not just embarking upon an academic exercise. After all, much had been made of the theme that slaves were the creators of history[26] rather than (Lin Biao's) 'heroes'. It will also be remembered that the last time the issue of Confucius was debated openly in the press (the early 1960s), it concealed a bitter debate about how to interpret contemporary Chinese politics. Just as the Confucius debate of the early 1960s turned on the evaluation of the Great Leap Forward, so the debate of 1973 turned on the evaluation of the Cultural Revolution. The central issue, therefore, was the extent to which Confucian ideas might promote retrogression to the pre-Cultural Revolution situation.[27]

The association between the criticism of Confucius and the case of Lin Biao was not made explicit until the denunciation of Lin Biao became an open and public issue after the Tenth Congress.[28] At that point, the parallel with the early 1960s was even more striking and the anti-Confucius campaign came to bear a remarkable resemblance to the Socialist Education Movement. Both of these movements were alike not only in their general orientation but in the confusion which marked their progress.[29] The Socialist Education Movement of 1963–6 sought to oppose corruption and the degeneration of cadres. It focused on the reversion to old ways of thought. Similarly, the anti-Confucius campaign of 1973–4 attacked the Confucian values of reverence for the past, 'filial piety', 'righteousness' (transcending classes), particularistic loyalty and ritualism.[30] In both movements, there was probably general agreement on these goals and in both movements there was profound disagreement on how to achieve them.

At the radical pole were those who were determined to preserve at all costs the 'socialist new things' of the Cultural Revolution and to prepare the ground for a new upsurge in the process of 'continuous revolution'. The history of recent years had seemed to show that such preparation had to be in the field of culture. Such was the repeated theme of Jiang Qing which might be traced back to the 'superstructural push' interpretation of Mao's position in the early 1960s. There was nothing inherently 'ultra-leftist' in such a position, however one might define that term, though it does seem that it was implemented in such a way that there was often a concentration on the behaviour of particular persons rather than the line they were said to represent. Indeed, current (1976–9) interpretations seem to be correct in claiming that the proponents of the movement of 1973 were bent on discrediting Premier Zhou Enlai, his protégé Deng Xiaoping, and many other recently rehabilitated cadres. Frequently, when the radical critics spoke of 'Lin Biao and his ilk', they meant Zhou Enlai,[31] who was cast as the 'Duke of Zhou' (*Zhou gong*)—a paragon of Confucian virtues who symbolised Confucius's golden age of minority cultural excellence amid general slavery. Zhou, it will be recalled, had been identified as the representative of a 'red bourgeoisie' in Hunan in late 1967, when he had been ably defended by Hua Guofeng. The alleged perpetrators of the criticism in 1973, however, included Jiang Qing and Yao Wenyuan who had been very active in denouncing the *Shengwulian* at that time. Perhaps one might explain their behaviour as sheer opportunism, but it does seem that there was a crucial difference between the utopian rejection of all authority, which had characterised the Hunan rebels, and the behaviour of Jiang and Yao who now enjoyed very high rank in the reconstructed Party. There is no evidence, to my knowledge, that Jiang, Yao or for that matter Zhang Chunqiao or Wang Hongwen rejected the need for a strong centralised Party after the events in Shanghai in January 1967.

At the opposite pole to Jiang, Zhang, Yao and Wang were those who were concerned that radicalism might harm the economy. When they criticised Lin Biao, they meant precisely what they said—idealism was potentially very dangerous. Those who realised that the movement had been interpreted by some as a weapon with which to attack Zhou Enlai, probably attempted to select those aspects of anti-Confucian thought which supported Zhou's leadership. Indeed, one writer has suggested that what started as an attack on Zhou's policies finished up as an attack on his opponents.[32]

There is, therefore, a great problem in identifying the positions taken by various contributors to the debate. We know in general terms that people who wrote under pseudonyms such as Luo Siding (a Shanghai group) and Liang Xiao (named after the two tertiary institutions, Beijing and Qinghua Universities) were said to have adhered closely to the radical position. It is not always easy, however, to be precise about that orientation nor the orientation of other contributors to the debate. To illustrate this problem, I shall describe one salient feature of the polemics and suggest divergent interpretations. Much of the discussion in 1973 – 4 focused on the Qin dynasty, which in the third century BC unified China and from which our term 'China' is derived. The First Emperor of Qin had long been denounced as a tyrant by Chinese scholars, and the Lin Biao group had likened him to Mao Zedong.[33] The conventional wisdom had it that the Qin Emperor maintained his harsh rule by supporting a 'legalist' code of punishment and had ruthlessly put down an attempt at rebellion by his frustrated first minister Lü Buwei who sought to restore feudal states and the Confucian virtues. A later first minister, Li Si, persuaded the First Emperor to burn the Confucian books and bury Confucian scholars alive and such harsh action eventually occasioned the downfall of the empire.

A new interpretation maintained that 'legalism' was older than Confucianism and Confucius himself had brought about the murder of Shao Zhengmao, his contemporary 'legalist' opponent. 'Legalism' was held to be an ideology appropriate to the 'progressive' feudal system as opposed to the old slave system to which the Confucians wished to return.[34] The First Emperor of Qin, therefore, who lived three centuries after Confucius, was a progressive monarch who aimed at consolidating the feudal system and eradicating old ideas. Thus, Lü Buwei was a reactionary conspirator who organised a faction with the aid of forces outside Qin and launched an abortive coup.[35] The First Emperor's endorsement of Li Si's advice to burn the books and bury the scholars was indeed the appropriate response to conspiracy and his aim was merely to eradicate sedition and not creative thought. The Emperor was not opposed to literature; he loved it.[36] Li Si's advocacy of 'legalism' was a plea for the rule of law and the promotion of modernisation and economic development. Finally, the Qin Empire was brought to an end by the conspiracy of another Confucian, Zhao Gao, who thereby negated many of the progressive measures undertaken in the short dynasty.[37]

There can be no doubt that Lü Buwei was an analogue of Lin Biao and the First Emperor of Qin was Mao but one may interpret the other characters in vastly different ways. If Li Si's most notable contribution was his policy towards recalcitrants, then he could be taken as the analogue of someone who supported a harsh interpretation of the exercise of the dictatorship of the proletariat—perhaps Zhang Chunqiao or Yao Wenyuan. If, however, his most notable contribution was, in fact, technical modernisation, the promotion of centralisation and the abolition of independent military power, then he was Zhou Enlai or perhaps his putative successor Deng Xiaoping. These men were just as eager to get rid of conspirators, only they had a very different view as to who they were. Occasionally, Li Si was portrayed as a grey vacillating character[38] which might support either interpretation. The same confusion attends the identification of Zhao Gao, who flattered the First Emperor whilst he was alive and plotted for the overthrow of his system once he was dead, in the same manner as Lü Buwei.[39] One wonders who was being likened to Lin Biao. Was it Zhou Enlai or one of the 'Gang of Four'?

The above should not be taken just as another exercise in Pekingology. The policy implications of the Qin dynasty (and many other) analogues were of crucial importance. It is surely the case that most people fell somewhere between the two extreme groups outlined above, but sufficient argument has been presented to show that the support for the anti-Confucius campaign might come from very different sources with very different consequences—and this was precisely what had happened in the Socialist Education Movement a decade before. Just as various Party officials managed to divert the focus of criticism away from its original targets in the early 1960s, so those who were worried about the effects on the economy, in 1973–4, attempted to keep the movement of that time focused on Lin Biao's 'idealism' and to prevent the target shifting to the new 'Duke of Zhou'. By March 1974, they had succeeded and the intense poster campaign of the previous month receded. It was probably with confidence that Deng Xiaoping, as Zhou's choice for the next premier, could attend in April the United Nations General Assembly conference on raw materials and development.[40] From the time Zhou Enlai entered hospital in May 1974 to his death in 1976, Deng remained as unofficial acting premier, symbolising a policy in which politics should not be interpreted in such a way that the economy was harmed.

The movement to criticise Lin Biao and Confucius continued into the autumn of 1974 and did sometimes give rise to renewed fears about the effect on production.[41] It was clear, however, that it was not going to develop into a new round of the Cultural Revolution. As the movement went on, the journal and newspaper articles became more and more obscure to the point that, I am sure, the masses did not understand them. It had been feared that the Cultural Revolution in early 1966 might degenerate into an academic discussion of how to interpret history; the anti-Confucius movement did just that.

This is not to say, however, that the anti-Confucius movement had no impact. It may be that, amid the verbiage, there was some very sound historiography. But that cannot be the main point. It would be an academic conceit to claim that the result of months of poster campaigns and mass criticism was just a partial improvement in historiography. Undoubtedly, a movement which took as a main target the continuing influence of a gerontocratic, male-dominated Confucian ideology would have an impact on the field of social relations. It is not surprising then that, in a manner much more profound than the Cultural Revolution, issues such as the subordination of women[42] (a favourite theme of Jiang Qing) and the dangers of particularistic loyalties were examined in depth. Equally significant was the spur which the movement gave to the 'revolution in education'.

The 'Revolution in Education'

The debate on education, which intensified in the radical climate of 1973, focused on a refutation of the kind of position argued by people like Zhou Peiyuan in the autumn of 1972. Indeed, Zhou was to be subjected to attacks by student poster-writers.[43] It was felt by many that the retreat from the political criteria which had dominated educational policy since the Cultural Revolution had gone too far and that, if a new round of the Cultural Revolution was to begin, the orientation of students and teachers was crucial. Once again, therefore, in a manner similar to 1966, a furious polemic unfolded on the question of entrance examinations.

The new round in the polemic was opened by one Zhang Tiesheng, a rusticated youth in Liaoning province.[44] Zhang had apparently become the leader of a production team and the demanding duties of that post prevented him devoting adequate time to preparation for his college entrance exam. Instead of completing his exam in the natural sciences, therefore, he wrote a letter to the examiners protesting about the dominance of academic authorities who discriminated against hard-working people such as himself. Of course, Zhang maintained, he could have devoted a couple of days to preparing for the exam but that would have resulted in him neglecting his political duty to engage in production. Was that the kind of behaviour college authorities wanted to encourage? Contemporary accounts of Zhang's action portray it as a revolutionary gesture whilst post-1976 accounts claim that Zhang was part of a conspiracy headed by those people soon to be known as the 'Gang of Four'.[45] The latter explanation seems the more likely. Educational policy in the north-east, at that time, was said to have been greatly influenced by Mao's nephew, Mao Yuanxin, who had very close relations with Jiang Qing and her associates. It could only have been someone of very great influence who was able to get Zhang's 'examination answer' published in the Liaoning Party newspaper *Liaoning Ribao* and then republished in the Central Committee newspaper *Renmin Ribao*. Moreover, if the protagonists of radical reform were basing their actions on 1966, they would surely remember that, at that time, Mao's support to the protesters at Beijing University had been a major factor in getting the Cultural Revolution launched. It is significant, therefore, that, after August 1973, Zhang became something of a cult figure and the north-east (Liaoning and Jilin) became the centre of radical innovation in education.

To my mind, however, it does not matter much whether Zhang's actions were or were not part of a conspiracy to wrest power away from the educational authorities in Beijing. What is important is the issue which it raised. How far should political standards be employed in selecting college students and who should judge those standards? The post-Cultural Revolution formula, it will be remembered, was 'recommendation by the masses and approval by the local leadership'. In many cases, the masses were just too busy or too unfamiliar with what college education entailed to concern themselves much with university enrolment.[46] Thus, the local Party leadership became more and more important in assessing students and this led to charges of nepotism. A major theme of the anti-Confucius campaign, therefore, became the nepotistic behaviour of Party officials in college enrolment,[47] and large numbers of students who had got in 'by the back door' were persuaded to withdraw from college.[48]

If examinations were now to be played down and if nepotism was to be combated, there had to be some mechanism in the education structure which could check on the behaviour of local Party officials. In the immediate post-Cultural Revolution period, this task had been performed by the Mao Zedong Thought propaganda teams but, since 1971, these bodies had become somewhat ineffective.[49] Moves were made in early 1974, therefore, to revamp these teams and establish new ones,[50] not only to supervise enrolment but also to promote once again the spirit of 'open door' education which had figured so prominently in the 'flying leap'. The results were to be quite impressive and the 'revolution in education' was to survive the demise of the anti-Confucius movement in 1974.

The idea of 'open door' education was based upon the old Great Leap Forward idea of combining the formal and informal in a creative as opposed to a selective approach to education. In fostering the informal aspect, there was a tremendous reservoir of talent in the countryside among the rusticated youth whose treatment up to 1973 had fallen far short of the original political aims of the rustication policy. Now, certain remedial measures were taken to improve the conditions under which such youth were settled.[51] It seems, however, that the potential which those youth had for improving rural education was insufficiently tapped. One suspects that local hostility continued and that was why some of these remedial measures could be described by the post-1976 leadership as the 'Gang's' attempt to place its agents in positions of power in the rural areas.[52] There was, however, much more to the anti-Confucius campaign than that.

The Li Yizhe Dazibao

Despite the moderate successes of the anti-Confucius campaign in the fields of social relations and education, it was quite apparent, by late 1974, that the 'superstructural push' scenario had failed to materialise and not many significant changes had occurred in the economy. Though the criticism of Confucius and Confucian values continued into 1976, it is fair to say that the movement was concluded in November 1974. At that time, its achievements were officially summed up[53] and a renewed stress on unity was in evidence.

Unity was, of course, a prerequisite for the convocation of the National People's Congress which had not met for a decade. The Tenth Party Congress in August 1973 had announced the impending convocation of that body and various groups were eager to see what legal provisions it would enact. One such group of three young men, Li Zhengtian, Chen Yiyang and Huang Xizhe, prepared in September 1973 a *dazibao* dedicated to that congress and urging the enactment of a socialist legal system.[54] The turbulence of the anti-Confucius campaign, however, delayed its publication and it was not until November 1974, when at long last it looked as though the congress would be convened, that their hundred-metre-long publication was put up in the city of Guangzhou. The *dazibao*, written under the pseudonym Li Yizhe and entitled 'Concerning Socialist Democracy and the Legal System', was an ambiguous document capable of many different interpretations.[55] One cannot but feel, however, that, by combining some of what was felt to be the 'ultra-leftism' of the Cultural Revolution with elements of liberal democracy, it constituted a challenge to the vanguard role of the Communist Party.

The essential argument of the *dazibao* was that the Lin Biao system was still alive and well. The promotion of legalism, therefore, ought not to result in the continuation of a 'social fascist autocracy' but in the rule of law based on democracy. Though a nod was made to the 'dictatorship of the proletariat', it was felt that such dictatorship ought not to remain unconstrained (*wu fa wu tian*). That which was Confucian about Lin Biao and that which still persisted was rule by means of the 'rites' (correct manifestations of outward behaviour) rather than the law. Lin and other members of the new privileged 'bourgeois' class owed their legitimacy to their claim to be able to interpret the 'rites'.

The implications of the Li Yizhe group's position for the Party's vanguard role were quite profound. After all, it might be inferred that it was not just the Lin Biao group which manipulated the 'rites' but the Communist Party itself. Like Djilas[56] (who sees the Party leadership as a new ruling class) and Konrád and Szelényi[57] (who describe the growth of a new class of intellectual 'teleological redistributors'), the Li Yizhe group believed that the generation of 'new bourgeois elements' was systemic rather than merely behavioural. Thus the Party, it was implied, must inevitably become corrupt and seek privileges for its members. As manipulators of the 'rites', the Party leaders could engage in the old Confucian practice of 'rectifying names' (labelling as 'class enemies' people who challenged their position) and could legitimise any change of policy they liked without reference to any basic rights. Once it was acknowledged, however, that class enemies did exist within the Party, there could be nothing but the ritual submission to the 'genius' leader and loyalty to that 'genius' became the only test of whether one was 'taking the socialist or the capitalist road'. The only way out of such a situation was for the leadership to become more accountable to the masses. The Cultural Revolution had sometimes achieved this but that movement had also suffered from the 'Confucian' concentration on ritual loyalty. There was no recourse but to the restoration and development of a socialist legal system.

The Li Yizhe *dazibao* was dedicated to Chairman Mao and, in its argument, one does see elements of Mao's position of the early 1960s. Mao also had felt that the generation of 'new bourgeois elements' was systemic rather than merely behavioural. Yet, Mao had seen the generation of such elements as stemming from the structure of the economy rather than in the control by particular groups over the manipulation of the 'rites'. It was on these grounds that he was able to justify the leadership of the Party and the relatively unconstrained 'dictatorship of the proletariat'. It was perhaps because he had felt that his diagnosis could lead to the kind of conclusions reached by Li Yizhe that Mao had been reluctant to develop his ideas. For all its protestations of loyalty to Chairman Mao and the Party, the Li Yizhe group had posed a fundamental challenge to Party leadership and the response of that leadership was predictable. Indeed, the group itself seemed to have little doubt about what its fate would be:

> We also are trying to find out what will happen when we have violated the 'prohibition' of the newspapers and offended the 'taboo' of the journals. It might also be called an act of testing the 'rites' in one's own person.[58]

The result of that test was the arrest of at least one of the authors, the publication of a more orthodox *dazibao* in rebuttal and an official declaration by Vice-Premier Li Xiannian that the original *dazibao* was 'reactionary through and through, vicious and malicious in the extreme'.[59]

The Campaign to Study the Theory of the Dictatorship of the Proletariat

As has been noted, the Li Yizhe *dazibao* was published just prior to the convocation of the long-awaited Fourth National People's Congress. The winding down of the anti-Confucius campaign had seemed to signify that a new unity had been achieved in the central leadership and that the proponents of 'continuous revolution' had given up their attempt to promote a new round of the Cultural Revolution. The spirit of compromise in the congress, which met in January 1975, was reflected in the prominence of both Deng Xiaoping and Zhang Chunqiao, both of whom soon received senior posts in the PLA (chief-of-staff and head of the PLA general political department respectively). That spirit of compromise also permeated the major speeches to the congress by Zhou Enlai[60] and Zhang Chunqiao.[61] While stressing the importance of making China into a modern socialist state by the year 2000, Zhou also made mention of 'class struggle'. For his part, Zhang, whilst stressing the theme of 'continuous revolution', also laid stress on the rights and guarantees in the constitution which he introduced.[62] But such rights and guarantees, one would suspect, would not have satisfied the group known as Li Yizhe.

The spirit of compromise of January 1975 was to be short-lived. Within three weeks of the end of the Fourth National People's Congress, a movement was launched which was to be much more divisive than the anti-Confucius campaign. The case of Li Yizhe had shown that there was a pressing need to legitimise the 'dictatorship of the proletariat' and to make it relevant to China's current situation. The new campaign to study the theory of the dictatorship of the proletariat, therefore, was offered as an antidote to the historical obscurantism generated in 1974 and the heterodox views put forward by people such as the Li Yizhe group. Though that group was strongly condemned, it was probably the case that most of the Party leadership saw some truth in the charge that the 'rites' had been manipulated and realised that one had to offer a replacement for the use of a book of quotations from Chairman Mao as the sole source of theory. Yet to return to the works of Marx and Engels was to court trouble. Various Party leaders had learned how to render ineffective attacks by historical analogy but questions of political economy had a much more obvious and immediate relevance.

Almost as if to rebut the charge that the generation of new class cleavages resulted from a monopoly over the manipulation of 'rites', people such as Zhang Chunqiao and Yao Wenyuan now began to make pronouncements on the economic conditions for the generation of class struggle. In doing so, they began to develop the position explored by Mao in the early 1960s. Though not as heterodox (from a Leninist point of view) as the *dazibao* of Li Yizhe, the official position developed in 1975 was, none the less, quite heterodox. One wonders, therefore, the extent to which Zhang and Yao enjoyed the support of the aged chairman. Mao, it was later claimed, warned the 'Gang of Four' about its conspiratorial activities in July 1974.[63] Could it have been a response to Mao's warning that some members of the 'Gang' now moved from an area where they had a firm power base (cultural affairs) to one where they did not (political economy)? On the other hand, might the actions of Zhang and Yao be explained solely by the need for an explicitly Marxist legitimisation of 'continuous revolution' rather than the peculiarly Chinese historical analogies? Is it possible, moreover, that Zhang Chunqiao and Yao Wenyuan would have had the temerity to develop the chairman's ideas without Mao's active support?

As I see it, it is inconceivable that Mao did not give Zhang and Yao his blessing. Surely, Mao's failure to attend the Fourth National People's Congress was more than a preference for the delights of Hangzhou. He was, it seems, quite well at the time and had a conversation with Franz Josef Strauss.[64] A more likely explanation of Mao's failure to attend was that he was distancing himself from the modernisation call of Zhou Enlai, not perhaps because he disagreed with it but because he was determined that its implementation should be along lines he had charted in the early 1960s but did not have the courage to make explicit. In 1975, Zhang and Yao were to do the explication for him but we shall probably never know whether Mao agreed with their interpretation.

The detailed exposition of Zhang and Yao's position may be teased out of a political economy textbook published under Zhang's supervision in Shanghai in 1975.[65] It is a confusing book which consists of a mixture of Stalinist orthodoxy and Mao's contrary ideas of the early 1960s. Doubtless, the book was the result of a composite authorship. A clearer and more simple exposition of the new position may be found in two articles written by Yao Wenyuan[66] and Zhang Chunqiao[67] in March and April 1975 and published in *Hongqi*. Like the Li Yizhe group, Yao and Zhang turned to the systemic generation of classes in socialist society but, this time, tied their exposition to the need for the continuance of the 'dictatorship of the proletariat'. As they saw it, the most important thing to be studied in the current campaign was Marx's description, in the 'Critique of the Gotha Programme', of inequalities arising from the fact that workers in a socialist (lower-stage communist) society were paid according to the time they spent at work.[68] Since workers were not equally endowed, those with greater productive capacity got a greater income. This was legitimised by the principle 'from each according to his/her ability, to each according to his/her work'. Such a principle was a special case of the 'bourgeois' principle ('bourgeois right') where equal rights were given to people who had been made unequal because of their economic location. Those who received more of the social product because of their greater productive capacity were in a better position to improve their productive capacity further and so get more. Thus, unless restricted by the 'dictatorship of the proletariat', this 'bourgeois right' would affect all the relations of production. This was perhaps the point Mao had been groping for in his earlier criticism of the 1950s Soviet political economy textbook. The implication was that patterns of distribution were just as much an aspect of the relations of production as were patterns of ownership. Though the latter might be determinate in some ultimate sense, in everyday life their relationship was reciprocal. Unless restricted, stratification based on income might lead to class division defined in classical Marxist terms. This was what had happened in the Soviet Union and was happening in China. But it was not only distribution and ownership which existed in a reciprocal relationship. There was, it will be remembered, a third aspect of the relations of production, outlined by Mao in the early 1960s, and that consisted of the relationship between people at work. Again, the implication was clear. Unless that relationship was continually equalised, there was the basis for the generation of new classes.

Deng Xiaoping's Counter-attack

To get to the above position, it seems necessary implicitly to reject Stalin and most of the orthodox post-Stalin Marxist-Leninist positions. In exploring these ideas in the early 1960s, Mao must have realised what he was doing and pulled back before he had made an explicit open commitment. Zhang Chunqiao and Yao Wenyuan, for all their ritual obeisance to Stalin, had fewer reservations. They were soon to incur the ire of the orthodox Party leadership and Deng Xiaoping was on firm textual ground when he counter-attacked.

Deng was, of course, concerned with much more than Marxist-Leninist orthodoxy when he took Yao and Zhang to task. After all, Yao and Zhang's articles had been published at a time when strikes (guaranteed, for the first time, under the new 1975 constitution) had taken place at Hangzhou. Deng feared, therefore, that the articles might exacerbate the quite considerable industrial disruption. There is much debate about what exactly the cause of the Hangzhou strikes might have been. Current (1976–9) interpretations lay the blame on the machinations of the 'Gang of Four',[69] although some commentators have seen them as a protest at the erosion of the Cultural Revolution norms concerning participation.[70] Whatever their cause, it is rumoured that they were settled by Deng Xiaoping who, thereafter, felt compelled to issue a set of documents designed to prevent further industrial chaos.[71]

At the core of Deng's counter-attack was a stress on those aspects of

Zhou Enlai's January 1975 report concerning unity and the maintenance of production. He insisted that Mao's 'three directives' (on studying the theory of the dictatorship of the proletariat, on promoting unity and on furthering the national economy) should equally constitute the 'key link' (basic programme) for the next 25 years.[72] Here he took a line diametrically opposed to that of the 'Gang of Four' who argued that the stress on unity and maintaining production should be subordinated to class struggle. Impatient with those who sought to bring about turmoil under the rubric of restricting 'bourgeois right', Deng branded his critics 'metaphysicians':

> They emphasise only politics, not economics, only revolution, not production. Upon hearing others talking about grasping production well and pushing economic construction forward, they simply label them practitioners of the 'theory of productive forces' and thus 'revisionists'.[73]

Deng saw his opponents as sham Marxists, for the acid test for deciding whether a policy was correct or not was whether it 'liberated the productive forces'.[74] This was the essence of what the 'Gang of Four' criticised as 'the sinister theory of the productive forces'. In Marxist theory, these productive forces (the way nature is appropriated) consist in human productive activity, the subject of that activity, the instruments of production and the way these three elements are combined (co-operation, co-ordination etc.). Put at its very crudest, 'the theory of the productive forces' held that changes in the productive forces determined the whole field of social relations and ideology, not just in the last instance or under certain historical conditions but in all instances and under all conditions. One can think of few Marxists who were that crude and Deng was certainly not one of them. On the other hand, there was probably little accuracy in the way Deng saw the position of Zhang Chunqiao and Yao Wenyuan. Theirs was not the view that the relations of production were everywhere determinate nor that ideological orientation was always the most important thing to worry about. A change in ideological orientation was, as they saw it, important in the initial stage of any revolutionary upheaval, but such an ideological change was not simply the product of human will nor, in the long run, could ideology be decisive. In the debate about the 'theory of the productive forces', therefore, one is considering the relative emphasis given to what has been a major debate in Marxism ever since the time of Marx. The 'Gang of Four's' heresy, from a Stalinist point of view, was not really its idealism but the assertion, derived from Mao, that the three aspects of the relations or production (ownership, relations at work and distribution) could not be separated and were mutually dependent.

The stress on the interrelation between the productive forces and the relations of production, between each of their constituent elements and between base and superstructure, was a direct inheritance of the approach of Mao Zedong which was more dialectical than mechanical. Deng Xiaoping, however, had less of a totalist point of view. Deng saw the 'three major struggles' (class struggle, the struggle for production, and scientific experiment) as being governed by different laws.[75] He could thus affirm class struggle whilst advocating the more rigid implementation of the various programmes for industrial regularisation, the responsibility system in various sectors of the economy,[76] the strengthening of vertical controls[77] and the de-emphasis on political activity. He could affirm China's relatively autarkic stand in world forums[78] whilst asserting positively the importation of technology[79] and concluding credit agreements with foreign powers.[80] This, those of a more totalist frame of mind saw as 'empiricism'.

In the preceding chapter, I discussed why the importation of technology could cause concern. Though, from 1972−5, the contracted volume of complete plants to be imported into China (costing some $US2.2−2.5 billion)[81] only constituted some 6 to 8 per cent of China's overall technology accretion,[82] the effect on the policy of agro-industrial integration might be quite severe. Deng apparently did not worry too much about such things and felt that, if Zhou's modernisation plans were to go ahead, the importation of large amounts of foreign technology was essential. Unfortunately, we do not know exactly how much was envisaged. In 1978, the details of a ten-year plan were released, which, it was claimed, dated from 1975 and had been drawn up under the supervision of Zhou Enlai. This plan had apparently been attacked by the 'Gang of Four'[83] and we do not have access to the 1975 planned targets. One might, of course, doubt whether such a plan existed in 1975. After all, if Deng's ideas on modernisation could be released to a Party audience, why couldn't details of the plan?

Following its demise in 1976, the 'Gang' was accused not only of resisting the importation of foreign technology,[84] for which Deng had called in 1975, but also of damaging foreign trade in general.[85] How it could have done this escapes me. If, however, it was in such a position in 1974−5, the 'Gang' was singularly ineffective. China's foreign trade increased from some $US3.9 billion in 1969 to $US14 billion in 1975[86] and trade relations were established with almost every part of the globe (including such dubious countries as Rhodesia). Though the 'Gang' might conceivably have objected to some of the trade partners and might have objected to the use of vastly increased petroleum exports to finance the modernisation programme,[87] it is very difficult to see on what grounds an increase in trade could be opposed. Arguments about dependency could have had little validity when trade was only some 5 per cent of GNP[88] (a smaller percentage than the early 1950s).

Perhaps the source of contention was not the increase in trade in itself but the way trade was being conducted. Like all trading nations in the early 1970s, China was compelled to enter into advanced commitments at a time of global recession and high inflation.[89] As a result of this, China in 1974 and 1975 incurred, for the first time, sizeable trade deficits amounting to $US1.1 billion and $400 million respectively.[90] To finance that trade gap, China was forced to embark on what may only be described as disguised borrowing overseas. At that time, China entertained deferred payment schemes for deliveries of complete plants. At the same time, a number of West European and Japanese banks were invited to place deposits in the Bank of China at Eurodollar rates and, by 1974, these amounted to several hundred million dollars.[91] Though such actions may not seem very surprising to Western observers, they were a significant departure from the self-reliant policies pursued for many years. In 1965, it will be recalled, China had declared itself free from all internal and external debt. Though one cannot be sure that the 'Gang of Four' objected to disguised indebtedness in 1975, the tone of Deng Xiaoping's demand that credit arrangements be sought with foreign countries does suggest that he was responding to some internal opposition.

Though the policies pursued by the 'Gang of Four' might have contributed to the strikes in Hangzhou, it seems that the new interest of people like Zhang Chunqiao in matters of political economy did not do very much to halt the general policies of economic deradicalisation initiated in 1970. Hua Guofeng, however, has claimed that the 'Gang' did have a very great impact on the economy and that its activities, between 1974 and 1976, cost the nation about ¥100 billion in the total value of industrial output, 28 million tonnes of steel and ¥billion in state revenues.[92] One is not clear how these figures were calculated and the extent to which they might reflect bad harvests and natural disasters. Nor is one sure just what kind of economic developments here were attributed to the 'Gang'. How does one quantify the effects upon economic growth of the 'Gang's' stress on participation in industry? How, moreover, does one evaluate the charge that the 'Gang' interfered with the 'three-level system of ownership' in the communes by prematurely upgrading the unit of account to brigade level?[93] Evidence, cited in support of this, could be ascribed to anyone and might refer not to the period after 1973 but to the 'flying leap' of 1968–70. The same goes for the charge that the 'Gang' placed unreasonable constraints on private economic activity. It is extremely difficult to establish the association between the personal position of any member of the 'Gang' and basic-level economic problems. Such accounts that we do have, such as those which described Jiang Qing's attempts to set up Xiaojinzhuang as an alternative to

Dazhai,[94] tell us more about her personal foibles than her general effect upon the economy. Nevertheless, the removal of some planners and managers during the various campaigns must have had some effect and official (1977) comment has not been slow to magnify the situation.[95] If, however, one examines the political economy textbook, produced under the aegis of Zhang Chunqiao in Shanghai in 1975, the overwhelming impression one gets is the stress on gradualism and caution in basic-level economic policy.

The Campaigns Intensify (1975)

Deng Xiaoping's counter-attack was referred to, in 1976, as 'the right deviationist wind to reverse previously correct verdicts'. These verdicts concerned people as well as policy and, throughout 1974 and 1975, leaders dismissed in the Cultural Revolution were restored to high office. These included such senior PLA cadres as Yang Chengwu (July 1974) and Luo Ruiqing (July 1975). This 'right deviationist wind' was said to have reached its 'high tide' from July-September 1975[96] and was bitterly attacked by the 'Gang of Four' through its journal *Xuexi yu Pipan* (*Study and Criticism*). It was to give rise to a heated poster campaign in the universities concerning academic and technical standards. There was, therefore, a new upsurge in the 'revolution in education' and Deng's associate, the Minister of Education Zhou Rongxin, came under attack for his professional orientation. The crucial point was how to apply the 'dictatorship of the proletariat' to the field of education, and on this point Deng's position was quite unequivocal. As Deng saw it, there were some fields, such as science and technology, which he designated a 'productive force', where the dictatorship had absolutely no relevance at all.[97] Thus, one might assess positively some of the scientific achievements made before the Cultural Revolution regardless of the 'line' then in force. Most contentious of all was Deng's alleged support of those who criticised the 'open door' principle of education which sacrificed theory to practice. Indeed, Zhou Rongxin appeared to criticise Mao's notion of taking 'society as school' as the 'bourgeois' education theories of Dewey.[98] By the autumn of 1975, the stage was set for a major confrontation in the education field and Mao Zedong himself was called upon to mediate in a particularly acute debate at Qinghua University. He apparently refused to do so and, in November, sent a series of contentious documents back to Qinghua University 'for the comment of the masses'.[99] Whether rightly or wrongly, this action was taken as Mao's endorsement for accelerated criticism and Zhou Rongxin was openly denounced.

If Mao really was behind the attempt to get a new round of the

Cultural Revolution under way in late 1975, he had fewer resources at his disposal than a decade before. A potential student movement was in the process of forming and the press, said to be under the control of the 'Gang of Four', could be expected to give the necessary propaganda back-up. But, this time, there was no Lin Biao and no military support. It was subsequently alleged that the 'Gang of Four' attempted to disrupt the armed forces and to oppose their modernisation.[100] To prevent such a disruption, a fundamental reorganisation of PLA regional commands had taken place in late 1973 at the instigation of Deng Xiaoping. It is quite likely that the 'Gang' opposed the creation of a technocratic army divorced from the rest of society, though one does not know how much its members still endorsed the 'people's war' thesis. In any case, the Cultural Revolution had shown that a large part of the army was not prepared to go along with Lin Biao's mobilisation and had proved itself more concerned with law and order. This may have been why some people, associated with the 'Gang', gave great stress to developing the citizen forces and the Shanghai militia was soon to become notorious as the 'Gang's' embryonic power base.[101]

On the face of it, Mao's position on the new upsurge of the Cultural Revolution was ambiguous. Had it been less so, one might have expected Hua Guofeng to have taken a more definite stand. In September and October, Hua, emerging as the Party's major spokesman on agriculture, delivered an address to a national conference on learning from Dazhai in agriculture.[102] In his speech, Hua seemed to reflect Mao's ambiguity. Echoing the 'Gang's' position that 'new bourgeois elements' might appear in the rural sector, Hua nevertheless made the point that, in most cases, the contradictions were 'among the people' and not antagonistic. Such a position could not have endeared Hua either to Deng or to the 'Gang'. Indeed, it is said that the 'Gang' attacked Hua for his moderate position[103] and perhaps caused him to lean a little in Deng's direction, but not far enough to associate himself with those whom the chairman might attack.

One may only speculate upon Mao's ambiguity. I have already suggested why he might have been unprepared to endorse fully Zhang Chunqiao and Yao Wenyuan's position on 'bourgeois right'. It was probably also the case that he did not much like the conspiratorial style of Jiang, Zhang, Yao and Wang and this may have been why he was said to have criticised the 'Gang of Four' in May 1975.[104] But what did Mao mean when he cautioned those people not to act as a 'Gang of Four'? Was it that he felt that the four people had developed an inappropriate set of policies or because he was concerned that their actions might bring discredit to what were after all his own policies. It may also have been the case that the aged Mao was unwilling to take the final step in endorsing attacks on the dying Zhou Enlai. Zhou had perhaps been responsible for moderating the Cultural Revolution but he had also been one of Mao's major assets in promoting that revolution in the first place.

Mao's reluctance fully to support the 'Gang's' attacks was made quite clear in a rather strange movement, which began in September 1975, to criticise the *Water Margin* (*Shuihuzhuan*). This Ming dynasty novel had long been popular in China and had been a particular favourite of Mao himself. It portrayed the Robin Hood-type exploits of a group of worthy bandits during the Song dynasty. The names of the leaders of this group had, over the centuries, become household words in China and, when Mao urged people to criticise the 'capitulationism' of one of the most prominent, he could not fail to strike a chord. This 'capitulationist' was Song Jiang,[105] who abandoned the rebels. His action was said to have contemporary relevance for those who were guilty of 'class capitulationism in home affairs and national capitulationism in foreign affairs'.[106] The campaign may be interpreted in a way similar to the earlier movement to criticise Lin Biao and Confucius. The 'capitulationist' Song Jiang expressed loyalty to the bandit leader Zhao Kai but, after the latter's death, sold out to the imperial court. Thus, Song Jiang may be identified as Lin Biao. A contrary interpretation is that the target was not Lin Biao but Deng Xiaoping[107] and the movement was apparently launched without the premier's knowledge.[108] Nevertheless, it was subsequently reported that, when Mao was informed that some people saw the target of the movement as certain contemporary leaders, he uttered an obscenity.[109]

Foreign Policy (1973 – 5)

But what could the charge of 'national capitulationism in foreign affairs' refer to? If one focuses on the case of Lin Biao, this may be taken as a reference to Lin's alleged flight to the Soviet Union. If, however, there was a contemporary target, then it would appear that some people were objecting to the policy of reconciliation with the United States. Yet it was quite clear that Sino-American relations had not developed so rapidly as many people had thought possible at the time of the Shanghai communiqué and the establishment of liaison offices (April 1973). Responding perhaps to domestic radicalisation, Zhou Enlai had made it quite clear, in 1973, that the Chinese policy of seeking 'necessary compromises' with imperialist powers was not the same as the Soviet policy of 'superpower collusion'.[110] At the same time, China began to take a slightly tougher stand on the question of Taiwan, insisting on the 'one China' clause in the Shanghai communiqué.[111] From the American point of view, Taiwan was even more of an obstacle to the normalisation of relations. In response both to a hardening of the Chinese position and to domestic pressure, President Nixon allowed the Taibei government to open two new consulates in the United States and made a point of filling the vacant position of United States ambassador to Taiwan. It was the Taiwan issue, moreover, which prevented any Chinese moves to establish some kind of relationship with the World Bank and International Monetary Fund.[112]

Despite his hardening on the Taiwan issue, President Nixon continued to enjoy considerable prestige in China for his initial moves in improving Sino-American relations. After his resignation, in the wake of the Watergate scandal, the Chinese leaders appeared to be most conciliatory and no less a person than Jiang Qing made the point that his misdemeanours over Watergate were trivial compared with his successes in foreign policy.[113] Yet perhaps Nixon was being used as a symbol to embarrass the new President Ford and to force him to speed up the process of normalising relations. At the same time, the rather colourless Chinese Foreign Minister, Qi Pengfei (who had succeeded Chen Yi on the old minister's death in 1972), was replaced by Qiao Guanhua,[114] who was probably seen as a tough and persuasive negotiator able to do something about the impasse. It was in such an atmosphere that President Ford was to go to China in late 1975.[115] His visit, moreover, cannot be unconnected with the intensification of the *Water Margin* campaign which sought to prevent what might have been seen as further 'capitulation'. There were, of course, sound domestic reasons why Ford was unwilling to accelerate normalisation and, despite Secretary of State Kissinger's apparent optimism that an agreement might be concluded on the Japanese pattern,[116] the outstanding problems, such as frozen assets and the question of Taiwan, remained unsolved. All those Chinese leaders who wished to accelerate normalisation could do was attempt to embarrass Taiwan by releasing former Guomindang agents[117] and to take solace in the fact that the United States troops on Taiwan (although reduced) had prevented the creation of a vacuum which might be filled by the Soviet Union.

Throughout the early 1970s, China's main preoccupation in foreign policy was clearly the relationship with the Soviet Union. Border clashes had resumed once again in 1972,[118] the Soviet Far Eastern forces had expanded to over 50 divisions and rapid moves had been made to settle the Soviet Far East. In response, the Chinese stepped up their policy of tunnel-building. Throughout the period, border negotiations proceeded in fits and starts to the point where the Soviet negotiator Ilyichev seemed to be a regular commuter between Moscow and the conference table in Beijing. Not only was there no progress on the border question but the situation in the South China Sea actually deteriorated. There, China pressed its claims on the Xisha (Paracel) and Nansha (Spratley) Islands. This resulted, in early 1974, in fighting on the Xisha Islands between

Chinese and Saigon forces.[119] The Soviet response to the Chinese action was cool and, with the collapse of the Saigon régime in early 1975, it seemed highly likely that the Soviet Union would begin to take a more active interest in the South China Sea. Though China was obviously delighted at the victory of the North Vietnamese and National Liberation Front forces in Vietnam,[120] the possibility that the Soviet Union might establish a naval base in South Vietnam seemed a major area of concern. There was a danger too that the Soviet Union might capitalise on the growing estrangement between the Vietnamese government and the new régime in Kampuchea (Cambodia) or Kim Il Sung's enthusiasm about the Vietnamese model of unification by force.[121] As far as China was concerned, Korea could provide a source of considerable embarrassment. China was also concerned at the close relations which the Soviet Union maintained with India. The government of that country remained implacably hostile and accused China of fomenting border provocations.[122] For its part, China condemned the Indian annexation of Sikkim[123] and sought to maintain good relations with Pakistan and improve relations with Bangladesh. Indeed, two weeks after the assassination of Mujibur Rahman, diplomatic relations were concluded with that country.[124]

China's attitude towards the Soviet Union remained at the centre of its foreign policy. It dictated China's opposition to the Helsinki talks[125] and strengthened its desire to forge closer relations with Europe. It was also a major factor in China's attempts to woo Japan by granting cheaper oil prices and supporting Japan's opposition to the Soviet occupation of the northern islands.[126] At all costs, China wished to prevent the joint Soviet-Japanese exploitation of the wealth of Siberia. Yet there were still obstacles in the way of concluding a Sino-Japanese peace and friendship treaty, not the least of which was China's insistence on an 'anti-hegemony clause' directed at the Soviet Union. The continued concern with Soviet 'hegemonism' did much to promote China's continuing desire to foster some kind of Third World unity. Mao Zedong, it was said, had personally initiated the 'three worlds thesis'. These three worlds consisted of a First World comprising *both* the Soviet Union and the United States, a Second World comprising the developed capitalist countries and the developed socialist countries and a Third World which constituted the remainder.[127] Though the Lin Biao scenario of the world's countryside surrounding the world's cities had long been discarded, Lin Biao's 'Long Live the Victory of People's War' was his one work which was relatively free of official criticism. It was felt necessary to continue to proclaim the common interests of China and other Third World countries. Thus, diplomatic relations were established with many states including such hitherto hostile régimes as Thailand[128] and the Philippines.[129] Interestingly, China's relations with Thailand, the Philippines and Burma continued to improve whilst those governments still felt that China was promoting insurrection within them. In south-east Asia, only Indonesia remained hostile, since it had merely suspended (and not severed) diplomatic relations in 1966.

Though the above survey of foreign policy would indicate that the original idea of driving a wedge between the superpowers had degenerated into a mobilisation of all available forces to oppose the Soviet Union, there is no doubt that China had established good relations with countries in the Third World and the 'second intermediate zone' which may not have been particularly concerned about the Soviet Union. This is remarkable at a time when domestic politics were so turbulent. Whatever the *Water Margin* campaign had been designed to do, it did not alter fundamentally the foreign policy identified with Premier Zhou Enlai.

The Campaign to Criticise Deng Xiaoping

The escalation of polemics in late 1975 was climaxed by the new year joint editorial of *Renmin Ribao* and *Hongqi*. This editorial gave prominence to a statement of Mao: 'stability and unity do not mean writing off the class struggle; class struggle is the key link and everything else hinges upon it'.[130] The implications for Deng Xiaoping, who had maintained that Mao's 'three directives' constituted the 'key link', were quite profound.

One week after the appearance of the new year editorial, Premier Zhou Enlai died, leaving Deng in charge of the State Council. In his funeral eulogy on 15 January, Deng called upon people to 'turn their grief into strength' and seemed to call for a movement to emulate the qualities of Zhou Enlai.[131] Yet, on the same day, an article in *Renmin Ribao* called for an intensification of the campaign in education and for attacks to be made on those who attempted to restore any part of the pre-Cultural Revolution education system.[132] In the following months, press articles reiterated the Cultural Revolution's theme of 'top persons in authority taking the capitalist road' and indicated that the 'expert' position in education might constitute an attack on the Cultural Revolution itself. Wall posters appeared speaking of 'China's new Khrushchev' who erroneously put forward Mao's 'three directives' as the 'key link' and who had declared that 'it did not matter whether a cat was black or white so long as it caught mice'.[133] This famous quotation from Deng, of Cultural Revolution notoriety, made it quite clear that Deng was under considerable pressure and it was in such a climate that Hua Guofeng was appointed acting premier.[134]

There has been much speculation as to the exact position of Hua Guofeng on the various debates which had raged over the past six months and his assessment of the current situation. Suffice it to say that whilst the media, under the control of the 'Gang of Four', declared that a 'life or death struggle' was in progress (and Deng's opinion could not have been much different), Hua assured the visiting ex-President Nixon that this was just an example of 'extensive democracy'.[135] Indeed, the moderation of the polemics in March would suggest that Hua had achieved partial success in cooling down frayed tempers. Then, in April, matters came to a head. An attempt to remove wreaths, laid in Beijing's Tiananmen Square in honour of Zhou Enlai on the occasion of the traditional Qingming Festival, erupted into violence,[136] ushering in one of the more sordid periods in contemporary Chinese history.

An immediate consequence of the 'Tiananmen incident' was the dismissal of Deng Xiaopeng from all posts both inside and outside the Party and the elevation of Hua to substantive premier and first vice-chairman of the Party.[137] As a press campaign against Deng began to unfold, Beijing (and most other places) was alive with rumours as to what exactly had gone on in early April and who had staged the Tiananmen incident.[138] Allegations and counter-allegations of perfidious conduct, forgery of documents and all kinds of skulduggery abounded.[139] Such one might expect in the early stages of a mass movement and indeed such had characterised the early Cultural Revolution. Yet the atmosphere could not have been more different. Observing China at first hand in 1966 and 1976 and attempting to compare the two movements, I could not but conclude that the campaign against Deng Xiaoping was not a mass movement at all. Though the press of 1966 did not always accurately reflect what was going on at the basic levels, the tone of its polemics and that of the mass criticism was similar. In 1976, the press campaign against Deng rarely corresponded to mass activity. When I asked factory cadres just what the concrete manifestation of Deng's 'line' had been in their particular unit, I was frequently told that it had had little impact since he had been 'nipped in the bud in time' and that policy would not change. Such a reply might indicate that the cadre concerned did not share in the official condemnation of Deng or that he had not studied Marxist theory sufficiently 'seriously' to see Deng as the manifestation of a particular approach rather than just a 'bad egg'. The former was perhaps the more likely explanation. In the factories which I visited at that time, the leadership did not seem to envisage any operational implications of the re-evaluation of the man his opponents had begun to call 'China's Imre Nagy'.[140]

There are two possible explanations for such a state of affairs. First, one might hypothesise that the criticism of Deng was unpopular either because its substantive content did not strike a chord amongst ordinary people or because they were heartily fed up with the 'Gang of Four' which was behind the denunciation. This latter explanation is borne out by the apparent joy with which the subsequent ousting of the 'Gang of Four' was greeted. Yet there is another explanation which is much more ominous. The lack of mass enthusiasm in the anti-Deng movement might be explained by the fact that the movement was blocked by the recon-structed Party machine which was under no circumstances going to see the development of a new upsurge in Mao's 'continuous revolution'. This is what the Party machine had tried to do in early 1966 and had failed. Had it now succeeded?

Throughout the summer and early autumn of 1976, the anti-Deng movement continued, though the problems which had to be faced were often completely beyond the scope of the 'struggle between two lines'. The death of Zhu De in July[141] removed from the central leadership one of the rumoured architects of the compromise leadership formed earlier in the year and a force for unity around which different groups might rally. The massive Tangshan earthquake, later in the month, diverted energies, and *Renmin Ribao* could only make a plaintive appeal that concern for the earthquake relief operations should enhance rather than detract from the anti-Deng movement.[142] This massive natural disaster absorbed the energies of Hua Guofeng[143] and many of the top Chinese leaders throughout August. They were perhaps removed from the stresses and strains of the struggle, though it was subsequently alleged that the 'Gang of Four' engaged in an attempt to belittle their efforts.[144] Hua was probably very tired when he had to face the greatest crisis in his life following the death of Mao Zedong on 9 September.

The Arrest of the 'Gang of Four'[145]

Following Mao's death, attempts were made both by Hua Guofeng and the 'Gang' to establish their legitimacy by reference to Mao's last wishes. On 16 and 17 September, *Renmin Ribao* (allegedly under the control of Yao Wenyuan as *de facto* head of the Party's Propaganda Department) published a call for people to 'act according to the principles laid down'.[146] This was considered to be a rallying call for those who supported the 'Gang'. The present (post-1976) leadership has claimed that this slogan was a falsification of a statement of Mao's on 30 April 'to act according to past principles' and it failed to include Mao's injunction against conspiracy and the statement, directed at Hua Guofeng, in which Mao claimed 'with you in charge, I am at ease'. It was probably the case, however, that Mao's being 'at ease' with Hua concerned only the current stage of the anti-Deng campaign in late April. Nevertheless, the slogan was used to establish the legitimacy of Hua's succession.

Following a Politburo meeting in late September 1976 at which, it is claimed, Jiang Qing charged Hua Guofeng with incompetence, a slogan war began in the press, as oblique as any of the old battles by historical analogy. The present leadership maintains that the 'Gang's' use of slogans and the release of key articles to the press was to mobilise its supporters for a military coup. This coup was to result in the appointment of Jiang Qing to the post of Party chairman, Wang Hongwen to the post of chairman of the Standing Committee of the National People's Congress and Zhang Chunqiao to the post of premier.[147] The forces to be used in this coup were those of the Shenyang Military Region where Mao's nephew Mao Yuanxin was political commissar, together with the Shanghai workers' militia under the command of Wang Hongwen. To support this charge, the present leadership has released evidence concerning the Shanghai operation.[148] Such evidence is, however, quite fragmentary and it is very difficult to believe that any concrete moves were taken in support of a coup. Mao Yuanxin, it is said, requested permission from Yang Chengwu, the deputy chief-of-staff of the PLA, to move troops into Beijing.[149] One does not usually ask for official permission to carry out a coup. Secondly, not a shot seems to have been fired in Shanghai when things came to a head and such a state of affairs is hardly likely to have occurred if the plans had been backed up by operational orders.

The arrest of the 'Gang of Four', by the State Council guard unit 8341 under the command of Wang Dongxing, took place on 6 October. Shortly after that, Hua Guofeng became chairman of the Party and head of its Military Commission in addition to his post as premier.[150] Immediately, a massive campaign was launched which was to accuse the 'Gang' of a whole host of 'crimes'—the most ironical of which was that it had carried out the unauthorised arrest of senior cadres with the aid of the public security forces.

Conclusion

The arrest of the 'Gang of Four' was to usher in a period of considerable soul-searching, as the Chinese leadership sought a new developmental strategy. The virulence which was poured on the heads of the 'Gang of Four' was perhaps the only unifying factor in the new situation. The 'Gang' was accused of sabotaging the economy; but how one evaluates such a charge depends upon how one sees the relationship between economic growth and the restriction of 'bourgeois right'. It was denounced for sabotaging the armed forces; but one's assessment here depends on how one sees the relationship between national defence and an army integrated with society. The 'Gang' was also charged with damaging foreign trade; but on this score one's evaluation will depend upon how one sees the effect of external factors on national economic integration. It was also denounced for dominating the media and throttling culture; but how one assesses this will depend on how one sees the relationship between different levels of creativity. Above all, the 'Gang' was charged with conspiracy; but, faced with the intransigence of the State Council and the Party machine, what else could it have done? That the members of the 'Gang' were élitist seems to have been borne out by the way the campaign of 1976 was conducted. That they were incompetent is shown quite clearly by the failure of any of the mass movements since 1973 to have much impact. But this does not necessarily mean that they were unprincipled. They did act 'according to the principles laid down'. The trouble was that Mao had laid down many different and contradictory sets of principles but did not always have the courage to do so firmly enough.

NOTES

1. This chapter is an expanded version of the conclusion to Brugger, 1978. Some passages are identical.
2. *PR* 19, 11 May 1973, p. 6.
3. Ibid. 17, 27 April 1973, p. 11.
4. Ibid., p. 13.
5. Ibid. 16, 20 April 1973, p. 4. Deng appeared at a banquet celebrating Samdech Sihanouk's return from the liberated areas of Cambodia.
6. Ibid. 35 – 6, 7 September 1973, p. 9.
7. *SCMP* 5439, 20 August 1973, pp. 15 – 16; ibid.,pp. 17 – 24 (on the Qiliying People's Commune, visited by Mao on 6 August 1958).
8. Ibid. 5447, 31 August 1973, pp. 134 – 40.
9. Ibid. 5444, 28 August 1973, pp. 8 – 9; ibid.5445, 29 August 1973, pp. 39 – 44.
10. *PR* 34, 24 August 1973, p. 4.
11. Wang Hongwen, 24 August 1973, *PR* 35 – 6, 7 September 1973, p. 30.
12. Zhou Enlai, 24 August 1973, ibid., pp. 19 – 20.
13. Ibid., p. 18.
14. Ibid., pp. 17 – 18.
15. Ibid., p. 25.
16. For a discussion of leadership changes, see Wich,1974, pp. 234 – 9.
17. Ibid., pp. 238 – 9. There was, however, a marked increase in the representatives of mass *organisations*. Approximate composition of the 195 members and 124 alternates is as follows:

	1969 %	1973 %
Military	44	32
Party and government cadres	27	28
Revolutionary mass organisations	29	40

18. This point is made with reference to the Tenth Congress by Bradsher,1973, p. 993.
19. For a short profile of Wang, see Chang,1974, pp. 124 – 8.

20. Wich, 1974, p. 235. Note, some factory-level Party branches had been set up before the Ninth Congress.

21. Wang Hongwen, 24 August 1973, *PR* 35 – 6, 7 September 1973, pp. 29 – 33.

22. Zhou Enlai, 24 August 1973, ibid., pp. 17 – 25.

23. See e.g. Yang Rongguo, *SCMP* 5436, 15 August 1973, pp. 106 – 15.

24. Guo Moruo, *SCMM* 734, 8 August 1972, pp. 70 – 8.

25. Yang Rongguo, *Hongqi* 12, 1972, pp. 45 – 54.

26. *RMRB*, 7 November 1971, p. 1.

27. The following is taken from Brugger,1978, pp . 256 – 60.

28. See e.g. Shi Lun, *Hongqi* 10, 1973, pp. 33 – 43.

29. For different sets of documents relating to different views on the Socialist Education Movement, see Baum and Teiwes, 1968. On the different perspectives in the anti-Confucius campaign, see Goldman, 1975.

30. See the collection of articles in PFLP, 1974; Price,1977 (a).

31. CCPCC, *zhongfa* (1976) 24, 10 December 1976, *Issues and Studies*, Vol. XIII, No. 9, September 1977, pp. 89, 91, 100 *passim*.

32. Goldman, 1975.

33. CCPCC, *zhongfa* (1972) 4, 13 January 1972, *Chinese Law and Government*, Vol. V, Nos.3 – 4, Fall-Winter 1972 – 3, p. 48.

34. Yang Rongguo, *GMRB*, 24 August 1974, *SCMP* 5690, 6 September 1974, pp. 140 – 3.

35. Luo Siding, *Hongqi* 11, 1973, p. 36.

36. Ibid., p. 38.

37. *RMRB*, 8 September 1974, *SCMP* 5700, 20 September 1974, pp. 191 – 203.

38. Ibid., p. 193.

39. Ibid.

40. Deng Xiaoping, 10 April 1974, *PR* 16, 19 April 1974, pp. 6 – 11.

41. CCPCC, *zhongfa* (1972) 21, 1 July 1974, *Issues and Studies*, Vol. XI, No. 1, January 1975, pp. 101 – 4. The explicit message of this document was, in fact, that production had declined in certain places, because of failure to implement the movement properly.

42. See *PR* 10, 8 March 1974, pp. 16 – 18; *PR* 12, 22 March 1974, pp. 19 and 21; *PR* 13, 29 March 1974, pp. 15 – 17; *PR* 14, 5 April 1974, pp. 18 – 21. See also Croll,1977.

43. Chan, 1978, p. 120.

44. *RMRB*, 10 August 1973, p. 1, *SCMP* 5442, 23 August 1973, pp. 112 – 14.

45. *PR* 8, 18 February 1977, pp. 13 – 5; CCPCC, *zhongfa* (1976) 24, 10 December 1976, *Issues and Studies*, Vol. XIII, No. 10, October 1977, pp. 96 – 7; CCPCC, *zhongfa* (1977) 37, 23 September 1977, *Issues and Studies*, Vol. XV, No. 1, January 1979, pp. 107 – 9.

46. Chan, 1978, pp. 117 – 19.

47. Ibid., p. 118.

48. Editorial report. *SWB* FE/4534/B11/11 – 14, 23 February 1974.

49. Chan, 1978, pp. 118 – 19.

50. Shenyang, Liaoning Radio, 24 April 1974 and 27 April 1974, Xi'an Shaanxi Radio, 24 April 1974, Ürümqi, Xinjiang Radio, 28 April 1974, *SWB* FE/4590/B11/26 – 30, 3 May 1974.

51. Bernstein, 1977 (a), pp. 91 – 107.

52. NCNA, 24 January 1978, *SWB* FE/5723/B11/15, 26 January 1978.

53. *RMRB*, 28 November 1974, *PR* 49, 6 December 1974, pp. 5 – 6. Though this was a call to continue the movement, as Starr (1976 (a), p. 465) points out, the article reads like an official summary.

54. Text in *Issues and Studies*, Vol. XII, No. 1, January 1976, pp. 110 – 48.

55. For a detailed examination of the *dazibao*, see Shirk, 1979.

56. Djilas, 1966.

57. Konrád and Szelényi, 1979.

58. *Issues and Studies*, Vol. XII, No. 1, January 1976, pp. 130 – 1.

59. Ibid., p. 111.

60. *PR* 4, 24 January 1975, pp. 21 – 5.

61. Ibid., pp. 18 – 20.

62. Text in ibid., pp. 12 – 17. Excerpt in Selden, 1979, pp. 571 – 5.

63. *PR* 3, 14 January 1977, p. 28. Mao apparently repeated this criticism in December 1974. See Wang Hongwen's letter in CCPCC, *zhongfa* (1976) 24, 10 December 1976, *Issues and Studies*, Vol. XIII, No. 9, September 1977, pp. 101 – 2. The chairman was said to have enjoined Wang not to join a 'Gang of Four'. Mao allegedly gave a similar warning to Jiang Qing in November 1974, ibid., p. 102.

64. *PR* 4, 24 January 1975, pp. 5 and 26. Mao met Strauss on 16 January.

65. Shehuizhuyi Zhengzhi Jingjixue Bianxie Xiaozu, 1975.

66. Yao Wenyuan, *Hongqi* 3, 1975, *PR* 10, 7 March 1975, pp. 5 – 10.

67. Zhang Chunqiao, *Hongqi* 4, 1975, *PR* 14, 4 April 1975, pp. 5 – 11; Selden, 1979, pp. 654 – 9.

68. Marx, 1875, pp. 18 – 19.

69. *PR* 14, 1 April 1977, pp. 23 – 6.

70. See Andors, 1977, pp. 234 – 5.

71. These were referred to by the 'Gang of Four' as Deng's 'three poisonous weeds'. Deng Xiaoping, 2 September 1975, *Issues and Studies*, Vol. XIII, No. 7, July 1977, pp. 90 – 113; 7 October 1975, *Issues and Studies*, Vol. XIII, No. 8, August 1977, pp. 77 – 99; part of the third document is in *Issues and Studies*, Vol. XIII, No. 9, September 1977, pp. 63 – 70. They may be also be found in Chi Hsin, 1977, pp. 203 – 86.

72. Deng Xiaoping, 7 October 1975, *Issues and Studies*, Vol. XIII, No. 8, August 1977, p. 78.

73. Ibid., p. 90. Translation altered for stylistic reasons.

74. Ibid., pp. 92 – 3.

75. Ibid., p. 93.

76. Ibid., p. 94.

77. Deng Xiaoping, 2 September 1975, ibid., No. 7, July 1977, p. 102.

78. Deng Xiaoping, 10 April 1974, *PR* 15, 12 April 1974, Supplement, p. iv.

79. Deng Xiaoping, 2 September 1975, *Issues and Studies*, Vol. XIII, No. 7, July 1977, p. 107.

80. Ibid., p. 108.

81. Eckstein, 1975 (b), p. 140.

82. Heymann, 1975, p. 679.

83. Hua Guofeng, 26 February 1978, *PR* 10, 10 March 1978, p. 19.

84. CCPCC, *zhongfa* (1977) 37, 23 September 1977, *Issues and Studies*, Vol. XV, No. 5, May 1979, pp. 92 – 3.

85. *PR* 9, 25 February 1977, pp. 16 – 18.

86. Chen Nai-ruenn, 1975, p. 645; *FEER, Yearbook: Asia, 1977*, p. 159.

87. CCPCC, *zhongfa* (1977) 37, 23 September 1977, *Issues and Studies*, Vol. XV, No. 5, May 1979, pp. 93 – 5

88. Eckstein, 1975 (b), p. 139.

89. See the discussion in Cheng, 1978, p. 143.

90. Chen Nai-ruenn, 1975, p. 645; *FEER, Yearbook: Asia, 1977*, p. 159; Eckstein, 1975 (b), pp. 147 – 8.

91. Eckstein, 1975 (b), pp. 148 – 9.

92. Hua Guofeng, 26 February 1978, *PR* 10, 10 March 1978, p. 12.

93. See e.g. NCNA, 3 February 1978, *SWB* FE/5737/B11/15, 11 February 1978; Wuhan, Hubei Radio, 14 January 1979, *SWB* FE/6019/B11/11 – 12, 18 January 1979.

94. *RMRB*, 12 January 1978, p. 2.

95. CCPCC, *zhongfa* (1977) 37, 23 September 1977, *Issues and Studies*, Vol. XIV,

No. 11, November 1978, pp. 98 – 110.

96. Zhai Qing, *Xuexi yu Pipan* 4, 1976, p. 11.

97. Apparently, Deng's authority for this was a supposed statement by Mao in 1963 which Deng's opponents denied that Mao ever made. See Kang Li and Yan Feng, ibid., p. 26 which discusses the Marxist credentials of this statement.

98. The most contentious article for which Zhou was held responsible was published in *Jiaoyu Geming Tongxun* 10, 1975 and is translated in *Vento dell'est* (Milan) 42, 1976, pp. 124 – 7. This article purported to *contrast* 'open door' education with Dewey's notion of 'society as school'.

99. Gittings,1976, pp. 492 – 3.

100. *PR* 10, 4 March 1977, pp. 9 – 12. See also the evidence in CCPCC, *zhongfa* (1976) 24, 10 December 1976, *Issues and Studies*, Vol. XIII, No. 9, September 1977, pp. 93 – 9; CCPCC, *zhongfa* (1977) 37, 23 September 1977, *Issues and Studies*, Vol. XIV, No. 8, August 1978, pp. 91 – 104.

101. *PR* 6, 4 February 1977, pp. 8 – 9; ibid.13, 25 March 1977, pp. 10 – 12.

102. Hua Guofeng, 15 October 1975, ibid.44, 31 October 1975, pp. 7 – 10 and 18; Selden, 1979, pp. 674 – 81.

103. CCPCC, *zhongfa* (1977) 37, 23 September 1977, *Issues and Studies*, Vol. XV, No. 5, pp. 88 – 9.

104. *PR* 3, 14 January 1977, p. 29. What purports to be Mao's comments may be found in CCPCC, *zhongfa* (1977) 37, 23 September 1977, *Issues and Studies*, Vol. XV, No. 2, February 1979, p. 96.

105. *RMRB*, 4 September 1975, *PR* 37, 12 September 1975, p. 7.

106. Ibid.

107. CCPCC, *zhongfa* (1977) 37, 23 September 1977, *Issues and Studies*, Vol. XV, No. 4, April 1979, pp. 109 – 110.

108. Starr, 1976 (a), p. 474, from Taiwan sources.

109. *PR* 23, 3 June 1977, p. 22.

110. Zhou Enlai, 24 August 1973, ibid.35 – 6, 7 September 1973, p. 23.

111. Robinson,1974, p. 18.

112. Ibid., p. 20.

113. Starr, 1975, p. 18.

114. Ibid., p. 19.

115. *PR* 49, 5 December 1975, pp. 3 – 4 and 8 – 9; ibid. 50, 12 December 1975, pp. 3 – 4 and 6 – 7.

116. Starr,1976 (b), p. 58.

117. *PR* 39, 26 September 1975, pp. 9 and 27.

118. Robinson, 1974, pp. 18 – 19.

119. *PR* 4, 25 January 1975, p. 4.

120. *RMRB*, 1 May 1975, *PR* 18, 2 May 1975, pp. 13 – 14.

121. Kim Il Sung visited China at the time of the collapse of the Saigon and Phnom Penh régimes. See the speeches of Kim and Deng Xiaoping in *PR* 17, 25 April 1975, pp. 11 – 17.

122. Ibid. 45, 7 November 1975, pp. 4 – 6.

123. Ibid. 37, 13 September 1974, p. 16; ibid.47, 22 November 1974, p. 17.

124. Ibid. 36, 5 September 1975, p. 6.

125. On the Chinese attitude to US-Soviet *détente*, see ibid. 29, 18 July 1975, pp. 4 – 6.

126. Starr, 1976 (b), p. 55.

127. Deng Xiaoping, 10 April 1974, *PR* 15, Supplement, p.i.

128. Ibid. 27, 4 July 1975, pp. 8 – 9.

129. Ibid. 24, 13 June 1975, pp. 7 – 8.

130. Ibid. 1, 2 January 1976, p. 9.

131. Deng Xiaoping, 15 January 1976, ibid.4, 23 January 1976, pp. 5 – 8.

132. Liang Xiao, *RMRB*, 15 January 1976, p. 2.

133. Mao had allegedly criticised this statement. Kang Li and Yan Feng, *Xuexi yu Pipan* 4, 1976, p. 26.

134. *PR* 7, 13 February 1976, p. 3. Hua's meeting with the Venezuelan ambassador was the first official confirmation that he had been appointed acting premier.

135. Hua Guofeng, 22 February 1976, ibid.9, 27 February 1976, p. 5.

136. Ibid. 15, 9 April 1976, pp. 4–7.

137. CCPCC, 7 April 1976, ibid.15, 9 April 1976, p. 3.

138. Personal information gained in Beijing.

139. Liang Xiao, *Hongqi* 5, 1976, p. 22.

140. CCPCC, *zhongfa* (1977) 37, 23 September 1977, *Issues and Studies*, Vol. XIV, No. 9, September 1978, p. 93.

141. CCPCC, NPC Standing Committee and SC, 6 July 1976, *PR* 28, 9 July 1976, pp. 3–4.

142. *RMRB*, 11 August 1976, ibid. 34, 20 August 1976, pp. 5–6.

143. Ibid. 32–3, 9 August 1976, p. 7.

144. CCPCC, *zhongfa* (1977) 37, 23 September 1977, *Issues and Studies*, Vol. XIV, No. 9, September 1978, pp. 86–8.

145. The following is taken from Brugger, 1979 (b).

146. See the discussion in Onate,1978, pp. 545–51. See also the comment in CCPCC, *zhongfa* (1977) 37, 23 September 1977, *Issues and Studies*, Vol. XIV, No. 9, September 1978, p. 89.

147. Hua Guofeng, 12 August 1977, *PR* 35, 26 August 1977, pp. 27–8.

148. CCPCC, *zhongfa* (1976) 24, 10 December 1976, *Issues and Studies*, Vol. XIII, No. 11, November 1977, pp. 106–112, and in *Zhonggong Yanjiu*, Vol. XI, No. 7, July 1977, pp. 158–60.

149. Onate, 1978, p. 555.

150. *PR* 44, 29 October 1976, pp. 7–11 and 21.

VIII
THE SEARCH FOR A NEW
DEVELOPMENTAL STRATEGY
(1977-1978)[1]

The events of October 1976 came as such a shock to so many people that it was some time before the implications of the 'Gang's' demise were fully realised. What had to be determined was the extent to which the denunciation of the 'Gang' might also imply a criticism of the late Chairman Mao and his policies. In the period 1977 – 8, attempts were made to remove the influence of the 'Gang' whilst still adhering to the symbol of Mao Zedong. As long as the criticism focused merely on the behaviour of the 'Gang', the symbol of Mao could be preserved. However, once serious attempts were made to refute the theoretical position of people like Zhang Chunqiao and Yao Wenyuan and to devise new economic policies, the attempt to disassociate Mao from the 'Gang' became more and more difficult.

Initial Criticisms of the 'Gang of Four'

The torrent of articles which appeared in late 1976 and early 1977 criticising the 'Gang of Four' was reminiscent of the Cultural Revolution. This time, it seemed that the 'right' was using tactics characteristic of the 'ultra-left'—the concentration on personal vilification rather than criticism of policy. The life history of each of the 'Gang's' members was subjected to scrutiny and it was suddenly discovered that Zhang Chunqiao had been a Guomindang agent, Yao Wenyuan was 'an alien class element', Jiang Qing's counter-revolutionary misdeeds dated from the 1930s and Wang Hongwen was a 'new bourgeois element'.[2] What was perhaps most distasteful was the sexist abuse directed at Jiang Qing who had been something of a feminist. There was no doubt that, in recalling the élitist behaviour of the 'Gang', the Chinese leaders evoked more than a grain of truth and, by focusing on the memory of Zhou Enlai, they were able to mobilise a considerable amount of support. But such support could only last for a short period of time unless new developmental strategies were worked out.

For several months after the fall of the 'Gang', there was little discussion of theory or policy. This must surely have been because of disagreements within the leadership.[3] One major source of contention was whether the denunciation of the 'Gang' implied an acquittal of Deng Xiaoping. According to Beijing's mayor, Wu De, who had played a major part in suppressing the Tiananmen demonstrations in early 1976, the criticism of Deng and the 'Gang' should proceed in tandem.[4] This was also said to be the position, in late 1976, of Wang Dongxing who had carried out the arrest of the 'Gang'.[5] Yet other Party leaders were convinced that Deng had been wrongly accused and attempted to put pressure on Chairman Hua Guofeng to revise the official verdict. The former vice-chairman of the Party, Chen Yun, it is alleged, not only wished to see the immediate rehabilitation of Deng and an official re-evaluation of the Tiananmen incident but also demanded the restoration to office of Peng Zhen and the posthumous rehabilitation of Peng Dehuai.[6] Such a demand was tantamount to a repudiation of both the Cultural Revolution and the Great Leap Forward and was resisted by the new Party chairman. By December 1976, however, Hua, whilst maintaining that the struggles against both Deng and the 'Gang' should continue, had been compelled to declare that the principal contradiction lay with the 'Gang' rather than Deng.[7] His reluctance to go further than that was to result in his being cast, in some handbills, as a member of the 'Gang of Five'.[8]

It is not too difficult to understand why Hua Guofeng might have been reluctant to proceed with the rehabilitation of Deng. Attempts had been made in late 1976 to disassociate the 'Gang' from the late Chairman Mao, but one could not be too sure just how credible those attempts were. At the same time, Hua had been portrayed as Mao's chosen successor. Pictures of Hua together with Mao appeared everywhere on billboards and, in early 1977, the long-awaited fifth volume of Mao's *Selected Works* was published under the new chairman's editorship.[9] Hua, therefore, had everything to lose if people took the rehabilitation of Deng to signify an implied criticism of the man whose mantle Hua had inherited. But one must go further than mere Pekingological speculation. Indeed, it may be argued that, despite the 'Gang's' alleged attacks on him, Hua did not find the kind of analysis of Chinese society advanced by the 'Gang' as unconvincing as people like Deng Xiaoping. One cannot, of course, be too sure about the position adopted by Hua in early 1977 but it is clear that, by March 1977, those who pressed for the rehabilitation of Deng were getting their way and Hua acknowledged that all the charges against Deng made by the 'Gang' were unfounded.[10] By mid-year, Deng had, in fact, been rehabilitated and, at the Third Plenum of the Tenth Central Committee in July, was reinstated as vice-chairman of the Party.[11]

The Eleventh Congress of the Chinese Communist Party and the Campaign to Criticise the 'Gang of Four'

The Third Plenum was to prepare the ground for the convocation of the Eleventh Congress of the Party which met in August 1977. Unlike the congresses of 1956, 1958, 1969 and 1973, this congress was not characterised by an attempt to head off renewed radicalism. In the months before the congress, the commitment of the leadership to 'continuous revolution' had been gradually eroded. At the congress, while stressing the importance of class struggle and Mao's view that cultural revolutions would continue to occur in the future,[12] Hua gave greater weight to the theme of unity and stability. At the same time, Hua's report seemed to signify that the restoration of Deng had ended the moratorium on theoretical debate and that serious attempts were now to be made to refute the 'Gang's' position. In the new climate, Mao's theory of 'continuous revolution' was reinterpreted as the mid-1950s version of 'uninterrupted revolution', whereby revolution was said to consist merely in the resolution of social contradictions.[13] The view of Zhang Chunqiao and Yao Wenyuan that new classes would constantly be generated was thus changed out of all recognition. The position that 'new bourgeois elements' might appear within the Communist Party was caricatured as the allegation that the Party itself contained a discrete bourgeois class.[14] Now, a different explanation for the existence of 'new bourgeois elements' was offered. They arose not as a consequence of social structure but as a result of individual capitalist behaviour.[15] The separation of behaviour from structure permitted articles to concentrate on the need to develop the 'productive forces'.

The theme of developing these 'productive forces' under the rubric of the 'four modernisations' (agriculture, industry, science and technology and national defence), which had been raised by Zhou Enlai in 1975, was to dominate the congress and its aftermath. It was the Party's task to promote those modernisations though little was said, at first, about the theoretical implications of such a role. After all, once it was implied that modernisation might be governed by 'laws' which could not be determined by the Party, it is very difficult to see what the Party's ideological role might be apart from educating people in economics.[16]

To facilitate the process of modernisation, the Eleventh Congress and its First Plenum elected to positions of leadership a number of senior economic planners. Of the four vice-chairmen of the Party, Deng Xiaoping and Li Xiannian were particulary concerned with economic matters. The third, Ye Jianying, a former marshal of the PLA, was also concerned with orderly economic development and only the fourth, Wang Dongxing, might be identified with the ideas of Mao on economic development put forward after 1958. The new Politburo included such veteran economic ministers as Fang Yi and Yu Qiuli, as well as Zhao Ziyang (as alternate) who was to become something of a symbol of new economic policies in Sichuan. In the Central Committee, 'followers of the Gang of Four', who had a very different idea about modernisation, were removed from the leadership. Of the surviving 174 full members of the Tenth Central Committee, 59 were not re-elected to the Eleventh and of 123 surviving alternates, 51 failed to retain their seats. In the new Central Committee, 146 out of 333 full and alternate members were newcomers who might be expected to support the new interpretation of the 'four modernisations'.[17]

Of the 35 million Communist Party members, the congress announced that half had been recruited since the Cultural Revolution and seven million since the Tenth Congress in 1973.[18] There must, therefore, have been quite a few members who remained sympathetic to the policies, if not the behaviour, of the 'Gang of Four'. To deal with such people, the congress decided to set up 'commissions for inspecting discipline'. These were to carry out a thorough screening of Party members in a manner similar to the campaign to 'purify the class ranks' of the late 1960s (though with very different criteria). The commissions, which bore a striking resemblance to bodies set up in the early 1950s, were made subordinate to local Party committees (at *xian* level and above or, in the army, at regimental level and above). They therefore did not constitute a separate Party control hierarchy such as that which was formed in the mid-1950s according to the Soviet model. By late 1978, however, there is evidence that such a hierarchy might have been developing and this was eventually headed by a Central Commission for Inspecting Discipline.[19]

Initially, the commissions for inspecting discipline were to function something like the old Party organisation departments. It was felt imperative to improve the organisational structure of the Party. To facilitate this, an ever increasing number of old Party cadres were rehabilitated (or 'liberated')[20] and it became clear that no previous verdicts could be trusted any more, including those which had been associated with Chairman Mao himself. As the Party leaders saw it, the problem in the past had been that people were admitted to the Party too easily and all sorts of undesirable elements had become members. Now, strict criteria for probation and selection were imposed[21] and Party schools were re-established.[22] Party control over the mass organisations (labour unions, Women's Federation and Communist Youth League) was strengthened. The centralist component of the Mass Line was emphasised and Mao's 1962 essay on 'Democratic Centralism' became required reading.[23] This essay criticised the abnormal Party life which existed prior to that date and described the Party as a processing plant for mass inputs (though it will also be remembered that this essay contained passages which reflected Mao's generative notion of class).[24] Thus, both democracy and centralism were stressed, but in a much more orthodox Leninist framework than had existed under the 'Gang of Four'.

The rectification of the Party, inaugurated by the Eleventh Congress, was to change fundamentally the nature of the campaign to criticise the 'Gang of Four'. In the second half of 1977 and throughout 1978, the campaign widened to include a large number of people branded as 'the Gang's sworn followers'. For a year and a half, the press was full of accounts of the denunciation of 'local despots', 'egalitarians' or just simply 'capitalist roaders', all of whom were said to have owed their position to the 'Gang'. They were blamed for almost every conceivable deviation and all those criticised were uniformly considered to be 'ultra-rightist'. In that way, an association was made with the denunciation of Lin Biao. Doubtless, a lot of the criticism was just but much also was contradictory and might reflect little more than cadres humiliated during the Cultural Revolution seeking revenge on the 'upstarts' who replaced them. There was, it seems, much scope for arbitrary interpretation. How, for example, was one to determine who belonged to the 'wind faction'[25] (those who changed their position according to the way the political wind had blown) or the 'quake faction' (those who made political earthquakes to advance their own position)?[26] Furthermore, in a Party which maintained a degree of secrecy about its operations, how could one always adhere to the 'three principles' ('practise Marxism and not revisionism, be united and don't split, be open and above board and do not intrigue and conspire')?

Throughout the campaign, there seemed to be a contradiction between the repeated calls for unity and stability and the quite vicious criticism of more and more 'sworn followers of the Gang'. Perhaps the source of the confusion was the contradictory messages which emanated from the Party Centre. For example, Hua Guofeng announced that the investigations connected with the 'Gang's' conspiracy had basically been concluded in February[27] and again in July 1978.[28] In August of that year, however, Wei Guoqing, who was close to Deng Xiaoping, suggested that the movement still had some way to go.[29] It is not unreasonable to infer, therefore, that various leaders interpreted the scope of the movement in different ways. One would expect that Mayor Wu De was anxious to get the movement over and done with as soon as possible, and it is significant that Wu was to be replaced as mayor of Beijing by Lin Hujia whose major claim to fame was 'taking the lid off the struggle' in Tianjin.[30] With the removal of Wu, it seemed that at least one of Chen Yun's alleged demands could be carried out and, before long, the Tiananmen incident of 1976 was declared a 'completely revolutionary action'.[31] Revolutionary it may have been, but its preparations had hardly been 'open and above board'.

Economic Policy (1977–8)

The rehabilitation of Deng Xiaoping in mid-1977 and his confirmation in office at the Eleventh Party Congress, not only changed the nature of the campaign against the 'Gang of Four' and ended the moratorium on theoretical discussion but also made it possible to thrash out a new economic policy to realise the 'four modernisations'. Prior to Deng's reappearance, constant reference had been made to Mao's 1956 speech 'On the Ten Major Relationships', which had been published openly in the press for the first time in late 1976.[32] This speech, it will be recalled,[33] was made partly as a refutation of the 1950s (Soviet model) stress on a centralised economy. It was, however, quite ambiguous and lent itself to different interpretations. On the one hand, the speech affirmed the policy of 'simultaneous advance of all fronts' (agriculture, heavy industry and light industry) which became the rallying cry of the Great Leap Forward. On the other hand, great stress was laid on sectoral balance, in contrast to the subsequent Great Leap affirmation of creative imbalance. But there was no doubt that Deng Xiaoping adhered to the balanced interpretation of Mao's 1956 speech and, following his rehabilitation, attempts were made to fuse together the prescriptions of 'On the Ten Major Relationships' and Deng's 'three poisonous weeds' (now redesignated 'fragrant flowers').

The general strategy for economic development was put forward at the first session of the Fifth National People's Congress in February 1978. Though the congress was seen as a continuation of that of 1975, when Zhou Enlai had put forward his long-term modernisation proposals, the documents were perhaps more reminiscent of the 1950s than the 1970s. A new detailed constitution was published[34] which restored many of the features of the constitution of 1954. The number of ministerial-level institutions was now expanded to 37.[35] The Procuratorate was restored to check upon the activities of government cadres and revolutionary committees were abolished in all units of production. Henceforth, such revolutionary committees would only continue to exist in administrative units where they seemed to function in much the same way as the old people's governments. Echoing the 1950s, moves were undertaken to revive the Chinese People's Political Consultative Conference[36] and to restore the various 'democratic' political parties which might help in the task of economic modernisation. Interestingly, nothing was said about the theoretical rationale for such vestiges of the 'new democratic' stage,

20 years after the 'construction of socialism' was said to have begun. At roughly the same time, the spirit of the 1950s was again evidenced by the new stress on conscription into the armed forces[37] rather than the old 'people's war' concept of a citizen militia. All this was a far cry from the atmosphere of the early 1970s.

Most important of all, the spirit of the mid-1950s was clearly recalled in the details of the new ten-year plan which were released by Chairman Hua to the congress. As one might have expected, there was a close similarity between the new plan and Mao's twelve-year plan which first saw the light of day in 1955. The targets were equally ambitious.[38] By 1985, it was anticipated that grain production would increase from some 295 million tonnes to 400 million, with an annual increase in the agricultural growth rate from just over 2 per cent to between 4 and 5 per cent. Twelve key areas for grain production were marked out (there were previously eleven) and it was envisaged that 85 per cent of the total rural farmland would be mechanised by 1985. In industry, iron and steel production was to increase from some 30 million tonnes to 60 million with an industrial growth rate of 10 per cent; 120 large-scale projects were planned and 14 local industrial bases were to be developed and consolidated. To achieve all this, the investment target for the final eight years of the plan was to equal the total for the preceding 28 years. These were Great Leap targets indeed, and press comments were not slow in pointing out the parallels with 1958[39] in the new atmosphere of 'uninterrupted revolution'.

But, as the congress documents suggested, there was to be nothing like the Great Leap. The experiments of 1958–9 were conducted in the spirit of 'self-reliance', both regional and national. In 1978, it became clear that the policy of 'export-led growth', described in the last chapter, was being given a new stress and attempts were made to finance much of the modernisation programme by exports of oil and coal. On a visit to Tokyo in October 1978, Deng announced that the $US 20 billion Sino-Japanese trade agreement for the next eight years might be expected to 'double and double again'. It was even envisaged that, by 1985, exports of oil to Japan might reach 40 to 50 million tonnes which was almost half China's output in 1978.[40] There was therefore a need to accelerate the process of oil production. There seemed, moreover, no recourse but to raise loans to pay for the necessary technology or to invite foreign participation in oil exploitation. Such issues had featured in the polemic between Deng and the 'Gang' in 1975 and, once again, some leaders voiced their worries. The fact that many ingenious formulas were worked out for borrowing overseas, then rejected, then adopted once again, suggests a major cleavage on economic policy in 1978.

In industry, also, the detailed measures undertaken to achieve the targets present a picture very different from the Great Leap. Rather, the ambiguity in industrial policies reflects the period of soul-searching of 1956 – 7. This one would expect when policies were set within the framework of 'On the Ten Major Relationships'. In July 1978, an interim document governing industrial policy was published entitled 'Draft Decisions on Several Questions Concerning the Acceleration of Industrial Development'.[41] These 'thirty points' reflected not only the spirit of the mid-1950s but also Deng Xiaoping's comments on industrial development of 1975. In enterprise management, the formula 'responsibility of the factory general manager under the unified leadership of the enterprise Party committee' was reinvoked. There was a stress on strict fulfilment of the eight targets specified by the state, on discipline and on the responsibility system, but factory managers were still required to work for a time on the shop floor. There was also some provision for intra-enterprise democracy. Workers' congresses were promoted once again and it became possible for leadership at shop level to be elected.[42] But, though the 'thirty points' still stressed the value of Mao's Anshan constitution and talked about the 'two participations and triple combination', such democracy was seen more in a representative than in a participatory sense. Once again, there was a stress on payment according to work[43] and piecework methods were experimented with.[44] Bonuses were now promoted quite openly, though it was claimed that they had never really been abolished in the Cultural Revolution and had merely had their name changed to 'supplementary wages'.[45] Complaints about low wages had, in 1977, been met by a national wage rise, affecting half of all industrial workers, and little had been said about the effect of such a rise on the urban-rural gap. None of this was new, but it did mark a significant departure from the ideals of the Great Leap and the Cultural Revolution. Daqing had been the symbol of the industrial policy of those times but in 1978, when plans were put forward to establish one-third of all industrial enterprises as Daqing-type enterprises by 1980, the 1972 interpretation held. Daqing had become the symbol of tight and efficient management.[46]

One cannot be sure just how much debate arose from the above provisions for enterprise management. We do know, however, that there was considerable difference of views on macro-economic policy. For example, there was, once again, a protracted debate between advocates of what Schurmann has called 'decentralisation I' (to the level of the productive units) and 'decentralisation II' (to local areas). Throughout 1977 – 8, the official position supported 'decentralisation II' and Deng Xiaoping, in one of his 'poisonous weeds' of 1975, had made a point of demanding that the decentralisation of authority over industry should not be extended beyond provincial and municipal levels.[47] This position was enshrined in the 'thirty points',[48] though that document made some concessions to greater unit independence by allowing industrial enterprises to retain a much greater proportion of their above-plan profits.[49]

Arguments over the type of decentralisation, it will be remembered, were of crucial importance in determining the role of the market in integrating the economy. The mid-1950s advocates of 'decentralisation I' had been attacked in the Cultural Revolution as followers of Liberman and his alleged Chinese spokesman, Sun Yefang. By 1978, Sun Yefang had been rehabilitated and people such as Chen Yun and Xue Muqiao, who had been sympathetic to the arguments that enterprises should enjoy greater independence, had achieved very important state posts. The influence of such people was reflected at a national conference on finance and trade which met in June-July 1978. This conference made much of the operation of the 'law of value' which had apparently not been fully implemented in the past because of the 'mentality of small producers'.[50] The implication here was that there was to be a far greater stress on the market determination of prices.

The operation of the 'law of value', which had constantly been reiterated at the finance and trade conference, was taken up by the head of the newly established Chinese Academy of the Social Sciences, Hu Qiaomu, in a speech to the State Council in July 1978.[51] Rejecting categorically the 'Gang of Four's' point that ownership could not be separated from the other aspects of the relations of production, Hu maintained that, once the pattern of ownership changed, the objective economic laws, which operated in any economy regardless of governing régime, also changed fundamentally in content. There was no reason, therefore, why China should not emulate the advanced experiences in economic management practised in the West. In 1977 and early 1978, there had been much discussion in the Chinese press about Lenin's qualified approval of aspects of the Taylor system of time-and-motion management[52] (though no comment was made about Lenin's point that the Soviet Union, in 1918, was concerned more with constructing 'state capitalism' than socialism). There had also been much talk about the independent nature of technology. But Hu was going much further than that. Hu's claim was that there was a fundamental separation between the social and technical divisions of labour. The technical economy, therefore, operated according to laws which should not be interfered with in an arbitrary manner. Subsequently, advocates of Hu's position were to claim that most problems which had plagued the economy in the past had been due to administrative methods of running the economy and, whether these derived from the Yan'an or Soviet models, they were inappropriate and unscientific.[53]

Hu, of course, was no classical liberal who had faith in some 'hidden hand'. He did support planning (though more of an indicative than a command variety). He wished, moreover, to maintain control over the economy via the banking system.[54] To this end, proposals were put forward to modify the previous policy of direct state investment in favour of financing production through bank loans. Most commercial enterprises already derived most of their liquid capital from such loans. Now, people argued, this should be extended to industrial enterprises and, it was hoped, fixed capital might eventually be managed by the same means.[55] Of course, by manipulating interest rates and the availability of credit, any state is able to maintain some control over the economy. It is highly doubtful, however, whether such mechanisms can do much to serve all the *political* goals which Chinese planners had considered in the past. In separating the social and technical divisions of labour, however, Hu had rendered such a consideration irrelevant. Doubtless, Hu's proposals might eliminate waste by tying production more closely to consumer 'demand'. But, as many economic philosophers will assert, the economists' 'demand' has nothing to do with a consideration of human and social needs. The fact that the preceding system might have been inefficient is no argument against such an observation.

The kind of position outlined by Hu reflected the growing tendency in 1977–8 to see the 'four modernisations' only in terms of increasing output. The ambiguity in the economy at that time, therefore, not only reflected the continuing legacy of Mao's ideas but also the fact that different forms of economic organisation might serve the goal of output maximisation. Some of these types of organisation seem firmly within the Great Leap Forward tradition. One such example was the horizontally integrated trust, like that of the 'dragon' system of Changzhou, which was set firmly within the framework of locally co-ordinated economic integration.[56] Other forms which were now advocated, however, had been heartily condemned during the Cultural Revolution. An example here would be the vertically integrated trust. This had once been denounced for preventing local integration and negating Party leadership. In calling for the re-establishment of such trusts,[57] people such as Hu Qiaomu must have realised that they were challenging those who still held to Mao's ideas. But until the Party leadership could reach a verdict on Mao's economic ideas, Hu's proposals would remain unendorsed and compromise documents such as the 'thirty points' would remain in force.

The Rural Sector (1977–8)[58]

Like those in the industrial sector, policies towards agriculture tended to reflect a similar kind of ambiguity. Agriculture was still regarded as the 'base' of the economy and was to play a major part in financing the modernisation of other sectors. To do this, output had to be increased considerably. This could partly be achieved through bringing new land into cultivation and plans were made to increase the 100- million-hectare crop area by some 13 million.[59] The major source of increased output, however, had to come from increased crop yields. In 1977 and 1978, therefore, a major effort was made to reach the targets for yields per hectare specified in the National Programme for Agricultural Development (1960). Since the new high-yielding seed types needed vastly increased amounts of fertiliser and water, there had to be considerable investment in fertiliser production capacity and in irrigation. Mechanisation was also felt to be imperative since the rural areas (unlike the urban) suffered from a general labour shortage. All such considerations implied a much greater centralisation of decision-making in agriculture. The control of the major rivers and the diversion of waters from the Changjiang to the north[60] could only be implemented through national co-ordination. Economic logic, moreover, suggested the use of commune and *xian*-level machine tractor stations, which had only sometimes been abolished in the preceding radical periods. The new centralising tendency was also reflected in the new stress on the research activity of central institutes rather than field experiments in the communes.[61]

But the centralising tendency in the years 1977 – 8 must not be overstated. Throughout the period, rural development was still seen within the context of Schurmann's 'decentralisation II' and the campaign to establish Dazhai-type *xian* was carried on according to the spirit of self-reliance. What was changing in that movement was not so much the stress on local initiative but the political criteria employed to assess it. In his speech to the national conference on learning from Dazhai in agriculture in late 1975, Hua Guofeng had laid down criteria such as being 'united in struggle' against 'capitalist activities' and the 'determination to supervise and remould class enemies'.[62] By 1977, however, Hua's aim to transform one-third of China's 2,100-odd *xian* into Dazhai-type *xian* by 1980 seems exclusively to have been seen in terms of output and the 1985 targets, announced at the first session of the Fifth National People's Congress in February 1978, reflected the new view.

The concern with output led also to a new stress on the integrity of the production team. At first sight, the mechanisation targets would seem to suggest that the former moderate approach to upgrading the unit of account would not change. Although, at a national level, only 28 per cent of collective income was generated at brigade and commune levels in 1978,[63] there were a few communes where the higher levels had begun to generate more income than the lower and where one could think of upgrading. In 1977, therefore, some provincial authorities urged that a selective programme of upgrading be undertaken.[64] By 1978, however, it was felt that the interests of increasing output would best be served by affirming the integrity of the production team and only allowing for upgrading under exceptional circumstances. Teams were urged to enter into contractual agreements with higher levels and much criticism was directed at communes and brigades which took labour away from the teams and harmed their independence.[65] At the same time, restrictions were lifted on the private activity of team members and peasants were encouraged to sell the produce of their private plots on the open market. Particularly important here was the supply of meat, since some 73 per cent of the country's 300 million pigs were raised privately.[66] In Sichuan, for example, peasants were given special allocations of rice and cloth for the sale of pigs and eggs to state marketing agencies.[67] As far as private trading was concerned, there seemed to be no controls on the price peasants might ask for their produce[68] and there was even some private sale of grain. By the end of 1978, it was estimated that some 30,000 rural trade fairs had been restored and, in a survey of 206 such fairs over the whole country, the volume of transactions was 30 per cent greater than the same period in 1977.[69] If one's focus was on increasing output, the above picture was very encouraging. If, however, one was worried about 'capitalist tendencies', there was cause for alarm.

The new focus on the integrity of the production team, in 1978, would suggest that less attention was to be paid to the programme of rural industrialisation. There is not much evidence, however, that efforts in this direction slackened in 1977–8. After all, a lot of the fertiliser, so necessary for increasing output, was still produced in local plants. The huge imported nitrogenous fertiliser plants had made some impact, but large-scale production was still insufficient, and transport facilities were still inadequate to ensure the central distribution of fertiliser. In any case, so long as 'On the Ten Major Relationships' informed economic policy, one would expect considerable attention to be devoted to the light industry located in the countryside. Yet it was apparent that a new austerity drive in the countryside made it so much more difficult to raise loans for light industrial development (or anything else). In their desire to balance the books, local cadres not only clamped down on corruption and waste[70] (blamed on the 'Gang of Four' and its followers) but also on those households who had overdrawn supplies of grain in anticipation of a share-out at harvest time.[71] By the end of 1978, the availability of credit in the rural sector was very tight.

In the situation of 1978, when it seemed that Party control over the rural economy was slackening, educated youths voiced their reluctance to go to the rural areas. In more radical days, many youths could be persuaded that it was a moral duty to integrate with the peasants. Now that official policy was to keep the majority of youths in segregated villages and now that the Party seemed concerned less with moral exhortation than with economic efficiency, educated youths began to feel that their talents might be better used in the cities. Such disgruntled youths were, therefore, most interested in a national conference on rusticated youth which took place at the end of 1978. The conference still maintained the need for the rustication policy but stressed a more liberal interpretation.[72] At the same time, an influential article in *Zhongguo Qingnian bao* made the point that, in the 1950s, the policy of *xiaxiang* had been justified because urban jobs were insufficient. In the Cultural Revolution, however, too many youths had been sent to the countryside and now, as the 'four modernisations' developed the economy, the number of such youths in the countryside might be expected to diminish. In fact, the article went on to pour scorn on the 'Gang of Four's' comments on the moral purpose of the *xiaxiang* movement. Integrating with the workers and peasants, the article declared, did not necessarily mean physical integration; it could simply mean 'emulating the fine qualities of the workers and peasants, studying assiduously and working actively for the four modernisations'. When it came down to it, the main method of closing the gap between city and country was to 'develop the productive forces'. Because of the interference of Lin Biao and the 'Gang of Four', the *xiaxiang* movement had done nothing in this respect.[73] I have no doubt that Mao would have been shocked at such a statement. Yet what is more to the point here is that there was little wonder that, on reading articles such as the above, many youths left the countryside and were most annoyed when Party authorities, worried about the shortage of jobs in the cities, sent them back. Such frustration was to give rise to a frenzied poster campaign in late November in which some returned youths demanded jobs and a reversal of the rustication policy.[74]

Policy Towards Education (1977–8)[75]

Economic necessity, therefore, dictated the continuance of the *xiaxiang* campaign in 1977–8. The same may be said for the policy of encouraging schools to run workshops (which might contribute to funds), the continuance of 'part-work, part-study' schools and the promotion of July Twenty-First colleges. In almost every other respect, however, the 'revolution in education' was reversed. The arrest of the 'Gang of Four' took place after plans had been made for the academic year 1976–7 but, even so, immediate provision was made to reduce drastically the amount of time students spent participating in manual labour. By the following year, despite lip service paid to 'open door education', tertiary students were only spending some four weeks per year in the factories or the communes.[76] The time spent by teachers on manual work was even less and the Ministry of Education ordered that the salaries of teachers, who had left their 'rightful duties' to work elsewhere, should be stopped.[77] Now, much greater attention was to be paid to theoretical studies and scorn was poured on those schools where classes in physics consisted of the study of 'three machines and one pump'.[78]

In general, the education system in 1977 – 8 saw a rapid return to the pre-Cultural Revolution situation. The national education work conference in April 1978 took place in an atmosphere reminiscent of the early 1960s[79] and the draft outline programme for national education (1978 – 85), introduced by Minister of Education Liu Xiyao, had very little room for the innovations of the Cultural Revolution.[80] What was singled out for particular condemnation was the 'two assessments' made, it was alleged, by the 'Gang of Four', to the effect that a 'revisionist' line had existed in education prior to 1966 and that the majority of intellectuals produced during those years were 'bourgeois'.[81] On the contrary, it was suggested, in 1978, that the pre-Cultural Revolution system was better than that which existed in later years. In line with such a revised view, large numbers of tertiary students were recruited directly from secondary school. Efforts were made, once again, to standardise textbooks. There was a return also to unified entrance examinations for colleges and universities, conducted first on a provincial level in 1977 and on a national level in 1978.[82] Of the 5.7 million students who sat the college entrance examination in October 1977, some 278,000 were admitted.[83] Provision was made also for the enrolment of graduate students, after a 'rigorous examination'[84] and it was rumoured that the higher-degree system, abolished in 1957, would be restored. Once again, academic titles (professor, associate professor etc.) were introduced and all levels in the education system were enjoined to 'respect the teacher'.[85]

In the new climate there was some discussion about increasing, once again, the amount of time spent in school, though financial constraints seem to have prevented a return to the six-year system for primary schools and six years for secondary schools which China had inherited from the West in the 1950s. A more normal pattern, specified in the national plan, was five:five for the urban areas and five:three for the rural.[86] Since the completion of a full five years of secondary schooling was seen to be a necessary prerequisite for tertiary enrolment, it appeared that rural students were to be excluded from the tertiary sector almost entirely,[87] unless they were able to finish their secondary schooling in the towns. Perhaps the most controversial point in the changes of 1977 – 8 was the restoration of a system of 'keypoint' (priority) schools (*zhongdian xuexiao*) with a first claim on state resources, the best students and a guarantee that their graduates would go into the most prestigious academic jobs.[88] These schools had been denounced in the Cultural Revolution as 'little treasure pagoda schools' which would exacerbate the difference between the two tracks[89] and one wonders whether their restoration was universally acclaimed. In promoting them, the veteran educator Zhou Peiyuan was most active. Zhou welcomed not only the restoration of 'keypoint' schools at primary and secondary level but also called for the establishment of 'keypoint' universities.[90] He was soon to get his way and, in 1978, 88 such tertiary institutions were so designated (compared with 60 élite institutions prior to the Cultural Revolution).[91]

With the establishment of these élite institutions, attempts were made to draw up exchange agreements with counterparts in foreign countries, in order to raise the level of academic standards. To achieve the same end, the Chinese Academy of Sciences and the newly established Chinese Academy of Social Sciences acquired considerable power and prestige. Doubtless, there was much truth in the charges, made in 1977–8, that academic standards had declined since 1966 but, as has been noted, questions of breadth had in the past been considered more important than questions of depth. In the new climate, it was argued that inequalities had to be tolerated in order to develop the economic base.[92] Only that way could greater equalities be achieved in the future. This reversal of what was considered to be one of the fundamental characteristics of the pre-1976 education system has disappointed many liberal educators in the West. The change, however, does seem to have been popular amongst Chinese intellectuals who had much to gain. It might also have been popular among peasants who derived pride from those one or two students in their village who made it to a prestige institution. But is such apparent popularity the only thing that one should consider?

The New 'Hundred Flowers' Policy[93]

The new prestige enjoyed by intellectuals in the period 1977–8 was accompanied, as one might expect, by the toleration of a much greater degree of freedom in literature and the arts. There was, it seems, a veritable explosion of artistic creation. Traditional Beijing operas, Western-style plays, modern short stories and even the occasional new novel appeared. Intellectuals could now read their own copy of the translated works of Victor Hugo, Dickens or Shakespeare against the background of music such as the exceedingly popular 'Blue Danube'. They were no longer afraid to listen to foreign broadcasts and could even write letters to their favourite foreign radio station. They could read, once again, the works of Chinese writers formerly considered 'bourgeois' or, if such was their taste, the many short stories describing the sufferings of youth and cadres in the Cultural Revolution (the so-called 'literature of the wounded generation').[94] If they were lucky enough to get tickets, they could attend performances of foreign orchestras and artistic troupes. All this was profoundly exciting and little was said any more about the extent to which such activities might promote a 'slavish mentality'.

In the new climate, constant reference was, of course, made to the original 'hundred flowers' policy of 1957. Just as intellectuals were encouraged at that time to criticise the restrictive nature of the Soviet model, so intellectuals were now encouraged to criticise the restrictive policies of the 'Gang of Four'. Attempts were made, therefore, to link the 'hundred flowers' movement of 1957 with the 'second hundred flowers' movement of the early 1960s (which, as has been demonstrated, was very different). A number of productions censured by the 'Gang' (allegedly against Mao's wishes) were reinstated, including one famous film which portrayed the Daqing oilfield as a model for increasing production rather than implementing the ideals of the Cultural Revolution.[95] It was pointed out that it had been Zhou Enlai, rather than Jiang Qing, who had correctly interpreted Mao's position on art and literature and that Jiang had mercilessly persecuted writers simply for maintaining close relations with the late premier.[96] The implication seemed clear. What had previously been branded as 'Liu Shaoqi's sinister line on literature and art' was not really Liu's at all but was more properly that of Zhou Enlai. It was, moreover, far from 'sinister'. Such a conclusion could not be made explicit, however, without openly challenging Mao's many statements on literature and art made in the 1960s. But one would have to have been singularly obtuse not to have realised that many of the policies associated with Jiang Qing were in fact those of Mao.

Just like Mao's economic ideas, the former chairman's statements on literature and art were capable of varying interpretations. In the mid-1950s, the official position had been that writers and artists should have freedom to write about what they liked provided that they served the socialist cause. Similarly, the 1978 constitution declared both that 'a hundred flowers' should bloom and that Marxism-Leninism should exercise a leading role in cultural affairs.[97] All that had changed, therefore, was how the cultural authorities interpreted Mao's very nebulous 'six criteria' for distinguishing 'fragrant flowers' from 'poisonous weeds'.[98] Deng Xiaoping was thus quite accurate when he denied that what was taking place was a form of 'liberalisation'.[99] The Party was just somewhat more easy-going.

Though it seemed that the Party was not going to let people publish anything they liked, it was clear that most of the previous verdicts on pre-Cultural Revolution works and their writers were to be revised. Symbolic of this aim was the rehabilitation in October 1977 of Zhou Yang and Xia Yan—who had been key figures among the Chinese Communist Party's cultural authorities from the 1930s to the mid-1960s.[100] Zhou, in particular, was to enjoy considerable prestige in cultural affairs in the following year and appeared more influential even than the Minister of Culture, Huang Zhen.[101] Yet the rehabilitation of somewhat lesser-known figures was to be a protracted matter. In December 1977, *Renmin Ribao* urged that the process of reassessment be given greater attention,[102] and to rectify the situation a new party fraction had to be organised in the Ministry of Culture.[103] This may have been because of the obstruction of

Zhang Pinghua, the head of the Party Central Committee's Propaganda Department, who was apparently concerned about the erosion of Mao's position.[104] Eventually, Zhang was to be removed from office,[105] but not until long after large numbers of artists and writers had been rehabilitated and a decision had been taken to remove the label of 'rightist' from all those 'capped' since 1957.

Once the large-scale process of rehabilitation had got under way in April 1978,[106] it became possible to rebuild, at a national level, the All China Federation of Literary and Art Circles and the National Writers' Union. These bodies were to provide forums for those who sought, by means of pressure-group activity, to criticise people such as Wu De who were reluctant to go along with all the changes.[107] So long as the critics did not contradict official policy, such efforts were supported by the Party leadership.

By November 1978, however, it did seem that some instances of free expression were pressing dangerously close to the limits defined by the Party. Such was the case with the poster campaign in the major cities in late November, initiated by educated youths returning from the countryside.[108] Taking their cue from the official change of verdict on the Tiananmen incident of April 1976,[109] many youths considered that spontaneous gestures of protest had been declared legitimate and were not sparing in their criticism of all and sundry. Mao himself was openly branded as a tyrant.[110] Organisations such as the Society for the Promotion of Socialist Democracy were formed and new unofficial literature appeared.[111] This put forward arguments which some people in authority must have considered to be highly dangerous. In response, the authorities did detain some of the authors of the more inflammatory *dazibao*.[112] Yet, on the whole, the official attitude was tolerant. But was this because of a new-found confidence in the efficacy of freedom of expression or because the protesters were attacking the very people the dominant faction in the leadership also wished to denounce? It is no accident that the early outpouring of protest and criticism coincided with what, in retrospect, was one of the most crucial series of meetings in the history of the Party. These meetings which took place in Beijing in late 1978 were, at last, to give official sanction to a slow process of de-Maoification. However dangerous the *dazibao* on Beijing's Democracy Wall and elsewhere might have been and however inflammatory the unofficial magazines might prove, they did serve to indicate that there was some mass support for people who sought a decisive confrontation with those in the central leadership who were worried about the gradual abandonment of the policies of the late chairman.

The Meetings of Late 1978[113]

The first and most important meeting to be held in late 1978 was a work conference of the Party Central Committee. This met on 9 November and was originally scheduled to last for three days. In fact, it went on for 35 days[114] and was the scene of bitter disputes fuelled, no doubt, by the external poster campaign. Unofficial sources reveal that the main source of dissension at that meeting was the official evaluation of the role of Mao Zedong. The conflict was between what the victors were to call the 'whatever' faction (*fanshipai*) and the 'practice' faction (*shijianpai*).[115] The 'whatever' faction was said to have been headed by Vice-Chairman Wang Dongxing. As commander of the military unit which had arrested the 'Gang', Wang was obviously not one of its supporters. He had, however, played a major role in the dismissal of Deng Xiaoping in early 1976 and was particularly disturbed by the reversal of so many of Mao's policies in 1977–8. Wang's disquiet was caricatured by his opponents as the philosophy of 'whatever'—an injunction to act according to whatever Mao Zedong said or noted before he died, which had been the theme of a *Renmin Ribao* editorial back in February 1977.[116] Wang was joined, it is said, by a number of other leaders, including Zhang Pinghua who, as we have seen, was worried about the changes of policy in the Party's propaganda network. On the other side, the 'practice' faction, which included Chen Yun and Hu Yaobang, took its cue from a major slogan which derived from Mao but was associated with Deng Xiaoping—'practice is the sole criterion for judging truth'.[117] Though unobjectionable from a Marxist point of view, this slogan had been used to justify what seems very much like William James's pragmatic conception of truth (judged by its cash value). In the polemic, the criterion of 'practice' was used by those who wished to examine Mao's policies in the light of their immediate effects and thus to arrive at a more balanced (in their view) picture of Mao.

In the work conference of November-December 1978, it was this latter group which was to triumph and Wang Dongxing and a number of other senior cadres were demoted to merely a symbolic role. Amongst these cadres, however, were people whose association with the 'whatever' faction is problematic. Chen Xilian, for example, the former military commander of the north-east who had been transferred to Beijing, was criticised mainly for supporting Mao Yuanxin, the 'arch henchman' of the 'Gang of Four'.[118] Even more important, Chen Yonggui, the founder of the Dazhai production brigade, was forced into retirement.[119] Though the 1978 interpretation of the Dazhai model, in the campaign to establish Dazhai-type *xian*, was very different from that which had been propagated in the Cultural Revolution, Dazhai had still continued to symbolise Mao's spirit of 'self-reliance'. At the meetings of late 1978, the dominant 'practice' faction was to have little room for such a spirit. Accordingly, two policy documents concerning agriculture were tabled[120] in which the Dazhai experience was mentioned rather cursorily.[121] After all, one of the documents was in fact a modified version of the Sixty Articles on Agriculture, promulgated in the early 1960s and denounced in the Cultural Revolution. The decision to return to the economic strategies of the early 1960s was, of course, a rejection of the Great Leap Forward and it now became possible posthumously to rehabilitate Peng Dehuai and Tao Zhu.[122]

The decisions reached at the work conference of November-December 1978 were ratified at the Third Plenum of the Eleventh Central Committee which met on 18–22 December and at a meeting of the Politburo which had been enlarged to include, amongst others, Chen Yun as Party vice-chairman and first secretary of the Central Commission for Inspecting Discipline. The communiqué of the Third Plenum announced that 'large-scale turbulent class struggles of a mass character had . . . come to an end',[123] signalling the official demise of Mao's view of continuous revolution and the theoretical rationale for new rounds of the Cultural Revolution in the future. On the original Cultural Revolution of 1966–9, the Central Committee reserved its judgement,[124] though subsequent references to the events of that time were overwhelmingly critical. It was announced, moreover, that the main focus of the Party's future work would shift to the realisation of the 'four modernisations'.[125] Since there had also been a general endorsement of Hu Qiaomu's position on 'objective economic laws', this did seem to constitute a completely new formulation of the Party's role. Now, in a way which was much less contentious than had been the case in 1977–8, the Party was seen less as the embodiment of the long-term interests of the proletariat and more as the intepreter of economic laws. Once a separation was made, moreover, between the Party's role as vanguard and the existence of a body of economic law, it became easier to separate that role from law defined in another sense. The intention was expressed, therefore, to continue the work of devising a socialist legal system,[126] which had been abandoned in 1957. Though the plenum paid tribute to Mao's achievements, the policy changes could only have been achieved after the abandonment of Mao's ideas of the past 20 years.

The demotion of the role of Mao was reflected most clearly in the decision taken by the Third Plenum no longer to refer to leaders by their titles (except on diplomatic occasions). Mao was henceforth to be referred to simply as 'comrade'. Hua Guofeng also was no longer the 'wise leader' and object of a personality cult. Though it was said that Hua had proposed the change to the plenum,[127] one cannot but feel that he had much to lose from such a move. Deng, as the formulator of new strategy worked out in 1977–8, could outshine Hua by claiming that he was 'restoring' Mao's Thought. Hua had, after all, only 'inherited' Mao's mantle. Now it seemed that not only the inheritance but also the restoration had been devalued. Those who were important, in the new climate, were people who worked out new policies on the basis of current practice. Perhaps the real victor was Chen Yun who seemed to have gained, at last, all the demands he had put forward after the arrest of the 'Gang' and who saw an official vindication of the position he had advocated back in the 1950s. In such a situation, even Deng's 'fragrant flowers' of 1975 and the 'thirty points' for industry he promoted in 1978, were to become somewhat dated.

Foreign Policy—Once More 'Leaning to One Side'

Apart from initiating a general process of de-Maoification, the meetings of late 1978 also ratified the decision to enter into full diplomatic relations with the United States. An announcement to this effect was made on 16 December,[128] signalling a new stage in the deterioration of the policy, inaugurated in the early 1970s, to drive a wedge between the superpowers. China was now definitely 'leaning to the side' of the United States. Such a development had been prefigured earlier in the year in the establishment of diplomatic relations with Libya[129] when no specific renunciation of Taiwan was made by the Libyan side. Interestingly, the Libyan communiqué had urged China to maintain its ideological fervour.[130] Such was a telling comment on China's tendency to see the world merely in terms of a 'balance of power'.

The cementing of US-China relations was prefigured also by the agreement, after six years of negotiations, on a Sino-Japanese treaty of peace and friendship.[131] China had continued to demand the insertion of an 'anti-hegemony' clause directed against the Soviet Union, but the Japanese had insisted that another clause be added to the effect that the conclusion of the treaty did not reflect on the relationship between either party and any third state.[132] Each side could, therefore, conclude that it had won a victory, and the economic benefits of improved relations could be exploited to the full. Indeed, by late 1978, it seemed that Japan would play the major role in providing advanced technology for China's modernisation programme. Such a situation did not, however, alter the fact that serious problems remained under the surface. There was no agreement, for example, on the question of South Korea. Japan had supported the maintenance of United States troops in the area whereas China, concerned about relations with North Korea, supported their withdrawal.[133] It was thus probably out of concern for the future of Sino-North Korean relations that China adopted a particularly solicitious attitude towards the North Korean régime throughout 1978.

The interests of the 'four modernisations' and opposing the Soviet Union was to lead China, in 1977–8, to adopt an even more active policy of cementing relations with all countries outside the Soviet orbit. Slightly better relations with India had become possible after the demise of the Indira Gandhi government. China expressed approval for the activities of ASEAN.[134] Large numbers of Chinese leaders travelled to a host of countries shopping for technology in the Second World[135] and expressing support for all kinds of régimes in the Third. A much publicised trip by Chairman Hua Guofeng to Yugoslavia, Rumania and Iran, on the tenth anniversary of the Soviet invasion of Czechoslovakia, was designed to assess the resistance of those countries to the Soviet Union. Yet to say nice things about the Shah's régime in late 1978[136] was, to say the least, impolitic. More significant still was the discovery that Yugoslavia had always been a resolutely socialist country and considerable praise was given to its policy of self-management.[137]

China's discovery of the Yugoslav 'road to socialism' in 1978 could not have endeared its leaders to those of Albania. But by that time, Sino-Albanian relations had reached an all-time low.[138] In retrospect, it seemed that these relations had been deteriorating ever since Nixon's visit to China in 1972 and that the Albanians were profoundly worried about what became known as 'Chairman Mao's thesis about the three worlds'. As Enver Hoxha saw it, the 'three worlds thesis' weakened the global struggle against imperialism and the two superpowers ought to be considered equally dangerous. After the fall of the 'Gang of Four' in China, a purge of leaders in the Albania Party of Labour had taken place[139] and Enver Hoxha seemed much less eager to re-establish ties with the West. By mid-1978, China was to be indicted by name for abandoning the anti-imperialist struggle and had, according to the Albanians, become a 'social imperialist country' itself. Enver Hoxha, one was told, had maintained good relations with the Chinese Party for the sake of the struggle against the Soviet Union but Mao had always been a nationalist rather than a Marxist-Leninist.[140] In such a climate, one may understand why Chinese aid to Albania came to an abrupt end in 1978.[141]

Sino-Albanian relations were not the only ones to have been degenerating since 1972. Vietnam also had been hostile to the Nixon visit. Though the fall of Saigon had been greeted enthusiastically by China, much more attention seemed to have been paid to the victory of the Khymer Rouge in Kampuchea. Fearful of the implications of Le Duan's visit to Moscow in 1975, when it was announced that Vietnam and the Soviet Union would co-ordinate plans for economic development, China began to show more hostility towards Vietnam. This situation was, moreover, exacerbated by dissension in the Khymer Rouge régime between pro-Hanoi leaders and their pro-Chinese opponents. After Vietnam's appeals to the West for aid had been rebuffed and Soviet-Vietnamese relations improved even further, China began to fear the growth of another Cuba on its doorstep.

The ostensible source of hostility between China and Vietnam, in 1978, was first the disputed border. Since the land in dispute was only some 60 square kilometres, it was hardly likely to have been the major source of concern, though the possibilities of oil exploitation on the continental shelf and around the disputed islands were much more important. A second source of contention concerned the mass exodus of ethnic Chinese from Vietnam which reached flood proportions after April 1978. From early April to mid-May 1978 some 50,000 overseas Chinese crossed the border into China, [142] most of whom came from the north and were not remnants of the old Saigon régime. This exodus coincided with a new Chinese determination to foster better relations with overseas Chinese who might be able to provide a source of foreign exchange and a reservoir of talent for the 'four modernisations'. Though most of the refugees must have been destitute, China was perhaps worried that inadequate concern could damage the new policy. Remembering, perhaps, that the maltreatment of overseas Chinese in Indonesia in 1965 had provided fuel for internal dissidents, China's leaders wished to avoid a repetition of that state of affairs in the delicate political climate of 1978. Thus, protests were most vocal.

By June the situation was tense. After Vietnam had expressed its intention to join the Soviet-led CMEA and after the overseas Chinese question had become critical, all aid to Vietnam was cut off. [143] For its part, Vietnam accused China of fomenting the activities of a 'fifth column' in Vietnam and border clashes continued. In November 1978, Vietnam concluded a 25-year treaty with the Soviet Union. That treaty confirmed China's worst fears about Vietnam [144] and the conclusion of diplomatic relations between China and the United States confirmed Vietnam's worst fears. Furthermore, with the disintegration of the Kampuchean régime into factions variously pro- and anti-Chinese, the stage was set for a decisive confrontation.

Conclusion

This chapter has documented the general retreat from the policies pursued in China before 1976. Up to mid-1977, there was much confusion as to what should be done and press comments focused on the nefarious behaviour of the 'Gang of Four'. Following the restoration of Deng Xiaoping, however, a nationwide rectification campaign was launched and a serious debate occurred on China's future development. In this second period, policies were set within the framework of the strategy of 'uninterrupted revolution' of the mid-1950s. An all-out effort was launched to increase production within an economy decentralised to local areas. At the same time, there was a restoration of the policy of 'letting a hundred flowers bloom and a hundred schools of thought contend'. Yet, despite that, the new strategy proceeded within the new context of 'export-led growth'. There was also a reluctance to allow the destabilising tendencies, associated with the mid-1950s vision, to occur once again. By 1978, therefore, new elements began to enter into the developmental strategy to the point where the various meetings of late 1978 ended the generalisation of the mid-1950s and returned to policies first experimented with in the early 1960s. This was only made possible by the implicit rejection of all of Mao's economic policies pursued since 1957. The Third Plenum was to begin the process of de-Maoification. Throughout the period, however, there were some continuities with previous policy. The general deterioration of the early 1970s foreign policy perspective continued, to the point where China was leaning very far to the side of the United States. Such a move was dictated not only by the need to foster the 'four modernisations' but also by the fear of greatly increased Soviet power. In taking this stand, China was to alienate some former allies and seemed completely to have abandoned many of the principled positions taken in the 1960s in the polemic on the General Line of the International Communist Movement. The next and final chapter will note that China was to go even further than a mere generalisation of the early 1960s and was, in fact, to go to war with that country which, only a few years before, was said to be as close to China as 'lips to teeth'.

NOTES

1. Much of this chapter is taken from the various contributions to Brugger, 1980; Brugger 1979(a), (b) and (c).

2. Hua Guofeng, 12 August 1977, *PR* 35, 26 August 1977, p.30.

3. See Sullivan, 1980.

4. Wu De, 24 October 1976, *PR* 44, 29 October 1976, pp. 13–14.

5. *Dazibao* displayed in Guangzhou, 10 February 1977, purporting to be pledges and demands sought by Chen Xilian, Wu De and Wang Dongxing, 5 October 1976, *Chinese Law and Government*, Vol. X, No. 1, Spring 1977, pp. 52–3.

6. *Issues and Studies*, Vol. XV, No. 2, February 1979, p. 88.

7. Hua Guofeng, December 1976, *Chinese Law and Government*, Vol. X, No. 1, Spring 1977, p. 67.

8. See handbill dated 8 January 1977, *Issues and Studies*, Vol. XIII, No. 3, March 1977, pp. 112–15.

9. See *PR* 17, 22 April 1977, pp. 12–37; Hua Guofeng, ibid. 19, 6 May 1977, pp. 15–27.

10. This was not reported until after Deng's rehabilitation. See ibid. 31, 29 July 1977, pp. 9–10.

11. CCPCC, 21 July 1977, ibid., p. 5.

12. Hua Guofeng, 12 August 1977, ibid. 35, 26 August 1977, p. 32 and 39.

13. See Sullivan, 1980, p. 36.

14. See *PR* 1, 6 January 1978, p. 19.

15. Ibid. 7, 17 February 1978, p. 7.

16. Discussed in Young, 1980, pp. 54–9.

17. *CQ* 72, December 1977, pp. 881–2.

18. Ye Jianying, 13 August 1977, *PR* 36, 2 September 1977, p. 36.

19. See Young, 1980, pp. 61–3.

20. As Lee (1978, pp. 935–6) points out, liberation (*jiefang*) signifies the restoration of cadres who have rectified their mistakes. Rehabilitation (*pingfan*) implies that the original charge was wrong. In my use of these words, I have not made this distinction and prefer the word 'rehabilitation' for both cases.

21. CCPCC, 18 August 1977, *PR* 36, 2 September 1977, pp. 18–20. See also Ye Jianying, 13 August 1977, ibid. 36, 2 September 1977, pp. 36–7.

22. CCPCC, 5 October 1977, ibid. 43, 21 October 1977, pp. 6–7 and 14.

23. Mao Zedong, 30 January 1962, ibid. 27, 7 July 1978, pp. 6–22.

24. Ibid., p. 12.

25. See Xu Shiyu, *Hongqi* 9, 1978, *SWB* FE/5913/B11/4, 11 September 1978.

26. According to Xu Shiyu, Wang Dongxing was said to have been such a person. In China, it is alleged that the term 'maker of earthquakes' was applied to Khrushchev. See *Zhengming* (Hong Kong) 16, February 1979, pp. 5–8, *FBIS* CHI–79–21–N 3, 30 January 1979.

27. Hua Guofeng, 26 February 1978, *PR* 10, 10 March 1978, p. 15.

28. Hua Guofeng, 7 July 1978, ibid. 30, 28 July 1978, p. 7.

29. Wei Guoqing, *Jiefangjunbao*, 25 August 1978, *SWB* FE/5902/B11/8, 29 August 1978.

30. Bonavia, *FEER*, Vol. CII, No. 42, 20 October 1978, pp. 10–11.

31. *PR* 47, 24 November 1978, p. 6.

32. Reprinted in ibid. 1, 1 January 1977, pp. 10–25.

33. See *China: Liberation and Transformation: 1942–1962*, pp. 132–3.

34. Text in *PR* 11, 17 March 1978, pp. 5–14; excerpt in Selden, 1979, pp. 689–95.

35. NPC, 5 March 1978, *PR* 10, 10 March 1978, p. 42.

36. The new constitution of this body is in ibid. 12, 24 March 1978, pp. 31–5.

37. Ibid. 11, 17 March 1978, p. 4.

38. Hua Guofeng, 26 February 1978, ibid. 10, 10 March 1978, pp. 18–26; excerpt in Selden, 1979, pp. 695–701.

39. *PR* 20, 19 May 1978, p. 7.

40. Lauriat, *FEER*, Vol. CII, No. 40, 6 October 1978, p. 60.

41. Text in *Issues and Studies*, Vol. XIV, No. 11, November 1978, pp. 89–97; ibid., Vol. XV, No. 1, January 1979, pp. 69–98.

42. *PR* 49, 8 December 1978, p. 9.

43. See ibid. 7, 17 February 1978, pp. 6–8.

44. The 'thirty points' called for a cautious experimentation with this system. See *Issues and Studies*, Vol. XV, No. 1, January 1979, p. 94.

45. Watson, 1980, pp. 124–5.

46. *Issues and Studies*, Vol. XIV, No. 11, November 1978, p. 94.

47. Deng Xiaoping, 2 September 1975, ibid., Vol. XIII, No. 7, July 1977, p. 100.

48. Ibid., Vol. XV, No. 1, January 1979, pp. 77–9.

49. Ibid., p. 74.

50. Li Xiannian, 20 June 1978, *PR* 30, 28 July 1978, p. 16.

51. Hu Qiaomu, July 1978, ibid. 45, 10 November 1978, pp. 7–12; ibid. 46, 17

November 1978, pp. 15–23; ibid. 47, 24 November 1978, pp. 13–21.

52. Ibid. 14, 1 April 1977, p. 25.

53. See Watson, 1980, pp. 14–15.

54. Hu Qiaomu, July 1978, *PR* 47, 24 November 1978, pp. 16–17.

55. See Watson, 1980, p. 116.

56. See ibid.; *Hongqi* 11, 1978, pp. 47–52. This model was cited in the 'thirty points', *Issues and Studies*, Vol. XV, No. 1, January 1979, p. 76.

57. Hu Qiaomu, July 1978, *PR* 47, 24 November 1978, pp. 15–16.

58. This section is based on Brugger, 1980.

59. The figure of 107 ha. was given to a US Water resources delegation 1974, Perkins 1976, p. 598. Other figures have been given to other delegations. In late 1978, official sources gave the figure of 100 ha., noting that the area had declined by 7 million ha. due to capital construction work. CCPCC, *zhongfa* (1979) 4, 11 January 1979, pp. 105 and 109. See also the discussion in Stavis, 1976, pp. 95–6. *RMRB* (22 May 1978, p. 1) stated that it was planned to extend the area by 13 million ha.

60. Tianjin Radio, 10 April 1979, *SWB* FE/6102/B11/14, 27 April 1979.

61. Fang Yi, 18 March 1978, *PR* 14, 7 April 1978, p. 8.

62. Hua Guofeng, 15 October 1975, ibid. 44, 31 October 1975, p. 8.

63. CCPCC, *zhongfa* (1979) 4, 11 January 1979, *Issues and Studies*, Vol. XV, No. 7, July 1979, p. 116.

64. Harbin, Heilongjiang Radio, 17 March 1978, *SWB* FE/5772/B11/8, 24 March 1978.

65. E.g. *RMRB*, 3 September 1977, p. 1; Wuhan, Hubei Radio, 26 January 1978, *SWB* FE/5730/B11/11, 3 February 1978.

66. *PR* (42, 17 October 1975, p. 23) states that every peasant household in the country raised 1.3 pigs on the average. This gives some 220 million pigs. This was 73 per cent of the official 1979 figure of 301 million. State Statistical Bureau, 27 June 1979, *BR* 27, 6 July 1979, p. 38.

67. NCNA, 10 November 1978, *SWB* FE/5971/B11/17, 17 November 1978.

68. NCNA, 11 November 1978, in ibid.

69. NCNA, 11 March 1979, ibid. FE/6068/B11/9–11, 16 March 1979.

70. Guangzhou, Guangdong Radio, 17, 19 and 21 January 1978, ibid. FE/5722/B11/3, 25 January 1978.

71. Guangzhou, Guangdong Radio, 14 January 1978, ibid. FE/5717/B11/12–13, 19 January 1978.

72. *RMRB*, 15 December 1978, p. 1 and 4.

73. Beijing Radio, 23 November 1978, *SWB* FE/5980/B11/1–3, 28 November 1978.

74. See McLaren, 1979.

75. This section is based on Price, 1978; Price, 1979; Price, 1980; Pepper, 1978.

76. Pepper, 1978, p. 880; Price, 1979, p. 70. The official recommendation was four weeks for tertiary students, six to eight weeks for secondary students and four weeks for primary students above grade three.

77. Pepper, 1978, p. 878.

78. Ibid., p. 875.

79. See *PR* 18, 5 May 1978, pp. 6–12.

80. Liu Xiyao, 22 April 1978, Price, 1978, pp. 40–50.

81. Deng Xiaoping, 22 April 1978, *PR* 18, 5 May 1978, p. 6 and 12; ibid. 51, 16 December 1977, pp. 4–9; ibid. 5, 3 February 1978, pp. 16–21.

82. Pepper, 1978, p. 882.

83. *RMRB*, 12 May 1978, p. 3.

84. Pepper, 1978, p. 881.

85. See the discussion in Price, 1979, pp. 71–2; Price, 1980, pp. 219–21.

86. Liu Xiyao, 22 April 1978, Price, 1978, p. 41; Price, 1979, p. 58.

87. Price, 1979, p. 58.

88. Liu Xiyao, 22 April 1978, Price, 1978, pp. 44–5.
89. Price, 1980, pp. 213–14; Price, 1979, pp. 64–6.
90. Zhou Peiyuan, *Hongqi* 9, 1977, p. 86.
91. These were listed in *RMRB*, 2 March 1978, p. 3; Price, 1978, pp. 53–4.
92. See Pepper, 1978, pp. 888–9.
93. This section is based on Chan, 1980.
94. See the discussion of various examples of this genre in ibid. pp. 191–7.
95. This was the film *Chuangye* (*The Pioneers*). See the discussion in Chan, 1980, p. 178, and Hua Guofeng's comments, 12 August 1977, *PR* 35, 26 August 1977, p. 28.
96. *RMRB*, 2 January 1977, p. 5.
97. NPC, 5 March 1978, Article XIV, *PR* 11, 17 March 1978, p. 8.
98. Mao Zedong, 27 February 1957, *SW*, 1977, p. 412. These six criteria were: (1) they must be beneficial to the unity of all nationalities, (2) to socialist transformation and construction, (3) to the 'people's democratic dictatorship', (4) to democratic centralism, (5) to the leadership of the Party and (6) to the unity with other socialist countries and 'peace-loving people' in the world.
99. Chey, 1979, p. 107.
100. Zhou and Xia reappeared on the list of personages commemorating national day 1977, Chan, 1980, pp. 181–2.
101. Ibid., p. 182.
102. *RMRB*, 22 December 1977, p. 3.
103. Ibid., 14 May 1978, p. 1.
104. *Dongxiang* (Hong Kong) 4, 16 January 1979, pp. 14–17, *FBIS* CHI–79–16–N 3, 23 January 1979.
105. This probably did not occur until the Third Plenum in December 1978.
106. *RMRB*, 14 May 1978, pp. 1 and 3.
107. See Chan, 1980, p. 183.
108. See McLaren, 1979.
109. *PR* 47, 24 November 1978, p. 6.
110. McLaren, 1979, p. 5.
111. Parts of a number of these unofficial journals have been translated into English. See e.g. *TPRC* 532 (*JPRS* 73728), 20 June 1979; *TPRC* 534 (*JPRS* 73756), 26 June 1979; *TPRC* 536 (JPRS 73787), 29 June 1979.
112. McLaren, 1979, p. 7.
113. This is taken from Brugger, 1979 (c), pp. 92–4.
114. *Jingbao* (Hong Kong) 18, special supplement, 10 January 1979, *FBIS* CHI–79–11–N1, 16 January 1979.
115. See the discussion in *Zhengming* (Hong Kong) 16, February 1979, pp. 5–8, *FBIS* CHI–79–21–N 3–7, 30 January 1979; *Jingbao* 18, special supplement, 10 January 1979, *FBIS* CHI–79–11–N 1–5, 16 January 1979; *Dongxiang* (Hong Kong) 4, 16 January 1979, pp. 14–17, *FBIS* CHI–79–16–N 1–6, 23 January 1979.
116. *RMRB*, 7 February 1977, p. 1.
117. The opening shot of this faction was said to have been an article in *GMRB*, 11 May 1977. See *Zhengming* 16, February 1979, pp. 5–8, *FBIS* CHI–79–21–N 4, 30 January 1979.
118. *Dongxiang* 4, 16 January 1979, pp. 14–17, *FBIS* CHI–79–16–N 2, 23 January 1979.
119. *Mingbao* (Hong Kong), 12 January 1979, p. 3, *FBIS* CHI–79–12–E 1, 17 January 1979.
120. These documents are 'Decisions of the CCPCC on Some Questions Concerning the Acceleration of Agricultural Development (Draft)' and 'Regulations on the Work of the Rural People's Communes (Draft for Trial Use)'. They were issued in CCPCC, *zhongfa* (1979) 4, 11 January 1979, *Issues and Studies*, Vol. XV, No. 7, July 1979, pp. 102–19; ibid., Vol. XV, No. 8, August 1979, pp. 91–112; ibid., Vol. XV, No. 9,

September 1979, pp. 104–15.

121. Ibid., Vol. XV, No. 7, July 1979, p. 118.

122. CCPCC, 22 December 1978, *PR* 52, 29 December 1978, pp. 6 and 14.

123. Ibid., p. 11.

124. Ibid., p. 15.

125. Ibid., p. 7.

126. Ibid., p. 14.

127. Ibid., p. 16.

128. Ibid. 51, 22 December 1978, pp. 8 and 11–12. This was 15 December in Washington.

129. Ibid. 33, 18 August 1978, p. 3.

130. Kallgren, 1973, p. 3.

131. 12 August 1978. *PR* 33, 18 August 1978, pp. 7–8.

132. See Article IV, ibid., p. 8.

133. See ibid. 47, 24 November 1978, p. 26.

134. Ibid. 27, 7 July 1978, pp. 38–9.

135. See e.g. ibid. 48, 1 December 1978, pp. 3–4.

136. Hua Guofeng, 29 August 1978, ibid. 36, 8 September 1978, pp. 8–9.

137. Ibid. 35, 1 September 1978, pp. 13–15.

138. The discussion of Sino-Albanian relations is taken from O'Leary, 1980, pp. 252–8.

139. See ibid.; Pano, 1977 (a) and (b); Prifti, 1977.

140. See Hoxha, 1979, pp. 384–453.

141. *PR* 29, 21 July 1978, pp. 20–3.

142. Ibid. 22, 2 June 1978, p. 14.

143. Ibid. 28, 14 July 1978, pp. 27–8.

144. Ibid. 45, 10 November 1978, p. 23.

IX
THE LAW OF VALUE AND THE RULE OF LAW (1979)

The Third Plenum of the Eleventh Central Committee in December 1978 emphasised the rule of law in both senses of the word. Neither 'objective economic laws' nor the legal provisions of the constitution were to be violated. The task of the Party, therefore, in promoting the 'four modernisations', was to devise policy according to 'economic law' and to work out precise legal codes to deal with all aspects of economic and social life. The first task was to give an unprecedented prestige to China's social scientists[1] and the second was to revive the vanishing profession of lawyer.[2] Law, in the second sense, was felt to be essential not only to promote democracy but also in order that China's dealings with foreign economic agencies might be put on a regular footing. The various meetings of late 1978 seemed to have dispelled any doubts the Chinese leadership might have had about integration with the international capitalist economy and 1979 was to see remarkable moves in that direction. On the other hand, 1979 was not a successful year for Chinese foreign policy as the events in Indo-China were to demonstrate.

The Question of Political Line

The concern with law, in the first sense, was to see the demise of the old slogan 'grasp revolution and promote production'.[3] The promotion of production was now seen as itself a revolution. Thus, the line of the Eighth Party Congress of 1956 could be revived.[4] That line, rejected explicitly by Mao, had maintained that the basic contradiction in society was no longer a matter of class struggle but resided in the relationship between the 'advanced socialist system' and the 'backward productive forces'. It was implied, therefore, that an 'advanced socialist system' was already in existence. In the early 1960s, it will be remembered, Mao had

228

begun to define socialism less as a model or as a mode of production and more as a reversible programme of transition. The reaffirmation of the line of the Eighth Party Congress in 1979 was a rejection of this view. It signified a return to the position, outlined by Stalin in 1936, in which the transition to communism would be assured provided that the economy was sufficiently developed. Such had also been the position of Khrushchev in the early 1960s which had been criticised by the Chinese as 'goulash communism'. In 1979, therefore, there seemed to be no major theoretical difference between the Chinese Communist Party and the Communist Party of the Soviet Union.

One must stress that the official Chinese view in 1979 was not that all class struggle had come to an end. It was that 'large-scale turbulent class struggles of a mass character had in the main come to an end'.[5] What class struggle there was, however, was seen as a residue of the past, a result of foreign influence or simply a reflection of the backward state of the productive forces. According to such a conception, it was theoretically possible still to defend the Great Leap Forward. It was obvious, however, that China's leaders had no such intention and the whole of Mao's developmental strategy since 1957 came under criticism. No attempt was made any longer to associate 'ultra-leftism' with 'ultra-rightism'. It was now stated that the dominant line, in force since the Great Leap, had been 'ultra-left'. It had apparently been called 'ultra-right' by Lin Biao and the 'Gang of Four' in order to mask their own 'ultra-leftism'.[6] In the opinion of the newly rehabilitated Lu Dingyi, the criticisms made by Peng Dehuai at the 1959 Lushan Plenum had been quite correct and the defeat of Peng had been due to that 'ultra-leftist' line which then went on to cause considerable damage for a full 17 years.[7]

Of course, once Peng Dehuai could be exonerated, so could Wu Han and his play *Hai Rui Dismissed from Office*.[8] The same went for Deng Tuo and his *Evening Talks at Yanshan*.[9] Peng Zhen was also rehabilitated and was appointed to head a new commission to draft a body of socialist law.[10] It seemed that even Liu Shaoqi could no longer remain under a cloud, though here the leadership was still cautious due to what were referred to as 'historical reasons'. One is not too sure what those historical reasons might have been, but throughout 1979 they remained sufficiently important to prevent Liu's posthumous rehabilitation in any formal sense. Nevertheless, his wife Wang Guangmei was to be restored to a place of honour.[11]

The leadership in 1979 was, however, not merely content to rehabilitate people 'wrongly accused'. It now began to criticise the deceased accusors. Ke Qingshi and Kang Sheng,[12] for example, were considered to be accomplices of Lin Biao and the 'Gang of Four' and observers waited with baited breath to see if Mao Zedong would join their number. But here again the leadership was cautious. Mao's position continued to be upheld and, as if to signal that an open criticism of Mao would not be forthcoming after the Third Plenum, some of Mao's 1958 comments on 'uninterrupted revolution' were reprinted.[13] After all, to criticise Mao openly might provoke the same kind of dispute as had occurred at the meetings of late 1978 . Indeed, it is rumoured that debate on Mao's role did recur at a central meeting in April and the leadership seemed to have decided to tread very warily. Yet, looking back over 1979, one does get the impression that the role of Mao was progressively minimised and this was quite apparent when one compares the various speeches made to commemorate national day (1 October)[14] with those which had been made on similar occasions in the past. Remembering, perhaps, the traumas which Khrushchev's denunciation of Stalin had caused three years after the Soviet leader's death, China's leaders were determined that there was to be no precipitate haste in the process of de- Maoification and they constantly denied that it was occurring.[15]

Observing 'Objective Economic Law'

The rejection of Mao's post-1957 economic ideas also implied a partial rejection of the ambitious production drive, advocated by Hua Guofeng in early 1978. It was announced, therefore, that a three-year programme of economic readjustment would be undertaken.[16] There was a new stress on formulating targets realistically and, in early 1979, the targets announced at the first session of the Fifth National People's Congress were scaled down. It had originally been estimated that the modernisation plans (to 1985) would cost some $US600 billion. By 1979, this figure had probably been reduced to some $280 – 360 billion.[17] Significantly, the Central Committee documents on agriculture, approved by the Third Plenum, spoke of 80 per cent mechanisation by 1985 instead of 85 per cent.[18] This process of readjustment was eventually endorsed at the second session of the Fifth National People's Congress in June 1979 when, for the first time in two decades, a mass of economic statistics was released.[19] There was even a detailed breakdown of the state budget.[20]

The stress was not only on realistic targeting but also on honest and open reporting of the actual economic situation. Such was felt to be essential if there were to be a complete reassessment of the economy. The Central Committee documents of late 1978, therefore, revealed that 100 million peasants still did not get sufficient grain, that the 1977 average per capita income in the rural areas was only ¥60 and that in one-quarter of all production teams it was under ¥40.[21] The mid-1979 statistics were, however, much more encouraging, though they too reflected a new sober approach to reporting.

With the readjustment of the economy, the overwhelming emphasis was on profitability.[22] In fact, the readjustment policies were probably caused more by concern with this issue than the problem of foreign exchange, highlighted in many Western comments. According to the profitability criterion, some unproductive enterprises were to be closed down. Piecework, bonus systems and other methods of securing the principle of 'payment according to work' were given great prominence. It was stressed also that one would only get an accurate picture of profitability if profits were calculated on the basis of fixed assets rather than according to administratively defined targets.

Legitimising Hu Qiaomu's ideas of mid-1978, the central leadership now made much of the merits of 'market socialism'. This gave rise to an extremely interesting debate in economic journals. It was pointed out that there was a crucial difference between a planned economy (essential to socialism) and a 'command economy' (which was an unnecessary heritage of the past). The function of the state, in planning, was only to set the limits within which production should be carried on. It should not attempt to plan everything for China's 380,000-odd industrial enterprises. Once general guidelines had been set by the state, individual enterprises could be left to plan production as they saw fit. Those enterprises were to enter into legally binding contractual arrangements with other productive units and with retail organisations. It was proposed, moreover, that greater freedom ought to be allowed to the various parties to the contract in negotiating prices. Gradually, the law of value ought to take over and, though this might lead to a price rise for primary products, inflation might be avoided by regulating the money supply.[23] There was no doubt that, in China in 1979, the ideas of Milton Friedman would have found a ready audience. It was claimed, moreover, that in the past vertical rule had led to centralised stultification. Dual rule, however, had degenerated into administration by regions and had resulted in decentralised anarchy. Both of these methods were administrative rather than 'economic' methods of managing production and both ought to be replaced by the market, which would reward the productive, penalise the unproductive, and so enhance efficiency. Such was an 'objective economic law'.[24]

The above ideas were put forward as proposals for what ought to be done. They went far beyond the guidelines laid down in the 'thirty points' and, at the time of writing (December 1979), only a few have been acted upon. It was clear, however, in the new context of 'decentralisation I', that industrial enterprise management was to enjoy more freedom than at any time since the 1950s. A much greater amount of profit might be retained by enterprises and management had considerably more discretion over labour and financial matters. The official formula was still 'responsibility of the factory general manager, under the unified leadership of the enterprise Party committee', though some calls were put forward for the restoration of 'one-person management'.[25] At the same time, the principle of representative democracy was still affirmed, with elected worker congresses and, in some cases, elected shop supervisors.[26] In this context, the Yugoslav experiences were closely studied.

In line with the suggestions made by Hu Qiaomu, the leadership considered very seriously the replacement of administrative means of running the economy by indirect control via the banks. At a banking conference in February 1979, it was suggested that investment in industry might, in future, take the form of bank loans, with enterprises paying the interest out of retained profits.[27] A similar method of financial management was also proposed for the rural communes. By adopting such methods, it was felt that the waste of state funds might be minimised.

To enhance the role of the banking system, 1979 saw the restoration of a number of specialist banks with authority over various sectors of the economy. The People's Construction Bank, for example, was given wide powers. It was proposed that direct grants for capital construction would be phased out and applications for capital construction funds would be made directly to the bank.[28] Such loans would only be approved once the appropriate contract had been signed between the construction company and its client. The Agricultural Bank of China, likewise, was reconstituted to supervise the rural economy[29] and will, I suspect, become the principal organ of state control in the rural areas. Reflecting the enhanced role of the banking system, bank managers were encouraged to refuse unprofitable loans, even when they had been recommended by leading cadres.[30] At the same time, interest rates (low by world standards) were raised.[31] Interest rates were, of course, one of the new economic levers which were to be used to replace administrative methods of running the economy. The use of this lever was felt to be essential if savings were to be maximised and if the compensation paid to national capitalists for non-payment of fixed interest since the Cultural Revolution was to become productive capital.

Another indication of the increased power of the banking system was the decision to place the Bank of China (the main organ concerned with foreign financial dealings) directly under the State Council.[32] This bank, which now ranked at the same level as a government ministry, assumed direct responsibility for borrowing overseas. As we have seen, the Third Plenum seemed to have quashed any reservations various leaders might have had on this issue. Credit arrangements, therefore, amounting to $US20 – 30 billion, were concluded with the United States.[33] In December 1979, moreover, a huge $1.5 billion loan was made by the Japanese government, directly to finance a number of industrial and transportation projects.[34] Part of the modernisation programme, therefore, will be financed by foreign loans. A substantial part also might be financed by direct foreign investment.

The preceding chapter noted that the problem of foreign investment had also been a contentious one in the past and that the details governing such investment had to await the formulation of the new legal code. The priority given to joint venture operations, however, was such that, with the one exception of a forestry law published in February 1979,[35] this was the first item of economic legislation to appear. In the light of recent Chinese history, the Joint Venture Law[36] was truly remarkable. Contrary to all anticipations, the law did not preclude 100 per cent foreign ownership in certain types of enterprises and, in his comments on the law, Li Xiannian was quite specific about China not feeling the need to insist on the usual 51:49 per cent ownership formula.[37] In fact, China's concern about national sovereignty seemed to be limited to the stipulation that board chairmen had to be appointed by the Chinese side.

The Joint Venture Law was not only startling in its implications. It was also very vague and it was anticipated that it would have to be supplemented by a lot of additional legislation. It was not at all clear just how far enterprises governed by the law would be subject to the industrial and commercial consolidated tax which applied to all enterprises. Nor could one anticipate how far foreign managers and technical personnel might be required to pay an income tax. There was, after all, no tax law in China and seminars were held in Beijing to explore intricate questions concerning foreign income tax law, the legal provisions governing value added tax, foreign contract law, employment law and general company law.[38] Such a situation, unthinkable even in 1977–8, was very far from the thinking of Mao Zedong and the 'Gang of Four' on 'bourgeois right'.

Discussions concerning the Joint Venture Law were only initial steps on the way towards a much closer integration of the Chinese economy with that of the capitalist world. It was even proposed that export processing zones might be set up in Guangdong province and near Shanghai and Tianjin.[39] One wonders whether these will eventually take the same form as those which currently exist in other countries. If the obvious model—Taiwan—has been chosen, one would anticipate some disquiet.

Though foreign loans and foreign investment were to finance part of the importation of technology necessary for the 'four modernisations', it was clear that the bulk of funds would derive from the export of oil and coal. China produced some 104 million tonnes of crude oil in 1978,[40] which placed it eighth in the world in petroleum production.[41] It also produced 618 million (crude) tonnes of coal.[42] In 1979, plans got under way to accelerate petroleum production and China opted for concentration on offshore exploration in the South China Sea rather than in the Far West. This decision, taken with regard to the Japanese market, was a potential source of danger. The Sino-American concessions, marked out in the South China Sea, included one in the Gulf of Tonkin, right across the part of the continental shelf disputed between China and Vietnam. It was probably because of the foreign threat to these concessions that China made a point of choosing American consortia with which to deal. But the implications for a possible future clash between the American and Soviet navies are worth considering.[43]

China's involvement in the international capitalist economy in 1979, at last, made it possible to reach agreement on American and Chinese assets frozen during the Korean War. It also made it likely that China would successfully conclude its application to join the World Bank and the International Monetary Fund, despite the membership of Taiwan. China's membership, some would argue, might result in an even greater surrender of sovereignty than the various moves described above. The IMF and the World Bank usually demand of a member country that it undergo a comprehensive economic survey by IMF personnel, that it agree to set the exchange rate of its currency so as not to damage competing currencies, that it consult regularly with the World Bank on the state of its economy and that it meet the normal conditions for any borrowing.[44] After assuming power, Fidel Castro had been most reluctant to meet such 'normal conditions for borrowing' which, he thought, would completely distort his proposed socialist economic strategy. If China were now to do what Castro was unwilling to do, there would be many countries which would intepret such action as an abandonment of socialism.

The economic decisions taken by the Third Plenum and detailed at the second session of the Fifth National People's Congress, displayed a greater shift in emphasis towards agriculture and light industry than at any time since 'agriculture' was designated the 'base' of the economy some 20 years previously. In June, it was announced that state investment in agriculture was to increase from 11 per cent of budgeted investment in 1978 to 14 per cent in 1979. Similarly, light industry's share increased from 5.4 to 5.8 per cent.[45] This stress on agriculture and light industry was accompanied by a renewed effort to close the 'scissors' between the prices of agricultural and industrial products. Since 1949, the price of grain sold to the state had doubled in relation to the price of industrial products sold to the rural areas.[46] Now there was to be a further 20 per cent rise in the price of grain accompanied by a further reduction in the price of farm machinery. Similarly, there was a much greater rise in the price of above-quota grain sold to the state and large rises in the official prices of a number of other agricultural products.[47] In this respect, 1979 policy was very close to that advocated by Mao in the mid-1950s. In other respects, however, agricultural policy had diverged markedly from the pre-1976 situation.

First, there was, in 1979, a much greater stress on zoning and agricultural specialisation. It was said that the idea that 'only growing grain constituted socialism' was an erroneous idea put forward by Lin Biao and the 'Gang of Four'. Though it is very difficult to imagine anyone making such a statement, it is certainly true that the former policy demanded that areas became self-sufficient in grain before they diversified their crops. Now it was stated that areas should grow whichever crops promised the greatest return and were suitable to the area concerned. In the past, an excessive concentration on grain had resulted in insufficient raw materials being available for light industry and in serious soil erosion.[48] This was particularly important since the crop area had been declining and land was at a premium.[49] Though the above policy would seem eminently sensible, it must be pointed out that crop specialisation might be expected to produce considerable inequalities between regions. The richer areas would earn more and so qualify for priority in state investment. If this were to take the form of loans, these areas would find repayments fairly easy. The old programme of self-reliance also generated inequalities and the Dazhai-type *xian* were, by and large, those *xian* which had traditionally been better off.[50] The inequalities, however, might have been mitigated by the commitment evoked by self-reliant effort and also by discrimination against those areas which could have made a higher income by not growing grain. There is no doubt that the new policies might be expected to boost output but this has been achieved at a political cost.

A second crucial difference between the policies of 1979 and those implemented before 1976 was a consequence of the demand to make 'payment according to work'. In 1979, this was increasingly spelt out as a call for greater attention to piecework in the countryside. Of course, the work-points system was, at root, a system of piecework but, over the years, it had been modified by team discussion and the grading of peasants on grounds additional to the capacity to produce. Now production teams were enjoined to make all payments, above the basic ration, according to the amount of work performed. Since it was often too difficult to determine the work-points of each and every individual in the team, piecework groups were formed and these sometimes turned out to be individual households.[51] Though the 'sixty points' of late 1978 explicitly outlawed this manifestation of one of the elements of *sanziyibao*,[52] it was to occur in many places in early 1979. Indeed, it often seemed as though production teams were disintegrating. Thus, peasants were warned that freedom to form small groups should not result in some groups consisting only of able-bodied adults whilst others consisted only of old people or children.[53] Faced with such a situation, the Party authorities applied corrective measures and, by the second half of 1979, it seemed that the disintegration of the teams had been halted. Nevertheless, the permanent division of the teams into piecework groups might be expected to hinder their cohesion.

The third difference in rural policy concerned the new emphasis on 'market socialism' and the law of value. Teams were now asked to enter into contractual relationships with higher levels[54] and the flow of funds and labour between the various components of the rural communes and light industry (run by the *xian*) was organised on a businesslike basis. Such a contractual system might be expected to institutionalise inequalities and to result in the relationships between units in the countryside being governed exclusively by the cash nexus. This situation would undoubtedly be exacerbated by the marked increase in private activity, illustrated most graphically by the fact that even the Dazhai production brigade was persuaded to restore private plots and to expand private activity.[55] As in the industrial sector, the attempt to devise 'economic' methods of doing things rather than administrative methods had led to some startling new suggestions. It was even advocated in November 1979 that governmental activities at commune level should be separated from economic activities. Commune cadres were, after all, on the state payroll and were state cadres like the local government officials. They were not, therefore, it was said, sufficiently concerned with economic management.[56]

A final difference in rural policy was the new status given to the state farm sector.[57] State farms were now to be run on a much more business-like basis and were governed by much the same kind of regulations as industrial enterprises. In receiving priority in investment funds these state farms constituted an élite sector of agriculture. In Mao's and the 'Gang of Four's' opinion, the communes would eventually be transformed into state farms once the productive forces had been sufficiently developed. The new priority given to this sector (which comprised only four million out of the 100 million hectares of arable land)[58] implied that their productivity would increase by leaps and bounds and that communes would never catch up to their level. Interestingly, the state farm sector was another field in which the Yugoslav experiences were being studied.[59]

The new stress on economic efficiency resulted in much more than the use of economic levers, specialisation and the promotion of élite sectors of the economy. It led also to redoubled efforts to control the population. Symbolic of this determination was the rehabilitation of the 98-year-old Ma Yinchu,[60] once denounced as a disciple of Malthus (and amongst Marxists that was a grave charge). In June 1979, it was announced that the Chinese population (including Taiwan) was 975 million.[61] The population growth-rate had declined to 1.2 per cent per annum and it was planned to reduce this to 0.5 per cent by 1985 and zero by the end of the century.

Though the 1.2 per cent is impressive, the overall growth rate since 1949 was some 2 per cent, which meant that over 60 per cent of the population had been born since 1949. Commenting on these figures, Vice-Premier Chen Muhua noted that the cost of maintaining the children born since liberation had amounted to about 30 per cent of the national income for those years. Population pressure had resulted in a situation where 6 per cent of the children reaching school age could not go to school, 12 per cent of primary school graduates could not proceed to junior secondary school, more than one-half of the graduates of junior secondary school could not enter senior secondary school and only about 5 per cent of senior secondary school graduates could enter tertiary institutions. Because of population growth since 1953, the 3.8-fold increase in the funds alloted for consumption had, in reality, only resulted in a 2.3-fold increase per capita. Grain production since 1951 had increased by 97 per cent and yet the amount of grain per head had only increased by some 17 per cent.[62]

To achieve the targets for reducing population growth, therefore, the goal of the one-child family was proposed. Education in family planning was stepped up and a draft family planning law was put forward. It was proposed also to train larger numbers of family planning workers and to devise sets of rewards and penalties for adhering to or exceeding the one-child target.[63] In various provinces, a system of honour certificates was introduced, which conferred not just honour but tangible material rewards. In some places in Sichuan, for example, one-child families were awarded subsidies for the single child up to the age of 14. That child received free schooling, an adult's grain ration, and an allocation of private land one-and-a-half times that of an adult.[64] Other places adopted different incentives for having only one child and corresponding penalties for having more than two children. Such penalties might include a deduction of 10 per cent from the parents' wages.[65] In addition, moral incentives were given to those who underwent sterilisation.

China, therefore, was one of the few countries in the world actively to have propagated the one-child family. In the long run, however, the fundamental determinant of the population growth-rate must be the provision of welfare facilities for the aged and measures which make children no longer a necessity for rural families. Studies show that the availability of birth control technology, the intensity of propaganda and the draconian nature of birth control provisions make little difference to population growth. What is important is an atmosphere of economic security.[66] China's remarkable success in bringing the growth-rate down to 1.2 per cent was due precisely to that. There is no reason, therefore, why the population growth-rate should not reach zero by the first or second decade of the twenty-first century. But such an achievement will not be due to the legislation of 1979. It will be a consequence of economic development. One is surprised that the present leadership, with its faith in the 'productive forces', has not commented on research which demonstrates that conclusion.

A reduction in the population growth-rate is, of course, extremely important if China is to solve the urban employment problem. The vociferous return of educated youths to the cities, noted in the preceding chapter, did much to underline the seriousness of this situation. The policy of rustication, which was still promoted throughout 1979, was seen not only to be unpopular but also to be inadequate. It was supplemented, therefore, by a number of other measures. For example, when a family member retired, the state guaranteed to find an urban job for one of its members. Groups of youths were organised to form study groups which might spend part of their time in voluntary labour. At the same time, urban wards or street committees encouraged the formation of service co-operatives to employ youths at quite low wages (the average being some ¥20 per month[67] which was one-third that of an industrial worker). The encouragement of these street collectives was, of course, reminiscent of the Great Leap Forward. It is therefore quite ironical that a consequence of not following the Great Leap policy of sending youths to the countryside was the resurrection of Great Leap-type structures in the cities. In the meantime, however, the rustication policy still involved the majority of youths and the complaints continued. One might anticipate, therefore, the continual return of educated youths and an exacerbation of the petty crime and delinquency which became so marked in 1979.[68]

Democracy and the Legal System

One of the major activities of many educated youths who returned to the cities in late 1978 was to demand the extension of democracy. To many people, democracy was the 'fifth modernisation'.[69] The furious poster campaign and the flowering of unofficial journals at that time, coincided with the tense meetings of the central leadership at which the 'practice' faction also argued for the extension of democracy. Though a few of the activists were detained, most of the protest activity was tolerated. Was this because of the leadership's new faith in spontaneous mass activity or because the protests served, for a time, the interests of the 'practice' faction? One suspects the latter, since the victory of the 'practice' faction was soon followed by attempts to curb extreme protests. Of course, one might argue that once traffic was disrupted and the mass movement got out of hand in early 1979, the authorities had to move in and establish law and order. In March, they were to act quite decisively.[70] A number of protesters, including the famous Wei Jingsheng,[71] were arrested and poster displays were confined to a few designated areas. By the end of the year, those designated areas had shrunk further. Even Beijing's Democracy Wall, which had earned the attention of legions of foreign journalists, was abolished and poster writers in the capital were required to apply for a permit to display posters in a place where few passers-by would read them.[72]

The protesters of early 1979 were caught up in a paradox. In denouncing Lin Biao and the 'Gang of Four' for arbitrary government, they engaged in the same kind of 'extensive democracy' which had been pioneered by Lin Biao. Thus, the central leadership, when it no longer had any need for such protests, could with some justification denounce their behaviour as being exactly the same as the 'Gang of Four'. Like many political scientists in the West, the central leadership did not disassociate capricious rule and an appeal to participatory democracy. Commenting on the introduction of the new legal code in June 1979, the Chief Procurator Huang Huoqing was to remark:

> For a while, not very long ago, a few bad elements in the name of democracy spread rumours, caused trouble and disrupted work, production and social order. Some even publicly made clear that their intention was to overthrow the socialist system and subvert the dictatorship of the proletariat. The masses were most incensed by their activities and demanded that they be dealt with according to law.[73]

But what was the relationship between the dictatorship of the proletariat and the new thinking about the rule of law? With the promulgation of the criminal code in June 1979, it seemed that socialist law was set very firmly within what the 'Gang of Four' had considered to be 'bourgeois right' (the granting of equal rights to people made unequal by their economic location). The initial premiss was that all people should have equal rights. Thus, rehabilitation of most of the old rightists was followed by the restoration of the rights of former landlords and some other proscribed elements.[74] But there were still certain people who were deprived of rights. These were criminals and counter-revolutionaries. The code went to great pains to define certain crimes such as fraud, tax evasion etc. But when it came to 'counter-revolution', all that could be said was that is was 'an act which attempts to overthrow the political power of the dictatorship of the proletariat and the socialist system'.[75] The scope for arbitrariness here was immense. Yet, before one condemns the Chinese leadership too harshly, one must note that most legal codes contain clauses which might, under certain circumstances, be used for political persecution. The logic of the 'Gang of Four's' argument was that all criminal codes were *inevitably* used for political oppression and one had to be careful to see that it was the right kind of people who were being oppressed. Though one might disagree with the 'Gang of Four's' choice of targets and its personal élitism, there was a certain honesty about that position. The 'Gang' took it upon itself to decide whom to persecute. The 1979 leadership did exactly the same thing but under the camouflage of 'equal rights'.

To have a theory of human rights, one seems to need a theory of natural law. In Marxism there is no such theory. Recognising this, Chinese leaders were most critical of the popular idea of human rights which transcend classes and rejected the criticisms of those who said that human rights had been violated in China.[76] One is not at all sure, however, upon what theoretical basis the leadership justified its constitutional rights. It might be that the Chinese leadership will eventually solve that fundamental problem of Marxism—the relationship between basic rights and basic needs. At the moment, however, one sees no signs of it.

It would be churlish to deny that the new stress on a socialist legal system made life more secure for many Chinese citizens than that which they enjoyed in the past. One has, moreover, yet to see how the constraints will be defined. One is encouraged by the fact that some writers can actually print, in official literary journals, the view that the original hundred flowers policy implied the encouragement of both fragrant flowers *and* poisonous weeds.[77] But perhaps the acid test will come when Hua Guofeng's promise to put the 'Gang of Four' on trial is actually implemented.[78] Surely, after the case of Wei Jingsheng, no one will expect the 'Gang' to get a *fair* trial. Yet, sympathisers of the 'Gang' would say that the concept 'fairness' itself derives from considerations of 'bourgeois right'. Thus, if the trial is unfair, it will confirm their worst suspicions. If, however, it is fair, such people will be able to find the trial equally reprehensible.

It is also difficult to deny that the commitment of the 1979 leadership to formal representative democracy is quite genuine. The replacement of the old revolutionary committees by local people's governments in June 1979[79] was probably only a formal change and those committees had long since ceased to be 'revolutionary' in any normal sense of the word (and many, of course, never were). Though representative democracy might be better than some of the arbitrariness which existed in the past, the participatory criticism still stands. The fact that the 'Gang of Four' might have violated the spirit of participatory democracy is no argument against it. Perhaps, in the future, some degree of participatory democracy will be incorporated into the panoply of representative forms prescribed by the legislation of mid-1979[80] It might equally be the case, however, that some Chinese intellectuals, who once again have the opportunity to read Rousseau and the like, will find such democracy wanting.

When one considers the legislation of 1979, perhaps the most important issue of all concerns the role of the Communist Party. What, for example, is one to make of the statement that the function of the constitution is to protect the will as well as the rights of the people?[81] Previously the official position was that the people's will had to be mediated through the Party. Such was the rationale of the Mass Line, which was promoted most vigorously in 1979.[82] If the Party's role were bypassed in this respect, what kind of vanguard would it be? What, moreover, were the implications of the official rehabilitation in 1979 of the famous Li Yizhe *dazibao* of 1974?[83] In Chapter 7, it was noted that that poster was an implicit attack on the very notion of the Party's vanguard role. Clearly, that interpretation was no longer officially held in early 1979 but the poster is very difficult to interpret in any other way.

As one reads the arguments about the legislation of 1979, one gets the impression that, despite such escape clauses as those dealing with counter-revolutionaries, the role of the Party had been considerably restricted. The separation of the Party's role from the 'objective economic laws', moreover, also constituted a restriction. This had taken place in a general atmosphere of disillusionment with the Party's past performance and its current élite role. Part of that disillusionment was due to the behaviour of Party officials and, throughout 1979, all kinds of criticism circulated in Beijing about the luxurious living enjoyed by many of China's leaders (only Hua Guofeng and Chen Yun, it seems, escaped censure).[84] But one wonders whether that was the only source of disillusionment. Could it be that the new socialist legislation, though welcomed by so many people, had severely damaged the legitimacy of the Party? After a decade and a half of criticism of Khrushchev's implicit denial of the dictatorship of the proletariat in his 'state of the whole people', the Chinese Communist Party was creating the same thing. The point here is not whether or not people welcomed the changes. It is merely that the Party seemed not to have a theoretical leg to stand on.

The Sino-Vietnamese War

As has been noted, there did not really seem to be any theoretical basis of dispute between China and the Soviet Union in 1979. They disagreed wildly about 'Comrade Mao Zedong's thesis about the three worlds', but this was a strategic rather than a basically ideological matter. It was an issue related to a classic concern with the balance of power. By 1979, the deterioration of China's foreign policy into one of mobilising any available force to oppose the Soviet Union had led to close ties with a number of quite repressive régimes. China's relations with Iran under the Shah and Zaïre under Mobutu may only be explained by a desire to offset what was felt to be growing Soviet power in Asia and Africa. In Kampuchea, this policy resulted in support for the Pol Pot régime.

Though support was sometimes expressed in ideological terms, there is some evidence that the Chinese were embarrassed by the extremism of the Kampuchean government. In late 1978, therefore, it was rumoured that China might have been actively manoeuvring to support those who wished to replace the Pol Pot government by a more moderate régime headed by Norodom Sihanouk.[85] What was particularly feared was a Vietnamese invasion of Kampuchea and, to forestall such an eventuality, there was felt to be a need to establish a more stable and popular government.

Yet the Vietnamese invasion was to occur. In response, China immediately stepped up aid to the Pol Pot forces and reinforced its border defences. As Sino-Vietnamese relations reached crisis point, the border situation became very tense and China began to contemplate military action. Though one cannot be sure, it is possible that, on his visit to the United States to celebrate the normalisation of Sino-American relations, Deng Xiaoping sounded out official American opinion on a projected Chinese military action and, on 17 February, Chinese troops went to war with Vietnam.[86] The war, which was to last until 16 March,[87] has given rise to much debate as to which side actually won.

To answer that question adequately, one must be precise about what the Chinese objectives were. Unfortunately, however, there is no course but to speculate. The official Chinese explanation for the attack was that China wished to 'teach Vietnam a lesson'. It wished to show that Vietnam could not engage in border provocations with impunity. Presumably, China's model here was the Sino-Indian War of 1962 when Chinese troops managed to solve the border question by inflicting a severe defeat on the Indian army. But Vietnam was no India. The Chinese attack was contained, without Vietnam calling upon its élite fighting forces, and Vietnam managed to demonstrate that the Chinese army was somewhat less efficient than many had thought. After the withdrawal of Chinese forces in March, there was no guarantee that Vietnamese border provocations would not continue and the subsequent negotiations were not very fruitful.

A second Chinese objective was to show that China had not been cowed by the Soviet-Vietnam treaty and was prepared to take action to prevent the expansion of Soviet influence in Asia. Such an objective was fraught with considerable danger and, throughout the early fighting, much fear was expressed that the Soviet Union might launch a punitive strike in north China. But such a punitive strike never occurred and Soviet aid to Vietnam was somewhat less than observers had anticipated. In retrospect, it would seem that Vietnam was reluctant to call upon all the Soviet aid which might have been available. This may have been because of the fear of United States involvement or, more likely, because an excessive dependence of Vietnam on the Soviet Union would have had serious implications for Vietnamese independence. As long as Vietnam could hold its own, Soviet aid remained limited. Again, the evidence would suggest that the Chinese objective of resisting Soviet influence was also not achieved. There was much more likelihood, after the war, that the Soviet Union might be able to establish a naval base in Vietnam. Laos, moreover, had now moved much closer to the Soviet Union and thus was able to expel Chinese technicians.[88]

The third objective was, of course, to take pressure off the Pol Pot régime in Kampuchea. Doubtless, the Chinese invasion achieved some success in this respect though, throughout 1979, the areas held by the former Kampuchean government dwindled and, by the end of the year, there seemed little prospect that the Pol Pot forces would regain lost ground. It was probably the case, however, that the Chinese saw little hope of restoring the Pol Pot government. During the negotiations with Vietnam after the Chinese withdrawal, the Kampuchean issue was kept off the agenda and China merely put forward the general demand that all Vietnamese troops should be withdrawn from foreign countries. China's efforts, in late 1979, seemed confined to supporting the attempt by ASEAN to persuade various countries to withhold recognition from the Heng Samrin government in Phnom Penh and so prevent Vietnamese expansion. After all, China, which was increasingly anxious to establish economic ties with the West, did not wish to be associated too closely with what seems to have been a rather loathsome régime.

The above seem to be the most important objectives in the Chinese invasion of Vietnam. Some observers, however, have contemplated other possible aims. It has been suggested, for example, that the Chinese action might have been designed to test the commitment of the United States to *détente*. If the Soviet Union could be exposed as aggressive, the SALT II negotiations might collapse and China would have achieved a strategic victory. In fact, the forebearance of both the Soviet Union and the United States during the conflict probably strengthened the commitment of both parties to *détente* and the SALT II treaty was eventually initialled. It has been suggested also that the Chinese action might have been a way of engendering solidarity after the traumatic shift in domestic policies at the various meetings in late 1978 or that the war effort might legitimise the new policies of economic readjustment introduced in early 1979. The fact that the war did not result in a domestic mobilisation campaign, and that the Chinese press coverage of the fighting was somewhat less than one might have expected, would throw considerable doubt on such views.

In terms of the three major objectives outlined above, one must conclude that the Chinese military actions of February-March 1979 were a failure. It seemed also that China's attempts to restrict the power of the Soviet Union, throughout 1979, were less than successful. By the end of

1979, the whole of Indo-China was within the Soviet orbit and a renewal of the conflict was not beyond the bounds of probability. As I have indicated, it might next time involve a naval confrontation. Soviet influence in Africa, moreover, remained very strong. The fact that a conference of non-aligned nations could have been held in Cuba does not suggest that China's influence over that body was at all significant.[89] The visit of Hua Guofeng and other leaders to Europe[90] achieved little in mobilising opposition to the Soviet Union and the only West European leader to have responded actively to Hua's warnings was Britain's Margaret Thatcher. Furthermore, the world recession tended to favour the Soviet Union more than China, which was seeking more active involvement in the international capitalist economy. 1979 was not a good year for Chinese foreign policy.

It is too early to assess the domestic effects of the Sino-Vietnamese War of early 1979. Western observers looked in vain for signs of an anti-war movement in China and speculated as to the effect of the war on the policy of 'four modernisations'. What is significant, however, is a consequence of the shift in the focus of Sino-Soviet contention from north China to the south. So long as the People's Liberation Army was deployed in the north, it could engage in economic as well as military tasks. The tropical terrain in the south does not lend itself to such activities and thus the cost of maintaining troops in that area will be much greater.[91] The rather mediocre performance of the Chinese troops in Vietnam, moreover, when confronted with superior Soviet munitions, will no doubt lend weight to those in China who argue for the accelerated modernisation of the armed forces. Throughout 1979, Chinese military delegations toured the world looking at advanced military technology and the cost of such imports could be immense. These China can ill afford at a time when the ambitious economic plans of 1978 have been subjected to readjustment.

Conclusion

The above description of policies in China in 1979 suggests a very different picture from that of China under Mao and the 'Gang of Four'. Economic policies were even significantly different from those of Deng Xiaoping, either in 1975 or 1978. In Mao's terms, much of what they implied was the development of capitalist relations of production. In the short run, they will undoubtedly stimulate growth. But should one take it as axiomatic that the early decades of economic growth must necessarily lead to greater inequality? Mao did not think so, though there was quite a lot of inequality in his day too. There will now probably be more.

But the question is not just one of inequality. To what extent have the means chosen by the present leadership severely distorted the process of socialist transition? Will China develop like Taiwan which, for the time being, has a respectable level of economic growth, a reasonable degree of equality but also an exploitative capitalist system and a repressive and undemocratic government? To what extent will China become increasingly dependent upon the West? What we notice now is the infatuation with the Western way of life as shown in the moves to promote bread rather than traditional *mantou* and the like.[92] But is this very significant? When it comes down to it, China will never experience the degree of dependence of nations like Taiwan. China is, after all, a major oil-exporting country and foreign economic activity will, for a very long time, remain a very small proportion of GNP. Nor will China become like Taiwan so long as the memories of early attempts to construct socialism are borne in mind. Though Mao would not agree, it is possible to make something of a case for 'market socialism'. A lot of theoretical work, of course, needs to be done before any definitive conclusion is reached and I am not sure the East European theorists have done it. One thing, however, does seem certain: Yugoslavia is not a very impressive model.

In the old days of self-reliant development, China was criticised for making all the mistakes which had already been made in the West. Such was inevitable when many Western inventions had to be invented all over again. Now China seems to be making the opposite mistake. It has copied, for example, methods of educational administration which by Western standards are inefficient and antiquated. The trouble seems to lie in the fact that the technical élite is very old and was trained in the 1940s and 1950s. For the moment, the youth are not taken very seriously as technical innovators. But one might anticipate that the youth will soon learn. There can be no doubt that the relatively free atmosphere in scientific and cultural life can only enhance creativity. The throttling of such creativity was, to my mind, one of the real (as opposed to the many imagined) crimes of which the 'Gang of Four' was guilty.

No one, I am sure, will mourn the passing of what used to be called 'Liu Shaoqi's sinister line on literature and art'.[93] Few people also would wish to return to the rather squalid political movements of 1976. But there are other things which might be regretted and these are perhaps more important. The commitment to a centralised model of economic development in the 1950s certainly increased economic growth. So did the reversals made to Great Leap policies in the 1960s, once the bad climatic conditions had passed. These are the periods which the present leadership has considered favourably.[94] The other periods, however, suggested the road to a new form of society which was neither a form of capitalism nor the stultifying 'socialism' of the Soviet Union. One wonders, after the three years of readjustment, whether attempts will be made to get back to the spirit of those times—not the spirit of 'ultra-left' commandism but the spirit of creativity and mass involvement, the legacy of which still continues to impress most visitors to China.

NOTES

1. See Kelly, 1979.
2. *BR* 21, 25 May 1979, p. 7.
3. *RMRB*, 9 March 1979, p. 2.
4. Li Hong, *Lishi Yanjiu* 4, 1979, pp. 3-12.
5. Hua Guofeng, 18 June 1979, *BR* 27, 6 July, 1979, p. 10.
6. Wu Jiang, ibid. 15, 13 April 1979, pp. 13-16.
7. Lu Dingyi, *RMRB*, 8 March 1979, p. 2,
8. *BR* 10, 9 March 1979, pp. 6-7 and 27.
9. Zhang Yide, *GMRB*, 26 January 1979, p. 3, *FBIS* CHI-79-029-E 2-8; Su Shuangbi, *GMRB*, 28 January 1979, p. 3, *FBIS* CHI-79-029-E 8-11.
10. *BR* 9, 2 March 1979, p. 3.
11. Ibid. 5, 2 February 1979, p. 3. Liu Shaoqi was to be posthumously rehabilitated in 1980.
12. See Chan, 1980, pp. 80-1.
13. See *BR* 1, 5 January 1979, p. 11.
14. See e.g. Ye Jianying, 29 September 1979, ibid. 40, 5 October 1979, pp. 7-32.
15. Ibid. 42, 19 October 1979, pp. 10-11.
16. Ibid. 26, 29 June 1979, pp. 13-23.
17. Liu, *FEER*, Vol. CVI, No. 40, 5 October 1979, p. 76.
18. CCPCC, *zhonfga* (1979) 4, 11 January 1979, *Issues and Studies*, Vol. XV, No. 7, July 1979, p. 114.
19. State Statistical Bureau, 27 June 1979, *BR* 27, 6 July 1979, pp. 37-41.
20. Zhang Jingfu, 21 June 1979, ibid. 29, 20 July 1979, pp. 17-24.
21. CCPCC, *zhongfa* (1979) 4, 11 January 1979, *Issues and Studies*, Vol. XV, No. 7, July 1979, pp. 105-6.
22. The following discussion is taken from Watson, 1980.
23. See Xue Muqiao, *BR* 43, 26 October 1979, pp. 14-20.
24. See Watson, 1980, pp. 114-15.
25. Ibid., p. 124.
26. *BR* 23, 8 June 1979, pp. 17-20.
27. Watson, 1980, pp. 116-17.
28. *BR* 15, 13 April 1979, pp. 4-5.
29. NCNA, 2 March 1979, *SWB* FE/6061/B11/11-12, 8 March 1979.
30. NCNA, 8 March 1979, *SWB* FE/6065/B11/9, 13 March 1979.
31. NCNA, 28 February 1979, *SWB* FE/6060/B11/10, 7 March 1979.
32. NCNA, 11 April 1979, *SWB* FE/6092/B11/1, 13 April 1979.
33. Liu, *FEER*, Vol. CVI, No. 40, 5 October 1979, p. 77.
34. NCNA, 8 December 1979, *SWB* FE/6293/A3/14, 10 December, 1979.
35. Text in *RMRB*, 27 February 1979, p. 2.
36. NPC, 1 July 1979, *BR* 29, 20 July 1979, pp. 24-6.
37. Ibid. 30, 27 July 1979, p. 4.
38. Cohen, *FEER*, Vol. CVI, No. 40, 5 October 1979, pp. 54-6.
39. Liu, ibid., p. 78.
40. State Statistical Bureau, 27 June 1979, *BR* 27, 6 July 1979, p. 37.
41. Smil, *FEER*, Vol. CVI, No. 40, 5 October 1979, p. 81.
42. State Statistical Bureau, 27 June 1979, *BR* 27, 6 July 1979, p. 37.

43. Lauriat, *FEER*, Vol. CVI, No. 40, 5 October 1979, pp. 58−9.

44. Liu, ibid., pp. 75−6.

45. Zhang Jingfu, 21 June 1979, *BR* 29, 20 July 1979, p. 21.

46. NCNA, 23 November 1977, *SWB* FE/5682/B11/17, 2 December 1977.

47. CCPCC, 22 December 1978, *PR* 52, 29 December 1978, p. 13.

48. *RMRB*, 28 February 1979, p. 1; Beijing Radio, 16 April 1979, *SWB* FE/6096/B11/1, 20 April 1979.

49. CCPCC, *zhongfa* (1979), 4, 11 January 1979, *Issues and Studies*, Vol. XV, No. 7, July 1979, p. 105.

50. This is the tentative conclusion reached by Dernberger (1978, pp. 93−7).

51. E.g. Fuzhou, Fujian Radio, 16 March 1979, *SWB* FE/6074/B11/4−5, 23 March 1979.

52. Article 35. CCPCC, *zhongfa* (1979) 4, 11 January 1979, *Issues and Studies*, Vol. XV, No. 9, September 1979, p. 105.

53. See Guangzhou, Guangdong Radio, 21 March 1979, *SWB* FE/6079/B11/15, 29 March 1979.

54. E.g. Shenyang, Liaoning Radio, 18 December 1978, *SWB* FE/6013/B11/7, 11 January 1979.

55. *RMRB*, 3 October 1979, *SWB* FE/6243/B11/1−4, 12 October 1979.

56. GMRB, 6 November 1979, *SWB* FE/6724/B11/1−3, 17 November 1979.

57. See *BR* 20, 18 May 1979, pp. 5−6.

58. *RMRB*, 26 January 1978, p. 2.

59. NCNA, 2 March 1979, *SWB* FE/6061/B11/15−16, 8 March 1979.

60. *BR* 31, 3 August 1979, pp. 3−4.

61. State Statistical Bureau, 27 June 1979, ibid. 27, 6 July 1979, p. 41.

62. Chen Muhua, ibid. 46, 16 November 1979, pp. 17−20.

63. Ibid., pp. 19−20.

64. Ibid. 46, 16 November 1979, p. 24.

65. Ibid., p. 25.

66. See Commoner, 1979.

67. McLaren, 1979, pp. 14−16.

68. E.g. the various items in *SWB* FE/6085/B11/5−10, 5 April 1979; *Tianjin Ribao*, 7 October 1979, *SWB* FE/6260/B11/6, 1 November 1979.

69. See e.g. *Tansuo* 1, December 1978, *TPRC* 534 (*JPRS* 73756), 26 June 1979, pp. 6−23.

70. See McLaren, 1979, pp. 9−14; see also Beijing Municipal Revolutionary Committee Circular, 29 March 1979, *SWB* FE/6083/B11/1−2, 3 April 1979, and the other items in the same issue.

71. *BR* 43, 26 October 1979, pp. 6−7.

72. Beijing Radio, 6 December 1979, *SWB* FE/6293/B11/1, 10 December 1979.

73. *BR* 27, 6 July 1979, p. 36.

74. Ibid. 7, 16 February 1979, pp. 8−10.

75. Ibid. 27, 6 July 1979, p. 33.

76. Ibid. 45, 9 November 1979, pp. 17−20.

77. See Chan, 1980, p. 190.

78. *BR* 42, 19 October 1979, p. 9.

79. See amendment to constitution passed at the second session of the NPC, in ibid. 28, 13 July 1979, p. 10.

80. The second session of the Fifth NPC examined a draft Organic Law of the Local People's Congress, and a draft Electoral Law. See ibid., pp. 8−11.

81. *RMRB*, 13 November 1978, p. 3.

82. See Young, 1980, pp. 68−9.

83. *BR* 9, 2 March 1979, pp. 15−17.

84. Personal information gained from visitors to Beijing.

85. Nayan Chanda, *FEER*, Vol. CI, No. 36, 8 September 1978, pp. 11−12; ibid., Vol.

CII, No. 41, 13 October 1978, pp. 9–11.

86. *BR* 8, 23 February 1979, pp. 3 and 8–9.

87. Ibid. 12, 23 March 1979, p. 3.

88. Ibid. 11, 16 March 1979, p. 22.

89. See the Chinese comment in ibid. 38, 21 September 1979, pp. 21–5.

90. See ibid. 41, 12 October 1979, pp. 8–11; ibid. 42, 19 October 1979, pp. 14–16; ibid. 43 26 October 1979, pp. 8–14; ibid. 44, 2 November 1979, pp. 8–12; ibid. 45, 9 November 1979, pp. 8–14; ibid. 46, 16 November 1979, p. 8.

91. *FEER*, Vol. CVI, No. 40, 5 October 1979, p. 53.

92. See *PR* 28, 14 July 1978, pp. 18–19.

93. *RMRB*, 19 December 1978, p. 3.

94. *BR* 26, 29 June 1979, pp. 21–2.

CONCLUSION

The slogan 'never forget the class struggle', which was put forward in 1962, followed much thinking by Mao on the nature of socialist transition. By that time, he had come to the conclusion that class struggle in socialist society ought to be directed, not only against remnants of former exploiters, but also against newly generated classes which might be represented in the Communist Party itself. The same theme was taken up in that major contribution to the polemic against the Soviet Union, 'On Khrushchev's Phoney Communism and its Historical Lessons for the World'. Mao's thoughts on the generative view of class, together with his ideas about the importance of superstructural factors, ought to have provided him with the basis for a new theory of socialist transition which would have informed both the Socialist Education Movement and the Cultural Revolution. But such a theory was not to appear.

In the main, the Socialist Education Movement was directed against former landlords or rich peasants, against officials who had violated organisational norms, against cadres who were corrupt, or against bureaucratic Party committees. Not much attempt, it seems, was made to get to the root causes of capitalist behaviour. When, from Mao's perspective, things were seen not to be going well, the target shifted to 'top persons in authority taking the capitalist road'. But there was little examination of the factors which made that road possible to take.

When the Cultural Revolution erupted in 1966 in the campaign against the 'four olds', the specific targets were residues of the past rather than new sources of antagonism. A cultural revolution was necessary, it was said, because the transformation of the socialist economic base had not been matched by a similar transformation of the ideological superstructure. Such was the old Stalinist notion of cultural change which ignored the position Mao had been groping for in the early 1960s. Instead of discussing structural factors which facilitated capitalist behaviour there was a wholesale condemnation of people who were declared all along to have been diehard reactionaries who consciously sought to restore capitalism. Marxist theory was at a very low ebb.

The absence of a coherent theory of cultural revolution led to some extraordinary paradoxes. As Red Guards hacked at the Communist Party, they declared their allegiance to the first item in the widely disseminated red book of *Quotations from Chairman Mao Zedong* which affirmed that the force leading their cause forward was the Communist Party. They proclaimed allegiance to the Mass Line even though that very Mass Line, which was a technique for reconciling Party policy and mass sentiments, could not function without the Party organisation. Party leadership was even affirmed when attempts were made to set up Paris Commune-type organisations which implicitly denied the need for a Party at all.

Throughout all the confusion, a stream of exhortatory articles was published in the press and various leaders proclaimed their allegiance to Mao Zedong Thought. But Mao himself did not attempt to give any theoretical substance to his views on 'continuous revolution'. Why was that? One answer might have been that Mao had been taken aback by the torrent he had unleashed. Indeed, the chairman was often to express extreme surprise at the sheer scope of the movement. A more likely explanation, however, was that Mao was fully aware of the implications of the views he had come to and was too much of a Leninist to wish to go down in history as profoundly unorthodox. After all, the Soviet critics had called him 'idealist'. To be sure, there was a defence against that charge but, if the Cultural Revolution were to fail, any explicit theory of Mao's could have been used to make the charge stick.

At the core of the problem was Mao's view that the very vanguard of the revolution could constitute its most serious obstacle. Most Leninists stopped at exploring that dialectical (and probably quite accurate) proposition. A second heresy was that ownership relations, though usually determinant, could change as a result of the effect of the other two aspects of the relations of production—the relations between people at work and the pattern of distribution of the social product. Thus, a dictatorial 'one-person' manager did not just behave like a capitalist manager. He could, in fact, become one. A high-salaried intellectual, moreover, did not just behave like a professional in a capitalist society. He could, in fact, become in reality a bourgeois intellectual. To develop a theory, however, Mao would have had to examine, in the first case, the relationship between legal ownership and real appropriation and, in the second, the notion of 'intellectual capital'. Mao was not prepared to do that and left his adherents without much theoretical basis for what they were doing. What tended to develop, therefore, was a repetition of the old technique of defining social class in terms of behaviour rather than structural position. Though Mao's writings of the early 1960s were contradictory and contain much which would support the old behavioural notion, I am sure that was the very position Mao had been trying to get away from.

In short, the chairman's lack of theoretical courage resulted in an analysis, on the part of many Cultural Revolution activists, which was un-Marxist, and China's present leadership has not been slow to point that out. It may be that, eventually, they will reach the same verdict about Mao. That would not only be wrong. It would be a sad epitaph for a man whose thinking, in the early 1960s, about the contradictions in socialist society had shown such promise.

Mao's lack of courage in developing his own ideas was compounded by his entrusting Zhang Chunqiao and Yao Wenyuan to do the work for him, long after the Cultural Revolution was over. We shall perhaps never know whether Mao agreed with their conclusions but, even so, the two keynote essays of Zhang and Yao in 1975 were not without theoretical importance. The behaviour of the 'Gang of Four', however, in the movements of 1975 and 1976, was such that the present (1976 – 9) leadership could count on widespread support for the denunciation of their *theoretical* position. Of course, the post-Mao leadership would probably have denounced their theories anyway, but the fact that those theories were associated with people who seem genuinely to have been hated, does not augur well for any revival of thinking about the generative view of class.

When the post-Mao leadership talked about 'continuous revolution', it in fact did little more than endorse Mao's 1958 version of 'uninterrupted revolution', which was still cast in the framework of a positive model of socialism. Though, by 1958, Mao had rejected the formulation of the Eighth Party Congress that the principal contradiction in China was between the 'advanced socialist system' and the 'backward productive forces', the present leadership found it possible to reconcile that proposition with 'uninterrupted revolution'. This was done by prising 'uninterrupted revolution' apart from the Great Leap Forward affirmation of creative imbalance. Thus, elements of 'uninterrupted revolution' coexisted uneasily with an increasing adherence to 'market socialism' and the 'rule of law'. 'New bourgeois elements', in so far as they were still felt to exist, were probably defined simply as those who broke the law—a law before which all were theoretically equal, regardless of their economic position. Who remembered, any more, the comments, made by the Chinese in the early 1960s, about Khrushchev's 'state of the whole people'?

Though many of the results of the Cultural Revolution were extremely negative, from whichever perspective one cares to look at them, one cannot deny that, for many people, the events of that time were a truly liberating experience. People began to ask questions which they had never considered before and came to a new understanding about the nature of power in Chinese society. Contrary to the position of Zhang Chunqiao, they came to realise that the mass movement was not always rational, but neither was the Party. They began to understand that a belief in organisational 'correctness' might lead either to bureaucratic repression or else anarchic factionalism. Yet, without some notion of organisational 'correctness', there would have been no Chinese revolution, much less a 'continuing' one. This is a familiar political paradox and is often used to point out the futility of revolution. In my view, it should not so be used. For all its excess, the achievements of the Chinese revolution have been immense.

In contrast to *China: Liberation and Transformation* 1942 – 1962, this volume has documented the breakdown of leadership consensus. Once the process of socialist transition became problematic, mutual suspicion reigned and the only kind of unity which seemed possible was based on an unquestioned loyalty to the symbol of Chairman Mao. But did the affirmation of 'continuous revolution' necessarily lead to the promotion of the 'cult of the individual'? Max Weber would have thought so. As he saw it, the breakdown of legal rationality or bureaucratic rationality had to lead to charismatic leadership. For Weber, that was not necessarily a bad thing. But, inevitably, charisma would itself become routinised once again and so the process might continue. It were almost as though Weber entertained the possibility of 'continuous revolution'. In Weber's view, modernisation had to lead to bureaucratism. For Trotsky, on the other hand, modernisation was the only means to escape from bureaucratism. Mao adopted neither of those positions. As he saw it, the function of 'correct' leadership was to see that socialist goals were never subordinated to bureaucratic ones. Thus, when the Party seemed unduly bureaucratic, there was no course but for Mao to assume a personal rule, which became more and more dependent upon information provided by close advisers such as Lin Biao and the 'Gang of Four'. Because that rule was limited, a high degree of regional independence developed and some provincial first secretaries interpreted the goals of socialism quite differently. In some ways, what developed was a feudal-type of structure and centralisation was only achieved, once again, by a restoration of much of what had existed prior to the Cultural Revolution. In 1977 – 8, this was legitimised by reference to the policies of the mid-1950s, and in 1979, by the policies of the early 1960s. I am not arguing here that China simply oscillated between feudal and capitalist structures and, in the end, the latter triumphed. Throughout that oscillation, there was much profound change, and despite all the unfavourable statistics, much economic development. My point is simply that the socialist transition to a new decision-making structure has yet to be worked out. If one rejects the Soviet model, there has to be an alternative to either capitalism or feudalism. Mao was groping for a solution. I wonder how much the present leadership is prepared to carry on where he left off.

When China was the model for significant parts of the 'left' in many countries, there was a tendency to ascribe to China theories of socialist transition and patterns of decision-making which the Chinese had never articulated. That was perhaps the result of support for a foreign policy which seemed unambiguously revolutionary. But was it so revolutionary? In the early 1950s, China adhered to the Soviet formulation of the 'socialist camp'. By the mid-1950s, more and more contacts were established with the newly independent countries of Asia and Africa. In the Bandung period of diplomacy, however, the 'socialist camp' paradigm remained and only began to crack after the development of the Sino-Soviet polemic in the late 1950s and early 1960s. At the beginning of the period covered in this volume, a second strategy began to develop which Peck has called 'revised Soviet internationalism'. Attempts were made to foster the creation of a new Marxist-Leninist 'socialist camp' and Marxist-Leninist Communist parties began to spring up in many countries, in opposition to Soviet 'revisionism'. At the same time, China renewed its attempts to foster Third World solidarity.

A series of right-wing coups in 1965, particularly in Indonesia, together with the war in Vietnam, called into question the efficacy of 'revised Soviet internationalism' and it was replaced by a generalisation, on a world scale, of Lin Biao's essay 'Long Live the Victory of People's War'. According to Lin Biao, the 'world's countryside' was surrounding the 'world's cities' and China should adopt a policy of maximum hostility towards imperialism. At the same time, it was stressed that wars of national liberation were the concern of the countries themselves and any kind of global strategy was out of the question. As such, it has been argued, that a 'revolutionary' foreign policy position was, in fact, a recipe for passivity and did not do much beyond isolating China diplomatically.

Another strategy, which emerged in the 1970s, was very different from this. With the decline of United States power in Asia, attempts were to be made to drive wedges between the contending 'hegemonic' powers and between them and their client states and the Third World in general. To do this effectively, channels of communication had to be opened between China and the United States and kept open between Beijing and Moscow. That strategy was to be remarkably successful in restoring China's place in international bodies and in isolating Taiwan. It was achieved, however, at a cost. China began to tone down its support for national liberation struggles and to lean increasingly to the side of the United States. Indeed, the strategy was to deteriorate into China's supporting any state, organisation or movement which opposed the Soviet Union, be it Iran under the Shah, South African-supported guerrillas in Angola, or NATO. Such actions were justified on the grounds that the Soviet Union was expansionist. Writing at a time when Soviet troops are pouring into Afghanistan, such a claim is not to be dismissed lightly. Nevertheless, there does not seem to be much left of the Chinese theoretical position articulated in the polemic on the General Line of the International Communist Movement of the early 1960s. China seems now to be arguing in classic 'balance of power' terms. One sees here a mirror image of the Chinese treatment of domestic politics. When, domestically, attempts to move beyond the behavioural determination of class to a consideration of structural questions petered out, behaviour once again defined class. Similarly, in international politics, an attempt was made to explain why the Soviet Union behaved imperialistically, but no coherent theory was ever articulated. Now, all that is left is the argument that, because the Soviet Union behaves imperialistically, there must be structures within that country which explain it. To explore those structures, however, might challenge the Leninist orthodoxy, so discussions are couched in terms of 'balance of power'.

A major consequence of China's 'leaning to the side' of countries like the United States and Japan, has been its increasing integration with the capitalist world. That, it will be remembered, was the charge which China made against Yugoslavia in 1963. But now, we are assured, Yugoslavia was always a socialist country. The Chinese, of course, have every right to make mistakes, but if they think they have made one, why don't they acknowledge it? When Mao's 1962 speech at the conference attended by 7,000 cadres was published in *Beijing Review* in 1978,[1] all perjorative references to Yugoslavia were removed. Is this telling history 'as it was' or is it just a different version or 'making the past serve the present'?

As I write this conclusion at the end of 1979, there seems little doubt that China is heading in a capitalist direction. There seems little doubt also that life for many people in China is now less tense and precarious than it was in the mass movements of earlier years. That conclusion, however, should not be read as an endorsement of capitalism. My point is that the theory of socialist transition needs to be considered once again. Mao's contributions in the early 1960s were seminal. Perhaps in the new 'blooming of a hundred flowers', they will be added to. But I somehow doubt it. When it criticised the first hundred flowers movement in 1957, the Chen Qitong group remarked that new ideas were often swamped by the revival of the old.[2] That group seemed to be a rather élitist collection of people, but in this respect they were probably right. In the near future, we might expect more revivals of the mid-1950s and early 1960s and an ever increasing importation of ideas from the West. Some of these latter ideas will undoubtedly be good ones, but so were some of the Soviet ideas of the early 1950s; and look what problems were caused at that time by borrowing foreign ways of doing things!

NOTES

1. Mao Zedong, 30 January 1962, *PR* 27, 7 July 1978, p. 11. The original is in Schram, 1974, pp. 158–87.
2. Chen Qitong *et al.*, *RMRB* 7 January 1957, *SCMP* 1507, 9 April 1957, pp. 17–19.

BIBLIOGRAPHY

Letters (a, b or c) have been inserted after some dates to facilitate identification of notes.

Addy, P. 'South Asia in China's Foreign Policy—A view from the Left', *Journal of Contemporary Asia*, Vol. II, No. 4, 1972, pp. 403–14

Adie, W. 'Chou En-lai on Safari', *CQ* 18, 1964, pp. 174–94

Andors, S. 'Factory Management and Political Ambiguity, 1961–63', *CQ* 59, 1974, pp. 435–76

_____ *China's Industrial Revolution: Politics, Planning and Management, 1949 to the Present*, New York, Pantheon Books, 1977

Bastid, M. 'Economic Necessity and Political Ideals in Educational Reform During the Cultural Revolution', *CQ* 42, 1970, pp. 16–45

_____ 'Levels of Economic Decision Making' in Schram (ed.), 1973, pp. 159–97

Baum, R. 'China: Year of the Mangoes', *Asian Survey*, Vol. IX, No. 1, January 1969 (a), pp. 1–17

_____ 'Revolution and Reaction in the Chinese Countryside: The Socialist Education Movement in Cultural Revolutionary Perspective', *CQ* 38, 1969 (b), pp. 92–119

_____ 'The Cultural Revolution in the Countryside: Anatomy of a Limited Rebellion' in Robinson (ed.), 1971, pp. 367–476

_____ 'Elite Behaviour under Conditions of Stress: The Lesson of the "Tang-ch'üan P'ai" in the Cultural Revolution' in Scalapino (ed.), 1972, pp. 540–74

_____ *Prelude to Revolution: Mao, the Party and the Peasant Question, 1962-66*, New York, Columbia University Press, 1975

_____ and Teiwes, F. *Ssu-Ch'ing: The Socialist Education Movement of 1962–1966*, Berkeley, University of California, Center for Chinese Studies, *China Research Monograph*, No. 2, 1968

Bennett, G. and Montaperto, R. *Red Guard: The Political Biography of Dai Hsiao-ai*, New York, Doubleday, 1971

Bernstein, T. 'Urban Youth in the Countryside: Problems of Adaptation and Remedies', *CQ* 69, March 1977 (a), pp. 75–108

_____ *Up to the Mountains and Down to the Villages: The Transfer of Youth from Urban to Rural China*, New Haven, Yale University Press, 1977 (b)

Bettelheim, C. *Cultural Revolution and Industrial Organization in China*, New York, Monthly Review Press, 1974

_____ *China Since Mao*, New York, Monthly Review Press, 1978

Bradsher, H. 'China: The Radical Offensive', *Asian Survey*, Vol. XIII, No. 11, November 1973, pp. 989–1009

Bridgham, P. 'Mao's Cultural Revolution', *CQ* 29, 1967, pp. 1–35; *CQ* 34, 1968, pp. 6–37; *CQ* 41, 1970, pp. 1–25

_____ 'The Fall of Lin Piao', *CQ* 55, 1973, pp. 427–49

Broadbent, K. 'The Transformation of Chinese Agriculture and its Effects on the Environment', *International Relations*, Vol. IV, No. 1, 1972, pp. 38–51

Brugger, B. (ed.) *China: The Impact of the Cultural Revolution*, London, Croom Helm, 1978

_____ 'China Since the Fifth National People's Congress: 1978 or 1957?' *The Australian Journal of Chinese Affairs*, 1979 (a), No. 1, pp. 135–44

_____ 'The "Gang of Four" ', *World Review*, Vol. XVIII, No. 2, June 1979 (b), pp. 5–23

_____ 'China: The Struggle for a New Policy', *Arena* 53, 1979 (c), pp. 83–99

_____ (ed.) *China Since the 'Gang of Four'*, London, Croom Helm, 1980

Burchett, W. 'Lin Piao's Plot—The Full Story', *FEER*, Vol. LXXXI, No. 33, 20 August 1973, pp. 22–4

Burton, B. 'The Cultural Revolution's Ultra Left Conspiracy: The May 16 Group', *Asian Survey*, Vol. XI, No. 11, November 1971, pp. 1029–53

Chan, S. 'Revolution in Higher Education' in Brugger (ed.), 1978, pp. 95–125

_____ ' "The Blooming of a Hundred Flowers" and the Literature of the "Wounded Generation" ' in Brugger (ed.), 1980, pp. 174–201

Chang, P. 'Research Notes on the Changing Loci of Decision in the Chinese Communist Party', *CQ* 44, 1970, pp. 169–94

_____ 'Political Profiles: Wang Hung-wen and Li Teh-sheng', *CQ* 57, 1974, pp. 124–31

Chen, C. and Ridley, C. *Rural People's Communes in Lien-chiang: Documents Concerning Communes in Lien-chiang County, Fukien*

Province, 1962-1963, Stanford, Hoover Institution Press, 1969

Chen Guangsheng (Chen Kuang-sheng) *Lei Feng, Chairman Mao's Good Fighter*, Beijing, PFLP, 1968

Chen Nai-ruenn 'China's Foreign Trade, 1950–74' in US Congress, Joint Economic Committee, 1975, pp. 617–52

Cheng Chu-yuan 'China's Machine Building Industry', *Current Scene*, Vol. XI, No. 7, July 1973, pp. 1–11

Cheng, J. 'Strategy for Economic Development' in Brugger (ed.), 1978, pp. 126–52

Chesneaux, J. *et. al. China: The People's Republic, 1949-1976*, New York, Pantheon Books, 1979

Chey, J. 'Chinese Cultural Policy—Liberalization? (a personal statement)', *The Australian Journal of Chinese Affairs*, 1979, No. 1, pp. 107–12

Chi Hsin *The Case of the Gang of Four*, Hong Kong, Cosmos Books, 1977

Chien Yu-shen *China's Fading Revolution*, Hong Kong, Centre of Contemporary Chinese Studies, 1969

Commoner, B. 'How Poverty Breeds Overpopulation (and not the other way round)', *Ramparts*, August/September, 1975; in Mack, Plant and Doyle (eds.), 1977, pp. 272–85

Croll, E. 'A Recent Movement to Redefine the Role and Status of Women', *CQ* 71, September 1977, pp. 591–7

Croll, E. *Feminism and Socialism in China*, London, Routledge and Kegan Paul, 1978

Dallin, A. *Diversity in International Communism*, New York, Columbia University Press, 1963

Daubier, J. *A History of the Chinese Cultural Revolution*, New York, Vintage Books, 1974

Davin, D. *Women-Work: Women and the Party in Revolutionary China*, Oxford, Clarendon Press, 1976

Dernberger, R. 'The Program for Agricultural Transformation in Mainland China', *Issues and Studies*, Vol. XIV, No. 10, October 1978, pp. 59–97

Dittmer, L. 'The Structural Evolution of "Criticism and Self Criticism" ', *CQ* 56, 1973, pp. 708–29

_____ *Liu Shao-ch'i and the Chinese Cultural Revolution: The Politics of Mass Criticism*, Berkeley, University of California Press, 1974

Djilas, M. *The New Class: An Analysis of the Communist System*, London, Unwin Books, 1966

Domes, J. 'The Role of the Military in the Formation of Revolutionary Committees 1967-68', *CQ* 44, 1970, pp. 112–45

_____ *The Internal Politics of China, 1949–1972*, London, Hurst and Co., 1973

Donnithorne, A. *China's Economic System*, London, George Allen and Unwin, 1967
_____ *The Budget and the Plan in China: Central-Local Economic Relations*, Canberra, Australian National University Press, 1972 (a)
_____ 'China's Cellular Economy: Some Economic Trends Since the Cultural Revolution', *CQ* 52, 1972 (b), pp. 605 – 19
Dreyer, J. 'China's Minority Nationalities in the Cultural Revolution', *CQ* 35, 1968, pp. 96 – 109
_____ *China's Forty Millions*, Cambridge, Mass., Harvard University Press, 1976
Eckstein, A. 'Economic Growth and Change in China: A Twenty-Year Perspective', *CQ* 54, 1973, pp. 211 – 41
_____ *China's Economic Development: The Interplay of Scarcity and Ideology*, Ann Arbor, University of Michigan Press, 1975 (a)
_____ 'China's Trade Policy and Sino-American Relations', *Foreign Affairs*, Vol. LIV, No. 1, October 1975 (b), pp. 134 – 54
_____ *China's Economic Revolution*, Cambridge University Press, 1977
_____ Galenson, W. and Liu Ta-chung (eds.) *Economic Trends in Communist China*, Edinburgh University Press, 1968
Erasmus, S. 'General de Gaulle's Recognition of Peking', *CQ* 18, 1964, pp. 195 – 200
Erisman, A. 'China: Agriculture in the 1970's' in US Congress, Joint Economic Committee, 1975, pp. 324 – 49
Esmein, J. *The Chinese Cultural Revolution*, New York, Anchor Books, 1973
FEER, Yearbook: Asia, 1977
Funnell, V. 'The Chinese Communist Youth Movement, 1949 – 66', *CQ* 42, 1970, pp. 105 – 30
Gardner, J. 'Educated Youth and Urban Rural Inequalities' in Lewis (ed.), 1971, pp. 235 – 86
_____ and Idema, W. 'China's Educational Revolution' in Schram (ed.), 1973, pp. 257 – 89
Gayn, M. 'Who After Mao?', *Foreign Affairs*, Vol. LI, No. 2, January 1973, pp. 300 – 9
Gittings, J. *The Role of the Chinese Army*, London, Oxford University Press, 1967
_____ *Survey of the Sino-Soviet Dispute: A Commentary and Extracts from the Recent Polemics, 1963-1967*, London, Oxford University Press, 1968
_____ *The World and China: 1922-1972*, London, Eyre Methuen, 1974
_____ 'New Material on Teng Hsiao-p'ing', *CQ* 67, September 1976, pp. 489 – 93
Goldman, M. 'China's Anti-Confucius Campaign 1973-74', *CQ* 63,

Bibliography

September 1975, pp. 435–62

Gray, J. 'The Two Roads: Alternative Strategies of Social Change and Economic Growth in China' in Schram (ed.), 1973, pp. 109–57

Gurtov, M. 'The Foreign Ministry and Foreign Affairs during the Cultural Revolution' in Robinson (ed.), 1971, pp. 313–66 (also in *CQ* 40, 1969, pp. 65–102)

Halperin, E. 'Peking and the Latin American Communists', *CQ* 29, 1967, pp. 111–54

Heymann, H. 'Acquisition and Diffusion of Technology in China' in US Congress, Joint Economic Committee, 1975, pp. 678–729

Hinton, H. *Communist China in World Politics*, London, Macmillan, 1966

Hinton, W. *Hundred Day War: The Cultural Revolution at Tsinghua University*, New York, Monthly Review Press, 1972

Horn, J. *Away With All Pests*, New York, Monthly Review Press, 1969

Howe, C. *Wage Patterns and Wage Policy in Modern China, 1919-72*, Cambridge University Press, 1973 (a)

―――― 'Labour Organisation and Incentives in Industry, before and after the Cultural Revolution' in Schram (ed.), 1973 (b), pp. 233–56

Hoxha, E. *Imperialism and the Revolution*, Tirana, The 8 Nëntori Publishing House, 1979

Hsiao, G. 'The Sino-Japanese Rapprochement: A Relationship of Ambivalence', *CQ* 57, 1974, pp. 101–23

Hunter, N. *Shanghai Journal*, New York, Praeger, 1969

Institute of International Relations *Collected Documents of the First Sino-American Conference on Mainland China*, Taibei, 1971

Israel, J. 'The Red Guard in Historical Perspective: Continuity and Change in the Chinese Youth Movement', *CQ* 30, 1967, pp. 1–32

Joffe, E. 'The Chinese Army after the Cultural Revolution: The Effects of Intervention', *CQ* 55, 1973, pp. 450–77

Johnson, C. 'The Two Chinese Revolutions', *CQ* 39, 1969, pp. 12–29

JPRS (ed.) *Miscellany of Mao Tse-tung Thought (1949-1968)*, 2 vols. (*JPRS* 61269–1 and 2), Arlington, Va., 20 February 1974

Kallgren, J. 'China 1979: The New Long March', *Asian Survey*, Vol. XIX, No. 1, January 1979, pp. 1–19

Kelly, D. 'At Last, An Arena: Current Policies in Chinese Social Science', *The Australian Journal of Chinese Affairs*, 1979, No. 2, pp. 123–136

Konrád, G. and Szelényi, I. *The Intellectuals on the Road to Class Power: A Sociological Study of the Role of the Intellegensia in Socialism*, New York, Harcourt, Brace, Jovanovich, 1979

Kraus, R. 'Class Conflict and the Vocabulary of Social Analysis in China', *CQ* 69, 1977, pp. 54–74

Kuo, L. *The Technical Transformation of Agriculture in Communist China*, New York, Praeger, 1972

Lee Hong Yung 'The Politics of Cadre Rehabilitation Since the Cultural Revolution', *Asian Survey*, Vol. XVIII, No. 9, September 1978, pp. 934–55

Levy, R. 'New Light on Mao: His Views on the Soviet Union's "Political Economy" ', *CQ* 61, 1975, pp. 95–117

Lewis, J. (ed.) *Party Leadership and Revolutionary Power in China*, Cambridge University Press, 1970

_____ (ed.) *The City in Communist China*, Stanford University Press, 1971

Leys, S. *Chinese Shadows*, New York, The Viking Press, 1977

Lifton, R. *Revolutionary Immortality*, London, Weidenfeld and Nicolson, 1968

Lin Biao *Long Live the Victory of People's War*, Beijing, PFLP, 1965

Liu Shaoqi (Liu Shao-ch'i) *Collected Works*, Vol. II (1945–57), 1969; Vol. III (1958–67), 1968, Hong Kong, URI

Lu Yung-shu 'Preparation for War in Mainland China' in Institute of International Relations, 1971, pp. 895–920

Luo Ruiqing (Lo Jui-ch'ing) *The People Defeated Japanese Fascism and Can Certainly Defeat U.S. Imperialism Too*, Beijing, PFLP, 1965

Macciocchi, M.*Daily Life in Revolutionary China*, New York, Monthly Review Press, 1972

Mack, A., Plant, D. and Doyle, U. (eds.) *Imperialism, Intervention and Development*, London, Croom Helm, 1979

Mackerras, C. 'Chinese Opera after the Cultural Revolution (1970–72)', *CQ* 55, 1973, pp. 478–510

McLaren, A. 'The Educated Youth Return: The Poster Campaign in Shanghai from November 1978 to March 1979', *The Australian Journal of Chinese Affairs*, 1979, No. 2, pp. 1–20

Maitain, L. (trans. Benton, G. and Colliti, M.) *Party, Army and Masses in China*, London, New Left Books, 1976

Mao Zedong *Selected Works*, Beijing, PFLP, Vol. I, 1965; Vol. II, 1965; Vol. III, 1965; Vol. IV, 1961; Vol. V, 1977

_____ *Quotations from Chairman Mao Tse-tung*, Beijing, PFLP, 1966

_____ *Miscellany of Mao Tse-tung Thought (1949-1968)*, see *JPRS* (ed.), 1974

_____ *Mao Zhuxi Wenxuan* n.p. n.d. (probably 1967)

_____ *Mao Zedong Sixiang Wansui*, n.p., 1967 (a) p. 46

_____ *Mao Zedong Sixiang Wansui*, n.p., 1967 (b) p. 280

_____ *Mao Zedong Sixiang Wansui*, n.p., 1969

_____ *A Critique of Soviet Economics* (trans. M. Roberts with introduction by J. Peck), New York, Monthly Review Press, 1977

Marx, K. 'Critique of the Gotha Programme' (1875) in Marx and Engels, 1970, Vol. III, pp. 9 – 30

_____ and Engels, F. *Selected Works*, 3 vols., Moscow, Progress Publishers, 1970

Maxwell, N. *India's China War*, Harmondsworth, Penguin, 1972

Mehnert, K. *Peking and the New Left: At Home and Abroad*, Berkeley, University of California, Center for Chinese Studies, 1969

Meisner, M. *Mao's China: A History of the People's Republic*, New York, The Free Press, 1977

Meisner, M. 'The Shenyang Transformer Factory', *CQ* 52, 1972, pp. 717 – 37

Milton, D. and N. *The Wind Will Not Subside: Years in Revolutionary China—1964-1969*, New York, Pantheon Books, 1976

Moody, P. 'Policy and Power: The Career of T'ao Chu, 1956 – 66', *CQ* 54, 1973, pp. 267 – 93

_____ 'The New Anti-Confucian Campaign in China: The First Round', *Asian Survey*, Vol. XIV, No. 4, April 1974, pp. 307 – 24

Moseley, G. 'China's Fresh Approach to the National Minority Question', *CQ* 24, 1965, pp. 15 – 27

Munro, D. 'The Yang Hsien-chen Affair', *CQ* 22, 1965, pp. 75 – 82

Muthiram, T. 'China's Policy in South-East Asia', *Journal of Contemporary Asia*, Vol. III, No. 3, 1973, pp. 335 – 44

Nee, V. *The Cultural Revolution at Peking University*, New York, Monthly Review Press, 1969

Neuhauser, C. 'The Chinese Communist Party in the 1960s: Prelude to the Cultural Revolution', *CQ* 32, 1967, pp. 3 – 36

Nixon, R. 'Report to Congress', 9 February 1972, *Department of State Bulletin*, 13 March 1972, pp. 313 – 418

Oksenberg, M. 'Communist China: A Quiet Crisis in Revolution', *Asian Survey*, Vol. VI, No. 1, January 1966, pp. 1 – 11

O'Leary, G. 'Chinese Foreign Policy From "Anti-imperialism" to "Anti-hegemonism" ' in Brugger (ed.), 1978, pp. 203 – 52

_____ 'China's Foreign Relations: The Reintegration of China into the World Economy' in Brugger (ed.), 1980, pp. 231 – 61

Onate, A. 'Hua Kuo-feng and the Arrest of the "Gang of Four" ' *CQ* 75, 1978, pp. 540 – 65

Orleans, L. 'China: The Population Record', *Current Scene*, Vol. X, No. 5, May 1972, pp. 10 – 19

Pano, N. 'Albania in the Era of Brezhnev and Kosygin' in Simmonds (ed.), 1977 (a) pp. 474 – 94

_____ 'Albania in the 1970s', *Problems of Communism*, Vol. XXVI, No. 6, November-December 1977 (b), pp. 33 – 43

Peck, J. 'Why China "Turned West" ', *Socialist Register*, 1972, pp. 289 – 306

PFLP *The Sino-Indian Boundary Question*, Beijing, 1962 (a)

_____ *Workers of All Countries Unite, Oppose Our Common Enemy*, Beijing, 1962 (b)

_____ *Training Successors for the Revolution is the Party's Strategic Task*, Beijing, 1965 (a)

_____ *The Polemic on the General Line of the International Communist Movement*, Beijing, 1965 (b)

_____ *Important Documents on the Great Proletarian Cultural Revolution in China*, Beijing, 1970

_____ *The Seeds and Other Stories*, Beijing, 1972 (a)

_____ *Taching: Red Banner on China's Industrial Front*, Beijing, 1972 (b)

_____ *Three Major Struggles on China's Philosophical Front (1949 – 69)*, Beijing, 1973

_____ *Selected Articles Criticizing Lin Piao and Confucius*, Vol. I, Beijing, 1974

Pepper, S. 'Education and Revolution: The "Chinese Model" Revised', *Asian Survey*, Vol. XVIII, No. 9, September 1978, pp. 847 – 90

Perkins, D. 'Industrial Planning and Management' in Eckstein, Galenson and Liu (eds.), 1968, pp. 597 – 635

_____ 'An Economic Reappraisal', *Problems of Communism*, Vol. XXII, No. 3, May-June 1973, pp. 1 – 13

_____ 'A Conference on Agriculture' *CQ* 67, September 1976, pp. 596 – 610

Pfeffer, R. 'Mao and Marx in the Marxist-Leninist Tradition: A Critique of "The China Field" and a Contribution to a Preliminary Reappraisal', *Modern China*, Vol. II, No. 4, October 1976, pp. 421 – 60

Pien Hsi 'The Story of Tachai' in PFLP, 1972 (a), pp. 166 – 93

Price, R. 'The Part-Work Principle in Chinese Education', *Current Scene*, Vol. XI, No. 9, September 1973, pp. 1 – 11

_____ (ed.) *The Anti-Confucius Campaign in China*, Melbourne, La Trobe University, Centre for Comparative and International Studies in Education, *Asia Studies Papers, China Series, No. 1*, 1977 (a)

_____ *Marx and Education in Russia and China*, London, Croom Helm, 1977 (b)

_____ (ed.) *Education After Mao*, papers presented at a seminar held at La Trobe University, Melbourne, 3 December 1978, La Trobe University, Centre for Comparative and International Studies in Education and Committee for Australia-China Relations, 1978

_____ 'Schooling for Modernization', *The Australian Journal of*

Chinese Affairs, 1979, No. 2, pp. 57–76

_____ 'Education—Why a Reversal?' in Brugger (ed.), 1980, pp. 202–30

Prifti, P. 'The Dismissal of General Begir Balluku, Albania's Minister of Defense: An Analysis' in Simmonds (ed.), 1977, pp. 495-502

Richman, B. *Industrial Society in Communist China*, New York, Random House, 1969

Riskin, C. 'Small Industry and the Chinese Model of Development', *CQ* 46, 1971, pp. 245–73

Robinson, J. *The Cultural Revolution in China*, Harmondsworth, Penguin, 1969

_____ *Economic Management in China: 1972*, London, Anglo-Chinese Educational Institute, 1972

Robinson, T. (ed.) *The Cultural Revolution in China*, Berkeley, University of California Press, 1971

_____ 'Chou En-lai and the Cultural Revolution in China' in Robinson (ed.), 1971, pp. 165–312

_____ 'Lin Piao as an Elite Type' in Scalapino (ed.), 1972, pp. 149–95

_____ 'China in 1972: Socio-Economic Progress Amidst Political Uncertainty', *Asian Survey*, Vol. XIII, No. 1, January 1973, pp. 1–18

_____ 'China in 1973: Renewed Leftism Threatens the New Course', *Asian Survey*, Vol. XIV, No. 1, January 1974, pp. 1–21

Rossanda, R. 'Mao's Marxism', *Socialist Register*, 1971, pp., 53–80

Salaff, J. 'Urban Residential Communities in the Wake of the Cultural Revolution' in Lewis (ed.), 1971, pp. 289–323

Salisbury, H. *To Peking and Beyond: A Report on the New Asia*, London, Arrow Books, 1973

Scalapino, R. (ed.) *Elites in the People's Republic of China*, Seattle, University of Washington Press, 1972

Schram, S. (ed.) *Authority, Participation and Cultural Change in China*, Cambridge University Press, 1973

_____ (ed.) *Mao Tse-tung Unrehearsed*, Harmondsworth, Penguin, 1974

_____ 'Some Reflections on the Pfeffer-Walder "Revolution" in China Studies', *Modern China*, Vol. III, No. 2, April 1977, pp. 169–84

Schurmann, H.F. *Ideology and Organization in Communist China*, Berkeley, University of California Press, 1966

_____ and Schell, O. (eds.) *China Readings*, Vol. II, *Republican China*; Vol. III, *Communist China*, Harmondsworth, Penguin, 1968

Schwartz, B. 'The Reign of Virture: Some Broad Perspectives on Leader and Party in the Cultural Revolution' in Lewis (ed.), 1970, pp. 149–69

_____ 'The Essence of Marxism Revisited', *Modern China*, Vol. II, No. 4, October 1976, pp. 461–72

Selden, M. (ed.) *The People's Republic of China: A Documentary History of Revolutionary Change*, New York, Monthly Review Press, 1979

Shehuizhuyi Zhengzhi Jingjixue Bianxie Xiaozu *Shehuizhuyi Zhengzhi Jingjixue* (draft, 2nd printing), Shanghai, Renmin Chubanshe, June 1975

Shirk, S. ' "Going Against the Tide": Political Dissent in China', *Survey*, Vol. XXIV, No. 1, Winter 1979, pp. 82–114

Sigurdson, J. 'Rural Industry and the Internal Transfer of Technology' in Schram (ed.), 1973, pp. 199–232

_____ 'Rural Industrialization in China' in US Congress, Joint Economic Committee, 1975, pp. 411–35

Simmonds, G. (ed.) *Nationalism and the USSR and Eastern Europe in the Era of Brezhnev and Kosygin*, Detroit University Press, 1977

Snow, E. 'Interview with Mao', *The New Republic*, 27 February 1965, pp. 17–23

_____ 'The Open Door', *The New Republic*, 27 March 1971, pp. 20–3

_____ 'Aftermath of the Cultural Revolution', *The New Republic*, 10 April 1971, pp. 18–21

_____ 'Population Care and Control', *The New Republic*, 1 May 1971, pp. 20–3

Solomon, R. *Mao's Revolution and the Chinese Political Culture*, Berkeley, University of California Press, 1971

Stalin, J. 'On the Draft Constitution of the U.S.S.R.', 25 November 1936 in Stalin, 1947, pp. 540–68

_____ *Problems of Leninism*, Moscow, Foreign Languages Publishing House, 1947

_____ *Economic Problems of Socialism in the U.S.S.R.* (1952), Beijing, PFLP, 1972

Starr, J. 'China in 1974: "Weeding Through the Old to Bring Forth the New" ', *Asian Survey*, Vol. XV, No. 1, January 1975, pp. 1–19

_____ 'From the 10th Party Congress to the Premiership of Hua Kuofeng: The Significance of the Colour of the Cat', *CQ* 67, September 1976 (a), pp. 457–88

_____ 'China in 1975: "The Wind in the Bell Tower" ', *Asian Survey*, Vol. XVI, No. 1, January 1976 (b), pp. 42–60

State Statistical Bureau *Ten Great Years: Statistics of the Economic and Cultural Achievements of the People's Republic of China*, Beijing, PFLP, 1960

Stavis, B. 'China's Green Revolution', *Monthly Review*, Vol. XXVI, No. 5, October 1974, pp. 18–29

_____ 'A Preliminary Model for Grain Production in China', *CQ* 65, March 1976, pp., 82 – 96

Sullivan, M. 'The Politics of Conflict and Compromise' in Brugger (ed.), 1980, pp. 20 – 50

Tao Zhu (T'ao Chu) *The People's Communes Forge Ahead*, Beijing, PFLP, 1964

Teiwes, F. *Politics and Purges in China: Rectification and the Decline of Party Norms: 1950-1965*, White Plains, N. Y., M.E. Sharpe, 1979

Trotsky, L. *The Revolution Betrayed* (1937), New York, Pathfinder Press, 1972

URI (ed.) *The Case of P'eng Teh-huai*, Hong Kong, 1968 (a)

_____ (ed.) *CCP Documents of the Great Proletarian Cultural Revolution, 1966-67*, Hong Kong, 1968 (b)

_____ (ed.) *Communist China, 1967*, Hong Kong, 1969

_____ (ed.) *Documents of Chinese Communist Party Central Committee*, Hong Kong, 1971

US Congress, Joint Economic Committee *China: A Reassessment of the Economy*, Washington, DC, US Government Printing Office, 10 July 1975

Van Ginnekan, J. 'The 1967 Plot of the May 16 Movement', *Journal of Contemporary Asia*, Vol. II, No. 3, 1972, pp. 237 – 54

_____ (trans. D. Adkinson) *The Rise and Fall of Lin Piao* Harmondsworth, Penguin, 1976

Vogel, E. *Canton Under Communism, Programmes and Politics in a Provincial Capital 1949-1968*, New York, Harper and Row, 1971

Wakeman, F. 'A Response', *Modern China*, Vol. III, No. 2, April 1977, pp. 161 – 8

Walder, A. 'Marxism, Maoism and Social Change', *Modern China*, Vol. III, No. 1, January 1977, pp. 101 – 18; Vol. III, No. 2, April 1977, pp. 125 – 60

_____ *Chang Ch'un-ch'iao and Shanghai's January Revolution*, Ann Arbor, University of Michigan, Center for Chinese Studies, *Michigan Papers in Chinese Studies*, No. 32, 1978

Wang Gungwu *China and the World Since 1949: The Impact of Independence, Modernity and Revolution*, London, Macmillan, 1977

Watson, A. 'A Revolution to Touch Men's Souls: The Family, Interpersonal Relations and Daily Life' in Schram (ed.), 1973, pp. 291 – 330

_____ *Living in China*, London, Batsford, 1975

_____ 'Industrial Management—Experiments in Mass Participation' in Brugger (ed.), 1978, pp. 171 – 202

_____ 'Industrial Development and the Four Modernisations' in Brugger (ed.), 1980, pp. 88 – 134

Weber, M. *The Theory of Social and Economic Organisation*, New

York, The Free Press, 1964

White, L. 'Shanghai's Polity in Cultural Revolution' in Lewis (ed.), 1971, pp. 325 – 70

_____ 'Leadership in Shanghai, 1955-69' in Scalapino (ed.), 1972, pp. 302 – 77

Wich, R. 'The Tenth Party Congress: The Power Structure and the Succession Question', *CQ* 58, 1974, pp. 231 – 48

Wilson, D. *A Quarter of Mankind: An Anatomy of China Today*, Harmondsworth, Penguin, 1968

_____ 'China and the European Community', *CQ* 56, 1973, pp. 647 – 66

Witke, R. *Comrade Chiang Ch'ing*, Boston, Little, Brown, 1977

Woodward, D. 'Two Line Struggle in Agriculture' in Brugger (ed.), 1978, pp. 153 – 70

Wylie, R. 'Red Guards Rebound', *FEER*, Vol. LVII, No. 10, 10 September 1967, pp. 462 – 6

Yahuda, M. 'Kremlinology and the Chinese Strategic Debate 1965-66', *CQ* 49, 1972, pp. 32 – 75

_____ *China's Role in World Affairs*, London, Croom Helm, 1979

Young, G. 'Party Building and the Search for Unity' in Brugger (ed.), 1978, pp. 35 – 80

_____ 'Conceptions of Party Leadership in China: The Cultural Revolution and Party Building 1968-1971', unpublished PhD thesis, Adelaide, Flinders University, 1979

_____ and Woodward, D. 'From Contradictions Among the People to Class Struggle: The Theories of Uninterrupted and Continuous Revolution', *Asian Survey*, Vol. XVIII, No. 9, September 1978, pp. 912 – 33

Yu, G. *China and Tanzania: A Study in Co-operative Interaction*, Berkeley, University of California, Center for Chinese Studies, *China Research Monographs*, No. 5, 1970

Zagoria, D. *Vietnam Triangle: Moscow, Peking, Hanoi*, New York, Pegasus, 1968

INDEX

accounting, levels in agriculture 128–9, 151, 186, 211–12

Aeronautical Institute (Beijing) 72

Afghanistan 254

Afro-Asian Peoples' Solidarity Organisation 39

agriculture: 'eight character constitution' 149; fertiliser production 150, 155, 157, 211–12; livestock 151, 212; mechanisation 29, 31, 128, 151, 207, 211, 230, 234; NPAD 149, 211; 'sixty points' 219, 235; specialisation 234–5; tractor stations 29, 211; *see also* accounting, communes, co-operatives, grain, peasants, state farms

Aidit, D. 53

Albania 51, 120, 221

Algeria 51–2

Andors, S. 30

Angola 253

Anshan Iron and Steel Corporation, constitution 55, 130, 154, 156, 208

art and literature 22, 32–6, 49, 54–9, 65, 109, 158–9, 164–5, 170, 196, 215–17, 245

ASEAN 221, 243

'August Storm' (1967) 104–5, 107–8

Australia 39

Bandaranaike, S. 163

Bandung Conference, 51–2 (proposed second), 253

Bangladesh 163, 191

banking 125 (and ultra left), 186, 209–10, 232

Beijing opera 34–5, 55, 158–9, 215

Beijing Review 254

Beijing Ribao 57

Belgium 39, 135

'blooming and contending' *see* 'hundred flowers'

'bourgeois right' 182–4, 188, 195, 233, 239–40

Brazil 39

Britain 83, 104–5, 244

Bulgaria 38

Burma 39, 59, 100, 120, 191

cadres: as leadership type 13, 127; May Seventh Cadre Schools 133, 147; participation in manual labour 26–7, 44, 81, 154, 170, 208; rehabilitation after Cultural Revolution 97–8, 108, 124–6, 128, 133, 153–4, 187; rehabilitation atter 1976 202–5, 216–17, 229; rural 18, 21, 23–8, 32, 45–9, 55, 59, 62, 74, 77–8, 128–9, 236; salary scale 155

Canada 135

Cao Diqiu 78

capitalists: bureaucratic 15; comprador 15; national (domestic) 15, 75, 232; 'persons in authority taking the capitalist road' 46, 48–9, 58, 61, 64, 79, 95, 98, 100, 104, 107–8, 171, 180, 192, 205, 249–50

Castro, F. 234

Ceaucescu, N. 162

Ceylon *see* Sri Lanka

chairmanship of the People's Republic 137–8, 143

Chen Boda 19, 59–60, 72, 75, 79, 81, 86, 105, 123, 136–7, 143
Chen Muhua 237
Chen Pixian 88
Chen Qitong 254
Chen Xilian 110, 123, 218
Chen Yi 85–6, 88, 97, 99–100, 104
Chen Yiyang 179
Chen Yonggui 31, 218
Chen Yun 17, 99, 202, 205, 209, 218–20, 241
Chen Zaidao 103–4, 110
Chiang K'ai-shek *see* Jiang Jieshi
Chinese People's Political Consultative Conference 206
Chongqing negotiations 135
class struggle 15–16, 21, 26–8, 33, 36–7, 44–6, 59, 96, 158–9, 164, 171, 181–5, 192, 203, 211, 219, 228–9, 249–51, 254
Colombia 39
'commandism and tailism' 18, 126, 128–9, 151
communes: Paris 79, 82, 89, 99–100, 107–8, 111, 113, 250; production brigades 23, 26, 46, 74, 127–8, 132, 151, 161, 186, 211; production teams 26, 128, 151, 211, 235–6; rural 26, 28–9, 44–6, 73–4, 127–8, 131, 151, 153, 161, 171, 211, 232, 236; urban 31, 134
communism 16, 108; 'communist style' 15; 'goulash communism' 44, 229
Communist Party of China: Beijing municipal cttee 47, 56, 59–61, 104; commissions for inspecting discipline 204, 219; congresses, 8th 96, 228–9, 251; 9th 109, 115, 122–3, 145, 171; 10th 171–3, 179, 204; 11th 203–6; control cttees 204; membership 204; Military Commission 58, 90, 101; norms of debate 17, 19, 65, 252; plenary sessions and associated conferences, 8th of 8th CC (1959) 229, 10th of 8th CC (1962) 21–2, 33, 37, 64, 11th of 8th CC (1966) 64, 70, 12th of 8th CC (1968) 114–15, 122, 137, 1st of 9th CC (1969) 123–6, 130, 2nd of 9th CC (1970) 138, 143, 145, 148–9, 3rd of 10th CC (1977) 203, 1st of 11th CC (1977) 203–4, 3rd of 11th CC (1978) 218–20, 223, 228, 230, 232, 234; Politburo Standing Cttee 57, 59–60, 62; Politburo Standing Cttee

first and second fronts 16, 19; Propaganda Department 47, 62, 71, 194, 217–18; reconstruction after Cultural Revolution 106, 109, 123, 125–6, 129–30, 134, 136, 139, 145–6, 152–3, 172, 174; relations with state 106; schools 37, 204; Secretariat 59–60, 123
Communist Parties (ML) 39, 52, 253
'compare, study, catch up with and help' (*bi xue gan bang*) 27–8
complete plants, import of 150, 155, 185
Confucius and Confucianism 96, 173–6, 178–81, 189
Constitution: Party, 1969 122, 1973 172, 1977 204; State, 1954 206, 1969–70 (draft) 137, 1975 181, 1978 206, 216, 240–1
contracts 211, 231–3, 236; workers 30, 78, 81
contradictions: 'correct handling of' *see* Mao Zedong, important speeches; exploitation of on a world scale 135; internal and antagonistic 27, 33, 48, 57, 98, 125, 188, 251; leader-mass 144–5; urban-rural 30, 81, 152–3, 155, 208, 213, 234
co-operatives 14, 31 (rural), 134, 238 (urban)
CMEA 222
counter-revolutionaries, suppression of 28, 36, 46, 60, 74, 78, 102, 109, 239, 241
coup d'état: rumours of (1966) 58, 60, 64; 'Gang of Four's' alleged (1976) 195
Lin Biao's (1971) attempt 143, 146–8; credit, foreign 185–6, 207, 232–4
Cuba 37–8 (missile crisis), 121, 222, 244
Cultural Revolution: cttees 72, 77–8, 85; Group 59–60, 62–3, 70, 72, 76–8, 80, 83, 85, 87, 90, 94, 98, 102, 105, 136–7, 143
Czechoslovakia 38, 121–2, 135, 221

Daqing Oilfield 31, 55, 134, 148, 156–7, 208, 216
Dazhai Production Team 31–2, 55, 112, 128–9, 148, 150, 188, 218–19, 236; Dazhai-type *xian* 150, 211, 218, 235
Debray, R. 113
decentralisation: of urban services 133–4; Schurmann's decentralisation I 16, 208–9, 231, Schurmann's decentralisation II 16, 126–7, 208, 211, 223

pert' 131; Tongji 112; *see also* education
urban administration *see* street administration
urban-rural gap *see* contradictions

value, law of 209, 231, 236
Vietnam *see* Indo China

wages *see* incentive policy
Wang Dongxing 123, 130, 195, 202, 204, 218
Wang Enmao 101
Wang Guangmei 46, 62–3, 97, 229
Wang Hongwen 78, 148, 170, 172, 174, 188, 195
Wang Jinxi 31
Wang Li 85, 102–5, 110
Wang Ming 121, 124
Wang Renzhong 77
Wang Xiaoyu 125
Warsaw Pact 135
Water Margin (Shuihuzhuan) 158, 189–90, 192
Weber, M. 252
Wei Guoqing 205
Wei Jingsheng 238, 240
Wenhuibao 56, 80
'whatever' and 'practice' factions 218–19, 238
Witke, R. 159
women 23, 177, 201, 204
work-points *see* incentive policy
work-teams 18, 23, 26–7, 31–2, 46–7, 55–6, 62–5, 71–4, 81, 85, 89, 152
World Bank and International Monetary Fund 190, 234
World Federation of Trade Unions 39
World Peace Council 39
Wu De 202, 205, 217
Wu Faxian 123, 146
Wu Han 22, 33, 35, 37, 55–7, 60, 96, 229
Wuhan incident 103–4, 110

xiafang and *xiaxiang*, 13–14, 98, 112, 127–8, 131, 147, 152–3, 170, 178, 212–13, 217, 238
xian 29, 31, 49, 55, 59, 62, 74, 83, 125, 127, 145, 150, 153, 157, 161, 204, 211, 218, 235–6
Xia Yan 216
Xie Fuzhi 63, 99, 101–5, 112, 123
Xisha and Nansha Islands (Paracels and Spratleys) 190–1, 222

Xue Muqiao 209
Xuexi yu Pipan (Study and Criticism) 187
Xu Shiyu 110, 123, 147
Xu Xiangqian 87, 112

Yahuda, M. 52–3
Yan'an *see* models
Yan Hongyin 101–2
Yang Chengwu 58, 64, 103, 110–13, 187, 195
Yang Dezhi 110, 125
Yang Rongguo 173
Yang Xianzhen 37
Yao Dengshan 86, 100, 102, 104
Yao Wenyuan 35, 56–8, 60, 65, 78, 82–3, 105, 109, 123, 157, 170–1, 174–5, 181–4, 188, 194, 201, 203, 251
Ye Jianying 87, 123, 204
Ye Qun, 123, 146
yidasanfan (1970) 152
Youth League (Communist) 36, 50, 56, 61, 64, 71, 204
Yugoslavia 16, 21, 221, 236, 245, 254
Yu Lijin 103–4, 110
Yu Qiuli 204

Zagoria, D. 52
Zaïre (Congo) 51, 241
Zambia 120
Zeng Siyu 104
Zhang Chunqiao 56–8, 60, 65, 78–80, 82–4, 88, 105, 123, 157, 170–1, 174–5, 181–4, 186–8, 195, 201, 203, 251–2
Zhang Guohua 101
Zhang Pinghua 217–18
Zhang Tiesheng 177–8
Zhao Yiya 105
Zhao Yongfu 95
Zhao Ziyang 204
Zhenbao incident 121–2
Zhongguo Qingnianbao (China Youth News) 71, 213
Zhou Enlai 48, 51, 59, 70, 77, 81, 84–6, 88, 97, 99–104, 108, 113, 123, 134–5, 137, 161–2, 165, 170, 172, 174–6, 181–2, 184–5, 188–9, 192–3, 201, 203, 206, 216
Zhou Peiyuan 160–1, 177, 214
Zhou Rongxin 161, 187
Zhou Yang 35, 37, 55, 62–3, 71, 216
Zhu De 123, 194